BEYOND
JEWISH
IDENTITY

RETHINKING CONCEPTS
AND IMAGINING
ALTERNATIVES

BEYOND JEWISH IDENTITY

RETHINKING CONCEPTS AND IMAGINING ALTERNATIVES

Edited by
JON A. LEVISOHN
and ARI Y. KELMAN

BOSTON
2019

Library of Congress Control Number:2019943604

The research for this book and its publication were made possible by the generous support of the Jack, Joseph and Morton Mandel Center for Studies in Jewish Education, a partnership between Brandeis University and the Jack, Joseph and Morton Mandel Foundation of Cleveland, Ohio.

ISBN 978-1-644691-29-8 (paperback)
ISBN 978-1-644691-17-5 (electronic)

Book design by Kryon Publishing Services (P) Ltd.
www.kryonpublishing.com
Cover design by Ivan Grave

Published by Academic Studies Press
1577 Beacon Street
Brookline, MA 02446, USA
press@academicstudiespress.com
www.academicstudiespress.com

Table of Contents

Introduction

Jon A. Levisohn and Ari Y. Kelman

This book is motivated by the deep discomfort that we, the editors, feel with the way that the phrase "Jewish identity" is often used by educators, educational policy makers, and other leaders in the Jewish community, especially (although not exclusively) in the United States. To be sure, we have learned much from colleagues who have written rigorously and insightfully about the ways that Jews understand themselves, about how Jewishness is enacted in contemporary settings, and about the ways that Jewish identity coexists alongside other identities (to name a few key studies: Cohen, 1974, 1983; Cohen & Eisen, 2000; Dashefsky & Shapiro, 1974; Hahn Tapper 2016; Hartman & Hartman, 1999; Hartman & Kaufman, 2006; Hartman & Sheskin, 2011; Horowitz, 1998, 1999, 2002; Pomson & Schnoor, 2018; Sagi, 2016; Sklare, 1967). But we also regularly encounter assumptions about the fixedness of Jewish identity, about the quantifiability of Jewish identity, and especially about the role of Jewish education in strengthening Jewish identity—assumptions that generated the discomfort to which we have already alluded. We launched the project that led to this book when we discovered that the two of us shared this discomfort. We wanted to understand the uses of the phrase "Jewish identity" in Jewish educational discourse, to develop and articulate our concerns with greater precision, to invite others into a conversation about how and why the phrase "Jewish identity" is used, and most aspirationally, to generate alternative ways that we might understand the desired outcomes of Jewish educational interventions.

To be clear, there is no unified definition of Jewish identity and no single discourse (some of the more diverse discussions include Cadge & Davidman, 2016; Charmé, 2000; Charmé, Horowitz, Hyman, Hyman, & Kress, 2008; Cohen, E., 2010; Dashefsky, Lazerwitz, & Tabory, 2003; Gitelman, 2009; Harvey, Cohen, & Kopelowitz, 2001; Herman, 1977; Kaufman, 1999, 2005; Kelman et al., 2017a, 2017b; Liebman, 1999; Magid, 2013; Moore, 2008; Oppenheim, 1984; Prell, 2000; Reszke, 2013; Thompson, 2013). The *haredi* or utra-Orthodox world eschews the term altogether, and it is less common in the Modern Orthodox community than it is in liberal Jewish communities. Still, there are important patterns and trends. Since the late 1960s, the phrase has grown in popularity and stature, often appearing as an almost self-reflexive rationale for many Jewish educational and communal efforts. "It's Official," trumpeted a headline reporting on a study by Steven Cohen and his colleagues of Jewish summer camps (Cohen, Miller, Sheshkin, & Torr, 2011), "Jewish Camp Strengthens Jewish Identity" (Fishkoff, 2011).

The popularity of the phrase left us feeling more and more uncomfortable with the range of experiences, meanings, self-conceptions, expressions, and affinities to which it seemed to refer. The more popular it grew, it seemed, the less well-defined it appeared to become. As our sense of this development deepened, we were gratified to learn about other scholarly voices that expressed concern with or critical perspectives on the phrase, its meaning and its utility (Brubaker & Cooper, 2000; Comaroff & Comaroff, 2009; Fearon, 1999; Gleason, 1983; Nicholson, 2008), and we started to gather like-minded fellow travelers. In fact, our work on the project got to the point where some of our colleagues accused us, only half in jest, of starting a movement to ban the use of the phrase "Jewish identity" altogether.

This is not quite accurate. We affirm that there are good and important ways that the phrase "Jewish identity" can and should be used by scholars of contemporary Jewish life. There may even be ways that the term can and should be used by educators and scholars of education; some of these will be suggested in the chapters that follow. If so, then what do we mean when we suggest that we need to go "beyond Jewish identity"? What's wrong with the discourse of Jewish identity that we need to go beyond it? And what might lie beyond? Each of the contributors to this book has their own perspective on these questions, of course. But in general, we can point to some broad themes that tie together the chapters of this book.

First, the discourse of Jewish identity tends to treat identity as unified and relatively static. To be sure, Jewish communal discourse often describes or advocates efforts to "strengthen" or "build" identity, so nobody really thinks that identity is absolutely static. If it were, it could not be strengthened! The claim that a stronger Jewish identity is the appropriate desired outcome of Jewish educational projects and programs is predicated on the assumption that those interventions can change identity, somehow, in positive ways. Still, scholars, researchers, communal leaders, and philanthropists often treat identity as if it is a unified thing, which a person simply *has*. That's why studies often seek to distinguish "strong Jewish identities" from "weak Jewish identities," and why interventions seek to transform the latter into the former. Implicit in this framework is a moral hierarchy between supposed strength and perceived weakness. Having a "strong Jewish identity" comes to mean, roughly, being more normatively involved in Jewish life, or more interested in or committed to Jewish causes, communities, knowledge, etc. In order to measure the relative strength or weakness of an identity, one must first create a series of metrics that suggest objectivity. What often results, however, is the creation of an identity concept that ranks Jewish identities and, in the process, turns a group of people who identify as Jewish into lesser versions of some imagined gold standard of Jewish identity. They literally do not measure up.

Surely, one can *be* Jewish—one can identify as Jewish, one can "have a Jewish identity"—in both strong and weak ways, in combination, conflict, and conversation with other commitments to other identities that one holds. This is the nature of identity. It is not a zero-sum game; there is no finite amount of identity to go around, such that being *more* of x (more American or more Western; more of a male or a professor or a musician) means being somehow *less* Jewish. The question, therefore, is not about whether or not one has an identity, but about what conditions bring one to act upon it and not some other identity or combination of identities. Rather than thinking about *having* an identity, it makes more sense to us to think about *enacting* multiple and intersectional identities, in different ways at different times (Brettschneider, 1996; Boyarin, 1997; Crenshaw, 1991; Glenn & Sokoloff, 2010; Silberstein, 2000). This is not to argue that the Jewish community should avoid principled debates over the practices and commitments that it values. Instead, it is to caution against totalizing claims that people who identify as Jewish behave in ways that demonstrate their Jewishness either exclusive of other identities they may hold or in ways that supersede those identities. Consequently, as each of the following chapters examines, we reject the conclusion that identity is the proper or sole metric for assessing articulations of Jewishness.

So the first general critique of the discourse of Jewish identity is that, once we pay close attention to it, it is inconsistent with our best understanding of how identity in general, and Jewish identity in particular, actually works. The chapters in this book develop this critique by drawing our attention to particular ways that the discourse of Jewish identity functions, and to the assumptions that it makes. The closer attention we pay, the more these inconsistencies stand out and the harder they are to ignore.

In addition, a second general critique focuses on the way that the discourse of Jewish identity has become inseparable from Jewish educational interventions. The assumption we seek to destabilize is causal in a simplistic sense: x experience leads to y outcome. That is, Jewish educational programs, of various kinds, lead to more (or stronger or deeper) Jewish identity. In one sense, of course, this assumption is demonstrably true. Every responsible study of the impact of Jewish education indicates that Jews who participate in Jewish educational projects and programs are affected on pretty much every relevant measure, in ways that suggest a greater commitment to things Jewish: broader institutional affiliation (e.g., membership in synagogues or JCCs), more ritual practice (e.g., lighting Shabbat candles or attending a Passover seder), more communal Jewish involvement (e.g., donating to Federation), stronger Jewish social networks (e.g., percentage of Jewish friends), etc.

In fact, many of us involved in Jewish educational research find ourselves compelled to repeat these well-documented realities in the face of communal voices that worry that Jewish education is a failed enterprise. It is not. The simple truth, repeatedly corroborated, is that investments in Jewish education pay off in terms of Jewish involvements. Participants in Jewish educational programs emerge from those programs—almost all of them, with few exceptions—with more Jewish knowledge, broader Jewish connections, and deeper Jewish commitments (see, e.g., Cohen, 1974; Cohen, 1995; Cohen & Kotler-Berkowitz, 2004; Cohen, 2007). In general, if the question is whether Jewish education has an effect on participants, the answer is consistently positive.

So if we can affirm that Jewish education works to increase or deepen various Jewish attitudes and behaviors, what's the problem? The problem is that there is a world of difference between observing the effect of, say, Jewish camp on campers' patterns of affiliation, on the one hand, and asserting that the goal of Jewish camp, or anything else, is to strengthen Jewish identity. Proposing that the desired outcome of any particular Jewish educational project or program is more or stronger "Jewish identity" has the effect of dumbing down larger educational goals to the most superficial and the least meaningful. It sets a low bar, and fails to capture anything aspirational. At the communal level, Jewish policy makers have long noticed that the the goal of "Jewish continuity" is unhelpful, affirming nothing other than a thin survivalism (see, e.g., Cohen & Fein, 1985). But "Jewish identity" is the corollary, on the individual level, of "continuity" on the communal level, and likewise demands critical re-examination.

We live in a world where those who identify as Jews, even the "nones"—the famous "Jews of no religion," i.e., those who when asked their religion answer "none"—affirm that they are Jewish and proclaim that they are proud to be Jewish in incredibly high numbers: 83%, according to the Pew Report on American Jews (Pew, 2013). With all of the attention to various numbers in the well-reported Pew study of 2013, that number that did not get the attention that we think it deserves. 83% is an astonishingly high number of Jews who feel a sense of pride in their Jewishness. The discrepancy between that figure and the much lower rates of engagement in almost every area of Jewish life suggest both that Jewish identity is strong and, at the same time, that the simplistic understanding of "Jewish identity" tells us precious little about the lives of American Jews.

Consider the obvious point that almost everyone who enters into a Jewish educational program or who responds to a demographic survey or an evaluation already has a Jewish identity. To qualify for participation in a demographic study or a Jewish educational program means that one already self-identifies as a Jew. In this respect, Jewish identity is not an output or an educational outcome; it is a precondition for inclusion. What remains of efforts to measure Jewish identity, therefore, almost always reinforces the idea that Jewish identity can be measured on a scale that ranges from strong to weak, a scale that is imposed by researchers on the subjective experiences of participants. But what about the Jewish identity of someone who is alienated by the bourgeois materialism of her childhood synagogue? What are we to make of the self-described "Tikkun Olam Jews," or even more poignantly, of those who embrace the title of "bad Jews"? How might we understand the relative strength or weakness of someone who hides her Jewishness out of a fear of antisemitism? How might we measure the identity of a vociferous supporter of Israel who does not claim memberships in Jewish organizations of any kind and does not perform any holiday-based rituals? Conversely, how can we disentangle the efforts of Israel's Ministry of the Diaspora to "strengthen Jewish identity" from its effort to promote allegiance to the State of Israel and opposition to its perceived enemies? How should we think about a recovering alcoholic who finds spirituality in AA meetings but not in synagogue? What about Jewish kids who spend time in academic Jewish studies courses on college campuses—according to one study (Sales & Saxe, 2006), the numbers range from 25% of those with minimal Jewish educational background to 50% of those with more intensive Jewish educational backgrounds—courses that are sometimes taught by non-Jews and that typically do not provide opportunities for the expression of the Jewish identities of the students? How should we categorize the non-Jewish parent of Jewish children who drives them to Jewish youth group events and stands with them on the *bima* at their *b'nai mitzvah*? How might our measures misunderstand the pattern of nonaffiliation and nonmembership, so prevalent among both young Jews and non-Jews? How might these measures miss the life cycle patterns among people who are marrying later and having fewer children? Capturing the various complex modes of Jewish engagement on a hierarchical or linear scale seems impossible.

Whatever the goals of Jewish education may be, either generally or the specific goals of particular projects and programs, they must amount to more than an effort to move the needle of some composite called "Jewish identity." Identity seems both overinflated and ill-equipped to rise to the analytical task of this effort. The chapters of this book will develop this critique, examining a variety of modes in which identity has been understood and operationalized. The second half of the book will also begin to offer constructive alternatives, ways of thinking about our desired educational outcomes that are richer, deeper, more robust, and most importantly, more helpful to educational practitioners and policy makers than "Jewish identity."

* * *

In part one of the volume, contributors explore different constructions of and approaches to the concept of Jewish identity. Each chapter presents a different investigation into the construction or application of Jewish identity and raises questions about the elasticity or applicability of the term. The first two chapters of this section focus on the ways in which our language shapes how we think about Jewish identity, its possibilities and its limitations. In chapter 2, Eli Gottlieb takes a semiotic approach to conceptualizations of Jewish identity, exploring a set of popular metaphors that pervade the discourse. By focusing on the animating metaphors of Jewish identity, Gottlieb exposes some of the hidden logic behind the term, tracing the implications of the ways in which we talk about identity for the ways in which we imagine that it works (or fails to work). In chapter 3, Samira Mehta explores the conceptualization of Jewish identity across a few different sites—the 2013 Pew Report on Jewish Americans, a discussion about multiple identities in the Jewish press, and multiethnic Jewish memoirs—to illuminate how identity, even Jewish identity, can be multiple, and that people who identify as Jewish might, as well, identify as something else simultaneously. Focusing on the conceptual frameworks of Jewish identity across domains, Mehta argues that Jewish identity is articulated as multiple because it is part of the multiple ways in which people experience it, and that efforts to cleanly segment it sometimes do more harm than good.

Chapters 4 and 5 examine the historical emergence of the concept. In chapter 4, Jonathan Krasner traces the emergence of the concept of Jewish identity from its nascent phase in the 1950s through its growth in the late 60s and into its central locus in Jewish communal discourse in the 1980s and into the twenty-first century. Focusing on the contributions of Kurt Lewin, Erik Erikson, Will Herberg, Marshall Sklare, and others, Krasner offers insights into how the concept of Jewish identity came to occupy the position it does, and what is at stake in maintaining investments in Jewish identity. In chapter 5, Ari Y. Kelman focuses more closely on the emergence of Jewish identity as an educational outcome, highlighting the period from the end of the 1960s through the early 70s. Kelman argues that concerns about identity emerged in response to changes in the politics of college campuses and how those changes appeared to affect Jewish students. Fear of what was happening on college campuses led Jewish communal leaders to posit Jewish identity as a bulwark against the turmoil of social and political currents. Jewish educators responded by promoting education for identity in K-12 classrooms as a way of preparing Jewish youth for college life. Therefore, Kelman observes, the emergence of Jewish identity as a focus of K-12 Jewish education had to be retrofitted from observations of Jewish college students.

While the central focus of the book is on Jewish identity discourse in the United States, chapters 6 and 7 provide a helpful transnational perspective, focusing on Jewish identities in Poland and in between Israel and the United States, respectively. In chapter 6, Katka Reszke explores the experiences of "Generation Unexpected," a term she uses to describe Polish Jews who were raised as non-Jews and only discovered their Jewish heritage as teenagers or adults. Reszke's focus on young Polish Jews highlights the ways in which people come to identify as Jews as adults, and how they explain their Jewishness to themselves and others. Notably, Reszke's interviewees describe their exhaustion, as a result of having to communicate their own Jewish existence to Israeli and American Jews who are routinely surprised to find young Jews in Poland. Reszke's contribution to this volume highlights the very complex and site-specific dynamics of Jewish identity, and the ways in which it almost always bears transnational and historical freight. Shaul Magid then draws the first section of the book to a close with an analysis of the writings of Rabbi Menachem Froman, a central figure of the settler movement whose unorthodox perspectives on Zionism and Israel, Magid argues, might hold the key to the formulation of an American post-Zionism. Using Froman's writings, Magid critiques what he calls the "dogmatization of Zionism," which has become a kind of litmus test for participation in Jewish communal life in twenty-first century America, and for a normative conception of Jewish identity that Magid wishes to both interrogate and disrupt.

* * *

In part two of the volume, contributors pivot from presenting critical perspectives on Jewish identity and its usages in contemporary Jewish discourse to introducing alternative formulations of the range of Jewish commitments and expressions. In chapter 8, Tali Zelkowicz offers the negative argument that "Jewish educators don't make Jews." That is, Jewish educators often suffer under the delusion that their job is to make their students into Jews, to instill Jewish identity into them or to strengthen it if it exists only in a weakened state. But this, she argues, misunderstands how identity actually works. More importantly, she shows us through classroom examples that the delusion actually undermines their ability to carry out their educational responsibilities. What are those responsibilities? For Zelkowicz, the alternative to producing Jewish identity is for educators to become facilitators, "to help learners develop tools and strategies they need to engage in their own [ongoing] work of becoming Jews."

In chapter 9, sociolinguists Sarah Bunin Benor and Netta Avineri note the common laments about the weak levels of Hebrew proficiency among American Jews, often taken as a kind of proxy for a weak Jewish identity. They introduce us to two linguistic phenomena that are distinct from proficiency (or lack of proficiency) in Hebrew: the "meta-linguistic communities" into which American Jews are inducted (even in those settings where little Hebrew proficiency is attained) and the development of "Jewish English." In each case, we find a phenomenon that is fascinating for scholars, but that is also particularly intriguing for educators and educational policy makers. As lovers of language, they too wish for stronger Hebrew proficiency. But given the realities of language learning in America, they propose that educators might take these two phenomena seriously as goals in themselves, aspiring to induct students into metalinguistic communities and to teach Jewish English, and to do so consciously and thoughtfully. "These concepts represent a reimagining of the goals of language education," they argue, "a new understanding of the role of language in building community and fostering Jewish self-understanding."

The last three chapters share a common impatience with the generality and generic nature of Jewish identity discourse, and a common desire for specificity in describing educational goals. In chapter 10, Shaul Kelner calls our attention to the phenomenon of the Soviet Jewry movement, often taken as the heyday of American Jewish activism. For one thing, the movement represented a mobilization of Jews—especially young Jews—on behalf of the Jewish people in a way that seems hard to imagine today. More subtly, the movement entailed an astonishing degree of cultural creativity, repurposing sancta and inventing rituals out of whole cloth. Yet, he argues, these efforts always served the larger cause of liberating Jews from behind the Iron Curtain. The cultural engagement and mobilization that emerged were by-products of collective action, and he observes that these successes of the Soviet Jewry movement arose indirectly, not as the focus of the entire effort. Furthermore, he emphasizes the collective nature of the project, as a corrective to the relentless individualism of educational discourse. Finally, and most constructively, he proposes that we aim for "subjectivity," rather than identity, focusing "less on how people think and feel about being generically Jewish and more on training them in specific ways of engaging the world as Jews, and specific ways of behaving with regard to Jewish culture, institutions, people, etc."

In chapter 11, Jon Levisohn contributes an additional layer to the critique of Jewish identity discourse, noting the way that that discourse has the potential to instrumentalize Jewish education, operating as a kind of universal solvent that dissolves the passions and commitments of Jewish educators for their particular domains. Those domains, he argues, are best understood in terms of practices. But beyond proposing that "Jewish practices" is a constructive alternative to "Jewish identity," he also charts the relationship between the two concepts. Practice, after all, contributes to identity: over time, we become what we do, as we start to see ourselves as practitioners of a particular practice (Lave & Wenger, 1991). But sometimes, identity precedes practice: we learn to perform who we are, to move from empty affirmations to more robust enactments of those practices that constitute the identity as we understand it. In either case, however, the goal of Jewish education is not to promote or deepen Jewish identity, but to focus on the more specific outcomes of promoting particular Jewish practices.

Finally, in chapter 12, Jon Woocher (of blessed memory) and Lee Moore share their innovative effort to frame a new way of talking about Jewish educational goals, an alternative that they call "Jewish sensibilities." They do not claim that these sensibilities are uniquely Jewish, nor do they argue that they capture the essence of Jewishness. But they do argue that the specific sensibilities that they enumerate have a resonance within Jewish history and Jewish tradition. Jewish sensibilities can function as "an overarching goal that involves learners coming to be aware of and to adopt as valuable in their own lives some of the distinctive ways in which Jews have perceived and responded to life's challenges and opportunities over the centuries." And by naming them, we will be able to develop educational programs to promote them directly, and even to assess them in appropriate ways. "Jewish sensibilities," they conclude, "are our language."

* * *

Is there still a place for Jewish identity discourse? There is. Does the phrase "Jewish identity" have a coherent usage? It does. It is perfectly reasonable to talk about Jewish identity in terms of how a person thinks about who she or he is in the world. Similarly, it remains important to invest our energies into understanding how people configure their senses of self in terms of memberships in larger collectives or communities. It also makes sense to consider the ways in which Jewish identity, like other identities, is projected upon individuals and communities by others, whether those others are well-meaning or antagonistic. These questions are closely connected but are not quite congruent. The confusion between them contributes, in part, to the reification of identity and to continued investments in research that seeks to uncover its secret or identify a silver bullet solution to whatever issues appear to afflict American Jews and their communities. Whatever practical or conceptual innovations may be developed that contribute to the flourishing of Jewish individuals and communities, they will not rest on the uncritical use of identity as a formulation for Jewishness.

This volume, while not the first to explore and critique the concept of Jewish identity, makes two important interventions into contemporary understandings of American Jewish life. It is the first collection to critically examine the relationship between Jewish education and Jewish identity. Insofar as Jewish identity has become the most popular way to talk about the desired outcome of Jewish education, a critical assessment of the relationship between education and identity is both useful and necessary. It is useful because the reification of identity has, we believe, hampered much educational creativity in the rather single-minded pursuit of this goal. It is necessary because the nearly ubiquitous employment of the term obscures a whole set of significant questions about what Jewish education is and ought to be for in the first place.

Second, this volume offers responses that are not merely synonymous replacements for "identity." When we have spoken about this project in Jewish communal organizations and educational venues, we have often been challenged in response by the question, "Well, then, what do you propose as a replacement?" The point here is not to replace the concept of identity with some other term that will, invariably, do the same kind of rhetorical work that identity already does. That would merely be a semantic exercise. By offering an array of responses in conversation with a selection of more critical essays, we hope that we can begin to expand, rather than replace, the array of ideas that the term "identity" is so often used to represent.

As scholars of Jewish education, we hope this volume contributes to any number of new conversations about the relationship between Jewish education and Jewish life. Our intention here is to move from critical inquiry (Part I) to suggestive possibilities (Part II). The true measure of this effort, of course, lies in the hands of our readers, those who will advance our understanding of the complexities of American Jewish education and life—beyond Jewish identity.]

* * *

This volume is a product of a research project at the Jack, Joseph and Morton Mandel Center for Studies in Jewish Education at Brandeis University. The authors shared their initial ideas on the topic at a conference in March 2014, after which they developed draft papers that were then shared with colleagues in a collaborative process. We are grateful to the participants in that conference and in the collaborative process that followed. We are also grateful to the staff of the Mandel Center for their contributions that have enabled our scholarly activity, including Elizabeth DiNolfo, Pamella Endo, Sarah Flatley, and especially Susanne Shavelson, for her editorial acumen and attention to detail. Finally, we are grateful to the Jack, Joseph and Morton Mandel Foundation, for their ongoing support of scholarship on Jewish education, in the service of a thriving Jewish future.

Bibliography

Boyarin, Daniel. (1997). *A Radical Jew: Paul and the Politics of Identity.* Berkeley, CA: University of California Press.

Brettschneider, Marla. (1996). *The Narrow Bridge: Jewish Views on Multiculturalism.* New Brunswick, NJ: Rutgers University Press.

Brubaker, Rogers, & Cooper, Frederick. (2000). Beyond "Identity." *Theory and Society 29*, 1–47.

Cadge, Wendy, & Davidman, Lynn. (2006). Ascription, Choice, and the Construction of Religious Identities in the Contemporary United States. *Journal for the Scientific Study of Religion 45*(1), 23–38. doi.org/10.1111/j.1468-5906.2006.00003

Charmé, Stuart. (2000). Varieties of Authenticity in Contemporary Jewish Identity. *Jewish Social Studies 6*, 133–5.

Charmé, Stuart, Horowitz, Bethamie, Hyman, Tali, & Kress, Keffrey. (2008). Jewish Identities in Action: An Exploration of Models, Metaphors, and Methods. *Journal of Jewish Education 74*(2), 115–143.

Cohen, Erik H. (2010). Jewish Identity Research: A State of the Art. *International Journal of Jewish Education Research 1*(1), 7–48.

Cohen, Steven M. (1974). The Impact of Jewish Education on Religious Identification and Practice. *Jewish Social Studies 36*(3/4), 316–326.

Cohen, Steven M. (1983). *American Modernity and Jewish Identity.* New York, NY: Routledge:

Cohen, Steven M. (1995). The Impact of Varieties of Jewish Education Upon Jewish Identity: An Inter-Generational Perspective. *Contemporary Jewry 16*, 68–96.

Cohen, Steven M. (2007). The Differential Impact of Jewish Education on Adult Jewish Identity. In Jack Wertheimer (Ed.), *Family Matters: Jewish Education in an Age of Choice* (pp. 34–58). Lebanon, NH: University Press of New England.

Cohen, Steven M., & Eisen, Arnold M. (2000). *The Jew Within: Self, Family, and Community in America.* Bloomington, IN: Indiana University Press.

Cohen, Steven M., & Fein, Leonard J. (1985). From Integration to Survival: American Jewish Anxieties in Transition. *The ANNALS of the American Academy of Political and Social Science 480* (1), 75–88. doi.org/10.1177/0002716285480001007

Cohen, Steven M., & Laurence Kotler-Berkowitz. (2004). The Impact of Childhood Jewish Education upon Adults' Jewish Identity: Schooling, Israel Travel, Camping and Youth Groups. *United Jewish Communities Report Series on the National Jewish Population Survey 2000–01* (Report No. 3). Retrieved from https://www.bjpa.org/search-results/publication/2814

Cohen, Steven M., Miller, Ron, Sheshkin, Ira, & Torr, Berna. (2011). *Camp Works: The Long-Term Impact of Jewish Overnight Camp.* Retrieved from https://jewishcamp.org/campopedia/camp-works-the-long-term-impact-of-jewish-overnight-camp/

Comaroff, John L., & Comaroff, Jean. (2009). *Ethnicity, Inc.* Chicago, IL: University of Chicago Press.

Crenshaw, Kimberle. 1991. Mapping the Margins: Intersectionality, Identity Politics, and Violence against Women of Color. *Stanford Law Review 43*(6), 1241–1299. doi.org/10.2307/1229039

Dashefsky, Arnold, Bernard Lazerwitz, & Tabory, Ephraim. (2003). A Journey of the "straightway" or the "Roundabout Path": Jewish Identity in the United States and Israel. In Dillon, Michele (Ed.), Handbook of the Sociology of Religion (pp. 240–260). Cambridge, UK: Cambridge University Press.

Dashefsky, Arnold, & Shapiro, Howard M. (1974). Ethnic Identification Among American Jews. Lexington, MA.: Lexington Books.

Fearon, James. (1999). What Is Identity (As We Now Use the Word)? Retrieved from https://www.stanford.edu/group/fearon-research/cgi-bin/wordpress/wp-content/uploads/2013/10/What-is-Identity-as-we-now-use-the-word-.pdf

Fishkoff, Sue. (March 3 2011). It's Official: Summer Camp Strengthens Jewish Identity. Retrieved from https://www.jta.org/2011/03/02/life-religion/its-official-jewish-camp-strengthens-jewish-identity

Gitelman, Zvi. (Ed.) (2009). *Religion or Ethnicity?: Jewish Identities in Evolution*. New Brunswick, NJ: Rutgers University Press.

Gleason, Philip. (1983). Identifying Identity: A Semantic History. *The Journal of American History 69*(4), 910–931.

Glenn, Susan A. & Sokoloff, Naomi B. (Eds.). 2010. *Boundaries of Jewish Identity*. Seattle, WA: University of Washington Press.

Hartman, Harriet, & Hartman, Moshe. (1999). Jewish Identity, Denomination and Denominational Mobility. *Social Identities 5*(3), 279–311.

Hartman, Harriet, & Kaufman, Debra. (2006). Decentering the Study of Jewish Identity: Opening the Dialogue with Other Religious Groups. *Sociology of Religion 67*(4), 365–385.

Hartman, Harriet, & Sheskin, Ira M. (2011). *The Influence of Community Context and Individual Characteristics on Jewish Identity: A 21-Community Study*. Retrieved from http://www.jewishdatabank.org/Studies/details.cfm?StudyID=713

Harvey, E., Steven M. Cohen, & Kopelowitz (2011). *Dynamic Belonging: Contemporary Jewish Collective Identities*. New York, NY: Berghahn Books.

Herman, Simon N. (1997). *Jewish Identity: A Social Psychological Perspective*. California: Sage.

Horowitz, Bethamie. (1998). Connections and Journeys: Shifting Identities among American Jews. *Contemporary Jewry 19*, 63–94.

Horowitz, Bethamie. (2002). Reframing the Study of Contemporary American Jewish Identity. *Contemporary Jewry 23*(1), 14–34.

Kaufman, Debra Renee. (1999). Embedded Categories: Identity among Jewish Young Adults in the United States. *Race, Gender and Class 6*(4), 76–87.

Kaufman, Debra Renee. (2005). The Place of Judaism in American Jewish Identity. In Kaplan (Ed.), *Cambridge Companion to American Judaism*. Cambridge, UK: Cambridge University Press.

Kelman, Ari Y., Belzer, Tobin, Hassenfeld, Ziva, Horwitz, Ilana, & Matthew Casey Williams. (2017). Traditional Judaism: The Conceptualization of Jewishness in the Lives of American Jewish Post-Boomers," *Jewish Social Studies 23*(1), 134–167.

Kelman, Ari Y., Belzer, Tobin, Hassenfeld, Ziva, Horwitz, Ilana, & Matthew Casey Williams. (2017). The Social Self: Toward the Study of Jewish Lives in the Twenty-first Century." *Contemporary Jewry 37*, 53–79.

Lave, Jean, & Wenger, Etienne. (1991). *Situated Learning: Legitimate Peripheral Participation* (1st ed.). Cambridge, UK: Cambridge University Press.

Liebman, Charles S. (1999). *Choosing Survival: Strategies for a Jewish Future: Strategies for a Jewish Future*. Oxford, UK: Oxford University Press.

Magid, Shaul. (2013). *American Post-Judaism: Identity and Renewal in a Postethnic Society* (Rev. ed.). Bloomington, IN: Indiana University Press.

Moore, Deborah Dash. (Ed.) (2008). *American Jewish Identity Politics*. Ann Arbor, MI: University of Michigan Press.

Nicholson, Linda. (2008). *Identity Before Identity Politics* (1st ed.). Cambridge, UK: Cambridge University Press.

Oppenheim, Michael. (1984). A "Fieldguide" to the Study of Modern Jewish Identity. *Jewish Social Studies 46*(3/4), 215–230.

Pew Research Center. (2013). *A Portrait of Jewish Americans: Findings from a Pew Research Center Survey of U.S. Jews*. Retrieved from http://www.pewforum.org/files/2013/10/jewish-american-full-report-for-web.pdf

Pomson, Alex, & Schnoor, Randal F. (2018). *Jewish Family: Identity and Self-Formation at Home*. Indianapolis, IN: Indiana University Press.

Prell, Riv-Ellen. (2000). Developmental Judaism: Challenging the Study of Jewish Identity in the Social Sciences. *Contemporary Jewry 21*, 33–54.

Reszke, Katka. (2013). *Return of the Jew: Identity Narratives of the Third Post-Holocaust Generation of Jews in Poland*. Boston, MA: Academic Studies Press.

Sagi, Avi. (2016). *Reflections on Identity: The Jewish Case* (Batya Stein, Trans.). Boston, MA: Academic Studies Press.

Sales, Amy, & Leonard Saxe. (2006). *Particularism in the University: Realities and Opportunities for Jewish Life on Campus*. Retrieved from https://avichai.org/knowledge_base/particularism-in-the-university-realities-and-opportunities-for-jewish-life-on-campus-2006/

Silberstein, Laurence J. (Ed.). (2000). *Mapping Jewish Identities*. New York, NY: New York University Press.

Sklare, Marshall, & Joseph Greenblum. (1967). *Jewish Identity on the Suburban Frontier*. New York, NY: Basic Books.

Tapper, Aaron J. Hahn. (2016). *Judaisms: A Twenty-First-Century Introduction to Jews and Jewish Identities* (1st ed.). Oakland, CA: University of California Press.

Thompson, Jennifer A. (2013). *Jewish on Their Own Terms: How Intermarried Couples Are Changing American Judaism*. New Brunswick, NJ: Rutgers University Press.

Taking Jewish Identity
Metaphors Literally

Eli Gottlieb

In "Metaphors we live by," Lakoff and Johnson (1980) argue that, "the way we think, what we experience, and what we do every day is very much a matter of metaphor" (p. 3). They support their argument with linguistic analyses of dozens of examples of what they call "conceptual metaphors." For example, "ARGUMENT IS WAR":

> We don't just talk about arguments in terms of war. We can actually win or lose arguments. We see the person we are arguing with as an opponent. We attack his positions and we defend our own. We gain and lose ground. We plan and use strategies. If we find a position indefensible, we can abandon it and take a new line of attack ... It is in this sense that the ARGUMENT IS WAR metaphor is one that we live by in this culture; it structures the actions we perform in arguing. (p. 4)

To drive home their point, Lakoff and Johnson invite us to consider a culture other than our own in which argument is viewed, not as war, but as dance. In such a culture, they suggest, arguers would see themselves as performers, whose shared goal is to create an aesthetically pleasing recital. Participants in such a culture would not only talk about arguments differently to us; they would conduct them differently. In this sense, argue Lakoff and Johnson, the metaphor of argument as war is not "poetic, fanciful, or rhetorical; it is literal" (p. 5).

In what follows, I examine how Jewish educators talk about identity. In the spirit of Lakoff and Johnson, I do this by analyzing the metaphors they use when doing so. To investigate what educators mean by Jewish identity, or by identity education, I consider what it would mean to take their identity metaphors literally.

Metaphors of Jewish identity have multiple sources. Some derive from studies of the self and its development in the social sciences. Others derive from popular conceptions of learning and Jewishness. Once we put these metaphors to use, however, we are inveterate mixers. Like hyperactive cocktail shakers, we combine our identity metaphors into ever more exotic concoctions. And because we not only talk in metaphors but also think in them and act upon them, our resulting ideas and practice end up being, well, a little mixed up.

Sometimes, more than a little. Sometimes, the metaphors we use to talk about Jewish identity are so thoroughly mixed up that we literally don't know what we are talking about. That, more or less, is my argument below. I begin by comparing and contrasting three metaphors that have dominated the literature on identity development. Next, I examine tensions between these metaphors. I then analyze instances of metaphor use "in the wild" (c.f. Hutchins, 1995). These latter instances are all texts written by educators whose goal is to provide a rationale or framework for Jewish identity education. I conclude with some thoughts about the practical importance of metaphorical coherence.

Theoretical Metaphor I: Crystallization

I begin with Erik Erikson. Not because he said it all first or best (although some argue that he did both), but because his metaphors have stuck. Erikson coined many phrases (e.g., "identity crisis," "moratorium") which have seeped into everyday language. But I want to focus here on a metaphor that underlies almost all of his writing on identity, namely, "crystallization" (see e.g. Erikson, 1968, pp. 160–162). Crystallization is the process by which tentative, fluid elements of personality become a structured and stable whole. According to Erikson, crystallization is not something that happens suddenly, once and forever after. It is an iterative process, in which successive structures are broken down and reconstructed, with each new crisis and reintegration. Indeed Erikson's "eight stages of man" (see, e.g. Erikson, 1963/1950) is intended, among other things, to chart and characterize successive crystallizations.

Crystallization is a dominant metaphor in Erikson's writings in the sense that it pervades his account of identity, even when he does not use the term explicitly. In Erikson's writings, an identity is something that is "formed;" it has structure; it is a coherent whole built of previously disparate parts; it is integral, stable, and unified, as opposed to fluid and tentative.

This motif of structure, stability and coherence is further crystallized (if you'll pardon the pun) in the writings of Erikson's popularizers and appliers. James Marcia's influential operationalization of Erikson's theory, for example, defines four possible identity statuses: diffuse, foreclosed, moratorium and achieved. A person with an achieved identity, according to Marcia, is one who

... has experienced a crisis period and is committed to an occupation and ideology. He has seriously considered several occupational choices and has made a decision on his own terms, even though his ultimate choice may be a variation of parental wishes. With respect to ideology, he seems to have reevaluated past beliefs and achieved a resolution that leaves him free to act. In general he does not appear as if he would be overwhelmed by sudden shifts in his environment or by unexpected responsibilities. (1966, pp. 551–555)

Even without reading his descriptions of the three other statuses and the ways in which they fall short of this ideal, one gets a sense of what characterizes mature identity for Marcia: stability, continuity, resolution. These qualities emerge out of prior flux and flow. Once achieved, however, they provide structure and a center of gravity.

Theoretical Metaphor II: Masks

Erikson's account of identity, and the crystallization metaphor that underlies it, are still alive and well in the discourse and practice of contemporary educators. However, as early as the 1970s, some psychologists began to take issue with Erikson. These critical voices gained in volume, rising to a peak in the 1990s, when they combined with other proponents of postmodernism.

The writings of Kenneth Gergen are a good example of this critique and its evolution. Gergen sought not only to undermine Erikson's crystallization metaphor but also to replace it with an alternative one. Gergen was, and remains, refreshingly explicit about his goal. In 1972, he published an article in *Psychology Today* titled, "Multiple identity: The healthy, happy human being wears many masks." In it, he targeted for critique the following two assumptions of Eriksonian theory:

1. That it is normal for a person to develop a firm and coherent sense of identity, and
2. That it is good and healthy for him to do so, and pathological not to. (p. 31)

Gergen reports on various empirical studies that he and others conducted to demonstrate the fluidity of our self-conceptions and their susceptibility to change. "Taken together," writes Gergen, "our experiments document the remarkable flexibility of the self (p. 65). We are made of soft plastic, and molded by social circumstances." This does not mean that we should see ourselves as fakes, argues Gergen. For "Once donned, mask becomes reality" (p. 65).

Gergen encourages us to "abandon the assumption that normal development equips the individual with a coherent sense of identity" (p. 65). Rather than worrying about incoherence and instability, we should be more concerned

> when we become too comfortable with ourselves, too fixed in a specific identity ... we should learn to play more roles, to adopt any role that feels enjoyable ... [The] mask may not be the symbol of superficiality that we have thought it was, but the means of realizing our potential." (pp. 65–66)

Gergen was not the first to conceive of identities as masks (see, e.g., Shakespeare, 1599, 2.7.1037–1040). However, he was one of the first psychologists to argue that multiple identity is not only a fact but also a value. In other words, for Gergen it is not only *normal* for us to wear many masks but *desirable* for us to do so. He developed this prescriptive element further in his book, *The Saturated Self* (Gergen, 1991), arguing, in effect, that under conditions of postmodernity, in which everything is in flux, multiple identities are more adaptive than are fixed, coherent ones.

Theoretical Metaphor III: Stories

In the last two decades, as postmodern enthusiasms have waned, a third metaphor has gained in popularity: Identity as narrative. There seem to be several reasons for the shift. Not the least of which is the difficulty researchers have faced when attempting to operationalize metaphors like "crystallization" and "masks." As Sfard and Prusak (2005) write:

> After many hours spent in libraries and on the web, we concluded that we would not be successful unless we came up with a definition of identity more operational than those to be found in the literature. Lengthy deliberations led us to the decision to equate *identities with stories about persons*. No, no mistake here: We did not say that identities were *finding their expression* in stories—we said they *were* stories (p. 14; emphasis in the original)

The "story" metaphor shares something with the "crystallization" metaphor and something with the "masks" metaphor. Like crystals, stories have structure and coherence. Without these, they wouldn't be stories. Yet, like masks, the meaning of a story changes to some extent with each new telling, as goals and audience vary.

When Mixed Metaphors Lead to Muddled Theory

In terms of fashion cycles in social science, the above three metaphors have been presented in rough chronological order. However, one should not conclude from this that these metaphors are related to each other as Hegelian thesis-antithesis-synthesis, or that social-scientific theorizing about identity is somehow cumulative. Firstly, the three metaphors I have chosen to highlight are only some of the more prominent ones. Other popular metaphors for identity include, "negotiation" (Swann, 1987), "membership" (Tajfel, 1974), and "participation" (Lave & Wenger, 1991). Secondly, versions of each metaphor have appeared before. Something like Erikson's crystallization metaphor is implicit in the writings of William James (James, 2009/1890), while Gergen's mask metaphor is anticipated to a large extent by Erving Goffman's writing about self as performance (Goffman, 1959).

For our current purposes, it is sufficient to note that each of the three metaphors I have highlighted is still in current use—often by the same person, occasionally in the same breath. This is where the trouble starts.

Mixing incompatible metaphors, is, according to George Orwell (1946), "a sure sign that the writer is not interested in what he is saying." As he explains in his essay:

> A newly invented metaphor assists thought by evoking a visual image, while on the other hand a metaphor which is technically 'dead' (e.g., iron resolution) has in effect reverted to being an ordinary word and can generally be used without loss of vividness. But in between these two classes there is a huge dump of worn-out metaphors which have lost all evocative power and are merely used because they save people the trouble of inventing phrases for themselves.

According to Orwell, then, if we want to ascertain whether an educator means what he says when he talks about identity, we have simply to observe whether the metaphors he uses are mutually compatible.

Similarly, a good way to ascertain what precisely educators are trying to do to learners' identities is to consider the verbs they use to describe what they are doing. For example, if an educator talks of "strengthening" a learner's Jewish identity, we can assume that this educator considers a healthy, mature Jewish identity to be one that is robust and resilient in the face of attack or attrition. We can assume also that, according to this educator, Jewish identities *need* strengthening; left to their own devices, Jewish identities are somehow fragile or liable to collapse. As this example demonstrates, verbs often function in educational discourse as telescoped metaphors. One more thing before diving into the data: My aim here is not to criticize particular educators or institutions. It is, instead, to highlight confusions and internal contradictions of which we are all guilty, and to illuminate the power of the words we employ in the service of educational aims. The authors of the examples cited below are committed, thoughtful and well-intentioned colleagues. By carefully analyzing their uses of identity language, my aim is not to criticize them in particular, the values they hold dear, or their professionalism as educators. As a Jewish educator, I share many of their goals. If I point any fingers, therefore, it is at "us," not "them."

Practical Metaphors I: Strengthening Distant Identities

I begin with a text I received from the Jewish Agency, which served as background material for a lecture I was to give their senior professional leadership. With impressive courage and self-awareness, the Agency was in the midst of re-examining its goals with respect to Jewish identity. One of the documents (Jewish Agency for Israel, 2010) began thus:

> In June 2010, the Board of Governors approved new strategic directions for the Jewish Agency that focus on strengthening the Jewish identity of the younger generation as the central vehicle through which we can impact the Jewish future and address some of the major challenges facing the Jewish world. . . . Our new strategic directions . . . will . . . prevent young Jews from around the world opting out of the global Jewish collective and growing apart from Israel [and] prevent young Israelis who are increasingly distanced from their Jewish roots opting out of the global Jewish collective. (chapter 5)

For a policy document, the prose is admirably clear. Yet, even in these first few sentences, we are faced with ambiguities and tangled metaphors. Clearly, "strengthening the Jewish identity of the younger generation" (chapter 13) is a major goal. But is it an end or a means? Is it a proximate goal, the achievement of which will draw us closer to the ultimate goal of "addressing some of the major challenges facing the Jewish world"? Or is the supposed direction of causality reversed, with strong Jewish identity as the ultimate goal and facing the Jewish world's major challenges a means to that end?

Setting these ambiguities aside and moving on to the latter part of the excerpt, we note the introduction of a new set of not entirely compatible metaphors. We have young Jews "opting out," "growing apart," and becoming "increasingly distanced." And, correspondingly, we have "our new strategic directions" which will "prevent" these undesirable outcomes. Formulations like these are so familiar to us that we tend to gloss over them without pausing to worry over coherence or meaning. We can see where the authors are heading and we want to keep up. But, just once, let's pause and re-read. We started with talk of "strengthening" and now we're talking about "preventing." If what we were trying to prevent was "weakening," this would all make perfect sense. We'd be for strengthening and against weakening. But look closely. It's not "weakening" we're seeking to prevent: it's "distancing." And even here, we seem to be talking about several, distinct kinds of distancing. There's "opting out" and there's "growing apart" and there's becoming "increasingly distanced." It appears that the authors consider these phrases and ideas to be interchangeable, with variation introduced merely for literary effect. But they're not. "Opting out" suggests that Jewish identities are like newsletter subscriptions. You click on the "unsubscribe" box and you're done; a rational consumer exercising his freedom to choose. "Growing apart" assumes that Jewish identities are like relationships; despite the good will on both sides, it's just not working anymore; musical differences and the desire to see other people have grown too large to ignore; it's time to call it a day. "Increasingly distanced" suggests that it's not even our fault; some unnamed other is the culprit. Distancing isn't something we're doing; it's something that's happening to us.

It doesn't take much hermeneutical heavy lifting to realize we're confused. All we have to do is look at the text's surface structure. If you're in the mood to roll up your sleeves and get really stuck in, consider what a strong identity might look like. Is it strong like a password, strong like an ox, strong like a bridge, or strong like an alcoholic beverage? Is it strong because it's immovable or strong because it's flexible? Is strength acquired through exercise, distillation, or buttressing? And how is distancing prevented? By corralling the endangered into small spaces with high fences? By removing "opt out" boxes? By relationship counseling?

Practical Metaphors II: Bequeathing Commitment

The next text is from the Israel Defense Forces Education and Youth Corps' (2011) "Torat Hahinukh" (or "Education Doctrine"). The Education and Youth Corps provides training and enrichment courses for soldiers and commanders in the Israel Defense Forces (IDF) at various points in their careers. It also provides other corps in the IDF with embedded education officers, who are responsible for the ongoing education of soldiers in the units to which they are assigned. A key area in which the Education and Youth Corps is active in the development of soldiers' "Israeli-Jewish identity."

I begin with the authors' statement of the goals of education in the IDF:

> Ultimate Goal: Cultivation of a strong feeling of belonging and meaning among soldiers and commanders. Strengthening their commitment to service in the Israel Defense Forces through understanding the ties that bind them to the State of Israel as a Jewish and democratic state and to the Jewish people.
>
> Goals:
> 1. Strengthening the concept of military service as a meaningful act for the individual and as a conscious expression of his belonging to the State of Israel and the Jewish people;
> 2. Understanding the complex environments within which IDF commanders and soldiers operate, and assistance coping with issues of legitimacy and direction, in order to support the commitment of commanders and soldiers to fulfill the missions they are assigned;
> 3. Strengthening the components of personal identity, alongside the components of collective identity, and strengthening the individual's ability to distinguish between them. (p. 56)

As in the previous example from the Jewish Agency, "strengthening" features heavily. But here it plays a different role. Strong identities are means, not ends. The ultimate goal is that soldiers be committed to service in the IDF; the strengthening of their Israeli-Jewish identities is a means to that end. Second, strengthening is conceived here as an activity that involves meaning-making, understanding, and differentiating between different components of one's identity. These latter themes are developed further in a passage that describes the Education and Youth Corps' methods:

> The approach to work on Israeli-Jewish identity includes several complementary, interrelated components:

A. The educational mission: Building two supports on which the discussion will be based: Knowledge and emotion

B. The educational activity: The educational move that enables the creation of change based on the educational mission

C. The result: Strengthening and deepening commitment, based on integrated meaning work: Knowledge, emotion and clarification. (p. 59)

This description is followed by a diagrammatic representation of the educational process (see Figure 1):

From the above we see that the IDF sees its mission as to engage soldiers' hearts as well as their minds; to bring about change in the soldiers' identities through values clarification; and thereby to deepen their commitment to service in the IDF. Moreover, we are presented with a visual metaphor of construction, reinforcing the impression that Israeli-Jewish identity is made up of a particular set of building blocks and the IDF's role is to serve as a builder. Indeed, this metaphor of the IDF as a builder of Israeli-Jewish identities has deep historical roots, reaching back to David Ben Gurion's oft-quoted aphorism: *Am boneh tzavah boneh am* —"A people builds an army builds a people."

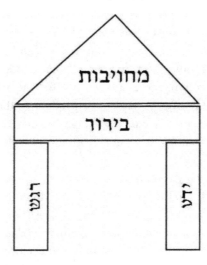

Figure 1 The IDF's approach to work on Israeli-Jewish identity (IDF Education and Youth Corps, 2011, p. 59). The left column represents "Knowledge," the right column, "Feeling," the horizontal bar "Clarification," and the triangular roof "Commitment."

Elsewhere in the text, the authors develop this approach in relation to specific "components" of Israeli-Jewish identity, such as "the people's heritage," "Zionism" and "bequeathing the memory of the Shoah" (pp. 48–49):

> Strengthening the sense of meaning and belonging of soldiers and commanders requires the development of a consciousness of shared fate and shared destiny. In these contexts, the goal is to understand that we are connected by memory of the past and a view of the challenges of the future. The work will focus on acquaintance with the components and characteristics of Israeli-Jewish identity, on cultivation of respect and tolerance for different approaches and streams in the world of Judaism and on processes of personal clarification. . . . When feet are planted deep in national, cultural and ethical heritage, there is a different power to the hand that holds the weapon. . . . To strengthen the sense of belonging among all who serve, the IDF seeks to advance acquaintance between groups and to cultivate tolerant and open discourse. The activity will address the common denominators and deepen also by clarifying the disagreements. . . . Bequeathing the memory of the Shoah in the IDF in these contexts strengthens the soldier's sense of belonging to the Jewish people, the State of Israel and the IDF. (pp. 48–49)

Of the three metaphors we reviewed earlier, the IDF's approach is closest to Erikson's "crystallization." Soldiers encounter ideas and groups that challenge their existing concepts of who they are and what matters to them. The IDF initiate and choreograph these encounters to encourage reflection and then commitment. Moreover, the desired product of the process is a firmly constructed identity, with all building blocks put together in such a way as to ensure that the resulting structure is strong enough to withstand future challenges.

So far, so clear. However, look a little more closely at the verbs used to describe the process. There's "strengthening"—which is to be expected. But there's also "development," "acquaintance," "cultivation," "clarification," and "bequeathing." These all appear in passive rather than active forms, obscuring who exactly is doing what to whom. Moreover, the actions to which they refer are not in any obvious sense interchangeable. For one thing, they entail different kinds of subjects, objects and relations between the two. Development happens to an individual. Acquaintance occurs between one individual and another, or between an individual and some other object. Cultivation occurs when one individual tends to the growth of another object or quality. Clarification is something one does to one's own thoughts or ideas. And to bequeath is to transfer one generation's property into the possession of the next. In other words, the process involves one, two, three or more actors, depending on the verb. Similarly, the objects on which the implied actors act vary from persons to ideas to cultural legacies. These are objects of a bewildering variety of shapes and sizes.

It is only when we pause to read slowly, and to take seriously the metaphors used here to describe identity education, that we realize how eclectic and vague the description is. The authors' use of passive, abstract formulations obscures tensions that become apparent the moment we attempt to translate them into concrete terms. Consider the relations between bequeathing and commitment. Commitment can't be bequeathed. This isn't an empirical fact but a logical one. Committing is something you do; it is active. Receiving a bequest happens to you; it is passive. Indeed, the overarching metaphor (made explicit in the diagram) of identity education as an act of construction, with the IDF as builder, is in fundamental tension with the doctrine's emphasis on individual reflection, meaning-making and commitment. If the soldier constructs his own identity, then the IDF isn't so much a builder as an architect and supplier of building materials. On the other hand, if the IDF *is* a builder, then acts of meaning-making, clarification, and commitment by individual soldiers are beyond its power to perform. Such acts of interior design are simply not the kinds of things that can be contracted out to a third party; they can be performed only as DIY (Do It Yourself).

At the Mandel Leadership Institute, we run an educational leadership program for senior IDF officers. When I ask these officers to describe the IDF's educational role in Israel, many reply: *lehaqnot arakhim*. The closest idiomatic translation I can offer for this phrase is "to impart values," but this doesn't do justice to the eccentricity of the formulation. The verb, "*lehaqnot*," is a *hiph'il* construction of the root, *kanah*—to acquire. Translated more literally, the term, "*lehaqnot arachim*," means approximately, "to cause others to acquire values." Consider this for a moment. The phrase acknowledges on one hand that values are something that a soldier—or any person, for that matter—can acquire only for himself. On the other hand, it places the IDF in the role of subject and the soldier in the role of object. In its mixture of active and passive, this linguistic move is similar to "bequeathing the memory of the Shoah." The fact that there are multiple phrases in the IDF's educational lexicon that contain built-in ambiguities about who is doing what to whom suggests that the ambiguity isn't accidental. Consciously or otherwise, the IDF is grappling with the question of how far it can or should intervene in the development of soldiers' Israeli-Jewish identities.

Practical Metaphors III: Connecting the Uninvolved to Authentic Jewish Personalities

My final example is from a report by Hillel International (Zwilling, 2010) on its recent initiatives to increase "Jewish engagement" among students in the USA. The report begins by defining the challenges these initiatives seek to address:

> In an era of extended emerging adulthood, where personal interests and social networks reign over institutions and organizational membership, organizations are being pushed to define new ways to connect the next generation to the richness of Jewish life. Hillel has taken this challenge to heart … In 2006, Hillel: The Foundation for Jewish Campus Life released a five-year strategic plan that enunciated a new mission: "Enrich the lives of Jewish undergraduate and graduate students so that they may enrich the Jewish people and the world." (pp. 4–5)

At the outset, we are faced with two distinct metaphors: "connection" and "enrichment." The "connection" metaphor is elaborated somewhat in the subsequent paragraphs:

> Rather than focusing on the number of participants in Hillel programs alone, Hillel now evaluates its success based on students' Jewish growth. Participation in one-off activities, it is felt, is a limited measure of success, as it only denotes attendance at a Hillel event. On the other hand, growth implies a meaningful transformation, laying the foundation for students to embark on lifelong Jewish journeys far beyond their four years on campus.
>
> Hillel embraced two methodologies to move its work beyond "the institution" and "the program" to help each student connect to, explore, and affirm their Jewishness: "Relationship-Based Engagement" and "Meaningful Jewish Experiences."
>
> Relationship-Based Engagement is an outreach method based on building relationships with students as individuals, learning about their stories, gaining an understanding of what is of interest and value to them,

and connecting them to Jewish life in ways that support their development and growth.

Meaningful Jewish Experiences are experiences that create positive Jewish memories, Jewish self-confidence, Jewish knowledge and connections to Jewish people/community. Meaningful Jewish Experiences lead students to develop ownership of their own Jewish experiences—making active choices to advance their Jewish journey and ultimately, although often later in the future, to make an enduring commitment to Jewish life. (pp. 6–7)

From these paragraphs we learn that the things to which Hillel seeks to connect young Jews are several and various. They include, "their Jewishness," "Jewish life," and "Jewish people/community." What Hillel means by "enrichment," however, is less clear. From the context, it appears to include some or all of the following: growth, meaningful transformation, exploration, affirmation, journeys, knowledge, self-confidence, ownership and commitment.

As in the texts by the Jewish Agency and the IDF, we are presented with a bewildering array of actions and relations. What does it mean to connect to one's Jewishness? Is it like getting in touch with your feminine side, spending quality time with your father, or logging onto a Wi-Fi hotspot? And how does one connect to Jewish life, if not by participating in "one-off activities?" (Zwilling, 2010). By participating repeatedly in routine activities? If so, which activities? And how many times must one participate in them to qualify as connected? Similarly, what is a meaningful transformation? How does it differ from a meaningless one? Is it a procedure you perform on yourself or something that someone else—preferably a licensed professional—performs on you? And how does one help a person "to explore"? (p. 6). By supplying the would-be explorer with the metaphorical equivalent of shoes? A GPS? A research grant? A native guide? Wanderlust?

None of these suggestive metaphors is developed or elaborated. However, additional clues as to the conception of Jewish identity underlying Hillel's approach appear later in the document, when two strategic initiatives are described: The Campus Entrepreneurs Initiative and Senior Jewish Educators:

Campus Entrepreneurs Initiative Interns are previously uninvolved Jewish students, from broad and diverse social networks, who are hired by Hillel and trained to use relationship-based engagement methods in building and developing their own social networks to connect their uninvolved Jewish peers to Jewish life. . . . Senior Jewish Educators are talented educators with deep Jewish knowledge and authentic Jewish personalities who serve as mentors and teachers for students' Jewish journeys, focusing particularly on those students who are not already involved in Jewish life on campus. . . . CEI Interns and Senior Jewish Educators encourage students to become an active part of defining or expanding their Jewishness. This principle of self-efficacy lays the groundwork for students to continue to find their own meaning in Jewish life long after they graduate. (pp. 7–14)

One striking feature of these descriptions is the implied gulf between those whom Hillel has recruited and the larger body of Jewish students that their recruits are expected to serve. The "involved" are contrasted with the "uninvolved." Senior Jewish Educators possess "deep Jewish knowledge and authentic Jewish personalities"—implying that others possess only shallow Jewish knowledge and personalities that are not (yet?) authentically Jewish.

Another striking feature is the difference between the before and after pictures of the target students. After being connected to their Jewishness by more involved peers and guided on their Jewish journeys by mentors more knowledgeable and authentic than themselves, they "become an active part of defining or expanding their Jewishness," and are able to "find their own meaning in Jewish life." How exactly this dramatic shift from passive to active is supposed to occur is not explained. In most of the sentences used to describe the two strategies, Hillel volunteers and professionals are the subject and target students the object. By what process do these latter, formerly passive individuals suddenly acquire agency? Moreover, if agency is a necessary condition for authentic Jewish identity, then, when Hillel professionals cast students as objects rather than subjects, they deny them—by definition—the very thing they say they wish these students to have. Hillel's mixed metaphors thus seem to lead to conceptions of identity education that are either circular or paradoxical.

The Importance of Being Literal

When I confront educators with their mixed-up identity metaphors, most do something remarkable: They acknowledge their discomfort and admit they have a problem. Indeed, they worry more about the moral implications of their everyday talk than about its logical consistency. It is uncomfortable to recognize that, while you prefer to think of identity education as a rational and noncoercive enterprise, your language casts you in the role of a planter or builder and those whom you teach in the roles of plants and buildings. That educators don't deny or ignore this discomfort is impressive. It would be all too easy to rebut my arguments as *pilpul* or nitpicking, the kind of "foolish consistency" that Ralph Waldo Emerson attributed to "the hobgoblin of little minds" (Emerson, 2007/1841). But, as these educators recognize, my critique is not about grammar or vocabulary; it's about ideas and actions.

When talking or writing about identity, I encourage us to take our metaphors literally, or at least to mix our metaphors responsibly. Not always or exclusively, but with sufficient regularity as to keep our heads clear and our feet within reasonable reach of the ground. As Orwell warned, when metaphors become unmoored from the images they were created to invoke, incoherence and banality follow. To paraphrase Orwell, our language of Jewish identity "has become ugly and inaccurate because our thoughts are foolish, but the slovenliness of our language makes it easier for us to have foolish thoughts" (Orwell, 1946). Let us endeavor to clean up our language and have wiser thoughts.

Bibliography

Emerson, R. W. (1841). *Self-Reliance*. Retrieved from http://www.emersoncentral.com/essays1.htm

Erikson, E. H. (1963/1950). *Childhood and Society*. New York, NY: W. W. Norton.

Erikson, E. H. (1968). *Identity: Youth and Crisis*. New York, NY: W.W. Norton.

Gergen, K. J. (1972). Multiple Identity: The healthy, Happy Human Being Wears Many Masks. *Psychology Today* 5(12), 31–35; 64–66.

Gergen, K. J. (1991). *The Saturated Self: Dilemmas of Identity in Modern Life*. New York, NY: Basic Books.

Goffman, E. (1959). *The Presentation of Self in Everyday Life*. New York, NY: Doubleday.

Hutchins, E. (1995). *Cognition in the Wild*. Cambridge, MA: MIT press.

IDF Education and Youth Corps. (2011). *Torat hahinukh (Hebrew)*. Retrieved from http://www.chinuch.aka.idf.il/SIP_STORAGE/files/0/1620.pdf

James, W. (1890). *The Principles of Psychology*. Retrieved from http://ebooks.adelaide.edu.au/j/james/william/principles/

Jewish Agency for Israel. (2010). *Securing the Future: Forging the Jewish Agency for Israel and the Jewish People (Part II: Operationalizing the Strategy)*. Jerusalem, Israel: Jewish Agency for Israel.

Lakoff, G., & Johnson, M. (1980). *Metaphors We Live By*. Chicago, IL: University of Chicago Press.

Lave, J., & Wenger, E. (1991). *Situated Learning: Legitimate Peripheral Participation*. New York, NY: Cambridge University Press.

Marcia, J. E. (1966). Development and Validation of Ego-Identity Status. *Journal of Personality and Social Psychology, 3*(5), 551–558.

Orwell, G. (1946). Politics and the English Language. Retrieved from http://www.orwell.ru/library/essays/politics/english/e_polit/

Sfard, A., & Prusak, A. (2005). Telling Identities: In Search of an Analytic Tool for Investigating Learning as a Culturally Shaped Activity. *Educational Researcher, 34*(4), 14–22.

Shakespeare, W. (1599). *As You Like It.* Retrieved from http://www.opensourceshakespeare.org/views/plays/playmenu.php?WorkID=asyoulikeit

Swann, W. B. (1987). Identity Negotiation: Where Two Roads Meet. *Journal of Personality and Social Psychology, 53*(6), 1038–1051.

Tajfel, H. (1974). Social identity and Intergroup Behavior. *Social Science Information/sur Les Sciences Sociales, 13*(2), 65–93.

Zwilling, J. (2010). *Emerging adults: The Hillel Model for Jewish Engagement.* Retrieved from https://www.bjpa.org/content/upload/bjpa/c___w/Zwilling-Emerging-Adults.pdf

You are Jewish if You Want to Be: The Limits of Identity in a World of Multiple Practices

Samira K. Mehta

In 2013, Paula J. Freedman published *My Basmati Bat Mitzvah*, a young adult novel about "just your average Jewish-Indian-American girl." Tara Feinstein, the narrator, is Jewish and also half-Indian, and she wants her bat mitzvah to acknowledge those facts. She also worries that having a bat mitzvah might somehow distance her from her recently deceased grandfather, Nanaji, especially after one of her Hebrew School classmates suggests that the statue of Ganesh in her bedroom is a false idol. Eventually, watching her Punjabi aunt doctor her Jewish grandmother's matzo ball soup while her grandmother traded knitting tips with her Muslim classmate's mother, Tara mused, "I thought again of Nanaji, how much he would have approved of Auntie's mixed-up little Punjabi-Bengali-American-Hindu-Muslim-Jewish Diwali potluck. And then I knew—it was going to be okay. . . . I could be Indian American and Jewish American all at the same time. I could have my bat mitzvah and still honor Nani and Nanaji. I was a spiritual person, like Nanaji. I was just me, and there was nothing weird about that" (p. 203). Tara's form of honoring her non-Jewish grandparents through her bat mitzvah meant more to her than simply keeping elements of Indian culture present in her life, like wearing a dress made out of a family sari or of putting *chat masala* on her popcorn. The novel suggests that in addition to having a bat mitzvah and taking her spiritual dilemmas to her rabbi, claiming both an Indian and a Jewish American identity also means that she will continue to be unsure she believes in God, to rub Ganesh's stomach and light incense in his honor for luck, and to not just celebrate Diwali but also learn about the significance of the holiday.

Freedman's novel depicts a world that is diverse and fluid, with friendships that cross boundaries and senses of self that contain many disparate elements.

Tara's identity is messy, and she pulls practices and ideas from any number of cultural and religious sources, but it also represents changes in the contemporary Jewish landscape and in the American landscape more broadly. If Tara's messy and multifaceted identity is increasingly the norm, then what are the repercussions of framing Jewish identity as singular, coherent, neat, or otherwise privileged over the other identities people hold at the same time?

This chapter seeks to examine this question by exploring some of the possibilities made possible by people who lay claim to multiple identities. It argues that Jewish identity can often lie alongside strong commitments to Christian (or other) practice, and sometimes even Christian (or other) belief. It demonstrates that Jewish identity can continue to exist even when it is not a primary identity. These findings posit the possibility that identity categories that assume Jewish exclusivity or primacy curtail our ability to recognize complex expressions of Jewishness, which are often articulated in concert with beliefs and practices associated with other religious and cultural traditions.

I want to pause here to offer two important caveats about this chapter and its claims. First and foremost, I am calling for an academic intervention. While I want to claim that it is vitally important for Jewish Studies scholars to look for Jewish practice, identity, and self-understanding wherever and in whatever forms it comes, I am not suggesting that every Jewish institution should do the same. In the end, religious and community institutions will decide whether they are interested in including or fostering hybrid Jewish identities. As they do so, they should have access to research that explores the complexities of contemporary Jewish life, including Jewish lives lived on the margins of Jewish community or lived in multiple communities. How organizations will react to that research will depend on their own identities, missions, and orientation towards religious law and culture. In order to make those decisions, however, religious and educational professionals and other community power brokers should have nuanced descriptive scholarship to draw on, scholarship that depicts the American Jewish landscape as it is, rather than as they (or some of their subjects) might wish it were. This chapter is one attempt to provide insight into such complicated and multifaceted identities.

Second, when thinking about Jewish identity, both Jews and scholars of Jews have a tendency to think about Jewish identity in terms of its religious and cultural markers. These assumptions appear in the 2013 Pew study that describes "Jews by Religion" and "Jews of No Religion" as well as in common parlance, where people refer to themselves and others as "secular Jews" or "cultural Jews." Often the distinctions between "religious Jews" and "cultural Jews" seem like common sense. A religious Jew might go to synagogue, light Shabbat candles, and pray; a cultural Jew would do none of those things, but would enjoy, for instance, bagels, lox, and Woody Allen movies (or less facetiously, feel a strong connection to Jewish history, literature, peoplehood, or the state of Israel). Even though a religious Jew might share all of those cultural markers of identity, and a cultural Jew might participate in some aspects of religious life, by and large these distinctions seem clear and obvious. Not only do they seem obvious in a Jewish context, but they sometimes seem applicable in a Christian one as well. (Belief in the divinity of Jesus, the Virgin birth, and the resurrection are religious. Santa Claus, Easter baskets and bonnets, and Flannery O'Connor are cultural.)

However, labeling practices as inherently "religious" or "cultural" is not useful in an academic context. First, scholars of religion often use definitions of religion that are much broader than "common sense" definitions, making arguments about, for instance, the religious nature of food—considering the memories and emotions that food might evoke, or the ethical systems that inform dietary choices as much as the ritual roles or legal restrictions connected to food. In these understandings of religion, the meaning or experience attached to a practice in any given context is what makes it religious, not the inherent qualities of the food in question. As a result, a practice cannot always be consistently said to be religious as opposed to cultural—a walk in the woods or Handel's *Messiah* might be a religious experience for some people and not for others. Likewise, going to worship services might prove alienating to someone not inclined to pray.

People often decide to label practices "religious" or "cultural" for strategic reasons. My research on Christian-Jewish interfaith families has found that when someone is advocating for keeping Judaism and Christianity separate, he or she tends to use language of religion to describe both the traditions and the distinct practices. On the other hand, those who want to advocate for practicing both traditions in a home tend to frame them as cultural (Mehta, 2015, pp. 82–109). So, for instance, imagine an interfaith couple who has decided to raise their children Jewish. They join a synagogue and enroll the children in Hebrew School and are trying to decide whether the spouse with Christian heritage must give up having a Christmas tree. Those who believe that Jewish families should abstain from Christmas, at least in their own homes, frame the Christmas tree and its festivities as religious, even if they are denuded of references to the birth of Jesus as the Savior (as opposed to Jesus as a character in a story). Those who want to suggest that Jewish families can have a Christmas celebration in their home tend to frame the holiday as cultural, and point out that for many Americans (and others), the holiday is about trees, gifts, and goodwill rather than about Christ. The specific practices in question, and the meanings attached to them may be the same in both cases and so the labels of "religion" and "culture" serve strategic rather than analytic purposes.

Both because of the broad net that scholars of religion have cast in naming practices and because, in conversations and debates about interfaith families, the terms religion and culture primarily serve strategic purposes, I am deliberately avoiding applying those labels to the practices I've described. Rather, I suggest that one must examine practices and worldviews, whether or not they might be identified as "religious," in order to understand the stories people tell about how they fit in the world.

In practical terms, for scholars of Jewish Studies, this means thinking very carefully about context. Clearly, not everyone who eats matzo ball soup is Jewish. (My Hindu, Indian father had very strong opinions about dill in matzo ball soup.) Matzo ball soup, however, might connect some people to their sense of themselves as Jewish—it might remind them of family recipes, of holidays, of trips to delis. For some, those connections might take on a religious cast—a way of connecting to beloved grandparents or a key piece of getting into a holiday frame of mind. For others, it might be a source of cultural pride—knowing all the soup options in the neighborhood delis. The issue at hand is less whether the practice is definitively religious or cultural, but whether it is part of what connects a person to their Jewishness, and whether and how they articulate that connection.

The Pew Portrait of American Judaism

In order to think carefully about how to examine the role of practices, community, and belief in shaping identity, we need to rely on more than just survey data to determine where Jewishness lies. In 2013, the Pew Research Center released its now much discussed *A Portrait of Jewish Americans: Findings from a Pew Research Center Survey of U.S. Jews*. The study is, in many ways, a study of Jewish identity, in which researchers divided the respondents into four demographic categories, based on the respondents' "self-identification" (p. 23). Those four categories were:

1. Jews by religion, that is, "people who say their religion is Jewish (and do not profess any other religion)" (p. 18).

2. Jews of no religion. In other words, "people who describe themselves (religiously) as atheist, agnostic or nothing in particular, but who have a Jewish parent or were raised Jewish and who still consider themselves Jewish in some way" (p. 18).

3. non-Jewish people of Jewish background, or "people who have a Jewish parent or were raised Jewish but who, today, either have another religion (most are Christian) or say they do not consider themselves Jewish" (p. 18).

4. non-Jewish people of Jewish affinity: a group defined as "people who identify with another religion (in most cases, Christianity) or with no religion and who neither have a Jewish parent nor were raised Jewish, but who nevertheless consider themselves Jewish in some way" (p. 18).

The Jewish affinity of this last group can be based on having Jewish friends and relatives, a sense of kinship through Abraham, or a sense of connection because "Jesus was Jewish" (p. 18).

The trouble with the sociological markers that the Pew Study used, however, is that they often do not reflect how people incorporate Jewish heritage (or other forms of identity) into their daily lives. In her personal essay comparing her own ecologically grounded food practices to her grandmother's kashrut, American author Thisbe Nissen (2006) reflects that she and Judaism "pretty much play in different leagues," with her knowledge of Judaism coming primarily from her grandmother: "her habits and rituals and her kitchen" (p. 50). Nissen does not identify as Jewish, because she frames Judaism as a religion and for her, she writes, Judaism is not about "religion, per se." Rather, she is interested in "trying to live each day as best [she] can, trying to be a good person, trying to do as little harm and as much good as [she] might in this lifetime, trying to seek out some evolving meaning in this life" (p. 50). To Nissen, those goals are not explicitly religious because she is not a person who "pray[s] and worship[s] and believe[s]" (p. 50). She does, however, see her practices as tied closely to her grandmother's: "I feel like I am doing right in the world by growing organic vegetables. My grandmother felt she was doing right by keeping kosher. I know one seems a lot more rational to me than the other, but that's because I believe what I believe" (p. 50). Does Nissen's association of her own gardening with her grandmother's kashrut cause her to identify as Jewish? No, certainly not in a way that she might mark on a survey. It does, however, suggest that Jewish heritage shapes her worldview, and her daily practice of gardening.

Though sociological studies and categories have their uses, they often fail to capture the complicated factors that inform people's practices and worldviews. As an ethnographer of the Jewish community farming movement, Adrienne Krone notes that, often, when she interviews people who are working on Jewish farms, they explain that they do not primarily identify as Jewish, nor do they belong to synagogues or engage in the kind of practices reflected by sociological surveys. When she asks them why, then, they chose to work at the farm, they will reference any number of parallels between the farm's explicitly Jewish values and their own worldviews. At the same time that they decline to be labeled as Jewish, their life choices reflect an orientation deeply informed by Judaism. What, then, do we see when we dig in and look at the Judaism that gets missed when one adheres strictly to sociological categories?

Multireligious Life in the Jewish Daily *Forward*

The fact that people with complex religious identities are often interested in claiming aspects of their Jewish identity can be seen in the fact that they sometimes turn to deeply Jewish locations to pose their questions about identity. From February of 2014 through December 2015, the *Forward* ran a column called "The Seesaw," which purported to answer "all your questions about interfaith life." The Seesaw was an advice column, in which a panel of experts (largely rabbis, authors, and scholars) responded from a range of perspectives. The column continued the *Forward*'s long tradition of providing a forum for Jews to discuss the challenges of life in America. The *Forward*'s original advice column, "The Bintel Brief," often addressed questions of Americanization, and other columns have addressed more short-term community tensions, such as the debate over whether observant Jews belonged in the socialist Workman's Circle. The *Forward*'s collections of letters have long provided scholars with insight into what historian Annie Polland (2007) refers to as "a more complex sense of yidishkeit" than one that was either religious or secular (p. 378).

More than one letter to the Seesaw raised the question of Jewish identity in ways that showcase some of the limits of the term when one is interested in complex senses of self. For instance, on March 1, 2015, the *Forward* printed an anonymous letter that said, "My family is originally from Ecuador but we have Spanish ancestry and Jewish roots. For the first eight years of my life I lived with my maternal grandparents in Ecuador. . . . Our Judaism consisted of occasional visits to the synagogue and the observance of a few holidays." After the age of 8, however, the letter writer moved to the United States to join her parents.[1] The author's father had always been Catholic and her Jewish mother had converted to Catholicism. The letter writer explained, "They are very religious and throughout the years I have come to embrace Catholicism as my principal religion." Embracing Catholic belief, however, did not mean abandoning Jewish practice. The letter continues, "whenever Passover, Yom Kippur, or Tisha B'Av arrives I always celebrate them with my grandparents, who also moved to the States. Although I do not practice Judaism, I still cherish it because it was part of my childhood." The author has a Hebrew name, but, as a baby, was baptized as a Catholic. She also explained that because her father's family is indigenous, whenever she attempted to claim Judaism, people were skeptical, noting that she did not "look Jewish."

This letter writer demonstrates the conundrum of identity for understanding contemporary Jewish life. As the 2013 Pew study points out, 60% of American Jews believe that a person cannot be Jewish if "he or she believes Jesus was the messiah" (p. 14). Pew itself would not consider the letter writer Jewish, as she has come to share her parents' Catholic faith. She, however, asks, "I am Catholic, but can I also be Jewish?" Despite the fact that her adoption of Catholic faith suggests a belief in Jesus as the Messiah, a position that the Pew study tells us most American Jews find incompatible with Jewish identity, the letter writer's observance of Jewish holidays, particularly Tisha B'Av, gives her a more robust Jewish practice than many people who might otherwise actively identify as Jews.

The answers in the *Forward* also affirm the letter writer's Jewish identity. The first respondent, Rabbi Scott Perlo of 6th and I Synagogue (a community that reaches out to Jewish and "Jewish adjacent" young professionals) wrote, "Because of your remarkable family history, I have a rather uncharacteristic answer to your question (for me at least), which is: you are Jewish if you want to be." Rabbi Perlo pointed out that, because according to Jewish law, one cannot renounce Judaism, and therefore the letter writer has a Jewish mother (despite her conversion to Catholicism) and is Jewish. The rabbi, however, went on to point out that the letter writer had "left the Jewish religion and embraced Catholicism." Because the Catholic faith clearly mattered to the reader, and because so many Jews (including Perlo himself) find belief in Jesus and "being Jewish" incompatible, he suggests that the letter writer identify as a person with "Jewish heritage."

---

[1]   The letter writer's gender is not obvious from the letter. I have chosen to use "she."

Both Susan Katz Miller, the author of *Being Both: Embracing Two Religions in One Interfaith Family* and Rebecca Lehrer, the co-Founder and CEO of *The Mash-Up Americans*—"a website and consultancy representing the hybrid culture and new face of America"—answered out of less mainstream positions. Both responded unequivocally that if one feels that one is both Catholic and Jewish, one can be. They offered suggestions for how to navigate life as a Jew of color and for understanding that while you can define your own identity, communities can draw their boundaries and that there will be Jewish communities that will not welcome someone with Catholic faith. Lehrer observed, "You clearly feel very connected to your Jewish roots and childhood. You grew up Jewish. You continue to celebrate holidays with your grandparents. Frankly, this is a lot more than many Jews who don't have other traditions! I'm not going to tell you how you can identify, but you sound pretty Jewish to me." Lehrer's barometer for defining someone as Jewish is a combination of upbringing, sense of connection, and adult practice. Her response, out of the individual's own self-description, was not concerned with whether his identity would be transmitted to future generations.

In saying, "I am not going to tell you how to identify," Lehrer rooted identity firmly in the realm of individual choice. Miller responded similarly, "Judaism has been formative in your life. There is disagreement in Judaism over who is a Jew. So if people try to tell you what you can or cannot be . . . you can gently explain that above and beyond these disagreements, you choose to claim Judaism as part of your identity." Miller's answer gives more weight to institutional designations of "who is a Jew," but suggests that since there is disagreement in "Judaism" over who gets the to claim the title, the letter writer can simply stake her own claim. Of course, the individual's self-definition of herself as a Jew might not meet community standards, because of her Catholic identity. She might well find that Hebrew Schools would not admit her children, if she were also teaching them about Catholicism. Similarly, while she might or might not be welcome to join a synagogue, she would likely experience continued pushback against her self-definition as a Jew in such institutional settings.

In the spread of responses to the Ecuadorian Catholic wondering if she is a Jew, we can see the pitfalls of treating identity as a category of scholarly analysis. For both Lehrer and Miller, the individual's response is what matters, over and above community norms. You have Jewish identity if you lay claim to Jewish identity, whether or not the broader community agrees. Perlo offers an answer that is only subtly different. Rather than claiming to be Jewish and Catholic, identities that will seem to many to be in contradiction, Perlo suggests Catholic with Jewish heritage as a way to name the letter writer's connection to her grandparents' tradition in a way that will make sense to other people who will see Jewish and Catholic identities as incompatible.

These responses, and the disagreement between them, highlight some of the challenges facing Jewish identity as a category of scholarly analysis, namely that it focuses on how people publicly label themselves (or are labeled by others), rather than about what they do, what they believe, how they experience the world, and how they understand that constellation of factors. First of all, despite the fact that most Jews see belief in Jesus as contradictory to being Jewish, the letter writer's clear connection to her Jewish heritage and observance, via grandparents, of Jewish holidays makes even the most conservative of the responders hesitant to completely deny her claim to the label. Depending on what definition of Jewish identity the interpreter uses and their own personal politics, we get very different answers to whether the letter writer is Jewish.

Though the letter writer was most interested in whether she could claim a Jewish identity and the respondents gave answers that addressed both how they articulate her truth and whether that truth is likely to be accepted by other Jews, scholars should not necessarily think about identities using the same criteria that people on the ground use. As a scholar of religious studies, I want to know what makes up her religious world and how her connection to Jewishness fits within that world. Is her dedication to Jewish holidays about a dedication to her grandparents or to the meaning and the content of the holidays? How does the presence of Jewish practice in her life or familial relationships with Jews shape her worldview? Asking this type of question moves beyond questions of identity or of traditional definitions of religion as it is "commonly thought of by modern people...as a medium, for explaining, understanding, and modeling reality" (Orsi, 2006, p. 3) and instead moves in the direction of understanding "religion as a network of relationships between heaven and earth involving humans of all ages and many sacred figures together. These relationships have all the complexities—all the hopes, evasions, love, fear, denial, projections, misunderstandings, and so on—of relationships between humans" (p. 3).

In this approach to understanding religion, one can also see hints of a way to ask questions about Jewishness. Rather than asking "to what community does the letter-writer belong?" we can explore what her desire to be both Catholic and Jewish means. How does that dual heritage locate her in a network of relationships with God and people, with practices and histories?

What is at stake for her in claiming a given identity, and what is at stake for communities in accepting or rejecting that identity? Scholars do not necessarily have to label these networks of relationships as "Jewish" or "Catholic" even though the letter writer would prefer to do so. Rather, we can map out the influences and constellations of multiple and overlapping religious systems and relationships in people's lives, giving us keener insight into how people experience a plurality of religious heritages, communities, and commitments. In this way, the scholarly agenda might be different from the agenda of differing communities. A Jewish community or a Catholic one might well be interested in excluding members who actively claim multiple identities, but another way of approaching this dilemma is to ask: "how does the person make sense of their multiple identities?"

Double Minority: an Increasing Literature of Self-definition

While a letter in the *Forward* can hint at the question of multiplicity, to fully explore these blended American identities, we need a mode of analysis that can accommodate their complexity. In recent years, a memoir literature has emerged as the children of interfaith, interracial marriages write about their experiences. Prominent memoirs such as Rebecca Walker's *Black, White, and Jewish* (2002) and James McBride's *The Color of Water: A Black Man's Tribute to His White Mother* (2006) tease out the relationships between blackness and Jewishness for an earlier generation, in ways that include strong connections to Jewishness without claiming an unambiguous Jewish identity. Ideally, Jewish studies scholarship would develop language to explore these elements of Jewish experience and to trace the complicated relationship between Jewish heritage and African American identity that such voices articulate. Both McBride and Walker experienced, either in their families or in the broader culture, blackness and Jewishness framed in opposition to each other, and any ability for them to coexist within a family came through personal reconciliation rather than through community support. These memoirs demonstrate conflicting sets of assumptions about what constitutes race, ethnicity, and religion and a clear sense that whatever they are, they are unstable in the lives of biracial children of interfaith marriages. In addition, while neither McBride nor Walker claim Jewish religious affiliation, they also carefully articulate Jewish aspects of their self-understanding.

James McBride's memoir, subtitled "A Black Man's Tribute to His White Mother" explores his mother's history, of which he was largely unaware while growing up. Ruth McBride Jordan was born Jewish in Poland, under the name Ruchel Zylska and grew up in Virginia, in a home that was both Orthodox and abusive. While staying with relatives in New York, she discovered Harlem, fell in love, and was largely disowned by her family for her relationship with and marriage to a black man, Andrew McBride. As a young woman, Ruth McBride found Jesus Christ, to whom she remained devoted until the day of her death. She and her first husband were founding members of a Black Baptist Church where he was a minister. After being widowed, Mrs. McBride married Hunter Jordan, who was also black.

Ruth McBride Jordan did not speak about her Jewish past, and, when her children asked about her race, claimed to be "light skinned." The only real hint of her Jewish background came when the family went to the garment district, where she was able to haggle with the Jewish merchants in Yiddish. Scholars such as Habiba Ibrahim and Phillip Harper argue that Jordan was not "passing," in that she did not claim to be black, except by implication to her children. They point out that the communities accepted her, but noted her racial difference. Rather, her association with blackness was "based on a chosen association with black community, as opposed to a performance of identity ownership or essence" (Ibrahim, 2012, p. 127). Like a God who does not have a race, but rather is the "color of water," Ruth McBride Jordan attempted to keep herself separate from the question of racial identity, both denying her whiteness but never explicitly passing by claiming blackness (Harper, 1998, p. 383).

This analysis of Ruth McBride Jordan's relationship to blackness provides Jewish Studies scholars a way to think about her son's Jewishness. Just as his mother associated with blackness without claiming to be black, so McBride does not claim to be Jewish, while claiming an association with Jewishness. Jordan did not tell her son that she was an Ashkenazi Jew until he was an adult, but the knowledge of her Jewishness has since shaped his understanding of himself (Ibrahim, 2012, p. 127). Reflecting on his mixed heritage, he highlights her Jewishness:

> I don't consider myself Jewish, but when I look at Holocaust photographs of Jewish women whose children have been wrenched from them by Nazi soldiers, the women look like my mother and I think to myself, *There but for the grace of God goes my own mother—and by extension, myself.* When I see two little Jewish old ladies giggling over coffee in a Manhattan diner, it makes me smile, because I hear my own mother's laughter beneath theirs. (McBride, 2006, pp. 103-104)

While his memoir talks about a childhood of struggles with his mother's whiteness, as an adult, he highlights her Jewishness. Through his mother's Jewish heritage, he relates to both an oppressed people and an ethnic group. Elderly Jewish ladies are not only identifiable as Jewish rather than simply as white, but also they are familiar and bring joy because they resemble his own mother. Jewish mothers dying in the Holocaust are more human to him because of their resemblance to his mother. Just as Jordan connected to aspects of African American culture and heritage and cast her lot with her black husbands, children, and church, McBride sees his own connections to Jewish people in similar terms.

While one could leave this as a vestigial heritage in McBride's past, the act of remembering Jewish heritage, and specifically doing so through the Holocaust is, as Laura Levitt has argued, a kind of Jewish practice. In using photos to connect the experience of the Holocaust to his own family, McBride makes a move similar to those of many American Jews without family histories of the Shoah. He connects himself to an act of communal remembering, a practice that Levitt argues is central to the contemporary Jewish attempt to create an identity and, perhaps more importantly, an emotional intimacy with a Jewish past, and, for some, with God (Levitt, 2007, pp. 21; 29; 40–41). While McBride is not, himself, a Jew, with his act of remembering through images and familial identification, he is participating in what is, in essence, a form of Jewish religiosity—articulating why it is that he has "something of a Jewish soul."

In describing his connection to Jewishness, McBride has to navigate the question of identities that are ascribed to him, which limit the ones that he can easily assume. McBride is black. That is an identity ascribed to him by the racial politics of the United States and one that sits in uneasy tension with the minority status of Eastern European American Jews who have access to many of the privileges of American whiteness. McBride does not dispute the whiteness of Jews, or their position in the racial hierarchy of American politics. He likely knew, as he wrote his memoir, that James Baldwin argued that no matter the history of antisemitism in the United States or abroad, by the time of the Civil Rights movement, in the United States, "the Jew's" "only relevance is that he is white" (Goldstein, 2007, p. 1). Jews have not always been white in the American racial schema, and their becoming white is inextricably linked to their entry into the middle class. At times, Jews have adopted white American racism as part of a process of assimilation. Similarly, Jewish leaders have at times chosen to distance themselves from African American political concerns and communities. As scholars such as Eric Goldstein (2013),

Jodi Eichler-Levine (2013), Jonathan Boyarin (2013), and Yvonne Chireau & Nathaniel Deutsch (1999) have argued, realities complicated the dynamic between Jewish and black communities.

McBride's memoir pushes scholars to consider how the histories of these communities shape people who exist in or adjacent to both of them. McBride, for instance, nuances this view of Jews as simply white, connecting, through his own history, with their persecution.[2] The tension between Jewish whiteness and the reality of Jewish persecution provides a recurring theme in the navigation of interfaith, interracial identity. McBride's response represents a desire to find commonality between his heritage and his identity as a black man. Importantly, McBride's identification is not simply a matter of connection, sparked by looking at photographs—it has shaped his political stance on complicated issues of Black–Jewish relations. This search gave him particular insight and a position from which to critique how both Jews and Blacks sometimes frame each other in popular discourse:

> [w]hen I hear black "leaders" talking about "Jewish slave owners" I feel angry and disgusted, knowing that they're inflaming people with lies and twisted history, as if all seven of the Jewish slave owners in the antebellum South, or however few there were, are responsible for the problems of African-Americans now. Those leaders are no better than their Jewish counterparts who spin statistics in marvelous ways to make African-Americans look like savages, criminals, drags on society, and "animals" (a word quite popular when used to describe blacks these days). (p. 104)

It is from his sense of dual identification that McBride, in the end, rejects both of these political stances. "I don't belong to any of those groups," he wrote. "I belong to the world of one God, one people" (p. 104). McBride moves back and forth between his particular identities to reach towards a kind of universalism—one in which minority groups ought not take swipes at each other, rather than at their shared oppressor.

It is hard to know what McBride's politics would be without his connection to his Jewish heritage. Perhaps he would have come to similar universalisms without exploring it. Certainly, however, through his mother's life story and

---

2 See chapter 2 of Jodi Eichler-Levine (2013) in which the author writes about similar links between Jewish and African American persecution, though the mode of identification is often, in examples, reversed.

his own connection to his mother's Judaism, he finds an expanded sense of his own self. "Now, as a grown man, I feel privileged to have come from two worlds. My view of the world is not merely that of a black man but that of a black man with something of a Jewish soul." But what does it mean to be a black man and a professing Christian with a Jewish soul? McBride is most certainly not an African American Jew. For one thing, he explicitly states that he does not consider himself Jewish (p. 103). In addition, the acknowledgments to his book note that he and his mother would both like to thank "the Lord Jesus Christ for His love and faithfulness to all generations" (p. 297). In the very text in which he names himself a "black man with something of a Jewish soul," he makes an explicit claim of Christian faith.

Scholars of American Judaism, then, would benefit from modes of analysis that can account for McBride's own conception of himself. How does Jewishness operate in his life, given the fact that it was a late discovery, in light of his Christian faith, and in light of American race relations and categorization of Jews as white? Being able to account for the Jewishness in McBride's life is distinctly different from labeling him as Jewish, or as forbidding him to claim such an identity. Rather, it takes seriously the possibility that his experience tells us something about the relationship between African Americans and Jews in the United States, about places where Jewish memory and memorialization exist outside of formal Jewish contexts, and about the role that Jewish heritage can play in the lives of children of interfaith marriage who hold Christian beliefs and participate in Christian communities.

It means McBride embraces both the participation in Jewish acts of remembrance and nostalgia and refuses to allow black and Jewish identity to be framed in oppositional terms. Because of that dual identity, he can see the antisemitism among African Americans as corrosive and largely based on an understanding of history that ignores historic Jewish marginalization. Unlike Baldwin, McBride cannot see Jews as, in the end, white, and he connects to his mother's heritage through its history of marginalization, through her Jewishness and not her whiteness.

The black and Jewish identity that Rebecca Walker, by contrast, constructed is considerably less stable, though her upbringing had much more explicit Jewish content than did McBride's. Walker is the daughter of Alice Walker, an African American author, and Mel Leventhal, a lawyer and civil rights activist. When the couple married in the 1960s, they did so in violation of Mississippi's miscegenation laws. They divorced in the 1970s, with Leventhal moving to New York City and then the suburbs with a Jewish woman, and Walker going on to write the Pulitzer Prize winning novel *The Color Purple.* Rebecca Walker grew up traveling between her parents and their dramatically different worlds. As an adult, she has built a career as an essayist and memoirist, trading in part on stories about her difficult relationship with both of her parents.

In her 2002 memoir, *Black, White, and Jewish,* Walker claimed to not see marginalization when she looked at the contemporary American Jewish experience, with "what Jewishness has become" (p. 313). Rather than the oppression of Jewish history, she saw the wealth in places like Riverdale, Westchester County, and Jewish summer camps. Both because she felt marginal in that community, as a person of color, and because she politically valued solidarity with the marginalized, she did not integrate Jewishness into her own self-understanding, and she resisted, in the memoir, seeing the possibilities that McBride pointed to in dual heritage. Rather than focusing on her Jewishness, she presented herself as biracial, noting that "hav[ing] white inside of me" kept her from feeling fully African American (p. 304). As a result, she worried about African American friends and communities rejecting her because of her white father. Similarly, though she did not want to claim Jewishness, she could not singularly identify with black people as her people, asking, "How can I feel fully identified with 'my people' when I have other people, too, who are not included in that grouping" (p. 306). Instead of feeling an affiliation with "my people," black or Jewish, she wrote that she feels "an instant affinity with people who suffer, whether they are my own, whatever that means, or not," with the "legacy of slavery and discrimination in this country," as well as with "the legacy of anti-Jewish sentiment and exclusion" (p. 306). The alliance with suffering might be rooted in aspects of African American and Jewish history, but is not, for Walker, focused on those heritages, extending out to the internment of Japanese-Americans during World War II and "struggle against brutality and genocide waged against the Native Americans in this country" (p. 306). Whether this compassion for those who suffer grew out of Walker's Buddhist practice or whether it led her to Buddhism, she does not say (Bolton-Fasman, 2001; Tolsky, 2009). Either way, however, suffering became central to Walker's self-understanding and allegiance, and she no longer saw suffering as part of the American Jewish experience, so in her memoir she rejected an identification with Judaism (Eichler-Levine, 2013, xiii–xxiv).

At seventeen, Rebecca Grant Leventhal chose to change her name to Rebecca Leventhal Walker. She wrote that she did so to increase her connection to her mother and to her heritage as an African American woman, a heritage that she saw as much more deeply connected to a political response to suffering.

She describes dialogue with her mother about the change, but that when she told her father about her decision, he interpreted her choice as growing out of her own inherent antisemitism. He saw her as choosing a "less Jewish" name, a move that for Jews has been part of the process of assimilation and essentially, an act of Jewish passing. He assumed that she wanted to downplay her Jewish heritage because, on some level, she did not like Jews (Rottenberg, 2008).

According to Walker, however, her problem is not with Jews in the traditional sense of antisemitism. Rather, to her, like to James Baldwin, American Jews are white and she is not. In changing her name, she did not reject Jewishness so much as she rejected whiteness. "When I change my name I do so because I do not feel an affinity with whiteness, with what Jewishness has become, and I do feel an affinity with blackness, with an experience of living in the world with non-white skin." (Walker, 2002, p. 313). Leventhal, who had once written to Alice Walker that "their children sure would be of minority groups," understood himself as a minority, as a Jew, and perhaps that sense of self shaped his 1966–1967 civil rights work. His daughter, however, associated Jewishness with whiteness, but, more to the point, with the apolitical middle class whiteness for which she understood her father to have abandoned his radical civil rights work. Walker's reasons for separating herself from Jewish identity in her memoir can provide scholarly insight into how Jewishness is constituted around concepts like race and class, but also around politics. What does it mean to isolate suffering as a key piece of Jewish heritage but not to see it in the contemporary Jewish moment? How do people with multiple heritages navigate conflicts between them and does the embrace of one automatically mean the rejection of the other, as with Walker's last name? Jewish Studies scholars could approach this fine-grained set of questions about how a multiplicity of identities are navigated and in doing so could sharpen their analysis of how Jewish identity is understood, defined, perceived, adopted, or rejected in the contemporary and multicultural United States.

Part of why Walker's story cries out for analysis is that her clear-cut rejection of a Jewish identity turns out to be far from stable. Beyond the memoir, she was not as clear that she could step apart from Jewishness (even the memoir, after all, is named *Black, White, and Jewish*). In her 2001 interview with Bolton-Fasman shortly after the memoir was released, Walker explained, "I feel extremely culturally Jewish. . . . I did a series of interviews [for this book] with black women and Jewish women, and I had an intuitive connection to each person. There was a different dynamic happening with each of them and it was strong and tangible." Similarly, in a 2009 interview about parenting on with Molly Tolsky, Walker observed that she did not think it was possible for her five-year-old son, Tenzin, to grow up "without some Jewishness." She argued that "like so many Jews in America," she understands her Jewishness as "so much more cultural than religious," that she focuses on sharing elements of "cultural" Jewishness with Tenzin. She intentionally "peppered" her conversation with him with Yiddish, explaining, "I feel like I'm bridging an old world connection there, because my grandmother's mother was from Kiev, and she always used—from *mensch* to *tuchus* to *meshugeneh*—a breadth of Yiddish words." Her Jewish insertions, then, are actually far removed from her political concerns for "people who suffer," and they expose a more positive valence of familial memories and ties.

The scholarly questions here are not focused on whether Walker is Jewish, or should be able to claim Jewishness. Rather, they seek to better understand how she, at different moments, take on aspects of Jewishness or put them aside and to what ends. What work do those choices do for her? Similarly, what does it mean to her for her child to be "a little bit Jewish?" What does she want to him to know about his "little bit" of Jewishness, and why does she value the connection to her grandmother's old world origins? How did Walker draw the connection between Jewishness and whiteness, and how does she reconcile alignments of whiteness and power against associations between Jewishness and suffering?

McBride and Walker do not intersect with Jewishness in the same way, despite the fact that they are both the children of Ashkenazi and African American marriages. They grew up in different communities and historical moments, in families that had distinct (if not necessarily carefully thought through) approaches to their blended identities. Perhaps they are utterly unique in their formation of identities or perhaps, as Emily Sigalow (2016) suggests in her work on syncretic identity, they fit within broadly drawn cultural patterns. Taken together, the memoirs do begin to suggest some patterns that are useful in thinking about this particular form of dual identity: Jewish and African American. Neither Walker nor McBride claims a conventional Jewish identity, though both see themselves as having a strong connection to Judaism. Both see themselves as having an affinity with Jews, but only in some contexts. Both have struggled with being of mixed race and have wondered whether and how to see Jews as white, as oppressor or oppressed. None of these observations are particularly surprising in light of both the experience of interfaith families and the history of Black–Jewish relations in the United States.

Conclusion

Multireligious, multiethnic, and multiracial families and individuals are increasingly part of the American landscape and therefore of the American Jewish landscape. Sometimes people who come out of these families actively claim Jewish identity. Sometimes they claim (or want to claim) Jewish identity alongside other identities—even other primary identities, as did the *Forward*'s Catholic letter writer who wondered if they could be both Catholic and Jewish. Other times, like Rebecca Walker, they both accept and reject Jewish or partially Jewish identities. And, like James McBride, others do not define themselves as Jewish, but still feel a connection and an association with Jewishness. The challenge for scholars of Jewish Studies, then, is to begin to explore all of the complicated ways that people intersect with Jewish thought and practice, taking on aspects of Jewishness and incorporating them into how they operate in the world. While claiming an identity is certainly one of the ways an individual might engage with Jewishness, it is not, potentially, the only way.

In this chapter, I have gestured towards some of the ways in which scholars might approach understanding these identities—I have pointed to expanded definitions of religion that might point also to expanded networks of looking for a kind of practice-based Jewishness, if not Jewish identity as such. I have explored James McBride as associated with Jewishness, while not Jewish, just as his mother associated with blackness without being black. And, in Rebecca Walker, I have suggested that the role that Jewishness plays in any given life may not be stable across a lifetime. The challenge, then, is to continue to theorize and explore these varieties of relationships to Jewish life.

Bibliography

Anonymous (2015). Can I Be a Jew-ish Catholic? Retrieved from https://forward.com/articles/215666/can-i-be-a-jew-ish-catholic/

Anonymous, L. (2015). Retrieved from https://forward.com/articles/215666/can-i-be-a-jew-ish-catholic/

Bolton, Fasman, J. (2001). Translating Between Two Worlds: An Interview with Rebecca Walker. Retrieved from http://www.interfaithfamily.com/arts_and_entertainment/popular_culture/Translating_Between_Two_Worlds_An_Interview_with_Rebecca_Walker.shtml

Boyarin, J. (2013). *Jewish Families.* New Brunswick, NJ: Rutgers University Press.

Chireau, Yvonne, & Deutsch, N. (Eds.). (1999). *Black Zion: African American Religious Encounters with Judaism* (1st ed.). Oxford, UK: Oxford University Press.

Eichler-Levine, J. (2013). *Suffer the Little Children: Uses of the Past in Jewish and African American Children's Literature.* New York, NY: New York University Press.

Freedman, P. 2013. *My Basmati Bat Mitzva.* New York, NY: Harry N. Abrams.

Goldstein, E. (Ed). (2007). *The Price of Whiteness: Jews, Race, and American Identity.* Princeton, NJ: Princeton University Press.

Harper, P. (1998). Passing For What? Racial Masquerade and the Demands of Upward Mobility. *Callaloo 21*(2), 381–397. doi:10.1353/cal.1998.0108

Ibrahim, H. (2012). *Troubling the Family: The Promise of Personhood and the Rise of Multiracialism.* Minneapolis, MN: University of Minnesota Press.

Leventhal, M. Letter from Mel Leventhal to Alice Walker. (1967/1966). Alice Walker Papers MSS1061 2/4, MARBL.

Levitt, L. (2007). *American Jewish Loss after the Holocaust.* New York, NY: New York University Press.

McBride, J. (2006). *The Color of Water: A Black Man's Tribute to His White Mother.* New York, NY: Riverhead Books.

Mehta, S. (2015). Chrismukkah: Millennial Multiculturalism. *Religion and American Culture 25*(1), 82–109.

Miller, S. (2013). *Being Both: Embracing Two Religions in One Interfaith Family.* Boston, MA: Beacon Press.

Nissen, T. (2006). Bury the Knife in Yonkers, Or Bibbity Bobbity Jew. In L. Snyder (Ed.), *Half Life: Jew-Ish Tales from Interfaith Homes.* New York, NY: Soft Skull Press.

Orsi, R. (2006). *Between Heaven and Earth: The Religious Worlds People Make and the Scholars Who Study Them.* Princeton, NJ: Princeton University Press.

Perlo, S. (2015). Can I Be a Jew-Ish Catholic? Retrieved from https://forward.com/articles/215666/can-i-be-a-jew-ish-catholic/

Polland, A. (2007). "May a Freethinking Man Help a Pious Man?": The Shared World of the "Religious" and the "Secular" Among Eastern European Jewish Immigrants to America. *American Jewish History 93*(4), 375–40.

Pew Research Center. (2013). *A Portrait of Jewish Americans: Findings from a Pew Research Center Survey of U.S. Jews.* Retrieved from http://www.pewforum.org/files/2013/10/jewish-american-full-report-for-web.pdf

Rottenberg, C. (2008). *Performing Americanness: Race, Class, and Gender in Modern African-American and Jewish-American Literature.* Hanover, NH: Dartmouth College Press.

Sigalow, E. (2016). Toward a Sociological Framework of Religious Syncretism in the United States. *Journal of the American Academy of Religion 84*(4), 1026–1055.

Tolsky, Molly. (2009). Five Minutes with Rebecca Walker. Retrieved from https://www.kveller.com/article/five-minutes-with-rebecca-walker/

Walker, R. (2002). *Black, White, and Jewish: Autobiography of a Shifting Self.* New York, NY: Riverhead.

On the Origins and Persistence of the Jewish Identity Industry in Jewish Education

Jonathan Krasner

Modern historian Jacob L. Talmon observed that "the links holding Jews together are—to use the words of Edmund Burke—as invisible as the air and as strong as the heaviest chains, and the Jewish ingredient to be as imperceptible to the senses, yet as effective in result" (1965, p. 69). The difficulties inherent in Jewish identity discourse are encapsulated in this poetic description. Yet, by and large, communal professionals, social scientists and educators have approached it with little prudence or humility. *The New York Times Magazine* dubbed 2015 as "the year we [Americans] obsessed over identity." But in American Jewish establishment circles, identity has long ago become a fetish, a preoccupation for Jewish social scientists, and the "holy grail" of Jewish education.

The discourse on Jewish identity and education is sufficiently ingrained and ubiquitous in American Jewish culture that it has an almost timeless quality. But, like most other buzzwords and phrases, it has a history that reveals much about its utility. Focusing on the years between 1940 and 1980, when the contemporary pattern was set, my purpose here is to historicize the term Jewish identity, to point out that it has a particular genesis and that the discourse on identity serves a particular purpose. It appeals to a set of needs that American Jews have felt, at least since the 1950s, which accounts for its popularity. Jewish educators have seized on identity formation, making it the raison d'être of their endeavor. But the ascent of identity discourse has also introduced a number of challenges for the Jewish educator that are conceptual, methodological, political, and even existential.

The Origins of Identity Discourse

The conventional wisdom in the academy is that the emergence of identity discourse was an outgrowth of the ethnic pride movements of the late 1960s. Some have connected the emergence of Jewish identity concerns with the Six Day War or the ethnic pride movements of the late 1960s and 70s. While these developments promoted increased public interest in heritage and a wave of cultural reclamation and refitting, the genesis of Jewish identity discourse is rightly located a generation earlier, in the anxiety-laden conversations about Jewish self-esteem during the 1940s, which gave way to creeping fears of assimilation in the mid-to-late 1950s and early 1960s.

Arguably, no scholar did more to bring identity into the consciousness of the American public than Erik Erikson. His book *Childhood and Society,* which was published in 1950, bequeathed to us the identity crisis. Erikson defined identity as "a subjective sense of continuous existence and coherent sameness" (p. 219). In Erikson's view, the individual negotiated a series of psychological struggles throughout the life course. Each of these developmental stages involved coming to terms with an existential question that contributed in a fundamental way to personality development.

Erikson recognized that identity had a psychosocial component that involved an appreciation of one's relationship to a larger group or groups and the internalization of the group's culture, values and philosophical outlook. But his work focused on the individual rather than social dynamics. Thus, it was left to others to develop his insights in the realm of social psychology. The adoption was rapid. Historian Philip Gleason observed that among the earliest writers to embrace the discourse of identity was Will Herberg, in his 1955 study of Americanization and religious group retention, *Protestant-Catholic-Jew.* Herberg's classic investigation of America's "triple melting pot" appropriated and repurposed identity as a sociological term of art. "Identity and identification are, in a sense, what the book is all about" (Gleason, 1983, p. 912). In Herberg's view, the process of white ethnic assimilation involved the dissipation of ethnic identity. In its stead the second and third generations came to identify with one of America's Judeo-Christian creeds. Religion, Herberg argued, was an acceptable way of retaining group distinctiveness.

Herberg's attraction to Erikson's conception of identity is notable given the role that Herberg's volume played in "affirm[ing] the arrival of Tri-Faith America" (Schultz, 2011, p. 85). Indeed, he implied that religious identification was an answer to postwar anomie. David Dalin asserted that *Protestant-Catholic-Jew* "served as a kind of 'scientific legitimation of the arrival of American Jews as partners on the national religious scene, bolstering Jewish self-respect and altering for better the perceptions of American Jews held by their non-Jewish neighbors" (Shapiro, 2003, p. 271; Dalin, 1988, p. 42). Dalin's characterization of the Herberg volume intimates why Erikson's psychosocial approach to identity development was appealing to a postwar Jewish community nursing the scars of antisemitism and preoccupied with its integration into American society.

Herberg was acutely concerned with what he characterized as "the perennial problem of belonging and self-identification." In particular, drawing upon sociologist Ruby Jo Kennedy's 1944 studies of ethnic and religious group endogamy and historian Marcus Hansen's "principle of third generation interest," he posited a metamorphosis in self-concept and sense of group belongingness among the descendants of European immigrants, the melting away of national characteristics and the persistence in the third and fourth generations of religious group cohesion. "They were Americans," Herberg wrote of the third generation, "but what *kind* of Americans?" Borrowing a line from immigration historian Oscar Handlin's 1954 volume, *The American People in the Twentieth Century*, Herberg asserted that the grandchildren of immigrants clung to group distinctiveness, "a sense of identity that would explain why they were different from 'One Man's family'" (Herberg, pp. 30–31). But whereas Handlin used the term identity in passing, Herberg fashioned it into a central descriptive and analytical frame (Gleason, p. 912). "Not to be a Catholic, a Protestant or a Jew is today, for increasing numbers of people, not to be anything, not to have a *name*," he wrote, with a bow to David Riesman. "To have a name and an identity, one must belong somewhere; and more and more, one 'belongs' in America by belonging to a religious community, which tells one *what* he is" (Herberg, p. 40).

At first glance, American Jews should have found Erikson's autobiography compelling. Erikson grew up feeling like a misfit and drew on his outsider-looking-in sensibility when formulating his conception of ego identity. A Jewish-born émigré to the United States whose concern about an ascendant German Reich compelled him to flee Vienna, in 1934, Erikson (*né* Homberger) changed his surname in a declaration of autonomy and a break with his European past. Yet, as Stephen Whitfield explained, Erikson was more intent on transcending the boundaries of Jewishness than reifying and celebrating them. "No one seemed less interested (or more ambivalent about [his Jewishness]) than the subject himself" (2002, p. 163). His biological father was most likely a gentile

Dane, a fact that Erikson's mother, Karla Abrahamsen Salomonsen, withheld from him during childhood. Theodore Homberger, the German Jewish doctor whom she married on Erikson's third birthday, raised the boy as his own. When the revelation came, it provoked a prolonged period of self-searching that only appeared to resolve itself after Erikson found a new surrogate father in Sigmund Freud. Erikson's biographer, Lawrence Friedman, recounts that later in life, Erikson, a convert to Christianity, was most intent on asserting his Jewishness as an act of defiance. When one of his graduate students inquired about Erikson's religious background, he reputedly replied, "If you are anti-Semitic, I'm a Jew" (Whitfield, p. 64; Friedman, 1999, p. 315).

Erikson's indifference did not stop others from recognizing the potential applications of Erikson's psychosocial exploration of identity to the Jewish condition. Kurt Lewin, whom we will discuss below, even compared the maladjusted Jewish adult to an "eternal adolescent" (Lewin, 1948b, p. 185). In particular, identity discourse served as a useful tool in discussing the post-war problems of Jewish adolescents, which dominated the writings and fears of Jewish educators. With the notion of "identity crisis," Jewish educators, rabbis and psychologists were handed an ideal construct to facilitate their exploration of the impact of antisemitism on Jewish youth's self-esteem. These Jewish professionals became focused on helping Jewish children and youth form positive emotional attachments to being Jewish. They wanted to make young people feel comfortable and proud to be American Jews (Furman, 2015).

Historian Philip Gleason contends that the term "identity" was typically used "casually" and in a loose and "unself-conscious manner" in earlier published writing (Gleason, p. 912). Yet even if it lacked analytical specificity, casual use of "Jewish identity" predated Erikson by more than a generation, at a time when it was seldom applied to other American racial or ethnic groups. In the interwar years it was sometimes employed in the course of anxiety-infused discussions of the negative affects of antisemitism on Jews' self-image. There was a panic around the phenomenon of passing, the suppression of identity in order to escape discrimination, and, it was supposed, as a consequence of self-loathing.[1]

---

1 An early but representative example of this discourse is found in Rabbi Hyman G. Enelow's 1920 volume *The Adequacy of Judaism*. Enelow, who was ordained by Hebrew Union College in 1898, and served for twenty-two years as the spiritual leader of Temple Emanu-El, in New York, decried those who "think they can ingratiate themselves with fashionable non-Jews by concealing their own Jewish identity, or by changing their original names or by transforming their native noses, or by belittling their inherited faith" (Enelow, p. 86)

Kurt Lewin: Champion of Jewish Belongingness

Not surprisingly, Jewish educators expressed alarm at the apparent pervasiveness of what contemporary scholars call "difference anxiety" (Malhotra, 2011, p. 25) and its attendant effects on the psyches of Jewish children and youth. As Joshua Fuhrman demonstrated in his recent dissertation, their concerns were given expression in the writings of prominent émigré psychologist Kurt Lewin, the father of group dynamics (Fuhrman, pp. 53–83). Not only did Lewin's theories speak to the Jewish condition, in the final decade of his life he pioneered the use of "action research," a model of investigation and intervention in response to social problems like prejudice and discrimination. And although Lewin did not use the term "identity," his scholarship laid the groundwork for how many social psychologists theorized Jewish identity in the 1960s and beyond.

The Prussian-born Lewin, described by Susan Glenn as "the pivotal figure in what might be called the Germanization of postwar American Jewish social thought," (Glenn, 2006, p. 102) was born in 1890, and was shaped by the antisemitism he experienced in Imperial and Weimar Germany. Recognized by the 1920s as one of the leading figures in the Gestalt school of psychology, he was nevertheless refused a tenure track faculty position at the Psychological Institute of the University of Berlin, due to his Jewish heritage, and was employed instead as a lecturer and, later, an untenured associate professor (Marrow, 1969, p. 54).

In 1933, when the Nazis moved to expel Jews from faculty positions at German universities, Lewin relocated to the United States and became a professor of psychology at the University of Iowa and, ultimately, the director of the Research Institute for Group Dynamics at the Massachusetts Institute for Technology, a position he held until his death in 1947 (Jackson, 2005, pp. 66–67). His most enduring intellectual contribution was in the area of social psychology, where he studied group behavior by applying the Gestaltists' insights into the integral nature of psychic organisms, that is, their insistence that they be treated as a unified whole rather than as a sum of their parts. He coined the term group dynamics, which he defined as the social and psychological processes and behaviors that characterize individuals' interactions within a collective, in response to internal or external forces (Dushkin, 1947, pp. 2–3; Nardi, 1947, pp. 7–10).

Lewin posited a link between group membership and healthy psychological development. "Whatever a person does or wishes to do, he must have some 'ground' to stand upon," Lewin wrote (Lewin, 1948, p. 145).

He warned that the burden of uncertainty about group membership as a child could metastasize into wholesale alienation and instability as an adult and perceptively understood the upsurge of antisemitism in interwar Europe and America as a reaction to the increasingly porous boundaries between Jew and gentile (Lewin, 1948, pp. 145–158). And while he declared forthrightly that self-hatred would be completely overcome only as a consequence of legal remedies to discrimination (Lewin, 1948c, p. 198), he believed that until then, Jews and other minorities could take steps in relation to their internal group life to minimize marginality's corrosive effects. "Only the efforts of the group itself will achieve the emancipation of the group," he wrote (Lewin, 1948a, p. 163).

For Lewin, the controlling factor in an individual's healthy sense of group belonging was a belief in a set of shared interests and an interconnected fate (Lewin 1948a, p. 166). While he acknowledged that overt self-hatred was rare, he insisted that its more subtle manifestations were all too common. The *coup de grâce*, he believed, was that Jewish "assimilation," a phenomenon that he equated with efforts by some light-skinned blacks to "pass" as white, hindered rather than facilitated their "friendly relations" with the majority. Efforts at deception would only be rewarded with heightened mistrust, whereas forthrightness would elicit respect (Lewin, 1948a, pp. 166–167).

Lewin's insights into marginality and group belonging had implications for inter- and intra-group relations writ large. But he popularized his scholarship in Jewish publication venues like *Jewish Frontier* and the *Menorah Journal*. To be sure, Lewin was only one voice among many in the late-1930s and 1940s warning about Jewish alienation and self-loathing. They included public intellectuals as varied as philosopher Horace Kallen, who described a generation of Jewish youth "in flight from their Jewish inheritance, and thus in flight from themselves," (Kallen, 1939, p. 84) and historian Salo Baron, who expressed alarm at the growing prevalence, in both Europe and North America, of "inverted Marranos" (Baron, 1942, p. 127). What distinguished Lewin's voice from the anxious chorus and made him the darling of Jewish educators was the combination of his scientific pedigree and reputation, and his conviction about the centrality of Jewish education in promoting Jewish psychological wellbeing. Andrew Heinze has written about the "therapeutic ethos that transformed American culture in the second half of the twentieth century" (Heinze, 2002, p. 32). Lewin's work on marginality and self-image emerged at the cusp of this revolution, and the Jewish public's yearning for a message of consolation after the Holocaust propelled it to even greater popularity after his death. Lewin had the credentials and the social psychology vocabulary to attract attention.

What is more, his message was essentially hopeful in that it coupled a diagnosis with a pathway to recovery, thus anticipating the self-help literature that appeared in its wake.

The cultural Zionist educators who dominated the Jewish education bureaus, community Talmud Torahs and synagogue center schools found in Lewin a kindred spirit. Although Lewin did not directly invoke Rabbi Mordecai Kaplan, who held outsized sway among the educators, the two seemed to share a functionalist concern with Jewish communal loyalty and collective consciousness. Religiously indifferent though he was, Lewin, nevertheless, believed in the power of Jewish education to promote a sense of common destiny, and thus facilitate group belonging. Similarly palatable was his dismissal of concerns about Jewish dual loyalties on the grounds that multiple group allegiances were natural and inevitable. Like them, he viewed the Yishuv in Palestine as a source of inspiration and pride rather than estrangement (Lewin, 1948b, p. 179; p. 185).

Prominent Jewish educator Alexander Dushkin became acquainted with Lewin in the course of recruiting an inaugural faculty for Hebrew University's Department of Education, in 1936. His efforts to lure Lewin to the fledgling institution were unsuccessful, but Dushkin renewed the acquaintanceship when he returned to the United States, in 1939, to direct the Jewish Education Committee of Greater New York (JECNY). Lewin was recruited as a featured speaker at educator conferences and his work appeared in the journal *Jewish Education*. His reputation was further burnished when he became director of the American Jewish Congress's Commission on Community Interrelations, where he was able to put into practice his model of action research (Jackson, pp. 67–68). At the time of his death, Lewin was working with the JECNY on an action research project focusing on teacher morale. In fact, he suffered his fatal heart attack while preparing an address on group dynamics for a JECNY-sponsored Jewish teacher professional development workshop (Dushkin, p. 3).

At the same time, Lewin's 1940 *Menorah Journal* article, "Bringing Up the Jewish Child," became a minor sensation and was reprinted posthumously by the United Synagogue for Conservative Judaism and the American Jewish Committee (Dushkin, pp. 2–3; Nardi, 1948a, pp. 10–11; 14–15; Furman, p. 71). While much of the article synthesized ideas that he presented in other venues, "Bringing Up the Jewish Child" was Lewin's first sustained argument for early intervention by Jewish parents and educators. Efforts to shield children from their underprivileged minority status were likely to backfire in the long run since they would inevitably encounter prejudice. Instead, caregivers and teachers should do their utmost to inoculate children from the sting of discrimination by imbuing them with positive feelings about their Jewishness and a sense of commonality with other Jews. "It is not similarity or dissimilarity that decides whether two individuals belong to the same or to different groups, but *social interaction and other types of interdependence. A group is best defined as a dynamic whole based on interdependence rather than on similarity,*" he wrote (Lewin, 1948b, pp. 182–184).

Lewin's wife, Gertrude Weiss Lewin, made efforts to promote Lewin's message after his death. She not only included Lewin's articles on Jewish social dynamics and marginality in an edited collection of his selected writings, but also interpreted Lewin for popular Jewish audiences. For example, in one article Mrs. Lewin compared the maladjusted Jewish child to the wicked son in the Passover Haggadah, who rejects his belongingness to the Jewish people. She also spoke candidly about the decision that she and her husband made to give their own children a Jewish education, acknowledging the backward pedagogic methods of some of her children's *heder* teachers, back in Germany, while reaffirming the value of their experience because it was "warm and intimate," and gave the children a "feeling of belongingness" (G. Lewin, 1947, pp. 14–16).

The American Jewish Committee and the Identity Campaign

Thus, Jewish education was charged with both an affective and a social aim. In this way, Lewin handed educators ammunition in their argument in favor of communal responsibility for Jewish education, a highly contested proposition during the interwar years. Federations and other communal charities tended to view Jewish education as a private matter, subject to parents' religious affiliation and personal convictions. Communal workers trained in social work and preoccupied with Jewish integration were particularly skeptical about the merits of including Jewish education among federations' funding priorities (Krasner, 2011, pp. 165–173; 407–408). By asserting a linkage between Jewish education and adjustment Lewin presented Jewish education as a social good.

Assessing Lewin's influence on Jewish education, Furman asserted that, "What originated under the shadow of Nazism as an approach to helping Jewish children overcome prejudice and unwelcome feelings of inferiority became, as the fundamental characteristics of American Jewish life changed dramatically in the 1950s and 1960s, the foundation of an approach to encouraging Jewish children and families to choose to identify as Jewish in an increasingly open and tolerant postwar society" (Fuhrman, p. 54). The theories of Lewin and Erikson were the sources of two tributaries that intermingled to create an impassioned Jewish identity discourse that inundated the communal landscape in the 1960s and 70s.

The two tributaries met up precisely at the moment when difference anxiety and attending fears of the psychological impact of self-hatred were giving way to concern about assimilation and Jewish survival. Identity discourse percolated as Jewish group belonging began to be experienced as voluntary. It provided a language to discuss a dynamic that had both social and psychological components, where interactions between the individual self-concept and group identification were bi-directional.

To gain an appreciation of how the invention of Jewish identity discourse was integrally related to this turn in communal priorities one need look no further than the case of the American Jewish Committee (AJC), one of the premier Jewish advocacy and defense organizations. Founded in 1906, in the wake of the Kishinev pogroms, by a coterie of well-connected, predominately central European Jewish establishment figures, the AJC became chiefly engaged during the 1940s and early 1950s in combatting anti-Jewish prejudice through education. Its celebrated five-volume *Studies in Prejudice* (1950) series, which included Theodore Adorno's *The Authoritarian Personality*, Bruno Bettelheim and Morris Janowitz's *Dynamics of Prejudice*, and Nathan Ackerman and Marie Jahoda's *Anti-Semitism and Emotional Disorder*, sought to convince a mass American audience to view racial and religious prejudice as a pathology.

Sitting at the head of the AJC, from 1943–67, was John Slawson, a Columbia University-trained psychologist and former director of the Cleveland Jewish Welfare Federation. Jewish communal workers in the interwar years tended to be divided between those who viewed the diminution of Jewish cultural distinctiveness as inevitable and desirable and those who valued cultural retention as a defense against social and psychological pathology. Slawson was firmly in the latter camp. Arriving in the USA from Ukraine as a child, in 1903, he received a meager Jewish education from a backward-looking *heder* teacher in Williamsburg, Brooklyn. He only developed an interest in Judaism and what he termed "a philosophical concern with identity" as an adult. But once he discovered the concept it became a professional preoccupation (Slawson, 1970). His first article addressing Jewish belongingness and its impact on psychosocial development, which utilized the term "Jewish ethnic identity," appeared in 1928, when Erik Erikson was still Erik Homberger and had not yet met Anna Freud nor begun his studies at the Vienna Psychoanalytic Institute.

Slawson was hardly an American rejectionist. Instead, he sought a middle path between what he considered to be the twin evils of wholesale assimilation and self-separation. An advocate of I. B. Berkson's "community theory" of ethnic adjustment in opposition to the melting pot process, he viewed ethnic identity retention as essential to forestalling potential psychological injuries associated with immigration and adjustment. "Indiscriminate assimilation," "'dressed up' Americanism," and the loss of "ethnic cultural values," could result in "demoralization," "neurotic effects," and the production of "grotesque personalities," he wrote (Slawson, 1928, pp. 87–88). Slawson brought this perspective with him when he became executive director of the AJC. In the early years of his tenure, which coincided with the final years of the Second World War and its aftermath, Slawson was concerned with the effects of antisemitism on the Jewish psyche. He wished to facilitate positive American Jewish adjustment, which he believed was hampered by Jewish expressions of ambivalence and self-devaluation. After the war, Slawson argued that the Jewish community desperately craved a program from the AJC that would "strengthen morale." He steered the AJC towards pairing its traditional defense agency function with initiatives to promote Jewish cultural effervescence. Jews could not fully participate in the program of "intercultural" and "interfaith education" that the AJC championed unless they were affirmed in their own Jewishness, he argued (Slawson, 1945).

It was Slawson who made possible the AJC's republication, in pamphlet form, of Lewin's "Bringing Up the Jewish Child," which was paired with an alternate perspective by Bruno Bettelheim. It is easy to discern Lewin's influence on Slawson's thinking, particularly in the way he connected group belonging to individual self-esteem. "The Jews of America want to obtain through [the AJC] a deeper sense of the reality of being Jewish, and wholesome pride in being Jewish—the kind of pride from which flows dignity, not chauvinism. In short, they want us to help them obtain a balanced perspective with regard to their Jewish identity, and they want us to contribute not only to their personal morale, but to the group morale of the Jewish community," Slawson argued in a widely circulated pamphlet. "They want to experience the feeling of togetherness—the strength that comes from working together—which American Jewry so greatly lacks at present" (Slawson, 1945). At the same time, Slawson approached collective belonging largely through a mental health prism. Group survival was at best an instrumental goal in the larger Eriksonian project of healthy ego-identity promotion and development.

Slawson was hardly the only Jewish communal leader to focus on the nexus between group belonging and individual psychological health. But his role as executive director of the AJC gave him outsized sway over the communal agenda. Slawson wielded this power not only through his access to the American Jewish community's power elite, but also via the organization's many levers of influence. These included its Office of Information and Research Services and its Division of Scientific Research, which was at that time the most active and well-respected producer of social scientific research on the Jewish community. According to Marshall Sklare, who served as Study Director and, later, Director of the Division of Scientific Research, from 1953–1965, Slawson played a critical role in bringing to fruition two community studies—in Riverton (Trenton, New Jersey) and Lakeville (Highland Park, Illinois)—that explored "the problem of Jewish identity," in postwar America. "It was [Slawson's] conception that the Committee could not rest on its contributions to the field of 'prejudice research' alone, but rather should go forward into the study of Jewish identity and thus complement the traditional emphasis of AJC's program" (Sklare & Greenblum, xiii). Only someone of Slawson's stature was able to overcome the skittishness of lay leaders who feared that the results of these studies could be exploited by hostile quarters. Equally important, Slawson unabashedly placed his support behind Sklare. As a Zionist and an observant Jew, Sklare was something of an anomaly at the AJC (Sklare, 1993, p. 10).

In contrast to the two-volume Lakeville study, which documented the impact of suburbanization on American Jewish ethno-religious behavior and practice, Riverton is hardly remembered today. But its publication presaged a refocusing of attention away from the impact of antisemitism on Jewish self-esteem and instead on the ways in which American Jews chose to understand and perform their Jewishness. Riverton sought to "obtain objective knowledge about the attitudes of American Jews toward themselves as Jews and toward their Gentile neighbors," by surveying two generations (parents and teenaged children) in a midsized, eastern industrial city. The headline that emerged from the study was respondents' overwhelming desire to "retain their Jewish identity." This finding cut across age brackets, with younger people even more likely than their elders to express pride in their heritage. While concern for ant-Semitism persisted, it was no longer viewed as disruptive to the nurturing of Jewish pride and a sense of collective belonging. The era when large numbers of Jews resorted to passing as a strategy for social and economic advancement was over (Sklare, Vosk, & Zborowski, 1955, p. 207).

At the same time, Sklare and his collaborators, Marc Vosk, and Mark Zborowski, found a decline in Jewish observance and an increasingly relaxed approach to boundary maintenance, particularly among the young, leading them to wonder aloud about the effect of the decline of antisemitism on Jewish survival. Antisemitism, they acknowledged, was historically among the most potent "forces, which bind Jews to one another." Here was an early instance, in the realm of social science research, of an argument that would become commonplace among Jewish leaders at the end of the century, that American freedom could be advantageous for Jews but ruinous for Judaism (Sklare, Vosk, & Zborowski, 1955a).

The sociologists' repeated use of "Jewish identity," a term that they utilized interchangeably with "Jewish identification," as did Herberg, is significant. Riverton was released the same year as *Protestant-Catholic-Jew*, and, in fact, Herberg's endnotes indicate that Sklare provided him with a paper based on the Riverton study, delivered at the Tercentenary Conference on American Jewish Sociology, prior to its publication in *Jewish Social Studies* (Herberg, p. 204n43). Whether their exchange of ideas also involved a borrowing of nomenclature is unclear. Conceivably, they both could have picked up the term independently from Erikson and applied it to social psychology, although Erikson's name is conspicuously absent from Herberg's index. Jewish group identification was clearly a concern of the AJC's Department of Scientific Research as early as 1951, when Zborowski prepared a literature review entitled "Jewish Belongingness and Group Identification." Implicitly arguing for the necessity of a study like Riverton, Zborowski concluded that few if any existing studies probed "the dynamics of Jewish group membership with its psychological, cultural and social implications" (1952, p. 2).

More important than whether Herberg borrowed "identity" from Sklare and his team is the question of why both authors reached for this term and made it central to their analyses at precisely the same moment. What was it about the American Jewish condition in the mid-1950s that cried out for identity as an analytical term of art? The answer can be gleaned from the Riverton study itself. The authors acknowledged the novelty of their inquiry during its rollout. "To our forefathers the answer to the question—what is a Jew?—was clear and unequivocal. A Jew was born a Jew and served God in the manner of his ancestors," the authors began. "Today we even phrase the question differently. We speak of identification with Jews and Judaism, of feelings of belongingness. This change in phraseology is not merely a byproduct of greater sophistication, nor is it a form of social science 'jargonization.' It reflects an awareness of the multifaceted nature of the several roles man must fill in life, of the many demands of sometimes conflicting loyalties which beset him, of the profound changes in group sanctions and individual values which have taken place in recent decades" (Sklare, Vosk, & Zborowski, 1955a). Sklare, Vosk, and Zborowski asserted that the question of Jewish identity could only be posed in an environment where group belongingness was voluntary, when it was neither assumed nor imposed. It only made sense when identity was perceived at once to be fragmentary and multidimensional.

The researchers contextualized identity historically as well as sociologically. They acknowledged its emergence as a logical conclusion of the granting of citizenship on an individual rather than a corporate basis. Isidor Chein made the same point in his response to the findings at the Tercentenary Conference. He lamented that Jewish rituals and traditions that were traditionally performed *"l'shem shomayim"* (for the sake of Heaven) were desacralized in contemporary America and reduced to "symbols of identification." Riverton pointed to the "reduced scope of Jewishness" from an immutable 24/7 lived reality to a compartmentalized set of beliefs, cultural markers, and group loyalties. Even the Orthodox, he argued, were not immune from the dissolution of an "all-pervasive Jewishness" (Chein, 1955, pp. 219–220).

Slawson seized on the Riverton findings to spread a gospel of "healthy integration" into American society that eschewed the extremes of "assimilation" and "self-segregation." In 1956, the AJC used a $30,000 grant from the Lilly Endowment to sponsor a Conference on Group Life in America, which brought together thirty-five academics, business leaders, and politicians to "seek new insights into problems concerned with integration, retention of group identity, etc." That same year, the AJC established a new department of Jewish Communal Affairs, which was headed up by Rabbi Morris Kertzer (AJC Administrative Board Meeting Minutes, September 25, 1956), and, in 1958, the organization's executive board passed a resolution that affirmed its support for the "fullest participation by Jews in the general American community, while retaining their distinctive heritage and religious identity" (AJC Executive Board Minutes, October 24–26, 1958). In a 1963 address at the Annual Meeting of the National Conference of Jewish Communal Service, Slawson presented the individual's pursuit of identity in developmental terms that were at once epic and universal. "Identity is one of the most important quests of man. Its realization is a lifelong development, beginning with childhood. It is in fact the consciousness of selfhood and the extension of the ego from the individual through the family to the more embracing groups—peer, religious, ethnic and national. Freud refers to Jewish identity as 'the individual's relatedness to the unique history of a people.'"

From Remedy to Safeguard: Jewish Identity Reconceived

In his "state of the Jewish community" address at the AJC's 1961 Annual Meeting, Slawson challenged his audience by rhetorically asking whether the Committee had been too focused on "proving our Americanism." "Are American Jews in danger of becoming Americans without a past?" Slawson wondered aloud. "Recognition of one's group identity instills a sense of surefootedness and tends to minimize feelings of uprootedness, unrelatedness, and aloneness in this modern mass society. It is essential to the unconditional acceptance of self, which in turn is basic to acceptance by others," he argued. "At this juncture in the history of Jews in America, grandfathers are crucial to our sense of continuity" (Slawson, 1961). Slawson, for his part, was unmoved by the pessimists, but he acknowledged "a cultural lag, sociologically speaking— between the expectancy and the actuality," which accounted for lingering fears about antisemitism and the persistence of "unhealthy" American Jewish behaviors such as voluntary social segregation and self-hatred.

Chein noted that a "by-product" of the conceptualization of Jewishness as an identity was "the tendency for the psychological isolation of Jewishness, its restriction to an island in the personal life space." The islanding of Jewish identity rendered it less consequential, Chein insisted, and compelled the individual to engage in an ongoing oscillation process between one's American and Jewish selves. Unlike some of his contemporaries, Chein saw little hope for identity integration. Jewishness in America would increasingly be experienced episodically. The more that Jewishness "becomes identified with certain activities at certain times, the greater is the tendency to experience one's identity as a Jew only in those activities and at those times. Jewishness becomes a sort of role that one plays, and one is only a Jew while playing this role." Observing that "the essence of meaning is that something is meaningful only insofar as it is tied up with other things in the outer world and with the mainsprings of feelings and motivations in one's inner self," he concluded that "the more circumscribed does Jewishness become, the less meaningful does it also become" (Chein, 1955, pp. 219–220).

Two factors prevented Sklare from indulging in a similar degree of pessimism about the long-term viability of the American Jewish community. The first related to American Jewish associationalism. Despite Riverton Jews' professed willingness to relax the boundaries between Jews and their non-Jewish neighbors, their social patterns suggested that they remained more comfortable around other Jews. Sklare and his collaborators concluded that, "This desire for individuation is so great as to constitute a strong obstacle to either assimilation or intermarriage." Thus, the taboo against interfaith marriage remained intact (Sklare, Vosk, & Zborowski 1955, p. 207). A second reason for Sklare's more measured interpretation of the data was the solace he took in knowing that Jewish identity affirmation in America increasingly came at little or no social or economic cost. Sklare understood that individuals inhabited multiple identities each of which came to the fore depending upon the social context. "Multiple roles are not necessarily contradictory," he argued, "in fact [they] may be complementary." Identity shifting created little or no psychic dissonance unless the various guises were in direct conflict. In the case of American Jews, Sklare noted that even if Jewish group identity was to some degree attenuated it was not in competition with American identity. There was little evidence of angst associated with an individual holding these two identities simultaneously, he asserted. Unlike a generation earlier, American Jews felt little need or desire to shed their Jewishness (Sklare, Vosk, & Zborowski 1955, p. 232).

Sklare's reassurances did not entirely assuage his own survivalist anxiety. "To some, the degree of belongingness which we have found would be considered ethnocentrism, but to others it would indicate that American Jews are perilously near assimilation," he acknowledged (Sklare, Vosk, & Zborowski, 1955, p. 218). One measure that Sklare's colleagues at the AJC, including Slawson, felt similarly uneasy was their increased attention to interfaith marriage, a phenomenon that up until then had been treated as a curiosity. Herberg's championing of the "triple melting pot" in *Protestant-Catholic-Jew* was premised on sociologist Ruby Jo Kennedy's finding of low interfaith marriage rates, particularly among Jews and Catholics. Even so, the AJC executive director began using public speaking engagements as an opportunity to defend endogamy. To some extent, the focus was understandable. Regardless of whether it was viewed as a gateway or a destination, there appeared to be an indubitable association between interfaith marriage and assimilation. The discourse around intermarriage in the 1950s and early 1960s became another opportunity for a synthesis of Lewinian and Eriksonian thinking. The American Jew's acceptance of endogamy and affirmation of Jewish identity as a personal choice was, in Slawson's view, an expression of Jewish psychosocial health. Intermarriage, on the other hand, could be a sign of pathology born of an unresolved adolescent identity crisis manifesting itself as persistent parental rebellion or self-loathing telegraphed by unrelenting social climbing. Slawson continued to employ the rhetoric of "personality health" well into the 1960s.

One should take note of the early relationship between the rhetoric of identity and fears of intermarriage, a linkage that predated 1964—the year of the infamous "Vanishing American Jew" cover story in *Look Magazine,* and the Broadway opening of *Fiddler on the Roof,* which reimagined Sholom Aleichem's Tevye stories as a paean to the inevitability of assimilation and intermarriage—let alone the 1990 National Jewish Population Study. Significantly, however, in the postwar years the emphasis was not yet on the "consequences" of intermarriage; that is on the transmission of Jewish identity to the next generation. Rather, the focus was on the individual himself—and it was usually a man—and what might drive him to reject his Jewishness through the act of intermarriage.

The Riverton findings set the stage for the more ambitious Lakeville study.[2] By choosing an established, Midwestern suburb, as opposed to an industrialized East Coast city, like Riverton, Sklare was deliberately focusing on a socially mobile, solidly middle- and upper-middle-class community heavily comprised of individuals at least two generations removed from immigration (Sklare, 1956). The study's conclusions were telegraphed in the subtitle of the book that summarized its findings: "A Study of Group Survival in an Open Society."

Among the most innovative and significant components of the Lakeville study was a series of attitudinal questions designed to ascertain respondents' "image of the 'good Jew'" (Sklare & Greenblum, p. 321). Twenty-two items in all were presented to the interview subjects, who were asked to rate their relative significance. Were these traits essential, desirable, neutral, or inimical to being a "good Jew"? Much has been written on the implications of the finding that Lakeville Jews privileged ethical conduct and Jewish self-acceptance over ritual observance, the maintenance of Jewish social ties, and other more particularistic behaviors and activities. Regardless, these items and a profusion of questions in the survey instrument about personal religious observances, institutional affiliations, friendship patterns, attitudes about the state of Israel, and the like, were designed to measure identification both qualitatively and quantitatively. Thus, the surveys represented an important

---

2 Interviews, which typically lasted between three and four hours, were conducted with a total of 432 Jews and 250 non-Jews. In Riverton, the sample included Jews only. 200 in all were surveyed with a more limited set of questions.

development in the conceptualization of Jewish identity. When identity was theorized and problematized from a psychological perspective within the context of studies on prejudice, its inherent subjectivity was assumed. After Lakeville, sociologists and Jewish communal professionals increasingly conceived of identity sociologically, that is in relationship to a package of measurable behaviors and attitudes. Sociologists devised indexes to gauge the relative strength or weakness of their subjects' identities. The implications of this shift on Jewish communal and education policy-making were profound, as programs, school curricula and even cultural productions were increasingly viewed as interventions, whose success or failure were determined on the basis of whether they could move the Jewish identity dial.

It is not an exaggeration to argue that, for better or worse, Sklare's publication of *Jewish Identity on the Suburban Frontier* (1967) was the moment when the idea of "strengthening" or "weakening" Jewish identity was born. In Sklare's work, identity was no longer primarily about how one sees oneself in the world, a distinguishing characteristic that defines relationships between the self and others. Instead, identity was indexed to a norm or set of norms. Since Lakeville, Jewish identity has become all about weights and measurements. Professional Jews spend much of their energies trying to find ways to tip the scales, while Jewish sociologists rush to measure the results. Whether or not Sklare intended it, he became the progenitor of an entire Jewish identity industrial complex.

And while Sklare assumed the role of impartial social scientist in his field work, his reports, articles and books left little doubt about his sympathies: Jewish survival was a desideratum. Sklare was hesitant to declare himself on the subject as an optimist or a pessimist. But he memorably compared himself to a Jerusalemite during the siege of 1947–48, who implored his fellow Jews not to "rely on miracles" but to dutifully recite *tehilim* (Psalms).

By the time sociologist Simon Herman wrote about American Jewish identity in the 1970s, he acknowledged that it could be understood either as "how the individual sees himself (self-identity) by virtue of his membership in the group," or "how the group defines itself," that is, "the pattern of attributes of the Jewish group as seen by its members" (Herman, 1977, p. 168). Herman was Lewin's student, so his receptivity to this latter conception of identity provides an indication of the distance that Jewish communal leaders and even some social scientists had traveled from conceiving identity as a psychosocial construct. Similarly, in his paper on American Jewish identity for the AJC Task Force on the Future of the Jewish Community in America, which met from

1969–72, sociologist Charles Liebman asserted that Jewish identity could be measured along two axes: Jewish values and Jewish affiliation (Liebman, 1973, p. 131).

The 1967 publication of Sklare's *Jewish Identity on the Suburban Frontier* coincided with a season of alarm about Jewish survival comparable to the fallout from the 1990 National Jewish Population Study and the 2013 Pew Report. Noting that the term "continuity" first entered the communal discourse in the mid-1960s, Marianne Sanua referred to these years as the period of "the first continuity crisis" (Sanua, 2007, pp. 113–116). Fears were fomented by a pair of studies by Erich Rosenthal, published in the *American Jewish Year Book* (Rosenthal, 1961, pp. 3–27; Rosenthal, 1963, 3–56), demonstrating declining birthrates and rising intermarriage rates, as well as a 1964 *Commentary* article on exogamy by Sklare. Rosenthal and Sklare's findings entered the popular consciousness through the notorious May 1964 *Look* magazine cover story entitled "The Vanishing American Jew" (Morgan, pp. 42–46).

In a series of high profile addresses, widely circulated pamphlets and a November 1964 Conference on "Jewish Identity Here and Now," Slawson and the American Jewish Committee made the argument that stimulating group identity was the surest counterweight to the allure of assimilation. To some extent, Slawson recapitulated established themes. But to his psychosocial approach he added a newfound conviction that group survival could only be ensured in an increasingly open society if Jews felt the imperative of identification as a positive value as opposed to an obligation and a burden. He acknowledged that the community had fallen short in efforts to showcase "its richness and everlasting vitality." And he insisted on the importance of education as a vehicle for identity enhancement (Slawson, 1967, pp. 10–11).

How Identity Became Both the Goal and the Elixir of Jewish Education

In retrospect, the 1964 gathering captured an important moment in the evolution of mainstream Jewish communal thought. Taking place only months after the Mississippi Freedom Summer, the disproportionate participation of northern Jewish youth in the voter registration efforts was understandably on the minds of many of the participants, as were the dimensions of black-Jewish relations more broadly. The consensus among the thirty participants was that young Jews' involvement in civil rights was in most cases an expression of belongingness to "a wider political, cultural and social world." Far from being in search of their Jewish roots or motivated by a Jewish imperative to bear covenantal witness, the Jewish civil rights workers were committed to building a utopian future that transcended their parents' clannish parochialism. Rabbi Arthur Hertzberg, who marched with Dr. Martin Luther King Jr., in 1963, recalled the discomfort his presence caused some of his activist coreligionists, who wanted to know: "What the devil is a rabbi doing in this thing, because we are in this business to get away from the rabbis and you have caught up with us" (Dawidowicz & Himmelfarb, 1966, p. 33).

Conference participants interpreted the disaffection of idealistic, college-educated youth as an ominous harbinger of assimilation. Nationally, it helped to accelerate the pace of Jewish institutional soul-searching. Not only was this in evidence at traditional defense and advocacy organizations like the AJC, which began rethinking its wary non-Zionist stance (Sanua, p. 152) and engaged in a vigorous internal debate about the advisability of upholding the liberal consensus on public policy issues like church state separation (p. 247), but also in the Jewish federation world. According to conference participant Robert Hiller, Executive Vice President of the United Jewish Federation of Pittsburgh, communal professionals recognized the need to reframe their work to appeal to the needs and values of third and fourth generation Americans. The era when federations were tasked with providing social welfare assistance had passed, Hiller insisted. The federations' client was no longer the poor but "the community itself" (Dawidowicz & Himmelfarb, p. 15).

Slawson took up his role as an apostle of Jewish identity in an increasingly tolerant American environment that welcomed expressions of ethnic distinctiveness. The conditions that characterized the late-1960s and 1970s were aptly described by Matthew Frye Jacobson, who argued that, "the example of Black Nationalism and the emergence of multiculturalism had provided a new language for an identity that was not simply 'American.' After decades of striving to conform to the Anglo-Saxon standard, descendants of earlier European immigrants quit the melting pot. Italianness, Jewishness, Greekness, and Irishness had become badges of pride, not shame" (Jacobson, 2006, p. 2). The so-called "ethnic revival" and the Six Day War made anxious parents, impetuous youth, and Jewish educators receptive to the prophets of Jewish survival who counseled greater emphasis on Jewish particularism.

To be clear, the embrace of ethnicity should not be conflated with a turn to identity or a newfound interest on the part of third and fourth generation European immigrants in group-belongingness. This was certainly not the case with American Jews for whom the problem of identity became a veritable postwar preoccupation, even before the term became part of the cultural lexicon. The "ethnic revival" was more a vehicle than a catalyst.

Moreover, as Herbert Gans recognized, the claiming of "symbolic ethnicity," in the late 1960s and 1970s, did not in any meaningful way represent a return to the immigrant ethnicity of the first generation (Gans, 1979, pp. 17–19). This iteration of ethnic identity was personally chosen rather than ascribed (Waters, 1990, p. 89). In adopting the icons and symbols of the ethnic group, the individual was typically more engaged in a process of self-discovery and personal meaning-making than in a profound and sustained desire to live in community. Thus, it was a superficial challenge, at best, to America's pervasive cult of individualism.

Revealingly, one area that received scant attention at the 1964 conference was Jewish education. In fact, when Marshall Sklare offered a tepid endorsement of Jewish summer camping as an agent of identity enhancement, Rabbi Seymour Siegel shot his point down, borrowing a quip from humorist Sam Levenson: "Jewish children never *go* to camp. They are sent." The nature of the problem was even more acute in relationship to the religious supplementary schools, he added. Siegel, a theologian at the Jewish Theological Seminary of America, the sponsor of the highly regarded Ramah camps, argued that in an era of freedom, there were no guarantees that compulsory education would keep young people in the fold over the long term. "The problem facing us is to teach them in such a way that when they reach the alleged age of freedom they will opt for Judaism" (Dawidowicz & Himmelfarb, p. 20). Sklare let the matter drop rather than arguing that Ramah and camps like it were better equipped than supplementary schools to promote affective educational objectives.

In fact, AJC staff members like Milton Himmelfarb and Manheim Shapiro were vocally skeptical about the efficacy of religious supplementary education, which represented the dominant form of formal Jewish education in the postwar era. Slawson appeared to share their suspicions, questioning whether the efforts of Jewish educators could be effectual in the realm of identity intensification: "War, as George Clemenceau observed, is much too serious a matter to be entrusted to generals; and Jewish continuity is much too important to leave exclusively to educators, rabbis or both. The entire community should be involved in the task" (Slawson, 1967, p. 14). Slawson's privileging of the home and the community as loci of identity formation made sense. Nevertheless, it is reasonable to read Slawson's remark in the light of the AJC's studious refusal to address the subject of Jewish education in any of its policy statements. Historically, the AJC's reticence in this area was premised in the conviction that education lay outside of its purview, a view that was shared by other defense and community relations organizations, including the National Jewish Community Relations Advisory Council. By the 1960s, however, this view was no longer operative. Yet efforts to formulate Jewish education policy remained stalled due to a lack of consensus on day schools. Opinion at the AJC spanned the gamut, from those who supported state aid to parochial schools to those who viewed day schools as a threat to public education and school desegregation efforts. Moderates hoped that a statement in support of Jewish philanthropic aid to day schools would help to forestall Orthodox efforts to push for government funding of their schools. But when AJC's department of Jewish Communal Affairs, under Yehuda Rosenman, tried in 1970 to convince the organization's National Executive Council to unequivocally endorse day schools in the context of a wider policy statement on Jewish education, the lay leaders recoiled (Sanua, pp. 249–250).

It took seven more years for the AJC to pass a statement on Jewish education and Jewish identity. In the meantime, the AJC sponsored a multi-year colloquium on Jewish education, which was cochaired by Rosenman and Columbia University professor of philosophy David Sidorsky. Taking as its point of departure Hebrew University professor of education Seymour Fox's warning that "the most urgent problem facing Jewish education" was "its lack of purpose and, consequently, its blandness" (Fox, 1970, p. 261) the thirty educators, social scientists and rabbis who comprised its membership determined to adopt as its focus the intersection of Jewish education and Jewish identity. Thirteen papers were commissioned from prominent and emerging scholars and rabbis on topics ranging from the goals and social context of Jewish education, to evaluation, to the relationship between Jewish education and Jewish identity. The recommendations that emerged included the prioritization of family education, as well as increased communal support for Jewish education on the high school and college levels. In expanding the focus of concern beyond the elementary school classroom, the colloquium signified an important evolution in communal thinking. But the colloquium was significant in two other respects: It offered an early articulation of the centrality of Jewish education in Jewish identity construction, while simultaneously problematizing that linkage, in part by casting doubt on the efficacy of the supplementary religious schools at the heart of the Jewish educational system (Sidorsky, 1977).

On the former point, the colloquium summary report pointed to a convergence of opinion among educators in all three major denominations that experiential education was vitally important in promoting healthy identity development in the younger generation. This concession by educators to a prioritization of affective outcomes signaled the recognition, even in the Orthodox community, that the family by itself was unequal to the task. As one participant observed, the homes of the third and fourth generations were often Jewishly impoverished, while the suburban communities in which they lived were devoid of the ethnic Jewish flavor that permeated the city neighborhoods where their parents and grandparents resided. Jewishness could no longer be picked up through osmosis. Moreover, Jewish communal leaders' fears about the youth's level of Jewish commitment were only reinforced as the civil rights activism of the early 1960s gave way to antiwar radicalism and an embrace of the counterculture.

The convergence was extraordinary in part because Jewish educators were initially slow to frame Jewish educational goals in terms of Jewish identity. While early twentieth-century Jewish educational progressives recognized the socializing potential of both formal and informal Jewish education, when it came time to formulate objectives, the emphasis was invariably on knowledge acquisition and patterns of behavior, such as ethical conduct, ritual observance, a love of learning, and Jewish civic engagement, rather than cultivating a sense of group belonging (Millgram, 1947, pp. 25–26). Perhaps they viewed collective belonging as an assumed overarching outcome. But by the mid-to-late 1960s, it was no longer safe to make any assumptions.[3] The intensification of Jewish education was essential to the safeguarding of Jewish continuity, Hebrew University social psychologist Simon Herman warned. The celebrated ethnic pride movements of the era were peddling thin gruel. Identification was not to be confused with identity, he insisted. The shallowness of Jewish home life left the third and fourth generations with little raw material from which to construct a meaningful identity. This view convinced Herman to shift his emphasis from the Lewinian psychosocial aspects of Jewish identity and focus instead on group norms and distinctive practices (Herman, 1977a; Sidorsky, 1977, pp. 16–17).

Notes of Skepticism and Caution

Yet the colloquium report also acknowledged that the goal of identity enhancement might be unachievable in a school setting. As colloquium

---

3 As one might expect, genuine curricular change on the ground lagged behind the pronouncements of educators and thought leaders. However, the dissemination of curricula and teaching materials explicitly designed to promote affective outcomes was facilitated by the creation, in 1976, of the Coalition for Alternatives in Jewish Education (renamed the Coalition for the Advancement of Jewish Education).

participant and Harvard University sociologist Nathan Glazer observed, "Jewish school is not really a central part of children's lives and links up with so little else." Furthermore, he added, Jewish teachers were themselves insecure about their Jewish identities. "Why should we expect Jewish teachers to be any better at this than Jewish parents?" Glazer's skepticism was reinforced in a couple of commissioned colloquium papers that assessed outcomes (Sidorsky, 1977, pp. 14–15).

And yet, the entry of Jewish identity into the mainstream American Jewish communal discourse was serendipitous for Jewish educators. For a variety of reasons both the traditional objectives of heritage transmission and social adjustment were becoming increasingly problematic in the postwar era. A byproduct of the shift from the communal Talmud Torah to the suburban congregational school was a decline in the number of days and hours per week of instruction. This forced a curricular reassessment and a scaling down of content and skills objectives. The relocation of the Jewish school to the congregation also encouraged an increased emphasis on performance over cognition, synagogue skills and b'nai mitzvah preparation over Hebrew fluency and text study. This trend coincided with the release of the First National Jewish Education Survey in 1959, which concluded that, "little has been accomplished toward teaching our children the literary-historic culture of their people" (Dushkin & Engelman, 1959, p. 5).

If the ambitious cognitive goals of the modern Talmud Torah, particularly its emphasis on Hebrew language acquisition appeared to be ever more elusive by the 1960s, the affective focus on social adjustment and the Americanization of Judaism also seemed increasingly misplaced as concerns about of the negative effects of antisemitism on the Jewish psyche gave way to fears of assimilation.

Walter Ackerman argued in the pages of the *American Jewish Year Book* that Jewish educators should take care not to exaggerate their power lest they create unrealistic expectations. Ackerman scoffed at "the rhetoric of nonsense that permeates most discussions of Jewish education today." According to Ackerman, the educators were only aiding and abetting their detractors whose exaggerated demands were beyond the capacity of any school (Ackerman, 1969, pp. 24–25). Ackerman's warning, coming in the midst of the community's anxious efforts to come to grips with the so-called "youth crisis," had little discernable impact. But his words were prescient.

Precious little research existed on the impact of education on identity formation. One important contribution of the AJC colloquium was the funding of two wide-ranging studies on the impact of Jewish education on identity conducted by sociologists Harold Himmelfarb, of Ohio State University, and Geoffrey Bock, of Harvard University Graduate School of Education. The results were chastening. Both researchers were interested in whether one could measure an independent effect of Jewish education on identification, and both approached the problem by looking at time as a variable. Essentially, their question boiled down to 'How much Jewish education is required to instill a sense of belonging independent of the impact of home, synagogue or other variables?' The researchers independently concluded that Jewish education needed to reach a minimum threshold of hours in order to have a discernable impact on identification. And while the two disagreed about where to set that threshold, both called into doubt the efficacy of the supplementary school as an identity booster. Only consistent attendance at an all-day Jewish school for eight or more years would meet the necessary criterion (Bock, 1977; Sidorsky, 1977, p. 24).

Equally important, the researchers found that home environment played a far more significant role in shaping personal identification and Jewish self-esteem than schooling, thereby vindicating Glazer's skepticism about the supplementary school's ability to act in loco parentis in promoting group belonging. The school had a more discernable impact on public behaviors, like synagogue attendance, participation in secular Jewish organizational activities and Jewish political engagement. But there, too, the role of the home was often equally significant. Moreover, Bock found a multiplier effect, whereby an intensively Jewish home environment enhanced the effect of schooling on public identification (Bock, 1977).

In retrospect, it is worthwhile to ponder the implications of the way in which these scholars and the organization that funded their research framed the research questions, if only because of the sweeping claims that they made and the outsized impact of their studies on Jewish education policy.[4] Himmelfarb went as far as saying that Jewish education had been "a waste of time" for 80% of those who were products of the system. By choosing to evaluate Jewish education's worth on the basis of whether it promoted a sense of communal belonging, as opposed to whether it inculcated skills and knowledge, or encouraged performance of mitzvoth and ethical behavior, the AJC was adopting narrow and arguably distorted criteria. Himmelfarb and Bock

---

4 A more recent study by Steven M. Cohen raises questions about the validity of Bock & Himmelfarb's findings about the negligible or even negative affect of supplementary education that did not reach the minimum threshold number of hours. See Cohen, 2007, pp. 34–56.

focused on the affective to the exclusion of the cognitive and the behavioral. To be fair, however, the colloquium's summary report took it as a given that "the achievements of personality are byproducts of an investment of energy in something other than self-development." In other words, Jewish identity could best be cultivated through the behavioral and cognitive realms. Colloquium member Rabbi David Lieber expressed the matter in this way: "Both Jewish identity and Jewish survival are by-products of a meaningful Jewish existence. As such, they should not be the focus of Jewish educational effort. Rather its goal should be to make the individual's Jewishness 'a source of vital personal significance,' by enabling him to participate to the full in the experience of Jewish living" (Sidorsky, p. 13).

Himmelfarb and Bock's research provided momentum for the development in the 1980s of family education initiatives, both in conjunction with and independent of congregational schools (Reimer, 1991, pp. 269–270). It also offered ammunition for supporters of day schools and *yeshivot*. However, the recognition that this educational model, while growing, would continue to hold limited appeal to a majority of non-Orthodox families compelled many policy makers to check their zeal. Many avoided the promotion of day schools as a one-size-fits-all solution to American Jewry's continuity crisis.

For the congregational school, the impact of the researchers' findings coming on the heels of declining enrollments, and brutal assessments of their efficacy in the cognitive domain was nothing less than devastating. If community leaders and policy makers were convinced that the congregational school model would endure for the foreseeable future, they were increasingly and openly skeptical of its capacity for renewal and redemption, thereby fomenting a crisis of confidence among teachers, administrators and parents.

On the positive side, the cloud over formal, congregational education prompted professionals and lay leaders to examine and experiment with novel and underutilized educational models, including camping, preschools and heritage tourism, that had the potential to provide a better return on investment. In the long run, the crisis forced innovation within the congregational school world, as well.

Conclusion

Identity was the quintessential conundrum for a community on the threshold of acceptance. The work of Lewin, Erikson, Herberg, Sklare, and others helped to shape the communal conversation. The reframing of that discourse from one that was essentially psychosocial and therapeutic to one that was sociological and survivalist reflected the community's growing sense of physical and socioeconomic security in the 1950s and early 1960s. The postwar intergroup relations movement and the pervasive rhetoric of "tri-faith America" facilitated American Jews' waning diffidence and self-consciousness.

The wider societal shift in the late 1960s and 70s away from Cold War conformism and towards a greater toleration for expressions of cultural diversity undoubtedly facilitated bolder expressions of Jewishness in the public sphere.

Likewise, the social upheavals that propelled the ethnic identity movement also created a sense of urgency within the Jewish community, shining a light on a flawed educational system and fueling the momentum for change. To the extent that the turn to identity compelled a reassessment of the delivery system of Jewish education, one might say that it provided a useful function, calling into question much of what had been taken for granted, including the relationship between means and objectives; bringing to the fore questions about systems and personnel; and inviting educators and policy members to think out of the box about the "grammar of Jewish schooling." On the other hand, as Ackerman warned, the emphasis on identity enhancement outcomes often encourages devaluing of the cognitive domain in favor of the affective and behavioral. Moreover, it carries with it the danger of Jewish education descending into rank tribalism. Finally, it abets the fallacious notion that parents can abdicate the cultivation of group belonging to the school.

The Jewish educator's role as a witting accomplice in the elevation of identity to a *sine qua non* in Jewish education has been a mixed blessing. While Jewish education has come to occupy an increasingly central position on the communal agenda, which has translated into increased funding for projects and programs, reductionist and often-unrealistic goals have too often defined success and failure. The matrix of philanthropic foundations, federations, Jewish schools, camps, Israel trips, Jewish campus organizations, service learning organizations, youth groups and the like has become a veritable Jewish identity industrial complex. And there is little to suggest that the obsession with identity is on the wane, within either the Jewish community or America at large.

Bibliography

Ackerman, Walter. (1969). Jewish Education—For What? *American Jewish Yearbook 70*, 3–36.

American Jewish Committee. (October 24–26 1958). *October, 24–26 Executive Board Minutes*. New York, NY: American Jewish Committee.

Baron, Salo. Summer (1942). Modern Capitalism and Jewish Fate. *Menorah Journal 30*.

Bock, Geoffrey. (1977). *Does Jewish Schooling Matter?, Jewish Education and Jewish Identity Colloquium Papers*. New York, NY: American Jewish Committee

Chein, Isidor. (July 1955). Comment on Forms and Expressions of Jewish Identity. *Jewish Social Studies 17*.

Cohen, Steven. (2007). The Differential Impact of Jewish Education on Adult

Jewish Identity. In Jack Wertheimer (Ed.), *Family Matters: Jewish Education in an Age of Choice*. Hanover, NH: Brandeis University Press.

Dalin, David. (July 1988). Will Herberg in Retrospect. *Commentary 86*.

Dawidowicz, Lucy, & Himmelfarb, Milton. (Eds.). (1967). *Conference on Jewish Identity Here and Now*. New York, NY: American Jewish Committee.

Dushkin, Alexander. (February–March 1947). Kurt Lewin. *Jewish Education 18*.

Dushkin, Alexander, & Engelman, Uriah. (Eds.) (1959). *Jewish Education in the United States*. New York, NY: American Association for Jewish Education.

Enelow, Hyman G. (1920). *The Adequacy of Judaism*. New York, NY: Bloch.

Fox, Seymour. (1973). Toward a General Theory of Jewish Education. In *The Future of the Jewish Community in America*. David Sidorsky (Ed.), New York, NY: Basic Books

Friedman, Lawrence J. (1999). *Identity's Architect: A Biography of Erik H. Erikson*. New York, NY: Scribner.

Furman, Joshua. (2015). *Jew and American in the Making: Education and Childrearing in the American Jewish Community, 1945–1967* (Unpublished doctoral dissertation). University of Maryland, College Park, MD.

Gans, Herbert. (January 1979). Symbolic Ethnicity: The Future of Ethnic Groups and Cultures in America. *Ethnic and Racial Studies* 2(1), 1–20.

Gleason, Philip. (March 1983). Identifying Identity: A Semantic History. In *Journal of American History* 69(4), 910–931.

Glenn, Susan. (Spring/Summer 2006). The Vogue of Jewish Self-Hatred in Post-World War II America. In *Jewish Social Studies* 12(3), 95–136.

Heinze, Andrew. (Winter 2002). Peace of Mind (1946): Judaism and the Therapeutic Polemics of Postwar America. *Religion and American Culture: A Journal of Interpretation* 12(1), 31–58.

Herberg, Will. (1955). *Protestant-Catholic-Jew: An Essay in American Religious Sociology*. Chicago, IL: University of Chicago Press.

Herman, Simon. (1977). Criteria For Jewish Identity. In *World Jewry and the State of Israel*. Moshe Davis (Ed.), New York, NY: Arno Press.

Herman, Simon. (1977a). The Components of Jewish Identity: A Social Psychological Analysis. In *Jewish Education and Jewish Identity Colloquium Papers*. New York: American Jewish Committee.

Jackson, John P. Jr. (2005). *Social Scientists for Social Justice: Making the Case Against Segregation*. New York, NY: NYU Press.

Jacobson, Matthew Frye. (2006). *Roots Too: White Ethnic Revival in Post-Civil Rights America*. Cambridge, MA.: Harvard University Press.

Kallen, Horace. (1939). Education of Jews in Our Time. *Journal of Jewish Education 11.*

Kaufman, David. (2012). *Jewhooing the Sixties: American Celebrity and Jewish Identity.* Hanover, NH: Brandeis/University Press of New England.

Krasner, Jonathan. (2011). *The Benderly Boys and American Jewish Education.* Hanover, NH: Brandeis/University Press of New England.

Lewin, Gertrude. (February–March 1947). Group Belongingness and Jewish Education. *Journal of Jewish Education 18.*

Lewin, Kurt. (1944). Jewish Education and Reality. *Journal of Jewish Education.*

Lewin, Kurt. (1948). Psych-Sociological Problems of a Minority Group. In Gertrud Weisse Lewin (Ed.), *Resolving Social Conflicts.* New York, NY: Harper and Rowe.

Lewin, Kurt. (1948a). When Facing Danger. In Gertrud Weisse Lewin (Ed.), *Resolving Social Conflicts.* New York, NY: Harper and Rowe.

Lewin, Kurt. (1948b). Bringing Up the Jewish Child. In Gertrud Weisse Lewin (Ed.), *Resolving Social Conflicts.* New York, NY: Harper and Rowe.

Lewin, Kurt. (1948c). Self-Hatred Among Jews. In Gertrud Weisse Lewin (Ed.), *Resolving Social Conflicts.* New York, NY: Harper and Rowe.

Liebman, Charles. (1973). American Jewry: Identity and Affiliation. In David Sidorsky (Ed.), *The Future of the Jewish Community in America.* New York, NY: Basic Books

Malhotra, Rajiv. (2011). *Being Different: An Indian Challenge to Western Universalism.* New Delhi, Indian: Harper Collins India.

Marrow. Alfred. (1969). *The Practical Theorist: The Life and Work of Kurt Lewin.* New York, NY: Basic Books.

Millgram, Abraham. (February–March 1947). Objectives of Jewish Education. *Journal of Jewish Education 18.*

Morgan, Thomas. (1964 May 5). The Vanishing American Jew. *Look Magazine 28.*

Nardi, Noah. (February–March 1947). Group Dynamics in Jewish Education. *Jewish Education 18.*

Nardi, Noah. (1948). Kurt Lewin: The Man and the Psychologist. *The Reconstructionist 14.*

Nardi, Noah. (1948a). Some Applications of Kurt Lewin's Social Dynamics. *The Reconstructionist 14.*

Oppenheim, Michael. (1984). A "Fieldguide" to the Study of Modern Jewish Identity. *Jewish Social Studies 46*(3/4), 215–230.

Reimer, Joseph. Summer (1991). Jewish Family Education: Evaluating its Course, Looking to Its Future. *Journal of Jewish Communal Service 67.*

Rosenthal, Erich. (1961). Jewish Fertility in the United States. *American Jewish Yearbook 61.*

Rosenthal, Erich. (1963). Studies of Jewish Intermarriage in the United States. *American Jewish Yearbook 63.*

Sanua, Marianne. (2007). *Let Us Prove Strong: The American Jewish Committee, 1945–2006.* Waltham, MA: Brandeis University Press.

Schultz, Kevin. (2011). *Tri-Faith America: How Catholics and Jews Held Postwar America to its Protestant Promise.* New York, NY: Oxford University Press.

Shapiro, Edward. (2003). *Will Herberg's* Protestant-Catholic-Jew: A Critique. In Jack Kugelmass (Ed.), *Key Texts in American Jewish Culture.* New Brunswick, NJ: Rutgers University Press.

Sidorsky, David, & Rosenman, Yehuda. (1977). *Jewish Education and Jewish Identity: Colloquium Papers—Summary Report and Recommendations*. Retrieved from https://www.bjpa.org/search-results/publication/13708

Sklare, Marshall. (November, 1956). *Memorandum on New Jewish Attitude Survey*. New York, NY: American Jewish Committee, Division of Scientific Research.

Sklare, Marshall. (April 2 1963). *The Quest for Jewish Identity in America. Draft Outline for John Slawson*. New York, NY: American Jewish Committee.

Sklare, Marshall. (April 1964). Intermarriage and the Jewish Future. *Commentary 37*.

Sklare, Marshall. (1993). *Observing America's Jews*. Waltham, MA: Brandeis University Press.

Sklare, Marshall, & Greenblum, Joseph. (1967). *Jewish Identity on the Suburban Frontier*. New York, NY: Basic Books.

Sklare, Marshall, Vosk, Marc, & Zborowski, Mark. (July 1955). Forms and Expressions of Jewish Identification. *Jewish Social Studies 17*.

Sklare, Marshall, Vosk, Marc, & Zborowski, Mark. (November 1955a). *Some Highlights of the Riverton Study*. New York, NY: American Jewish Committee, Division of Scientific Research.

Slawson, John. (May 1928). Jewish Education as a Jewish Social Work Function, Proceedings of the National Conference of Jewish Social Service.

Slawson, John. (1945). *Our Objectives*. New York, NY: American Jewish Committee.

Slawson, John. (1961). *The Realities of Jewish Integration*. New York, NY: American Jewish Committee.

Slawson, John. (1967). *Toward a Community Program for Jewish Identity*. New York, NY: American Jewish Committee.

Slawson, John. (March 20, 1970). Autobiographical Sketch. American Jewish Archives.

Talmon, Judah Leib. (1965). *The Unique and the Universal: Some Historical Reflections*. London, UK: Seeker & Warburg.

Whitfield, Stephen. (Spring 2002). Enigmas of Modern Jewish Identity. In *Jewish Social Studies* 8(2/3), 162–167.

Zborowski, Mark. (c. 1952). *Jewish Belongingness and Group Identification. Draft Report*. New York, NY: American Jewish Committee.

Identity and Crisis: The Origins of Identity as an Educational Outcome

Ari Y. Kelman

"It is dubious whether identity can be manufactured, as it were, in a classroom"
(Marshall Sklare, *America's Jews*, p. 161)

Early in the twenty-first century, there is probably no educational outcome so widely embraced and pursued across the American Jewish denominational and political spectrum as identity. In one characteristic mission statement, a school identifies itself as "a modern Orthodox Jewish day school providing excellence in Jewish education to the entire Jewish community. Our focus is on the needs of the whole child, fostering a love of learning and a strong sense of Jewish identity." A large Reform congregation presents its educational programming in similar terms. "We strive to provide a positive Jewish identity and a personal understanding of the history, mission, and social conscience of the Jewish people, while appreciating that diversity and respecting each student." The webpage of a national overnight camp system states, "Our staff encourage the growth of Jewish values in each of our campers, and our programming is carefully created to nurture a positive Jewish identity through all that we do." Israel travel programs offer a similar educational vision: "Taglit-Birthright Israel seeks to ensure the future of the Jewish people by strengthening Jewish identity, Jewish communities and connection with Israel via an educational trip to Israel for the majority of Jewish young adults from around the world." Regardless of movement affinity or educational program, identity is ubiquitous.

Presenting identity as an educational outcome assumes that it is possible to teach someone to have an identity. But is it? Sociologist Marshall Sklare, who helped bring wider acceptance of the concept of identity to scholars and leaders of American Jews (Krasner, 2015), had his doubts. "Education is a very bad way of creating identification. Education, and especially Jewish education," says Sklare, "is geared to creating mastery of certain textual materials. . . . Jewish education has always been devoted to creating educated Jews. . . . Trying to create both educated and identified Jews within our present afternoon Hebrew school structure, we run the risk of creating neither" (quoted in Arian, 1972, p. 35). Others who advocated for increased investments in Jewish education agreed, claiming that Jewish schooling, whether supplemental or day, "is not the best vehicle for identity formation" (Sidorsky, 1973, p. 41).

Nevertheless, the promise that Jewish education could promote Jewish identity has become something of a truism, and this chapter examines how it came to be that way. It examines Jewish communal leaders' discussions of education between the mid-1960s, when identity barely registered in discussions of Jewish education, and the mid-1970s, when the two concepts became inextricably linked. Over those ten years, identity moved from the margins of thinking about Jewish education to become one of its most significant concepts and outcomes. Building on Jonathan Krasner's insights into the growth and development of the "identity industry," this chapter focuses in on the dynamics that fused education to identity, specifically. It demonstrates that the driving force behind this change in orientation toward identity was a rising fear for Jewish communal survival born of concerns about Jewish college students whom many felt were ill-equipped to face the social and political pressures of campus life during the late 1960s. The proposed solution to this situation was to foster a stronger sense of Jewish identity in adolescents and teenagers who would become the college students in the future.

Fears of Youth, Fears of Survival

Jewish communal institutions turned concerns about Jewish college students into a spate of articles, studies, commissions, reports, investigations, and other attempts to assess and address the situation on campus. By the early 1970s, the emerging obsession with Jewish education and Jewish identity had become the subject of its own running commentary. In 1969, Samuel Dinin wrote wryly, "There is hardly a conference, national regional or local or a major address which does not have as its theme—the revolutions, crises, challenges—facing Jewish life and Jewish education" (p. 3). As if to illustrate Dinin's point, at an American Jewish Congress convening in 1971, Earl Raab noted that American Jews are in a state of "disarray" or "ferment," depending on how one understands the situation. "Among the ways in which this ferment is being expressed is in an organized quest for 'Jewish identity.' Commissions on Jewish identity are multiplying on the American landscape" (1972, p. 14). These were taken up both by communal organizations like the American Jewish Committee (AJC) and the American Jewish Congress (AJCongress), as well as Bureaus of Jewish education, charitable organizations, and others. They were also taken up by Jewish baby boomers, many of whom understood identity to be the issue of the day. When *Response* magazine convened a symposium on "Jewish action," Joseph Reimer responded by noting that "The questions posed by the symposium seem clearly directed to the dilemma of Jewish identity in our times" (1970, p. 59). There were so many studies and reports on American Jewish "youth" that the American Jewish Committee commissioned an annotated bibliography to keep track of all of them (Rosenfield, 1970).

One of the first reports on Jewish college students was prepared by Geraldine Rosenfield of the American Jewish Committee in the wake of the 1967 National Conference for New Politics (Rosenfield, 1967; Hall, 2003). Much of the report is an unremarkable accounting of campus groups, but its formulation of the concerns that motivated the report reveals the burgeoning anxiety about Jewish students on campus and the fear that college campuses had fostered a climate detrimental to American Jewish students. Rosenfield reported that "the Jewish community is concerned about three things: the alienation from the Jewish tradition of many bright, socially conscious young people; the self-destructiveness of the hippy way of life; and the possible support the youthful dissenters seem likely to give to anti-Israel factions and black antisemitism [sic]" (p. ii). Rosenfeld understood these possibilities as functions of the broader sweep of youthful rejection of all things "establishment." "For the young dissenter," she concluded, "the synagogue and temple are so integral a part of the middle-class structure that he casts these aside with the other philistine abhorrences" (p. 40). Her slightly mocking tone notwithstanding, she reinforced the power of Jewish communal concern about younger Jews who, it seems, were ready to jettison their Jewishness in favor of more suitable options.

The American Jewish Congress also expressed its concern for Jewish college students in a special issue of *Congress Bi-Weekly* focusing on "Jewish Youth and the College Campus." For insight, the AJCongress turned to Irving Greenberg, a young Orthodox rabbi and professor at Yeshiva University. He opened his contribution, "Jewish Survival and the College Campus," by provocatively claiming, "The future of American Judaism is being shaped on the college campus." (1968, p. 5). He called campuses a "disaster area for Judaism, Jewish loyalty and Jewish identity" (p. 5) concluding, "The failure of Jewish identity on campus must also be seen as a further revelation of the insufficiency and irrelevance of much of Jewish education in America" (p. 7). Students, he argued, arrive on campus under-equipped Jewishly, and thus come under the "negative influence of the college experience on Jewish identity" (p. 8), which he traced to Ericksonian claims about the pressures of "personality integration." Though he was among the first to connect Jewish education to identity in a causal way, Greenberg's emphasis lands not on identity per se, but on survival. "If this [college campus life] is the major arena of Jewish survival," he proposed, "then we are engaged in nothing less than a battle for Jewish survival—and flowering" (p. 8). Greenberg responded to this situation with a proposal for the creation of a "Center for Jewish Survival" that can work on the challenges to Jewish identity that attend campus life.

Greenberg's contribution was paired with one by folk singer Theodore Bikel, who published a more impressionistic account of college life drawn from his perspective as an indefatigable touring performer and frequent visitor to college campuses. Bikel also framed his "evaluation of the campus experience in terms of Jewish identity" in the language of survival. He reflected on campus radicalism, the anti-war movement, the "hippies" and the "straights," and the generation gap. He did not find evidence of Greenberg's "disaster area." Instead, he noted, "There is little cause for alarm about the youth situation since the paramount concern of youth in rebellion seems to be precisely with the very issues Judaism projects: social justice, freedom of conscience, protection of the individual, and peace" (p. 13). Nevertheless, Bikel also concluded his report from campus with a turn to the question of survival. "Survival has been our chief concern for two thousand years of diaspora. . . . We have survived genocide; we rightfully rebel against cultural homicide. Not to know how to deal with ethnic suicide would be ludicrous" (p. 16). Bikel nodded to "the study of Jewish literature, Talmud, etc.," but he made no substantive mention of Jewish education as part of his vision for survival.

From the Reform Movement came another portrait of college students in crisis. Writing in *Dimensions*, a publication of the Reform Movement, Sara Feinstein offered a more pointed formulation that explicitly connected Jewish education and the concerns of the Jewish community, using identity as a kind of fulcrum. "The anxiety [about survival] is again echoed in the hearts and minds of many contemporary Jews, and campus youth is not exempt from it. Interpolating this question in the context of the identity conflicts of campus Jews, the crux of the matter becomes whether or not young Jewish radicals will again give up their own stake in the struggle" (1970, p. 8). She continued, "with the onslaught of ambivalence and self-doubt that grow out of the flux of campus tensions, even the best combination of positive factors is often rendered ineffectual. Institutions and individuals in the Jewish community are often disheartened in the seeming futility of their most earnest efforts to prepare college-bound youth for what awaits them on campus" (p. 7). "With no foothold, many lose touch with themselves. American Jewish youth," Feinstein concluded, "is by and large a paragon of Jewish miseducation" (p. 9).

The Miseducation of American Jewish Youth

Critiques of the failures of Jewish education were as popular as they were fierce, and they often resonated with larger critiques of American education and ideas about how to reform it, as articulated by theorists like Ivan Illich and Paolo Friere. College students were among the sharpest in their dismissals of Jewish education, but they were hardly alone.

As a student at Columbia University, Howard Sticklor wrote, "The prime instrument of such distortion [of religious wisdom] is the synagogue or, more precisely, the synagogue school, for it is that institution that sets, the tone and level of most of the activity of the Jewish youth community" (1969, p. 3). Similarly, Executive Vice-President of the American Association for Jewish Education Isaac Toubin wrote that few people are learning anything in Jewish education, and that what "we what we are generally engaged in is more correctly called 'playing school'" (1970, p. 49). Student leader James Sleeper wrote that "Jewish education misses its unique opportunity to meet the searching young with both the style and content of its own modes of learning" (1971, p. 137). Sleeper certainly felt that Jewish education could be salvaged, as long as it "provides hints of a viable cultural, spiritual, and interpersonal alternatives to the emptiness of students' current pressured, cram-packed, instrumental, goal-oriented, and fragmented lives" (p. 138). Marc Triebwasser, a young observer on the scene, explained that, for many students, the result of realizing that "he's not black" was that "he begins to realize that he is Jewish." (1970, p. 17). Activists responded by "peel[ing] away most of their early Jewish miseducation" in order to discover that "Judaism has much to offer as a vibrant alternative to laissez-faire liberalism" (ibid.).

Members of the Jewish educational establishment shared this understanding of Jewish education's shortcomings. Professor of Jewish Education Walter Ackerman expressed his displeasure with characteristic bluntness, deriding religious school curricula as "an affectation which obscures more than it reveals and hinders more than it helps" (1970, p. 21). Seymour Fox dismissed much of Jewish education for its "blandness" (1973). Samuel Dinin observed, "There is usually a blanket indictment an assumption made, explicitly or implicitly, that the failure of Jewish education is due to its lack of relevance to the world in which we live, and that this irrelevance of what is taught in our schools is the cause of one of the crises facing Jewish life today" (1969, p. 3) William Chomsky felt similarly. "The conclusion is clear and obvious. We cannot hope to succeed in our educational program unless we relate it to the experiences and problems of our youngsters. In a culturally denuded community, schools operate in a vacuum, and the educational program is meaningless and irrelevant." (p. 7). Alvin Schiff explicitly connected events in Israel to the weaknesses of American Jewish education, wondering aloud about its prospects in the wake of Israel's 1967 victory. "The paradox is that Israel (the existence of Israel) has achieved, particularly after the Six-Day War, what synagogues, Jewish schools and Jewish organizations not been able to accomplish" (p. 6). For Schiff, Israel's success highlighted the shortcomings of American Jewish educational endeavors.

Despite these dismissals and condemnations, almost all of Jewish education's critics found in it the potential for reviving Jewish life in the United States. Typically, these were formulated in terms of the liberatory potential of education, and they were juxtaposed with what they understood to be its moribund, irrelevant, and staid conditions that they claimed characterized their own experiences. Hillel Levine, who addressed the 1969 Council of Jewish Philanthropies and Welfare Funds on behalf of a group of students who protested the meetings, claimed that the priorities of American Jewish communal organizations have been mislaid, arguing that "quality Jewish education will help the individual remain whole in a society which denies sanctity to the human vessel" (1973, p. 190). James Sleeper qualified his critique of Jewish education as it has been taught with a more positive vision of its potential. "To engage in Jewish education may be to 'corrupt the young,' for such education would surely support a measure of their alienation from the suburban cultural nets we've described. Such Jewish education will surely not bring the young to membership in empty suburban temples." (p. 138) Bill Novak's article "The Making of a Jewish Counter Culture," concluded, "All the good will and interest in the world will lead us nowhere if young Jews remain ignorant" (1970, p. 10). Even Walter Ackerman formulated his vision for Jewish education in terms that resonated with those of his younger interlocutors, arguing that Jewish education could only succeed if it *resisted* the tendencies of

American schooling in both content and structure, and if it stopped supporting American education and tried to counter it instead:

> If not by choice then by circumstance, Jewish education is both in fact and theory the exact antithesis of general education in our time.... The Jewish school serves no pragmatic ends and can have no other real function than to help its students understand and appreciate the intrinsic value of education (1969, p. 35).

Jewish education, he argued, was "*torah lishma*" at its highest, and contained within it the kernel of a deeper critique of American culture and a salve from the career and skill-oriented approaches of American compulsory schooling. The way to do that was to "provide experience radically different than non-Jewish schools" (p. 36).

These visions of Jewish education shared a common belief that the success of the endeavor could be traced to its ability to offer an alternative vision of society and the place of the individual within it. In other words, Jewish education would succeed, they believed, if it provided people with the tools and knowledge necessary to resist the assimilation and uniformity of American middle-class life.

This vision was articulated early and powerfully by Irving Greenberg, who found a formulation that turned on his conception of identity. As part of a 1967 symposium on "Jewish distinctiveness" published in *Congress Bi-Weekly*, Greenberg wrote that American Jews were "at a moment of pivot— before the tide begins to run remorselessly" against the maintenance of Jewish particularism. The situation facing American Jews was one in which "the continuing breakdown of social barriers and increasing integration of the Jew as colleague and coworker in American life is removing the ethnic shelter of Jewish identity" (p. 16). This was true, he observed, in "intellectual-academic-government-cultural circles, where an abnormal percentage of Jews are found" (p. 9). The effects of higher education, he noted, benefitted Jewish individuals but worked against a sense of membership in a Jewish collectivity (see also Liebman, 1973), which were being worn away by the opportunities of a more open, tolerant society. While he noted the maintenance of Jewish distinctiveness across a number of areas, he shared concerns about what could sustain it in the longer term. For this, he proposed "A more positive force for survival is the potential strengthening of Jewish education" (p. 14). Greenberg agreed that there was a crisis facing American Jews, and that the lack of Jewish education was to blame. His response was to strengthen Jewish identities through education, so that American Jews could both avail themselves of the benefits of higher education and white collar professions it promised, while retaining their commitments to the Jewish collectivity and its purported distinctiveness.

Genealogies of Identity

Running through these critiques of Jewish education lay a thread of concern about the precarious state of Jewish identity. James Sleeper opened his essay with a comment about how he imagined that in the past, "Jewish parents had no more to decide to give their children a sense of Jewish identity or a working Jewish education than modern American parents have to decide that their children shall speak English" (1973, p. 121). Sleeper shared this pastoral view of the educational past with many other critics who imagined Jewishness of the past to have been organic, domestic, and interwoven into a person's everyday life and general worldview. Whether one believed, like Sklare, that schools were not adequately equipped for the task, or like Sleeper, that Jewish education could make up for what has been lost over time, both approaches are shadowed by a sense that younger American Jews had either lost or were never given the experiences necessary for a fully developed Jewish identity. Education, they believed, was both to blame for its failures and held the potential for its revival.

The emerging concern for Jewish identity coincided with an expansion of identity discourse more generally. The political and cultural upheavals of the late 1960s and the fragmentation of the New Left along lines of race, gender, religion and sexuality, identity helped stoke the furnaces of identity politics and thrust it to the foreground of American cultural and political discourse (Brubaker & Cooper, 2000; Fearon, 1999; Nicholson, 2008; Jacobson, 2008). Behind slogans like "the personal is political," and "black is beautiful," identity became increasingly politicized as minority groups argued for equal treatment under American law, grounded in classic liberal formulations of the neutral state. One's identity, however expressed, articulated through a minority community on whose behalf activists lobbied, protested, argued, and advocated for the recognition of their rights. In the late 1960s, wrote historian Phillip Gleason in an historical analysis of the concept, "the national crisis translated itself to the ordinary citizen as a challenge to every individual to decide where he or she stood with respect to the traditional values, beliefs, and institutions that were being called into question, and with respect to the contrasting interpretations being offered of American society" (1983, p. 928). Questions of identity mapped along concerns for individual, communal and civic distinctions and played out, often in competing rhetorics of rights.

Coincidentally, identity also came to be understood as the object of a "crisis" due to Erik Erikson's uncannily titled *Identity: Youth, and Crisis* (1968). Crisis, for Erikson, was inherent to the development of identity in and around adolescence. He defined crisis in terms of self-doubt and role confusion, predicated on the developmental awakening that the world of childhood was not necessarily the world of young adulthood or beyond. For Erikson, the adolescent crisis of identity was no mere developmental stage nor was it simply youthful frivolity. "The search of youth," he wrote, "is not for all-permissibility, but rather for new ways of directly facing up to what truly counts" (p. 37). However, they manifest—in fashion or music or drugs or politics—articulations of identity crises represented a deeply existential urge to both articulate and seek solace from confusion with respect to one's place in the world. Erikson's crisis was not fatal, however. It was "a necessary turning point, a crucial moment, when development must move one way or another, marshaling resources of growth, recovery, and further differentiation" (p. 16). Identity crises were serious and nearly ubiquitous, if overused (Erikson, 1994, p. 15). As a result, at an American Jewish Congress convention, Walter Kaufmann, a professor of Philosophy at Princeton, ironically observed that having an "identity crisis" had become a new status symbol. "You can be with it without a beard and without taking drugs, without reading Hesse and without civil rights work and you certainly do not have to occupy a building; but if you are not concerned about your identity, you are really out of it" (1969, p. 31).

The emergence of American Jewish identity as an educational outcome coincided with these events in both politics and psychology, and its early formulations aligned with the collective dimensions of both burgeoning identity politics and Erikson's sense that young adult identity was characterized by crisis. These two streams came to a head in the wake of Israel's military victory in 1967, which contributed to the fracture of New Left coalitions and left many American Jewish college students wondering where the realignment of politics left them. Israel's victory may have been the precipitating event, but its impact was not fully felt or articulated among Jewish college students until it emerged as the source of a fissure among members of the New Left at the National Conference for New Politics in the fall of 1967 (Hall, 2003). The split that emerged, largely between members of the New Left and members of an emerging black nationalist coalition, left many Jewish students feeling caught between their affinity for Israel and their commitments to liberal student politics (Feldman, 1967). A resurgence of anti-Zionism and antisemitism left many Jewish New Leftists feeling excluded from the New Left, in which they had previously played a significant role. It was as much a feeling of personal betrayal as political turnabout. Columbia undergraduate MJ Rosenberg, writing to "Jewish uncle toms," sharply outlined the dilemma facing Jewish college students. "If I must choose between the Jewish cause and the progressive anti-Israel SDS, I shall always choose the Jewish cause" (1969).

Jewish communal leaders responded by framing the situation facing Jewish students as a crisis. They believed that most Jewish college students were ill-equipped to counter critiques of Israel or build a vibrant response to the allures of countercultural life. Students felt similarly, and both attitudes emerged in critiques of Jewish education and visions for its potential to stoke stronger identities. Writing about "secular" Jewish college students, Richard Narva wrote, "Most tragic of all [about Jewish life on campus], is the consequent lack of opportunity for Jewish students to confront the problem of their Jewish identity in tension with a vital Jewish community" (1968, p. 13). Jewish campus life was weak and the majority of students were ill prepared to formulate their identities on their own.

The Reluctant Embrace

Not all Jewish educators were excited about the prospect of identity, but even the most skeptical could not ignore the rising resonance of the term. Alexander Dushkin offered a new historical model for Jewish education that now culminated in the orientation of education toward identity. "In our generation we have witnessed a twofold shift in the formulation of the overall purpose of Jewish education from *massoreth*, transmission of the religious cultural tradition, to *histagluth*, social environmental adjustment, and now to *Hizdahuth*, personal identification" (1973, p. 21). This marked a stark shift from his work a decade earlier, which paid little heed to identity in Jewish education, as the concept shifted from a marginal concern to a prevailing preoccupation. Similarly, Shraga Arian recognized the popularity of the concept and grudgingly encouraged his colleagues to pay attention. "Identity is the new magic word, and Jewish Federations Jewish Community Centers are already engaged in such programs. If the Bureaus of Jewish Education do not embrace these new identity programs, we stand a good chance of becoming irrelevant and ultimately superseded by other communal structures" (1973, p. 36).

For Airan, identity was just the term of the day, and if education was to remain a part of the Jewish communal conversation, it needed to invest in identity discourse. "The Bureau must assume these roles, because Jewish destiny has thrust this task upon it. Responding to the needs of this era impel our Bureaus of Jewish Education to become Bureaus of Jewish identity as well" (p. 37). Arian read the currents correctly, and partially owing to his influence, the 1969 conference of the National Council for Jewish Education took as its theme "Coping with Challenges in Jewish Education: Identity and Commitment." Four years later, the New York Bureau of Jewish Education organized its "pedagogic conference" around the theme of "Jewish Studies and Jewish Identity."

Questions about the promise and prospect of identity arose from other quarters, as well. In his introduction to the special issue of *Congress Bi-Weekly* on college students, the AJC's president, Arthur Lelyveld explained that identity itself could not be the issue. "We [the older generation] want them [the students] and our grandchildren to be Jews in more than identity. We want them to be Jews who will *carry on*" (1968, p. 4. Italics in the original). Though he raised the question of intergenerational transmission, Lelyveld was not satisfied with a vague sense of identity. For Leon Spotts, then editor of the *Journal of Jewish Education*, the issue revolved around the possibility that Jewish education could speak to the needs and interests of the younger generation. He asked, "Can the Jewish school succeed in making its program pertinent and meaningful in terms of life today in the real world?" (1969, p. 43). The implication being that its success was not a foregone conclusion. Similarly, Simon Greenberg, Vice-Chancellor of the Jewish Theological Seminary, noted, "The fundamental goal of Jewish education has from time immemorial been that of training the young so that they would identify themselves as Jews and with the Jewish people (a) rather than merely by the accident of birth; (b) happily—rather than reluctantly; and (c) significantly rather than peripherally" (1967, p. 164). But he qualified his observation by adding, "We would find it more difficult to agree on a definition of happy Jewish, self-identification, and most difficult to arrive at a consensus regarding the meaning of significant Jewish self-identification" (1967, p. 164). People might agree on Jewish identity as an educational outcome, but he acknowledged that reaching consensus on what that meant would prove difficult or even impossible.

Questions arose from the younger generation, as well. Arthur Green, a rabbi involved in havurat shalom, a pioneering Jewish co-op and house of study, was one of these critics. Speaking for baby boomers, he wrote, "Most American Jews of my generation, I must observe, do not care whether the

Jewish people survives as the Jewish people. Most do not care about Jewish *identity* as a value" (1970, p. 8. Italics in the original). Harold Weisberg, a philosophy professor at Brandeis, affirmed Green's claim and offered his own dismissal of identity as its own end. "I think Jewish identity is one of the myths of our time. . . . I wonder how much it helps us in putting such a stress on the fact that you ought to have a Jewish identity. . . . The question of identity is hardly sufficient here. The question is not simply one of identity, but the whys of survival. What is the point? What is the value" (1970, p. 16). He concluded, "I think all of this talk of confused identity in a mass society indicates a certain lack of moral strength, an excuse for not facing up to problems" (p. 17). In short, Green and Weisberg agreed that neither identity nor survival promised a compelling enough vision of Jewish life in the United States and beyond, regardless of the emerging consensus around the fission of the two concepts. Their objections, while notable, nevertheless indicate the depth to which identity had become part of communal discourse about American Jewish youth.

These challenges suggest that even during the period in which Jewish identity and Jewish education fused together, there were voices in the Jewish community that wondered aloud whether or not identity had either the conceptual depth or the consensual agreement to shoulder the load of Jewish communal survival. Nevertheless, both identity and survival became focal points for Jewish communal investment from the 1970s onward, as ongoing concerns about college students came increasingly to shape investments in Jewish education. In response to the student protests at the 1969 convention of leadership of Jewish federations and welfare funds (CJF), Jewish charitable organizations increased their investments in education in the name of communal survival. The students, for their part, advocated for more education. One Harvard student provoked the leadership of the assembled groups with a sign that read simply, in Hebrew "I bet you can't read this." Another student sign curtly captured the demands of the protesters. "Pay up for Jewish education." Remarkably, the assembled CJF leadership responded approvingly to the students and increased its allocations to Jewish education in the name of survival. "Prodded by student demonstrators and by a handful of academics," reported the *American Jewish Yearbook* in 1971, "many welfare federations managed some shift in their priorities and allocated a greater proportion of their funds for education." The article went on to note, "some welfare federation executives now prognosticate the abandonment of the 'health and welfare' model in Jewish life in favor of what is euphemistically termed a 'survival model' emphasizing education." (Weinberger, 1971, p. 231; See also Cohen & Fein, 1985).

Education for Survival

The preoccupation with Jewish survival and the commitment to Jewish education and Jewish identity as its guarantor found its most powerful formation in two initiatives of the American Jewish Committee. First, in 1969, the AJC convened a Task Force on Jewish Education, which brought together 36 Jewish community professionals, lay leaders, rabbis and scholars and was charged with exploring "new questions regarding the continuity of Jewish identity and the quality of Jewish life" (Gold, 1973, p. ix). David Sidorsky, a young professor of philosophy at Columbia University, served as a consultant to the Task Force and took primary responsibility for synthesizing and summarizing its work, which the AJC published in 1972. The Task Force focused on Jewish education and its supposed ability to foster or foment Jewish identity. The Task Force addressed an array of issues, turning most of its attention on the "third generation" of American Jews, who would have been "Jewish youth involved in the counterculture, either of the 'radical' or 'hippie' variety" (1973, p. 34). Resulting from concerns about college students, the Task Force advocated for increased attention to Jewish identity. "On any view of the future, however, the concern with youth culture should be directed toward the general field of research and programs that relate to Jewish identity" (p. 36).

The connection between education and identity was further solidified when the AJC followed the Task Force with the creation of the Colloquium on Jewish Education and Jewish Identity that grew directly out of the Task Force. Launched in 1972, the Colloquium included many members of the original Task Force, with new additions including representatives of the three major Jewish religious movements, three psychologists who had written about Jewish identity and Geoffrey Bock, a young Harvard EdD who had written his dissertation on the impact of Jewish schooling. Sidorsky again formulated the Colloquium's course of action around the production of Jewish identity, asking how Jewish communities might better "provide experience[s] and environment[s] conducive to the formulation of Jewish identity?" (1977, p. 11). The question was a practical one, but more than that, it reflected the emerging conventional wisdom that Jewish education would invariably lead to a stronger Jewish identity and that this was the best course for ensuring the survival of the Jewish people. As Sidorsky wrote of the Colloquium's recommendations, they represented a "response to the reformulation of the goal of Jewish education with a recognition of the primacy of the question of Jewish identity" (1977, p. 23).

The emerging consensus around education as the engine for identity was especially notable given that some of the members of the Colloquium expressed concerns about the effectiveness of Jewish education in general. Semyour Fox's contribution hung on his assertion that Jewish education had no stated purpose (p. 261). Although he advocated for Jewish education that cultivated a sense of communal membership, Walter Ackerman, like Fox, refused to entertain "proposals for the improvement of the current state of affairs" until stakeholders disabuse themselves of "the rhetoric of nonsense that permeates most discussions of Jewish education today" (1970, p. 24). Sidorsky himself hedged on the expectation that education could or should shoulder the burden of identity.

> Cultural continuity rather than cultural adjustment is now the central problem of American Jewish life. . . . Sixty years ago, Jewish educators and parents alike assumed that Jewish schooling simply enriched an indigenous cultural heritage. Jewish educators never claimed that their efforts would insure cultural continuity and this task has only recently been thrust upon them (1972, p. 2).

Meanwhile, Geoffrey Bock, the only member of the Colloquium to have conducted original research on the relationship between education and identity, found that Jewish schools are better at influencing "public" affinities than they are at cultivating "private" values.

> Because schooling has a greater affect on public behaviors it is easier for educators to teach people to identify with the formal institutions of group life than to accept the intrinsic, personal ethnic group values. As an ethnic group comes to rely on its formal educational institutions for the continuity of group life, it stresses identification with specific ethno-religious institutions, rather than with personal values and beliefs (p. 8).

Bock concluded that schools succeed at cultivating relationships with institutions but they were far less successful at changing personal attitudes, feelings, or beliefs. Jewish schooling may create Jews with strong patterns of affiliation or membership, but, he warned, "they will not be especially Jewish in personal outlook" (p. 8). Put slightly differently, Jewish schools promote communal identification, but they do not significantly impact individual identity (see Himmlefarb, 1982).

Despite Bock's subtle distinction between public and private attitudes, by the mid 1970s the work of the American Jewish Committee's Task Force and Colloquium helped solidify the causal relationship between identity and education. Much of this effort, however, was not based on research on students in K-12 education, where much of the emphasis in Jewish educational circles lay, but on college students. The Task Force was explicit about this, as was the American Jewish Committee and the American Jewish Congress. *The Journal of Jewish Education* tended to focus on K-12 efforts, but it took a great deal of direction from the commentary and concern brewing around college students.

The influence of observations of college students informed an emerging research stream on Jewish identity, as well. Steven M. Cohen, who published one of the first studies (based on a survey of students at Barnard) connecting Jewish education and Jewish identity, found that Jewish schooling exerts a limited influence over students' Jewish attitudes (1974, p. 326), a finding confirmed by Arnold Dashefsky and Howard Shapiro (1974). As the decade wore on, the focus of research into education and identity migrated away from whether or not a connection existed to how to make it more effective. The question was no longer, "did education foster identity," but by what mechanism could it do so better. The relationship between the two had become something of a truism. Harold Himmelfarb (1974) and Geoffrey Bock (1976) both argued for more time in the classroom, though they differed as to how much would make a difference. As the decade wound down, the connection between Jewish education and Jewish identification grew increasingly stronger such that in 1978, Dashefsky and Shapiro argued, "There is no doubt that it is possible to introduce improvements in the Jewish educational system in the United States, in methods and curriculum as well as in the administrative structure and the teaching faculty, but to conclude that there is no relationship between Jewish education and Jewish identification is untenable" (p. 90).

Conclusion

A close examination of the discourse around "Jewish youth" during the pivotal years in which identity became a Jewish educational outcome reveals a growing concern over Jewish college students. The on-campus political repercussions of Israel's victory in 1967 shook the political alignments of the New Left, leaving many Jewish students searching ways to make sense of a political reality in which former alliances no longer held. Jewish communal leaders from across the political and denominational spectrum responded with an array of analyses, investigations, and initiatives designed to better understand what was happening to Jewish students on campus, and, as a result, how to help them. What emerged was a consensus around the failures of Jewish education to prepare students for college, and a sense that the best outcome of a successful education would be an identity that was strong enough to weather the volatility of campus life. Investing in education at the K-12 level would, in turn, shore up the Jewish identities of future students.

The perceived weaknesses of Jewish identity could be counteracted by greater investment in Jewish education for the express purpose of strengthening or emboldening Jewish identity. Identity gave Jewish education a purpose, of sorts, at precisely the moment when few of its leaders could articulate one. It filled a need for Jewish communal leadership as much as it did for the students who would be the recipients of new programs, mission statements, and investments. By the mid-1970s, Jewish education for Jewish identity had become a communal truism and a cottage industry.

It was, however, not born of a positive articulation of the purpose of Jewish education or the purpose of Jewish communal belonging, generally speaking. Rather, it emerged out of a larger concern for the survival of the American Jewish community. The logic and language of survival pervade Jewish educational and identity discourse in the late 1960s, and they serve as a kind of binding matter that provided urgency and continuity between the two concepts. Preparing Jewish students for campus life was a question of survival, emerging from the fear that Jewish students, when faced with conflict, might abandon their Jewish lives entirely. Education was supposed to provide for identity, and identity was supposed to enable students to defend against the forces on campus. Identity had become a crisis, and solving it would require investing in Jewish children who would soon become college students themselves.

Identity therefore emerged from a defensive logic, one formulated to protect Jewish college students from being swept under the changing tides of campus politics. Identity, Jewish communal leaders imagined, could provide an anchor, a safe harbor where Jewish students could find themselves and, as a result, identify a way out of the complex politics that emerged in the wake of 1967. While campus battles about Israel waged on into the 1970s (see Breirah) and continue to do so in the early years of the twenty-first century, Jewish educators still discuss the present and future of Jewish education, and Jewish college students still negotiate complex political alliances. American Jews still go looking for ways to engage, to participate, to enact, and to learn about being Jewish, while the concept of Jewish identity remains firmly ensconced in the vocabulary of American Jewish education.

Bibliography

Ackerman, Walter. (1969). Jewish Education, For What? *American Jewish Year Book 70*, 3–36.

Arian, Shraga. (1972). Structuring a New Bureau of Jewish Education for the 70s. *Journal of Jewish Education 42*(1), 34–37.

Bikel, Theodore. (1968, October 28). Report on Jewish Campus Youth. *Congress Bi-Weekly*, 32(11), 1 –16.

Bock, Geoffrey. (1976). *The Jewish Schooling of American Jews: A Study of Non-Cognitive Educational Effects* (unpublished doctoral dissertation). Harvard Graduate School of Education, Cambridge, MA.

Bock, Geoffrey. (1977). *Does Jewish Schooling Matter?* Retrieved from http://www.bjpa.org/Publications/details.cfm?PublicationID=2229

Brubaker, Rogers, & Cooper, Frederick. (2000). Beyond "Identity." *Theory and Society 29*, 1–47.

Chomsky, William. (1969). This I Believe: The Credo of a Jewish Educator. *Journal of Jewish Education 39*(1), 6–10.

Cohen, Steven M. (1974). The Impact of Jewish Education on Religious Identification and Practice. *Jewish Social Studies 36*(3/4), 316–26.

Cohen, Steven M., & Fein, Leonard J. (1985). From Integration to Survival: American Jewish Anxieties in Transition. *The ANNALS of the American Academy of Political and Social Science 480*(1), 75–88.

Dashefsky, Arnold., & Shapiro, Howard. M. (1978, Summer). Hinukh Yehudi V'hizdahut Yehudit B'artzot Habrit (Jewish Education and Jewish Identification in the United States). *B'tfutzot Hagolah, 19*, 90–94.

Dashefsky, Arnold, & Shapiro, Howard M. (1974). *Ethnic Identification Among American Jews*. Lexington, MA: Lexington Books.

Dinin, Samuel. (1969). Crisis and Relevance. *Journal of Jewish Education 39*(3), 3–5.

Dushkin, Alexander. (1973). Israel and the Teaching of Jewish Identity. *Journal of Jewish Education 42*(2/3), 21–26.

Erikson, Erik H. (1994). *Identity: Youth and Crisis*. New York, NY: W. W. Norton & Company.

Fearon, James. (1999). What Is Identity? (As We Now Use the Word)—DRAFT. Retrieved from https://www.stanford.edu/group/fearon-research/cgi-bin/wordpress/wp-content/uploads/2013/10/What-is-Identity-as-we-now-use-the-word-.pdf

Feinstein. (1970, Winter). A New Jewish Voice on Campus. *Dimensions in American Judaism, 4*(2), 4–11.

Feldman, Paul. (1967, October 16). The New Politics Fiasco: A Study in Manipulation. *Congress Bi-Weekly, 34*(13) 13–16.

Fox, Seymour. (1973). Toward a General Theory of Jewish Education. In David Sidorsky (Ed.), *The Future of the Jewish Community in America*. Philadelphia, PA: Jewish Publication Society.

Gleason, Philip. (1983, March). Identifying Identity: A Semantic History. *The Journal of American History 69*, 910–31.

Gold, Bertram. (1973). Preface. In David Sidorsky (Ed.), *The Future of the Jewish Community in America* (1st edition). Philadelphia, PA: Jewish Publication Society.

Green, Arthur. (1970). American Jewish Youth. *Congress Bi-Weekly*, 37(5), 6–8.

Greenberg, Irving. (1967, April 3). Identity in Flux. *Congress Bi-Weekly*, 34(7), 8–16.

Greenberg, Irving. (1968, October 29). Jewish Survival and the College Campus. *Congress Bi-Weekly*, 35(11), 5–10.

Greenberg, Simon. (1967). New Approaches in Jewish Education. *Journal of Jewish Education* 37(4), 162–68.

Hall, Simon. (2003). 'On the Tail of the Panther': Black Power and the 1967 Convention of the National Conference for New Politics. *Journal of American Studies* 37(1), 59–78.

Himmelfarb, Harold S. (1974). The Impact of Religious Schooling: The Effects of Jewish Education upon Adult Religious Involvement (unpublished PhD dissertation). University of Chicago, Chicago, IL.

Himmelfarb, Harold S. (1982). Research on American Jewish Identity and Identification: Progress, Pitfalls, and Prospects. In Marshall Sklare (Ed.), *Understanding American Jewry*. New York, NY: Transaction Publishers.

Jacobson, Matthew Frye. (2008). *Roots Too: White Ethnic Revival in Post-Civil Rights America*. Cambridge, MA: Harvard University Press.

Kaufmann, Walter. (1970, April 3). The Future of Jewish Identity. *Congress Bi-Weekly*, 37(5), 31–35.

Krasner, Jonathan. (2016). On the Origins and Persistence of the Jewish Identity Industry in Jewish Education. *Journal of Jewish Education* 82(2), 132–58.

Lelyveld, Arthur J. (1968, October 28). Jewish Youth: Our Fears and Our Responsibilities. *Congress Bi-Weekly*, 35(11), 4, 17–18.

Levine, Hillel. (1973). To Share a Vision. In Jack Nusan & Peter Dreier (Eds.), *Jewish Radicalism: A Selected Anthology*. New York, NY: Grove Press, Inc.

Liebman, Charles S. (1973). *The Ambivalent American Jew: Politics, Religion and Family in American Jewish Life*. Philadelphia, PA: Jewish Publication Society of America.

Narva, Richard. (1968). Judaism on the Campus—Why It Fails. *Response: A Contemporary Jewish Review* 2(2), 11–17.

Nicholson, Linda. (2008). *Identity Before Identity Politics* (1st ed.). Cambridge, UK: Cambridge University Press.

Novak, William. (1970). The Making of a Jewish Counterculture. *Response: A Contemporary Jewish Review* 7, 5–10.

Raab, Earl. (1972, March 10). Futuring the American Jew: A Presentation. *Congress Bi-Weekly* 39(5), 14–17.

Reimer, Joseph. (1970). Contribution to the Symposium. *Response: A Contemporary Jewish Review 9*, 59–62.

Rosenberg, M. Jay. (1969), February. To Jewish Uncle Toms. *Jewish Frontier.*

Rosenfield, Geraldine. (1967). *Interim Report on the New Left and Alienated Youth.* New York, NY: American Jewish Committee.

Rosenfield, Geraldine. (1970). *What We Know About Young American Jews: An Annotated Bibliography.* New York: American Jewish Committee. Retrieved from https://www.bjpa.org/bjpa/search-results?search=rosenfield+Jewish+youth

Schiff, Alvin Irwin. (1969). The Campus Rebellion, Jewish Youth and Jewish Education. *Journal of Jewish Education, 39*(3), 5–6.

Sidorsky, David. (1972). *The Future of the Jewish Community in America: A Task Force Report.* New York, NY: The American Jewish Committee. Retrieved from http://www.bjpa.org/Publications/downloadFile.cfm?FileID=13558

Sidorsky, David. (1973). *The Future of the Jewish Community in America.* Philadelphia, PA: Jewish Publication Society.

Sidorsky, David. (1977). *Colloquium on Jewish Education and Jewish Identity: Summary Report and Recommendations.* New York: American Jewish Committee. Retrieved from https://www.bjpa.org/search-results/publication/13708

Sklare, Marshall. (1971). *America's Jews.* New York, NY: Random House.

Sleeper, James A. (1971). Authenticity and Responsiveness in Jewish Education. In James Sleeper, & Alan L. Mintz (Eds.). *The New Jews.* New York, NY: Vintage Books.

Spotts, Leon H. (1969). The Challenge of Jewish Youth. *Journal of Jewish Education 39*(4), 43–47.

Staub, Michael E. (Ed.). (2004). *The Jewish 1960s.* Waltham, MA: Brandeis University Press.

Sticklor, Howard. (1969). Education and Self-Deception. *Response: A Contemporary Jewish Review 3*(1), 2–6.

Toubin, Isaac. (1970, April 3). The Means of Transmitting Jewishness in the United States. *Congress Bi-Weekly, 37*(5), 49–51.

Triebwasser, Marc A. (1970, March 6). The Jewish Activist Youth Movement. *Congress Bi-Weekly, 37*(4), 15–19.

Weinberger, Paul. (1971). The Effects of Jewish Education. *The American Jewish Yearbook 72*, 230–49.

Weisberg, Howard. (1970, April 3). Permanence and Change. *Congress Bi-Weekly, 37*(5), 14–16.

Regarding the "Real" Jew: Authenticity Anxieties Around Poland's "Generation Unexpected"

Katka Reszke

Since the fall of the communist regime in Poland in 1989, we have been hearing more and more about a "renaissance" of Jewish culture in what many Jews still refer to as the Old Country. As numerous Poles developed an interest in Jewish history and heritage, thousands discovered their own Jewish ancestry or embraced Jewish ancestry they may have known about but had not explored before. Today, Poland is home to the largest Jewish culture festival in the world and it may feature probably more Jewish artistic and intellectual enterprises than any other European country. Rather than defining it as a "renaissance," it is important to stress that what we are witnessing in today's Poland is the creation of a distinct contemporary Polish Jewish culture whose authorship is now shared by Jewish and non-Jewish Poles and which takes place in conjunction with an evolving revitalization of the Polish Jewish community. Moreover, we can now also observe how more and more Jews around the world, including the many who can trace their family roots to Polish lands, are becoming actively interested and increasingly involved in Poland's contemporary Jewish life and culture. This too poses a much-appreciated challenge to the long-dominant narrative which had the Jewish story in Poland ending with the Holocaust and the remaining traces of Polish Jewish life disappearing under communism. Few would have dared to predict that following the end of the communist regime, the grandchildren of World War II survivors would begin discovering and embracing their Jewish roots. I refer to this generation as Generation Unexpected.

Between 2001 and 2011, I conducted semi-structured in-depth interviews with fifty young adults who can be considered members of the third post-Holocaust generation of Jews in Poland. I talked to people born between the mid-1970s and the early 1990s. The majority of them had learned about their Jewish roots while in their teens or twenties. For the sake of positioning the researcher, let me note that I too am a representative of Generation Unexpected and I too only began discovering my Jewish roots in my teens.

In this chapter, I focus on how young adults in contemporary Poland who discover or "stumble over" their Jewish roots make sense of their experience as they struggle to legitimize or authenticate their membership in the Jewish collective. I look at how individual narratives maneuver discursive landscapes and I focus on the theme of authenticity, which resonates far beyond the Polish context.

We live in a climate of skepticism about the authenticity of just about anything, yet both individual and collective Jewish identity narratives continue to rely on the often vaguely defined idea of "the authentic Jew."

Peculiar patterns of Jewish deassimilation and identity construction, which have surfaced in the Polish context during the past three decades, continue to generate novel analytical categories and shed light on how historical and geographical context utterly transforms the way the same heritage can be experienced by very different heirs. They offer different perspectives on both the perceived "essence" of Jewishness and its perceived periphery and boundaries. Understanding contemporary Jewish Poland calls for a reevaluation of some of the most fundamental philosophical questions regarding Jewish identity. The discourse around the seemingly most obvious truths about being Jewish, being "authentically" Jewish, or being a "real" Jew in today's Poland, is turning the "Old Country" into a prolific source of educational opportunities and a hotbed of debate about the nature and parameters of contemporary Jewish identity.

Between the end of World War II and the early 1990s, there never seemed to be a right time to deliberately "come out" as a Jew in Poland (see Stratton, 2000). For our parents' and grandparents' generations, to identify as a Jew was often nothing but a stigma. Since the fall of the communist regime, the number of Jews in Poland has been constantly growing and it seems fair to say that for the majority of the younger generation—those, who began their identity quest in the 1990s or later—Jewishness is a primarily positive experience.

For some, the idea that there are Jews living in Poland today is still a matter of faith. The notorious question of how many Jews may actually live in Poland also appears to be subject to interrogation. In 2012, the World Jewish Congress estimated the Jewish population of Poland at a mere 5,000. The American Jewish Joint Distribution Committee had it at 25,000. However, if we take into account all Poles with at least one Jewish grandparent and so much as consider the ones who have yet to discover their Jewish roots, these modest numbers would need to be tripled, if not quadrupled. In 2011, when interviewed about Jewish life in Poland, the country's chief rabbi, Michael Schudrich, said, "Over the last 21 years, thousands of Poles have discovered that they have Jewish roots and nobody knows how many thousands they are." When asked how many Jews there are in Poland today, he answered, "Pick a number; double it. It is too small. I don't know, but tomorrow there will be more" (Zwalman Lerner, 2011). And he was not wrong about that.

Both the so-called "renaissance" of Jewish culture in Poland, as well as the growing number of people seeking a Jewish affiliation, have become much-debated phenomena (Gruber, 2002; Lehrer, 2013; Reszke, 2013). People express concerns about the authenticity of the new Polish Jewish culture, and that extends to a certain skepticism about the authenticity of the new Jewish identities.

Identity and Authenticity

The notion of authenticity has been present in philosophy for centuries. However, only in the past several decades has it become central to the discourse of identity and the construction of the "modern self." My interest in authenticity is a socio-anthropological one. In my interviews with representatives of Poland's "Generation Unexpected," a peculiar rhetoric transpires as a defense mechanism against accusations of inauthenticity. In their narratives, the participants maneuver between the primordial and the constructed in response to "threats" posed to the authenticity of their identities. These responses reveal some of the complexities involved in being Jewish in Poland, as well as being recognized as "real Jews" by multiple "others."

The postmodern rise of multiculturalism, pluralism and globalization can be held responsible for the dethronement of a particular traditional understanding of culture. The shift altered conceptions of culture from a normative, regulating, coherent system that determines the lives of individuals who participate in it, or are indeed "bearers" of it, toward a theorization of culture as unstable, fragmented, and subject to reinterpretation and change (Boas, 1940; Levi-Strauss, 1974; Mead, 1964). Under this new paradigm, individuals were considered free to choose their own ways of participating in a given culture. They were free (or more free, anyhow) to actively construct their cultural identities, and they could claim more than one at a time. Moreover, these identities were now understood to be fluid, dynamic, self-reflexive and continuously reordered against the backdrop of shifting experiences of day-to-day life (Hall, 1996; Gidden; 1984; Lifton, 1993). Erik Erikson's pioneering theory of individual identity rooted in developmental psychology would face fierce challenges, but the discourse he put forth would prove persistent. Erikson described identity as "a subjective sense of an invigorating sameness and continuity" which unfolds through time according to an innate schedule (Erikson, 1968, 19; Schachter, 2005b). "Achieving" identity was seen as a mark of maturity—the end result whereby we become who we are supposed to be. The postmodern belief is that rapidly changing social reality and circumstances relentlessly challenge the individual, rendering sameness, coherence, or stability not only practically unachievable, but in fact perhaps not so much desired (Burszta, 2004). One of the chief theorists of postmodern identities, Robert Jay Lifton (1993), claims that people structure a fluid, constantly changing identity with multiple, often contrasting elements, and that while continuous self-recreation of identity "is by no means without confusion and danger, it allows for an opening out of individual life, for a self of many possibilities" (Lifton, 1993, pp. 4–5). Along similar lines, Stuart Hall's well-endorsed definition of identity frames it fragmented, multiple, flexible and ever shifting (Hall, 1992). In post-traditional social orders—as argued by sociologist Anthony Giddens—identity is not inherited or static. Instead, it has become a reflexive project (Giddens, 1984).

By its own nature, the postmodern identity discourse would now have to face questions regarding authenticity. On the one hand, culture no longer fully controlled who we are, but on the other, culture and social context conditioned how we might choose who to be. In other words, individuals were "free within a context," but not "free of context" (Tamir, 1996, p. 47). This distinction would become one of the central predicaments of the modern condition and—in effect—one of the major themes in the discourse of identity. After all, questions would stubbornly resonate about which of the many changing identities available to us are in fact more "authentic" than others and how do we "authentically" maneuver between them.

Inspired by Jean-Paul Sartre (1948), in his analysis of the notion of an "authentic Jewish identity," Stuart Charmé distinguishes between what he describes as essentialist authenticity and existential authenticity. He points out two different qualities: the essentialist reference to "Jewish content" and the existential quality of a personal identity. The latter involves asking about the authenticity of the Jewish qualifier of one's self, whereas the previous asks about one's own sense of authenticity (Charmé, 2000). When we say "authentic Jewish identity," is our main concern the authenticity of a person who happens to be Jewish? In other words, are we wondering if a given Jewish person is living an "authentic" life, if she or he is being "true to herself"? Or are we in fact wondering about the authenticity of their Jewishness and whether or not they are being "true" to it, in some fashion?

The two divergent paradigms of thinking about identity resonate soundly in the controversy between primordialism and circumstantialism in theories of ethnicity. The basic assumption of primordialism is that individuals are born as involuntary members of a given community, where belonging is secured by birth or—yet more bluntly—by blood. Primordial traits are described by Geertz (1963) as "givens" of social existence, which possess an "overpowering coerciveness" and are compelling, determinist, involuntary, and inborn. The circumstantialist perspective on the other hand (otherwise referred to as mobilizationist, situationalist, or instrumentalist) emphasizes the socially constructed nature of ethnicity, and interprets ethnic mobilization in terms of indications of concrete interests, whether political, social or economic. This view acknowledges the possibility of changing ethnic identifications, as well as the emergence of new ethnicities (Gil-White, 1999). In the most extreme scenario, circumstantialists see individuals as rational actors and ethnicity as a means of accessing social, political or economic resources (Barth, 1969; Gil-White, 1999).

To sum up, according to the traditional paradigm, there is an unchangeable core to ourselves, an essence, which is determined by birth and governed by the rules of the culture we were born into. Our identity is secure and "authentic," as long as we remain faithful to our birthright. The alternative paradigm assumes no essence of the self. We may be born into a culture, but we are free to construct our identities. Because they happen in dialogue and in response to ever-changing circumstances, our identities are never fixed, never stable and remain forever in the process of becoming.

* * *

The worst thing to be in Poland is to be a Jew who isn't one. (Sara)

Since the democratic changes in Poland in the late 1980s, thousands of young people have discovered their Jewish roots. Some learned about them from their grandparents' death bed confessions, others by uncovering hidden old documents, overhearing conversations, pursuing a hunch, or simply taking steps toward learning more about one's family's background. Others, aware of a Jewish link in their family's past, decided to embrace and explore that knowledge and actively pursue a Jewish affiliation. For many of their grandparents, being a Jew was associated with a stigma. They developed survival strategies that often involved obscuring or falsifying civil documents, baptism, intermarriage, or name changes. More often than not, in post-communist Poland, one could discover partial Jewish roots, in many cases on the father's side of the family, and in even more cases, such discoveries would be followed by the realization that it may be difficult or impossible to find hard evidence of those roots and that—regardless of how hard the evidence might be—there will be many who will not give credence to one's newly discovered Jewishness.

> *There are those who feel more Jewish, those who feel less Jewish, and those who take away from others that right to feel like anybody at all.* (Anabela)

Members of Generation Unexpected speak extensively about the different ways in which other people question their Jewishness and tell them that they are not "real" Jews. This first type of questioning pertains to the question of whether a given person is "really Jewish," in the "biological," primordial sense. This line of inquiry stems from the assumption that a person is Jewish if she or he was born to a Jewish mother, but it also involves having to support one's Jewish origins with some kind of satisfactory genetic or familial evidence. This kind of evidence is hard to produce no matter where one lives, and especially in Poland. Another line of questioning circles around the notion of pursuing a Jewish identity relatively late in life and in "a country like Poland." While the primordialist questions are posed by people both within and outside of Poland, the assumption that Poland is fiercely antisemitic and nothing beyond a vast Jewish graveyard and therefore Jews should not "choose" to live there, is one held primarily by non-European Jews.

Aleksandra points out how common it is for foreign Jews to start the conversation with the blunt question "Are you Jewish?":

> *You know… for them it's the first thing—it's after the mother that you are Jewish, it's always like this…* (Aleksandra)
> *As a Polish Jew I didn't feel recognized or respected enough by American institutions and of course not by Israeli institutions… it was as if we were second quality Jews.* (Bożena)

Some members of Generation Unexpected resort to arguing that if they had been born before World War II, they would not have to debate their own Jewishness. They stress the fact that they would qualify as Jews according to Nazi laws:

> If someone falls under the Nuremberg Laws, then they are Jewish to me. (Jadwiga)

Traditional Jewish law holds that Jewishness is passed down through a person's mother. There is no such thing, according to the Jewish law in its orthodox interpretation, as a "non-halachic Jew." Nevertheless, more than half of young Jews in today's Poland are in fact considered "non-halachic Jews." This is a phenomenon whose significance cannot be overestimated, and it opens up new vocabularies and poses challenges to existing dominant narratives of Jewishness and intergenerational transmission. Poland's Generation Unexpected is a product of unprecedented processes of deassimilation taking place in that part of Europe:

> For a long time I wondered what this being Jewish meant, what attracted me in it. Is it some kind of romanticism with regard to the war and to loss of family? Or with regard to the fact that from something negative Jews had turned into something positive, into some kind of fashion ... I could not answer any of this for myself. (Sara)
>
> People talk about a trend, but I don't particularly like to think about it this way, because I don't think that it's a trend, because most people who do it, don't do it because they fancy Jews, but because they have a certain need. (Szymon)

Questioning her own motives, Sara wonders whether she had fallen prey to fashion and whether her own Jewishness might be just another case of following a "trend." Szymon, by contrast, dismisses that possibility out of hand, while nodding to the deeper concerns that claiming Jewishness might address. Yet, Sara has been an active member of the Polish Jewish community for many years now, and her own usage of the past tense suggests that her "self-suspicions" no longer haunt her. Moving from the past to the present, Sara continues,

> I feel authentic in that I doubt, in that uncertainty about who I am, about whether I am connected, whether I have the right to this tradition. (Sara)

Sara seems to identify doubt and self-questioning with authenticity. In a prominently existential remark, she becomes an advocate of a particular understanding of identity, which sees it as unstable and unfixed, and a particular understanding of authenticity, which assumes instability of identity (Charmé, 2000) as part of its very authenticity. Jean Paul Sartre wrote about authenticity carrying an "ontological insecurity" and being beyond that which is fixed and established (Sartre 1948). Stuart Charmé paraphrased the French philosopher in saying that what makes Jewish identity authentic is an assumption of the instability of all identities (Charmé, 2000). As Max explains,

> It isn't like that, that it's [being Jewish] so super-fixed, it is NOT fixed, and that is super for me, that it isn't fixed, and that is what is most important for me. (Max)

Max appears to be endorsing the kind of existential approach to identity which appreciates its fluctuating, unfixed nature and where being Jewish can be seen as an ongoing process of becoming.

The important observation here is that very few members of Generation Unexpected were actually raised to be Jewish. Rarely was Jewish tradition actively transmitted to them, and—for the most part—nobody expected them to embrace their Jewish heritage:

> Can I allow myself to call myself a Jew-Jew, if because of deepest cultural assimilation I was totally deprived of that culture, raised in a Polish home ...? (Wiktor)

In Wiktor's terms, his generation does not feature many "Jew-Jews"— Jews born and raised as Jews. Consequently, when entering any area of Jewish life, they confront their own sense of unfamiliarity; they are confronted by their own lack of knowledge of Jewish traditions and lack of any "practical" Jewish background. In a similar tone, Magda expresses concerns about not being "equipped" with the right "tools" to be Jewish:

> How am I supposed to know Jewish prayers if in my home nobody ever prayed in the Jewish way? How am I supposed to know what is what if I never saw the things before in my life? I'd like to learn Hebrew, but then again I'm not sure if that isn't trying to fill up my identity with something external. (Magda)

Magda seems to be saying that beyond the feeling of inadequacy due to her "Jewish illiteracy," there is an existential void, an existential inadequacy, which, as I believe she suggests, cannot be fixed by Hebrew lessons alone:

> *I regret I was never that annoying Jewish kid who disturbs everyone in the synagogue and who never had to learn the difference between the Torah and the Talmud...* (Ewelina)

Ewelina regrets never having the opportunity to be a Jewish child who came to know the difference between the Torah and the Talmud by cultural osmosis. Today, Ewelina does know the difference between the two. She wishes, however, for that difference to have been a self-evident one—one she would have naturally been raised with, one that would have been elemental to her upbringing. Her personal Jewishness begins in early adulthood; it "missed" her childhood. Her existential void, if I may, is not in not knowing the difference between the Torah and the Talmud. It is in never having been a Jewish child. In longing for a Jewish childhood, Ewelina expresses a longing for a personal Jewish past—one that she could remember as her very own. Such personal Jewish pasts are very often missing from the experience of the members of Generation Unexpected, and it is a profound source of anxieties about identity and authenticity:

> *If it weren't for persecutions and antisemitism, I think my family would be totally Jewish and I wouldn't have to struggle with what to do in order to live a normal life.* (Natalia)
>
> *To discover that which could have been if it weren't for... How I would have turned out if someone back there hadn't converted to Christianity, hadn't chosen the assimilationist way.* (Wiktor)
>
> *... I would like to be part of that world, the one I would surely have belonged to from the beginning if it weren't for the Second World War.* (Hana)
>
> *As I began identifying with it, I felt that this world, my world, was totally taken away from me.* (Teresa)
>
> *I never knew it. I miss that [world] in Poland before the war so much.* (Natalia)
>
> *I embraced an identity that isn't there.* (Marek)

Each of the above speaks to the notion of embracing a potential identity—one that would have been theirs in an alternative version of history. The idea then is to be Jewish *as if* history had not severed Jewish ancestries. The narratives bring about the question of what would have happened had history unraveled completely differently—had there been no Holocaust, no World War II, no persecutions, and no communism. In other words, our participants talk about embracing a Jewish identity as an act of reclaiming or perhaps "rescuing" an identity that "could have" or "should have" been theirs. It is, in a sense, a very personal counter-history.

Beyond Blood

Members of Generation Unexpected make various references to an understanding of Jewish identity in distinctly primordialist terms. They include statements about identity viewed as something we are born with—something, which is ascribed, and not chosen, something we cannot reject, because it is already determined by our personal history, our heritage, our genes, or—more bluntly—by our blood. They also speak about the nature of belonging to the Jewish people, about a perceived essence of Jewishness and perceived boundaries of Jewish identity:

> Blood. There's something in it, which attracts us. Ancestors. We want to be the descendants of our Jewish ancestors. (Łukasz)

Unlike Łukasz, Danuta does not associate the "essence" of being Jewish with the physicality of blood, but rather—as she calls it—with "something metaphysical":

> ...That Jewish spark... It is something that draws you to other Jews and something that makes you want your life to be bound with Jews and with Jewishness. (Danuta)

In the following example, what is emphasized is the unconscious and—*ipso facto*—involuntary nature of Jewishness as something, which is inherited:

> Some things are simply inherited... it doesn't matter whether you know that you're Jewish or not, you will inherit it anyway. (Joanna)

The involuntary component of Jewish identity is even more clearly accentuated in Eryk's statement:

> You know... it's these kind of blood ties, some kind of tribal ties... So if you have some [Jewish] ancestor, then you're Jewish whether you want it or not. (Eryk)

Robert claims that blood is "naturally" the most important component when talking about Jewishness:

> It is my choice that I talk about it [about being Jewish], that I don't hide it … ,
> but the fact that I'm Jewish is not something I had anything to do with … I'm
> Jewish because that's how I was born. (Robert)

Robert argues that he "had nothing to do" with his being Jewish. In other words: he did not choose it. He also says he had a "feeling" that he was Jewish before he actually knew that he had Jewish ancestors.

Jadwiga also suggests that her life was influenced by her Jewish roots even before she had any awareness of her father's ancestry:

> Even when I didn't have that [Jewish] identity, I mean when I didn't know
> that I was Jewish, we lived as if the way we lived was influenced by the fact
> that we were Jewish. It isn't something you choose, for me Jewishness is not
> something you choose. (Jadwiga)

Aside from the generally positive responses to the discovery of Jewish roots, what seems to transpire in the narratives is a common uncanny feeling of having "something inside," an indescribable intrinsic attribute, a mark of difference that they could not quite articulate. For many, it was only a matter of time before they would discover their Jewish roots because they had a "hunch" and always felt that "there was something there," just waiting to be discovered.

An interesting description of this involuntary aspect in the experience of being Jewish was offered by Max:

> My experience of Jewishness is the experience of being determined by tradition,
> and very much by my ancestry … My experience of being a Jew is the experience
> of not being able do otherwise … that it determines me, that it is important to
> me and that it has to be important to me, that it is not a simple choice. (Max)

Beyond Poland

As members of Generation Unexpected, many Polish Jews find themselves objects of fascination and curiosity. As a result, they are called upon by Jews and non-Jews to explain or justify their identities as Jews in a place where Jews are not expected to exist. This plays out differently depending on who is asking. In the following fragment, Bożena expresses her disappointment about other

Jews failing to acknowledge the existence of a contemporary Polish Jewish community. She also talks about how Polish Jews do not have the opportunity to try to explain to other Jews what sort of a challenge it is to be Jewish in Poland:

> *I want to show them* [foreign Jews] *that we exist and that we are human beings and that we have a lot to say about our struggle with discontinuity of Polish Jewish community and about our disconnectedness from the entire Jewish world.* (Bożena)

According to Joanna and many others, foreign Jews cannot seem to grasp how one can suddenly find out that they are Jewish and, worse yet, pursue being Jewish in a country like Poland:

> *According to Jews in the United States and in Israel, there are no Jews in Poland, and this is a huge problem, because . . . those groups come here, and they look at you like you're a monkey in a ZOO and "what do you mean you found out that you're Jewish when you were fifteen?!" But we should talk about this, so that they have an awareness of this . . . It pisses me off when Israelis say: "How can you live in this huge cemetery?" . . . and so on, but I think it's important for Jews to live in Poland.* (Joanna)
>
> [*They ask me*] *"How can you live in a country where three million Jews were killed?" And then I say: This is my country, this is where I was born, this is where my family is, so what do you want me to do? Go to Israel? "Yes!" So I say "This is my country and my mission. . . . Jews living in the Diaspora is also a solution." I educate in this way, this whole propaganda drives me nuts, I feel like there is something I should do about this, that these people need to be educated.* (Odelia)

All participants stressed the significance of the specifically Polish context—the cultural and historical landscape where their Jewish identities came about. Analyzing some of their interactions with foreign Jews, it appears that Generation Unexpected is being accused of being "strange." This approach places younger Polish Jews in a position to have to justify the particularity of their Jewishness in the Polish context:

> *It's this specificity of Polish Jewry . . . it is an immanent feature: 90% of the people we have here* [in the community of young Polish Jews] *are baptized Catholics who had their First Communion.* (Magda)

In an attempt to explain some of the complexities of being a Jew in contemporary Poland, Szymon describes his generation in terms of people with "messed up biographies" who are nevertheless, a natural "historical consequence." He goes on to say that only the idiosyncrasies of Polish Jewish history could yield a generation of people who did not realize that they were Jewish, and who now have children who suddenly "want to" be Jewish:

> *Being raised to be a Jew is to be told at home that we are Jewish, or to be sent to a Jewish summer camp, or to be sent to a Jewish school. As you know, there were no such options in Poland...* (Bożena)

Similarly, Max, Magda, and Franka all point to certain characteristics of Polish Jews, which they attribute to the contingencies of Polish history:

> *Polish Jews (...) are a very specific group [. . .] There won't be people among them raised in Jewish religious culture, because there were no such people in Poland for fifty years...* (Max)
>
> *I got used to this type of Jews we have in Poland. The stories of young Polish Jews are absolutely unique, and they couldn't happen anywhere else. And that's what's interesting.* (Magda)
>
> *Such stories only happen in Poland, one better than the other.* (Franka)

What seems to be a consequence of Polish Jews' uniqueness is the fact that the resultant claims on Jewishness are difficult if not impossible to understand in other contexts. Being Jewish in post-communist Poland does not fit existing models—this is what accounts for its obscurity and incites questions of authenticity:

> *Our problems are often completely obscure for Jews from other countries. We have problems that occur only here really. Our problems and struggles, that you don't know if you should live at a cemetery, or is it a cemetery, or is it not... for them it's completely abstract.* (Eryk)
>
> *If I grew up in the States I wouldn't have this sort of sensitivity... For Jews from abroad it is kind of weird, that we want to be here, that we want to go on...* (Aleksandra)
>
> *All this* [history] *makes Jewish life here abnormal, not as simple as it is in the States and maybe that is why so many people decide to live it, because they weren't raised in Judaism, because nobody forced them to run to shul...* (Elza)

Regardless of who is asking, members of Generation Unexpected fiercely defend their claims on Jewishness and their articulations of Jewish identities that seem so unusual to many of their interrogators:

> It doesn't matter how someone found out, or how many percent... mom, dad, grandma, grandpa... But that someone who is aware that somebody in his family was [Jewish], first and foremost has the desire to somehow explore it. (Wiktor)
>
> Every situation in which someone tells me that I'm not a Jew is very hard, it devastates me, it destroys everything that I had managed to work out for myself, that identity, that sense of identity. (Łukasz)

Authenticity is conceived of as strongly contextualized and conditioned by the unusual circumstances of Polish history. As a result, attempts to define "the essence" of Jewish identity in Poland seem futile. Members of Generation Unexpected talk about the specific Polish context and point to the fact that, because of their idiosyncrasies as a group, they are largely misunderstood, especially by North American and Israeli Jews:

> To be a Jew, to be a Jew from here, yes, from Warsaw, from this city where you walk on corpses, where you walk on human skulls, yes. . . . This is no ordinary city, this is the New Jerusalem. . . . It's not an ordinary city; it's a very important city, and a very important country. . . .It is that feeling that this is your legacy, that you cannot forget, that it is important and that nobody will remember it for you. I have a part in the legacy of the Holocaust and my part in it is to try to understand. I ought to, I feel that I should, I feel this responsibility, this duty . . . to remember, to think about it, to understand, and to somehow transmit that memory. It is some kind of absurd reaffirmation of the covenant. (Max)

Max goes on to make a seemingly shallow statement which contains within it a rather reflective and profoundly existential claim:

> Young Jews in Poland drink beer and nobody else can do it for them. And in that sense they can feel important, very important. (Max)

What Max appears to be saying is that the mission the of members of the third generation of Jews have in Poland is essentially to exist. In this Shakespearian "to be or not to be," the mission of young Polish Jews is "to be." In that sense, he points out that the most important thing here is the very idea that there can be another generation of free (beer-drinking) and—dare we say—"real" Jews in Poland. And that whether they do anything beyond drinking beer together is secondary to the very fact that they simply are, that they exist against everyone's boldest expectations.

Beyond Choice

The stories of the participants in this study may create the impression that being Jewish in today's Poland is a matter of choice. After all, we are dealing with people who, on the most part, grew up in Christian or atheist environments, largely unaware of their Jewish ancestry. Furthermore, most of them could and in fact did "pass for" a non-Jewish Pole and could likely continue to do so even following the discovery of Jewish "roots." In fact, nobody expected of our participants to suddenly pursue a Jewish life and rarely did anyone encourage them to do so. This is why it appears to be the default assumption made by scholars, writers and journalists that the phenomenon we are dealing with in Poland is that of choosing to be Jewish (Pinto, 1996; Rosenson, 1996). And yet, primordial references were made by the participants in many different contexts and the notion of being Jewish as a matter of autonomous individual choice was not commonly endorsed by members of Generation Unexpected. Rather, they tend to describe their Jewishness as something imperative, given, determined, and compelling—something stemming from their "roots," from "blood" even, as was mentioned by many.

I want to suggest that primordial identity discourse is commonly endorsed by Poland's Generation Unexpected because it appears in response to their individual identities being questioned. Being as they are new and constantly challenged, such identities could be described as uncertain or insecure. These identity anxieties or perhaps anxieties over the authenticity of personal Jewish identities come both from outside—in the form of questions and accusations posed by others with their ideas about what is "real" or "authentic," as well as from within—in the form of self-questioning and insecurities about one's own sense of authenticity. And so who they are and who they think they should be and who others think they are and who others think they should be are all questions, which transpire in these personal identity narratives and provide a glimpse of how representatives on the third post-Holocaust generation of Jews in Poland manage their relationships with themselves, with one another, and with the world at large.

Most of the literature on primordialism and circumstantialism presents them as tools for researchers to explain ethnic identity and rules of membership in ethnic groups (Geertz, 1963; 1999, Isaacs, 1975; Gil-White, 1982; Thompson, 1989). My approach does not apply primordialism and circumstantialism as theories explaining Jewish affiliation, but rather I recognize them as discursive themes, which appear in individual narratives. In other words, I am not interested in defining the nature (or "essence") of Jewish identity, but rather I try to look at ways in which individuals make sense of their experience of Jewish identity. Here is where the dialectic of choice and ascription comes to play (Melchior, 1996).

We cannot reject the idea of primordialism as unattractive in the study of identity, because no matter how socially constructed people's identities may be, or we would like to believe that they are, many of those same people also employ primordial rhetoric. I want to emphasize that primordialism's power (just as circumstantialism's power) reveals itself primarily in discourse. We constantly witness people making decisions that very often come across as conscious or rational. Nevertheless, those same people often perceive and describe their decisions in terms other than voluntary—in terms of a subjective feeling of being compelled by blood, roots, or fate. The critical point here is that primordialism is in fact circumstantial. In the simplest words, there are circumstances in which people are likely to try to make sense of their identities in primordial terms.

Representatives of Generation Unexpected assign more significance to the primordial because they seek something strong, unquestionable and unshaken to guard their security as Jews. And they seek it precisely because their Jewishness is under constant scrutiny. The physicality or tangibility of blood offers a domain of reference, which seems fixed and inescapable, "given by nature," "real." One of the important factors in the pursuit of authenticity is the desire to be recognized as authentic by others (Taylor, 1992). Primordialism can thus be recognized as a "strategic choice." In other words, for a given group, interference from the outside that can be perceived to be an "existential threat" to the authenticity of the community, may cause a "primordialist backlash" (Tempelman, 1999, pp. 30–31).

All of our participants were born into Polishness. Polish is their mother tongue, and Poland is where they grew up. Furthermore, Christianity was often the first religion they came into contact with, whether actively or passively. They were educated in Polish schools; they were familiarized with Polish literature, music, cinema, and theater. It is evident then that we are dealing with people who are Polish. In public discourse, the ethnic model of Polishness prevails over the civic (Zubrzycki, 2001). This is partly due to the fact that Poland is considered one of the most ethnically homogenous countries in the world (Levinson, 1998). Although members of Generation Unexpected do not question their Polishness, none claims to have "Polish blood" or "Polish lineage." Moreover, in their narratives they do not position being Polish in conflict with being Jewish. Most refer to themselves as Polish Jews, and in that sense they see themselves as a specific (and endangered) species. To ask them whether they are more Polish or more Jewish would be as impractical as to ask Siberian tigers whether they are more Siberian or more tiger. However radical this transition may seem, the discovery narratives of our participants show that their "sudden Jewishness" becomes "naturally" contained in their "well-established Polishness." They describe their Polishness in a rather commonsensical way. They see it as a matter of fact. And, consequently, they do not feel the need to resort to primordialist references in order to justify being Polish. Members of Generation Unexpected regard their Polishness as a self-evident and secure aspect of their identity. This is true not only for the younger generation; most Jews in today's Poland take their Polishness "for granted" (Krajewski, 2005, p. 101). They "do not need to aspire to being Polish" because they were raised Polish (Krajewski, 2005, p. 17). Their Jewishness, on the other hand, remains prone to questions—those posed by others, as well as those from within. It is important to note, however, that self-questioning is also a product of dialogic interaction with other people, and it takes place within a framework of prevailing social-cultural representations and discourses (Billig, 1993; Harré & Gillett 1994).

The phenomena which take place in the contemporary Polish Jewish community implore the employment of the discourse of deassimilation, or disassimilation, as Diana Pinto calls it (Gudonis, 2001; Krajewski, 2005; Pinto, 1996). Taking place most prominently in Europe, and particularly in Eastern Europe, deassimilation is reflected in the processes of embracing partial Jewish ancestries and creating new, public frameworks of Jewish life (Gudonis, 2001 Pinto, 1996). It represents individual and communal investments in numerous forms of Jewish affiliation that are granted open publicity. Yael Tamir (1996) proposes the term "renewal of identity" understood as the reverse proces of assimilation. She talks about "renewal of Jewish identity," referring to Jews of Eastern Europe recapturing a space within the social structure. Tamir suggests that individuals who choose to embrace Jewish identity are in fact embracing an identity that "could have been" theirs (Tamir, 1996). They are not returning to an identity that they used to have, but to an identity their ancestors once had. In other words, they are not renewing their own identity, but rather they are claiming an identity rooted in their family history, a "potential" identity offered by their past. In this context, Tamir wonders why we seem to perceive it to be "less strange" for an individual to adopt an identity of his or her ancestors—if it is no longer expected of a shoemaker's son to be a shoemaker, why then do "we still think it is *natural* for the son or grandson of a Jew to be one too?" (Tamir, 1996, p. 34).

If we employ Barth's (1969) model of ethnicity or other social identities, which assumes that people may change or adopt new ethnic identities, then the phenomenon of constructing new Jewish identities in contemporary Poland could be explained in terms of situationalism or circumstantialism. Identity here is seen as situationally contingent and individuals are said to be able to change their ethnicity under certain circumstances. Our case may certainly appear to embody such a model. However, if we want to move beyond frantic attempts at defining the nature of ethnicity and toward an understanding of the experience of ethnicity as it reveals itself in personal narratives, we need to appreciate contradictory patterns in the ways individuals make sense of their stories.

As I already mentioned, my concern is not the "pursuit of authenticity" as an ethical imperative that philosophers struggle to define. Rather, I look at how individuals narrate their experience and discursively deal with the question of authenticity or lack thereof. While our participants emphasize the significance of being "compelled to be Jewish" by their roots, they also commonly refer to a "sense of mission" wherein their Jewishness appears to increase in importance because it "takes place" in Poland. In other words, while primordialist references account for one of the ways in which they make sense of their Jewish experience, "mission" provides an alternative interpretative trajectory. Representatives of Generation Unexpected make clear that for them, Jewishness is all the more significant because it "happens" in Poland. While primordial discourse is based on the assumption that being Jewish is "essentially" inherited "through blood," "mission discourse" seems to emerge from the idea that being Jewish is contextually and historically contingent. The notion of mission here can be seen as deriving from an appreciation of the uniquely Polish backdrop for their Jewishness. While they emphasize Jewish identity's social and historical situatedness, the Polish circumstances seem to solicit primordial discourse. In other words, the case of Generation Unexpected suggests that the notion of Jewish blood acquires new meanings in post-Holocaust, post-communist

Poland. The participants are challenged with regard to their authenticity and confronted with questions about whether they are "really Jewish" and about why they "insist on being Jewish" in Poland. These threats to identity prompt a "primordialist backlash" (Tempelman, p. 1999). In attempts to legitimize or authenticate their belonging in the Jewish community, individuals stress the unquestionable, stable, given, involuntary, and determinist aspects of their identities.

Susan Glenn notes how "throughout all the de-racializing stages of twentieth-century social thought, Jews have continued to invoke blood logic as a way of defining and maintaining group identity. . . It is one of the ironies of modern Jewish history that concepts of tribalism based on blood and race have persisted not only in spite of but also because of the experience of assimilation" (Glenn, 2002, p. 140). This irony appears to be no less salient in the experience of deassimilation. The point must be made, nevertheless, that this "blood logic" takes on different forms in different socio-historical circumstances. For instance, in *The Jew Within*, Cohen and Eisen point out that American Jews prefer to see themselves as individuals who consciously choose to be Jewish and do so in an appreciation of the self and family, rather than out of concerns about Jewish survival (Cohen & Eisen, 2000). On the other hand, members of Generation Unexpected prefer to see their Jewishness as an imperative and not as a choice precisely because it is perceived as a call for ensuring Jewish survival.

Inasmuch as Generation Unexpected appears to be a community of individuals who actively choose to identify as Jewish while often failing to meet the "objective" criteria of belonging to the Jewish collective, when speaking for themselves they nevertheless stress the more determinist and essentialist view of Jewishness. This invites another question: Why, despite the proposals of social constructionism and postmodernism, are identities often felt and described as if they were essentialist? (Bernstein, 2005; Benhabib, 1999; Calhoun, 1994; Epstein 1987). Yngvesson and Mahoney (2000) talk about the "subjectively experienced desire for rootedness," which occurs among adoptees who set on to find their birth parents. Shneider's (1968) classic study of American kinship explains, "The relationship which is "real" or "true" or "blood" or "by birth" can never be severed. . . . It is culturally defined as being an objective fact of nature, of fundamental significance and capable of having profound effects, and its nature cannot be terminated or changed." (Schneider, 1968, p. 24; see also Modell, 1994, and Yngvesson & Mahoney, 2000). Hence, the "relationship of blood" is what "secures" identity and belonging. Yngvesson and Mahoney (2000) quote from one of the adoptees: *A person who does not know her ancestry is denied access to who she really is.* Here, again we can see the assumption that an authentic self requires a primordial connection. In this sense, adoptees express difficulties reconciling between who they are (in the sense of who they were raised as by their adoptive parents) and who they "could have been" (had they been raised by their birth parents). For the most part, the participants in my study were raised by their birth parents. However, the late discovery of Jewish roots poses for them the question of who they "could have been" had their ancestors not suppressed their Jewishness in the past. We could say then that, by embracing Jewish identity later in young adulthood, they are in fact "becoming" who they "could have been." In Cheng's (2004) discussion of the complexities involved in adoption we read: "Does the past or the heritage you didn't know about change the solidity or reality of the life you did actually experience?" (Cheng, 2004, p. 68). The narratives of the young Polish Jewish adults provoke a similar question: Does the new awareness of "alternative roots" pose a moral imperative of some sort to "re-root" oneself?

It seems unsatisfactory to argue that the participants' Jewishness is merely a strategically deployed identity in the form of collective action aimed at achieving political interests (Bernstein, 2005). It is rather difficult to envision potential political interests in the pursuit of Jewishness among representatives of Generation Unexpected. As full-fledged Polish citizens, they could in fact choose whether or not to reveal their Jewish roots to other people. If falling for essentialisms is part of identity politics and a strategy to achieve better identity status (Kimmel, 1993), then in our case perhaps the better identity status, to which young Polish Jewish adults may aspire, is that of the fully legitimate status as Jews within the global Jewish community. And yet, essentialism employed as a strategy proves rather ineffective. Allow me to mention one more example from an interview, which illustrates essentialism's ineffectiveness, or perhaps even counter-effectiveness:

> *Authentic Jewishness is when you're at your window, peeping through the curtain, looking curiously at goyish apartments, wondering what it's really like to be a goy . . .*
>
> *I'm not on the opposite side either. I don't wonder what the Jews are doing over there. I am neither here, nor there . . . there are two situations like this in Jewish folklore, when characters like that appear. The first one is the Dybbuk, a soul, who could enter neither here nor there. Not holy enough to go to heaven,*

and not sinful enough to be damned. One might say then, that I might feel like
such a cultural Dybbuk. And the other character is in "Fiddler on the Roof,"
there is this beautiful scene. . . . I know a bird can fall in love with a fish, but
where are they going to live? And now, I am such a birdfish, and where should
a birdfish live? (Sara)

Sara's "self-defeating" discourse becomes apparent when she acknowledges that her own definition of "authentic Jewishness" leaves no room for her. In other words, Sara falls outside her own essentialist categories; she excludes herself from her own definition. It seems that her hybrid "birdfish" identity—in her own essentialist approach—can never actually be authentic. In this sense, Sara appears to be endorsing the idea that individuals embody the norms and values of the culture they were "born into." Therefore, the authentic way is for those individuals to comply with the roles ascribed to them by their culture and not to deviate from them by rejecting what was 'primordially intended' for them. Such essentialist authenticity assumes that "a person's real or authentic identity derives from some sort of cultural, ethnic, or biological core element" (Charmé, 1998, p. 3). Of course, the problem with our Generation Unexpected is that while they may carry the "biological core element," they nevertheless were not exactly born into Jewish culture. And it is precisely that paradox, which seems to be of Sara's concern. Regardless of the imminent contradictions, the essentialist model of authenticity is one which sanctions notions such as "authentic" or "real" Jew, "authentic" or "real" Judaism, and it assumes the existence of some kind of "essential," "real" Jewishness.

In view of the existentialist model, on the other hand, culture does not fully determine how we should live, and an authentic life is that, which is freely chosen by the individual herself (Stevenson, 1974, see also Tamir, 1996). Existential authenticity, as described by Charmé, "lies in an awareness and acceptance of our identities' unstable process of becoming" (Charmé, 1998, p. 3). This model was proposed by Sartre (1948) who, as noted by Charmé, appears to have anticipated contemporary non-essentialist approaches to identity in general. Self-determining freedom presents itself as one of the central notions here (Taylor, 1989). However, whereas in essentialist authenticity self-determining freedom is out of the question, in the existentialist model it is burdened with certain limitations. First, Yael Tamir's assertion that individuals may be free *within* a context, but not *of* context suggests that individuals are always situated in particular socio-cultural circumstances that necessarily shape, albeit to a degree, the choices they will make (Tamir, 1996). To put it in Heideggerian terms, *being-towards-death* cannot be separated from *being-in-the world*, from being already situated in a socio-historical context or in a primordial past, which condition one's existential potentiality (Heidegger, 2008. See also Aho, 2003). The second source of limitation for self-determining freedom is the fact that identity is necessarily formed in dialogue, and for it to be authentic we must ensure recognition by others (Taylor, 1991). Charles Taylor argues that authenticity requires self-definition in dialogue (Taylor, 1989). Ferrara (2004) makes a similar point, when he says—following Hegel (1976) and G. H. Mead (1934)—that identity grows out of interaction and mutual recognition. He goes on to say that, while it can be expected that the authenticity of one's identity may not be recognized by some people, it "makes no sense" to imagine that one's identity may never be recognized by anybody else (Ferrara 2004, p. 20).

Around 267,000 Jews are believed to live in England and Wales according to the 2001 census. That same census returned as many as 390 thousand Jedi Knights of the fictional *Star Wars* film universe. But does my authenticity as a Jedi require that others perceive me as an authentic Jedi? In other words, if I choose to be a Jedi Knight, and consider myself to be a Jedi Knight, and have some 390 thousand fellow Jedi Knights in England and Wales alone to share my Jedi experience with, why then—if at all—should I be bothered if everyone else thinks I am insane, and not a Jedi at all?

The expansion of the social context of cultural phenomena causes a transformation of the factors involved in identity construction. The individual in society became endowed with wider access to different choices leading to the formation of various identifications, which go beyond the historical foundations of the construction of particular identities (Castells, 1997). It has been noted that in democratic pluralist societies individuals are free to choose their cultural belonging (Melchior, 1993). At the same time, such freedom is necessarily conditioned by the dialogic nature of identity construction, the significance of social and political circumstances, as well as the distribution of powerful discourses (Bakhtin, 1981; Bernstein, 2005; Taylor, 1989). Moreover, certain assumptions with regard to what kind of identities "make some kind of sense" appear to prevail in the social world (Appiah, 2005, p. 18). As observed by Tamir (1996), "we think that it is more "natural" or less strange for individuals to adopt an identity embraced by their parents or grandparents" (Tamir, 1996, p. 34). This suggests that it "makes sense" to embrace a heritage we can claim birthright to. How do Jedi Knights reconcile this?

For decades following the end of World War II the prevailing assumption was that there would be no more Jewish life in Poland. In this sense, members of Generation Unexpected inhabit lives which came close to never happening:

> We may be free people, but maybe we're potentially a little less free than others. (Max)

I would like to suggest that our attempts at determining exactly how much freedom individuals really have in their relationship to culture, sociability or even birthright may make for a great debate, but are rather unavailing. What we are able to access and assess is how people exercise their freedom to choose how they talk about their freedom or lack thereof and how they talk about the relationships they have with their cultural, social and personal realities.

Following Max's reflection, discovering and embracing Jewish roots may be less of a free choice when taking place in Poland. But perhaps Jews in Poland today are also captive to the notorious racializing primordialist discourse, which reverberates throughout the Jewish world and sanctions our Jewish identities with the blood of our mothers. On the one hand then, young Polish Jews embark on an identity quest, which presents itself as *par excellence* constructivist and existentialist—they learn, they struggle to construct new models, and they and ask relentless questions about what it means to be Jewish in general and about what it means to be Jewish in the prolific and anguished landscape of today's Poland. On the other hand, they find themselves measured against existing foreign models of being Jewish and while they resist them, they still find themselves having to respond to dominant narratives and assumptions about what it means to be Jewish among "real" Jews, as part of a global diaspora.

"We are never more (and sometimes less) than the coauthors of our own narratives" (MacIntyre, 2007, p. 213). In this sense, partial authorship of Jewish identity narratives in Poland should be attributed to those outside voices, whether supportive or critical, who play a significant role in the ongoing process of dialogic interaction. In the early 1990s, Marek Edelman—one of the leaders of the Warsaw Ghetto uprising—expressed his skepticism with regard to younger Jews "emerging" in post-transition Poland in a conversation with Konstanty Gebert—one of the intellectual leaders of the Second Generation: "You guys are a fraud, a literary fiction. The Jewish people is dead, and you have simply thought yourselves up" (Gebert, 1994, p. 165). Edelman's comment serves as an excellent example of accusations of inauthenticity, which younger generations of Jews in Poland were likely to hear from Holocaust survivors.

But it also offers a keen rendering of Jewish identity construction in the post-Holocaust world.

We cannot aspire to remove the language of identity from social sciences. Nor can we actually remove it from "real" life. We are forever stuck with the notion of Jewish identity, and we can no longer aspire to remove the vocabulary of authenticity in our studies of Jewish culture. But we can aspire to recognize the discursive hegemonies these words are capable of creating. In our liberal democratic open pluralistic postmodern bubble, our discourse is full of inconsistencies and ironies.

Regina Bendix point out that "the notion of authenticity implies the existence of its opposite, the fake, and this dichotomous construct is at the heart of what makes authenticity problematic" (Bendix, 1997). Jewish leaders, policy makers and—sadly—educators around the world are fond of the qualifying notion of a "strong Jewish identity," as if identity was a measurable power of some kind. But if we agree that identity is a process of becoming rather than of being, that it cannot be measured, that it is never fixed, that it is dialogic in nature, and that it ought not be rendered good or bad, then the notion of a "strong identity" is reduced to an idle slogan. The postmodern or—if we must—the post-postmodern anxiety over the (in)authentic can effectively sabotage the modernist, romantic longing for the authentic. Much like today's hegemony of the notion of a strong Jewish identity can sabotage individual experiences of being Jewish.

"Whether one takes a modernist position that authenticity was born and lost simultaneously in the swirl of modernity, or the postmodernist position that authenticity was always a myth, the use of signifiers of authenticity has proliferated. And while defining the authentic may be an impossible task in the postmodern swirl of simulations and signs and styles, as a culture we seem to still agree that it is better to be authentic than inauthentic" (Goldman & Papson, 1996, pp. 185–186).

Could it be that in our frantic attempts at capturing and defining the ineffable, the ultimate goal, the absolute, we have in fact turned authenticity into a god? Better yet: doesn't our discourse around Jewish identity and around its authenticity suggest that we have created a religion of Jewish identity with a god in the form of authenticity? (For an interesting take on Jewish identity as ideology, see Rokhl Kafrissen, 2014).

Fanatic worship of authenticity and zealous observance of the religion of Jewish identity create an uneasy fantasy about what makes a Jew a good Jew or—worse yet—a "real" Jew. Still, it is not identity as a concept that we should dread or mock, but rather the definitional confusion around it (see Krasner, 2016). Our failure to define or to avoid the most obvious semantic inconsistencies when talking about identity is precisely what leads to discursive constructs as dreadful as "strong Jewish identity," "authentic Judaism" or "good Jew" versus "bad Jew." Just as the notion of identity is not the culprit, neither is authenticity. It is how we use them in the stories we tell and the conversations we have.

The Jewish identity experience in Poland hosts questions and contradictions. Jews in post-communist Poland resist existing models of being Jewish. They construct their own—insecure, fragile or confused as they may be. They try things on; they embrace, abandon, question, and ask. During our interview, Sara recalled her first steps toward "figuring out" her Jewishness. "I am not sure I had the identity"—she said—"But I definitely had Jewish questions." If I may suggest a very non-essential "essence" of post-transition Polish Jewish identity, let me identify it as being-in-discussion—in an ever-changing configuration of the individual inner discussions, the relentless discussions with one another, and the passionate and challenging discussions with the outside world. This Polish-Jewish being-in-discussion or—better yet—becoming-in-discussion is unique to the times and the land but it resonates far beyond them. And as Jews in Poland struggle to be recognized as legitimate, authentic or real, they will be subjected to close scrutiny—from outside, as well as from within. But although they may not be as numerous as Jedi Knights, they are no better, no worse, and no more "real" than history made possible for them to be.

Obscured in Jewish memory by decades of oppression, Poland has over the past few decades become an increasingly popular travel destination for thousands of North American and Israeli Jews. At the same time, Polish Jewish heritage and contemporary Polish Jewish experience have become a backdrop for countless research ideas, art projects, collaborations and educational opportunities. Being Jewish in Poland will likely forever exude an air of disquiet, whether social, political or emotional. Anxiety may just have to be that fundamental existential quality which continues to fuel those unexpected Jewish identities and ensure that they never run out of questions.

Bibliography

Aho, Kevin. (2003). Why Heidegger Is Not An Existentialist: Interpreting Authenticity and Historicity in *Being and Time*. *Florida Philosophical Review* 3(2), 5–22.

Appiah, Kwame Anthony. (2005). *The Ethics of Identity* (1st ed.). Princeton, NJ: Princeton University Press.

Bakhtin, M. M. (1981). *The Dialogic Imagination: Four Essays*. Michael Holquist (Ed.) & Carly Emerson (Trans.). Austin, TX: University of Texas Press.

Bakhtin, M. M. (1986). *Speech Genres and Other Late Essays*. Caryl Emerson, Michael Holquist (Eds.) & Vern W. McGee (Trans.). Austin, TX: University of Texas Press.

Barth, Fredrik. (Ed.). (1969). *Ethnic Groups and Boundaries: The Social Organization*. New York, NY: Little, Brown & Company.

Bekerman, Zvi. (2001), Constructivist Perspectives on Language, Identity, and Culture: Implications for Jewish Identity and the Education of Jews. *Religious Education* 96(4), 462–73. doi:10.1080/003440801753442375

Bendix, Regina. (1997). *In Search of Authenticity: The Formation of Folklore Studies* (1st ed.). Madison, WI: University of Wisconsin Press.

Benhabib, Seyla. (1999). Civil Society and the Politics of Identity and Difference in a Global Context. In Neil J. Smelser & Jeffrey C. Alexander (Eds.), *Diversity and Its Discontents: Cultural Conflict and Common Ground in Contemporary American Society*. Princeton, NJ: Princeton University Press.

Bernstein, Mary. (2005). Identity Politics. *Annual Review of Sociology* 31(1), 47–74. doi:10.1146/annurev.soc.29.010202.100054

Boas, Franz. (1940). *Race, Language and Culture*. New York, NY: Free Press.

Breakwell, Glynis Marie, & Canter, David V. 1993. *Empirical Approaches to Social Representations*. Oxford, UK: Clarendon Press.

Calhoun, Craig. (Ed.). (1994). *Social Theory and the Politics of Identity* (1st ed.). Oxford, UK: Wiley-Blackwell.

Castells, Manuel. (1997). *The Power of Identity*. Malden, MA: Blackwell.

Charmé, Stuart L. (2000). Varieties of Authenticity in Contemporary Jewish Identity. *Jewish Social Studies* 6(2), 133–55. doi:10.1353/jss.2000.0001

Charmé, Stuart Z. (1998). Alterity, Authenticity, and Jewish Identity. *Shofar: An Interdisciplinary Journal of Jewish Studies* 16(3), 42–62.

Cheng, Vincent J. (2004). *Inauthentic: The Anxiety over Culture and Identity*. New Brunswick, NJ: Rutgers University Press.

Cohen, Steven M., & Eisen, Arnold M. (2000). *The Jew Within: Self, Family, and Community in America*. Bloomington, IN: Indiana University Press.

Epstein, Steven. (1987). Gay Politics, Ethnic Identity: The Limits of Social Constructionism. *Socialist Review* 93/94(9), 9–56.

Ferrara, Alessandro. (2004). The Relation of Authenticity to Normativity A Response to Larmore and Honneth. *Philosophy & Social Criticism* 30(1), 17–24. doi:10.1177/0191453704039396

Gebert, Konstanty. (1994). Jewish Identities in Poland: New, Old, and Imaginary. In Jonathan Webber (Ed.), *Jewish Identities in the New Europe* (pp. 161–67). Washington, DC: Littman Library of Jewish Civilization.

Geertz, Clifford. (1963). *Old Societies and New States* (1st ed.). New York, NY: Free Press.

Giddens, Anthony (1984). *The Constitution of Society: Outline of the Theory of Structuration*. Cambridge, London: Polity Press.

Gil-White, Francisco J. (1999). How Thick Is Blood? The Plot Thickens . . .: If Ethnic Actors Are Primordialists, What Remains of the Circumstantialist/Primordialist Controversy? *Ethnic and Racial Studies* 22(5), 789–820. doi:10.1080/014198799329260

Goldman, Robert, & Papson, Stephen. 1996. *Sign Wars The Cluttered Landscape of Advertising*. New York, NY: The Guilford Press.

Gruber, Ruth Ellen. (2002). *Virtually Jewish. Reinventing Jewish Culture in Europe*. Berkeley, CA: University of California Press.

Hall, Stuart, & du Gay, Paul. (1996). (Eds.). *Questions of Cultural Identity*. London, UK: Sage Publications.

Harré, Rom, & Gillett, Grant. (1994). *The Discursive Mind* (1st ed.). London, UK: Sage Publications.

Hegel, G. W. F. (1977). *Phenomenology of Spirit* (A. V. Miller, Trans.). Oxford, UK: Oxford University Press.

Heidegger, Martin. (2008). *Being and Time*. New York, NY: Harper Perennial Modern Classics.

Horowitz, Bethamie. (2003). *Connections and Journeys: Assessing Critical Opportunities for Enhancing Jewish Identity*. New York, NY: UJA-Federation.

Isaacs, Harold R. (1975). Basic Group Identity: The Idols of the Tribe. In Nathan Glazer & Daniel Patrick Moynihan (Eds.), *Ethnicity: Theory and Experience* (pp. 29–52). Cambridge, MA: Harvard University Press,

Irwin-Zarecka, Iwona. (1990). *Neutralizing Memory: The Jew in Contemporary Poland*. Piscataway, NJ: Transaction Publishers.

Kaffrisen, Rokhl. (2014, April 3). A Few Thoughts on the Roots of the Identity Discourse. Retrieved from www.rokhl.blogspot.com/2014/04/a-few-thoughts-on-roots-of-identity.html

Kimmel, Michael S. (1993). Sexual Balkanization: Gender and Secuality as the New Ethnicities. *Social Research* 60, 571–88.

Kosmin, Barry Alexander, & Kovács, András. (2003). Jewishness in Postmodernity: The Case of Sweden. In Zvi Gitelman, Barry Kosman, & András Kovács (Eds.), *New Jewish Identities: Contemporary Europe and Beyond*. Budapest, Hungary: Central European University Press.

Krajewski, Stanislaw. (2005). *Poland and the Jews: Reflections of a Polish Jew* (1st ed.). Kraków, Poland: Austeria.

Krasner, Jonathan. (2016). On the Origins and Persistence of the Jewish Identity Industry in Jewish Education. *Journal of Jewish Education* 82.

Lehrer, Erica T. (2013). *Jewish Poland Revisited: Heritage Tourism in Unquiet Places*. (New Anthropologies of Europe.) Bloomington, IN: Indiana University Press.

Levinson, David. (1998). *Ethnic Groups Worldwide: A Ready Reference Handbook*. Phoenix, Ariz: Greenwood.

Levi-Strauss, Claude. (1974). *Structural Anthropology*. New York, NY: Basic Books.

Lifton, Robert J. (1993). *The Protean Self: Human Resilience In An Age Of Fragmentation*. New York, NY: Basic Books.

MacIntyre, Alasdair. (2007). *After Virtue: A Study in Moral Theory, Third Edition*. Notre Dame, IN: University of Notre Dame Press.

McKay, James. (1982). An Exploratory Synthesis of Primordial and Mobilizationist Approaches to Ethnic Phenomena. *Ethnic and Racial Studies* 5(4), 395–420. doi:10.1080/01419870.19 82.9993387

Mead, Margaret. (1964). *Continuities in Cultural Evolution*. New Haven, CT: Yale University Press.

Mead, George H. (1934). *Mind, Self & Society from the Standpoint of a Social Behaviorist* (1st ed.). Chicago, IL: University of Chicago Press.

Melchior, Malgorzata. (1996). Jewish Identity in Poland: Between Ascription and Choice. In Yitzhak Kashti, D. Schers, & D. Zisenwine (Eds.), *A Quest for Identity. Post War Jewish Biographies*. Tel Aviv, Israel: Tel Aviv University.

Modell, Judith S. (1994). *Kinship with Strangers: Adoption and Interpretations of Kinship in American Culture* (1st ed). Berkeley, CA: University of California Press.

Pinto, Diana. (1996). *A New Jewish Identity for Post-1989 Europe. JPR Policy Paper 1*. Retrieved from http://www.bjpa.org/Publications/details.cfm?PublicationID=4333

Polonsky, Antony, Bartal, Israel, Hundert, Gershon, Opalalski, Magdelena, & Tomaszewski, Jerzy. (Eds.). (1996). *Poles, Jews, Socialists: The Failure of an Ideal*. Liverpool: Liverpool University Press.

Reszke, Katka. (2013). *Return of the Jew: Identity Narratives of the Third Post-Holocaust Generation of Jews in Poland*. Boston, MA.: Academic Studies Press.

Rosenson, Claire. (1996). Jewish Identity Construction in Contemporary Poland: Dialogue Between Generations. *East European Jewish Affairs* 26(2), 67–78.

Sagi, Avi. (2002). *A Critique of Jewish Identity Discourse*. Ramat Gan, Israel: Bar Ilan University.

Sartre, Jean Paul. (1948). *Anti-Semite and Jew*. New York, NY: Schoken Books.

Schneider, David M. (1968). *American Kinship: A Cultural Account* (1st ed.). Upper Saddle River, NJ: Prentice Hall.

Stevenson, Leslie. (1974). *Seven Theories of Human Nature*. Oxford, UK: Oxford University Press.

Stratton, Jon. (2000). *Coming Out Jewish* (1st ed.). London, UK: Routledge.

Tamir, Yael. (1996). Some Thoughts Regarding the Phrase: "A quest for identity." In Y. Kashti, F. Eros, D. Schers, & D. Zisenwine (Eds.), *A Quest for Identity. Post War Jewish Biographies*. Tel Aviv, Israel: Tel Aviv University.

Taylor, Charles. (1989). *Sources of the Self: The Making of the Modern Identity*. Cambridge, MA.: Harvard University Press.

Taylor, Charles. (1992). *The Ethics of Authenticity*. Cambridge, MA.: Harvard University Press.

Tempelman, Sasja. (1999). Constructions of Cultural Identity: Multiculturalism and Exclusion. *Political Studies* 47 (1), 17–31. doi:10.1111/1467-9248.00185

Thompson, Richard H. (1989). *Theories of Ethnicity: A Critical Appraisal*. New York, NY: Praeger.

Trotzig, Astrid. (2001). *Blod Är Tjockare Än Vatten*. Sweden: Pocket.

Yngvesson, B., & Mahoney, M. A. 2000. "As One Should, Ought and Wants to Be": Belonging and Authenticity in Identity Narratives. *Theory, Culture, and Society 17*(6), 77–110.

Zubrzycki, Genevieve. (2001). "We, the Polish Nation": Ethnic and Civic Visions of Nationhood in Post-Communist Constitutional Debates. *Theory and Society 30*, 629–68.

Lerner, Zwalman, & Deceber, Jessica. (2010). Rabbi Michael Schudrich on the Opportunity for Renewed Jewish Life in Poland. Retrieved from http://www.jewishtimesasia.org/one-to-one-topmenu-45/rabbi-michael-issue-december

Re-Thinking American Jewish Zionist Identity: A Case for Post-Zionism in the Diaspora (Based on the Writings of R. Menachem Froman)

Shaul Magid

I

In the past decade there has been increased attention on the vexing question of Jewish "identity" among American Jews. The 2013 Pew Research Center Survey of US Jews, as well as other studies and indicators, suggest that American Jewry is in a significant state of transition. The ostensible twin towers of Jewish identity in the past half century, the Holocaust and Israel, are no longer anchors of a stable Jewish identity. The Holocaust is inevitably moving from a lived reality of witnesses to an event in Jewish history. For anyone under the age of forty-five, Israel is a much more complicated place and for many young American Jews the nostalgia and romanticism that is depicted, for example, in Otto Preminger's 1962 film version of Leon Uris' novel *Exodus*, no longer resonates.[1] This is all to say that the question of Jewish "identity" in America is indeed an important topic for scholar consideration.

But the very notion of "identity" requires some clarification. How does identity function in a minority community that is largely accepted in the majority society in which it lives? Does identity function as a way of drawing boundaries between "insiders" (American Jews) and "outsiders" (the American public)? Does it serve to draw boundaries between who is "inside" and who

---

1 There is understandably a great deal of anxiety about this transition of the Holocaust from memory to history. For one recent example see Rosenfeld (2013).

is "outside" the American Jewish community? American Jews today live in an ostensibly pluralistic community, largely of their own creation, a community that acknowledges and accommodates difference on many levels of Jewish existence. But those differences also must have boundaries. What are those boundaries and who gets to decide? Here the question as to the relationship between Jewish identity and Jewish discourse is pertinent; that is, between markers of inside and outside versus boundaries of what is considered part of legitimate Jewish conversation.

Below I examine and critique what I consider to be a phenomenon in contemporary American Jewish identity discourse that I call the "dogmatization of Zionism." This is not a critique of Zionism per se but rather its contemporary reception. Zionism has been a part of American Jewish discourse for many decades. American Jews debated it, embraced it, resisted it, and in many cases rejected it. Until the 1930s Zionism was not supported by the majority of American Jews. And until the Biltmore Platform in May 1942 even most American Zionists were not statists (Gal, 1992). Zionism was always one among various alternatives of Jewish identity in America. I suggest that today the Jewish *discourse* about Zionism has become Jewish *identity* itself; Zionism defines Jewish legitimacy and is no longer part of a larger conversation. Rather, it has become the very boundaries of the conversation. I am less concerned below about how and why this happened and am more interested in questioning whether Zionist hegemony is healthy for American Jewry. My constructive suggestion is that creating a Jewish space—or perhaps better put, reviving a Jewish discourse— that is outside Zionism's hegemony is an important part of reconsidering the boundaries and possibilities of Jewish identity as we move further into the twentieth-first century in a robust American Jewish community that is less willing to play the auxiliary role than it has in the past, both toward European Jewry that is no more, and toward Israel that continues to demand its reflexive allegiance. That is, I think we should try to make Zionism part of a more multivalent and robust Jewish discourse and not the very contours of Jewish identity.

In her opening remarks at a session at the 2015 JStreet Conference, Rabbi Sharon Kleinbaum noted that a Jew today can walk into almost any non-Orthodox synagogue in America and profess his or her atheism or lack of Jewish practice and be embraced and accepted. But if a Jew enters that same synagogue and professes to be an anti- and even non-Zionist, he or she will likely be shown the door. While perhaps somewhat exaggerated for affect, Kleinbaum's point is well-taken. Lest I be misunderstood, I fully acknowledge Zionism as a viable and important form of Jewishness in the diaspora.

This is not meant to undermine diaspora Zionism. Rather, I hope to challenge its hegemony, to resist, even negate, its ostensibly totalizing nature and argue for the creation of a diasporic post-Zionism

To begin: How did this happen? How did Zionism in America go from being part of Jewish discourse to policing Jewish identity? In the early 1970s, referring to American Jews, Norman Podhoretz proclaimed in the pages of *Commentary Magazine*, "We are all Zionists now." He was likely correct. In the aftermath of the Six-Day War, the remnants of anti- or even non-Zionism among American Jews (excluding the ultra-Orthodox) collapsed with the thunder of military triumphalism and political reality.[2] What was later to become "the occupation" was in the early 70s considered by most American Jews, and Jews worldwide, as "the liberation" of lands that were tied to Israel's biblical past and offered a security buffer against its neighbors.[3] The fear that this young country, the refuge for so many Holocaust survivors, was so quickly threatened with annihilation, and the exuberance and relief of Israel's ability to defend itself against that threat resulted in a collective sigh of relief and celebration of Jewish survival. But something else happened in 1967 that few took the time to examine. Through no fault of its own Israel became a different country, the occupier of another people whose claim of self-determination increasingly challenged their own. It took some years for the smoke of war to clear to reveal a new set of circumstances that would change the contours of American Jewish identity in response to this change of circumstances in Israel.[4] When a small cadre of Jewish progressives in America in the aftermath of the Yom Kippur War initiated an organization in 1973 called Breira to challenge the language of "liberation" and to call for the end to the occupation, they were summarily dismissed and forcefully shut down by the American Jewish establishment (Staub, 2004, pp. 80–308). By 1977 Breira was gone. American Jews could not see the dark side of liberation. The time was not right.

---

2 For a history of American anti-Zionism, specifically "The American Council for Judaism." see Kolsky (1990).

3 The turn to Zionism occurs quite a bit earlier in America. By the mid-1930s Zionism began to gain ground in the US and by the early 1940s it begins to dominate American Jewish discourse.

4 In Israel, the reality became apparent much earlier. See, for example, Sprinzak (1991); Goremberg (2007, 7–41); Zertal & Eldar (2004). An interesting addition to this literature is the 2015 film *Censored Voices* directed and produced by Mor Loushy. Loushy obtained the uncensored tapes of interviews made with Israeli soldiers immediately after the June 1967 war by Amos Oz and Avraham Shapira. The censored tapes appeared after the war as a book *Siah Lohamim* (Conversations with Soliders).

The next forty years saw the growth of a strong and vocal foundation of support for Israel in America headed by the Zionist Organization of America, the American Jewish Committee, and later AIPAC. The latter was contentiously referred to "The Israel Lobby" in the controversial book by that title by political scientists John Mearsheimer and Steven Wald (2002).[5] Mearsheimer and Wald argue that Zionism, largely in the form of the Zionism of the pro-Israel lobbying group AIPAC, had become one of the most powerful ideological forces in American foreign policy even in cases where it is ostensibly at odds with American self-interest. While one can certainly contest their conclusions regarding American foreign policy and Israel, I think it is safe to say that by 2002 Zionism did indeed become a dominant, almost exclusive, form of American Jewish identity.[6] The political and geopolitical implications notwithstanding, by the turn of the twenty-first century American Jewish identity became fused with Zionism. Below I consider the implications of that hegemony. While Zionism is defined in many different ways, today mostly as supporting Israel as the nation state of the Jewish people, the term itself has become a marker that defines the boundaries of legitimacy in the American Jewish conversation.

For obvious reasons, Israeli society has a much more vexed relationship with Zionism. Israelis generally know much more about the complex nature of Zionism, an ideology that was at war with itself for most of its existence as is demonstrated by the proceedings of the Zionist Congresses in Basil, Switzerland (Berkowitz, 1996, pp. 8–76). For many Israelis, Zionism is the Jewish ideology that founds their political existence. For American Jews it is more often an identity defined by the support of a country they choose not to live in. There are those in Israel who are much more strident in their Zionism than most American Jews and there are those who are much more ambivalent. And then there are those, who often identify as "post-Zionists," who are involved in constructing an Israeli identity outside the conventional Zionist narrative. Gershom Scholem, the great scholar of Kabbalah and a lifelong Zionist (although his Zionism was quite complicated, or as he would say "dialectical") was adamant that Zionism needs to be self-critical in order

---

5   On "the Israel lobby," c.f. Foxman (2007).
6   Scholars have depicted the development of American Zionism in many ways; see Raider (1998), Cohen (2003), Gal (1998), and more recently, Sasson (2013). Ezra Mendelsohn (1992) notes that at the turn of the twentieth-century Zionism was a minority faction in a plethora of Jewish ideologies competing for the Jewish populace including Orthodoxy, Socialism, Territorialism, Diaspora nationalism, Bundism, Yiddishism, etc.

not to become hegemonic (Magid, 2015). In Scholem's view, Zionists need to understand that Zionism contained contradictions at its very core and thus it needs constant reflection and reexamination. This sentiment was also shared by a lesser-known contemporary of Scholem in America, Simon Rawidowicz, a professor at Brandeis University and lifelong Zionist, who wrote a scathing critique of Zionist policies in the early 1950s entitled "Between Jew and Arab" that was included in his Hebrew magnum opus *Bavel ve-Yerushalayim* in 1957. Rawidowicz writes, "Is there any nation on the face of this earth that has the authority to admonish Israel? But 'Israel' should admonish itself. The source of wisdom is morality; the first principle is that rule which governs the relationship between man and his neighbor" (Myers, 2008, p. 146). To some degree, Israeli post-Zionism, and also some forms of Israeli Zionism, provide some of that self-criticism. Post-Zionism, therefore, is born from Zionism itself.

This self-critical awareness has arguably not happened among most contemporary American Zionists today (except in the relatively small American Zionist left), although that was certainly not the case in earlier iterations of American Zionism (Kolsky, 1992, pp. 1–35; Gal, 1992, pp. 15–47, pp. 99–136). One could counter my claim of Zionist hegemony by stating that Jewish groups such as Jewish Voice for Peace who support BDS (Boycott, Divestment, and Sanctions against Israel) are non- or anti-Zionist and yet are free to express their views. While this is true, these groups are largely considered outside the Jewish mainstream and are not invited into the American Jewish conversation; for example, there is considerable support among American Jewish Zionists toward the bill now being considered in the Knesset that would make supporting BDS a criminal act. Beyond the Jewish community, New York Governor Andrew Cuomo issued an executive order in June 2016 boycotting any organizations that backs the BDS movement. Cuomo said, "If you boycott against Israel, New York will boycott you."

Non- or anti-Zionists have no real share in American Jewish discourse because Zionists police the boundaries of that discourse (thus groups such as J-Street and individuals such as journalist Peter Beinart have to constantly reiterate their Zionist credentials). For example, non-Zionist groups such as Jewish Voice for Peace cannot participate in Hillel activities on most American college campuses that follow the National Hillel Guidelines.[7] In some cases, even center-left organizations such as JStreet are excluded from participation

---

7 For discussion of these policies, see my essay in *Zeek* (2014) and on Judith Butler's work (2014).

in Hillel activities, depending on the Hillel director at a given campus. In 2015 National Hillel director Eric Fingerhut withdrew from speaking at the JStreet conference because of the "anti-Zionist" views of some of the participants there such as Palestinian negotiator Saeb Erekat (JTA, 2015). In America, there appears to be a vacuum between Zionism and anti-Zionism, between a Jewish identity where support of Israel occupies the center and a Jewish identity where it exists on the periphery or not at all. In short, there is not yet space for a diasporic post-Zionism.[8] This space would move Zionism from being American Jewish *identity* itself to reviving Jewish *discourse* that could include non- or post-Zionist alternatives.

I begin with the working assumption that a society where one ideology has hegemony over all others, where one ideology gets to define the terms of legitimacy, even if there may be good historical reasons why this state of affairs has transpired, opens itself to the dangerous possibility of a kind of cultural totalitarianism whereby dissent is considered a modern form of heresy. Regarding religion more generally, Catholic theologian David Burrell recently put it this way. "What history has shown is that the presence of other-believers can help the faithful in each tradition to gain insight into the distortions of that tradition: the ways it has compromised with seductions of state power, or ways in which fixation on a particular *other* effectively skewered their understanding of the revelation given them" (Burell, 2014, p. 135).[9] When the other, in our case, non-, anti-, or even post-Zionism, is considered the enemy, and thus excluded, largely by means of accusations of antisemitism, it cannot function as a means toward revealing the weakness of one's position (i.e. Zionism).[10] What I am suggesting then is that an American post-Zionism is primarily about challenging the hegemony of the term as a litmus test for legitimacy. The creation of this space is an imperative even for those who consider themselves

---

8 The language of exclusion in reference to non- or anti-Zionism begins in America as early as 1942. The anti-Zionist American Council for Judaism is defeated at the 1942 CCAR conference and the Zionist Organization of America (which Ben Gurion earlier on did not think was very Zionist) declares in 1942 that any Jewish organization fighting Zionism was now guilty of "blasphemy." See Kolsky (1992, pp.73–74).

9 Interestingly, American Jews have been quite progressive in terms of religious belief in regards to inclusion. To bring one example, every year on Shavout the Manhattan JCC hosts a large gathering of Jews of all stripes to partake in learning from many teachers of all branches of Judaism. I wonder if the organizers would consider allowing an openly anti-Zionist to speak about his/her position?

10 On the equation of anti-Zionism (or post-Zionism) and antisemitism see Yakira (2009) and my review in *The Journal of Religion* (Magid, 2012).

anti-Zionists. For example, Daniel Boyain, a notable anti-Zionist writes, "Zionism is a particular reading of Jewish culture and especially of the Bible. I do not, and could not, given my hermeneutical theories, argue that it is a wrong reading or that there is a right reading that can be countered to it. I do argue, however, *that it is not the only reading*" (Boyarin, 1994, 246, emphasis added). What Boyarin is challenging here is not the *possibility* of Zionism as one reading of the tradition but the hegemonic claim that it is the *only* legitimate reading of the tradition.

While post-Zionism in Israel is certainly not part of the Israeli mainstream, it is nevertheless part of Israeli discourse, and, in my view, it makes Israel a healthier society.[11] Can American Jewry cultivate a distinctive brand of American post-Zionism, and if so, what would it look like and how would it function? Below I explore this possibility of creating a critical space between Zionism and anti-Zionism through reading a series of essays by R. Menachem Froman (1945–2013), an eclectic and iconoclastic religious Zionist and close reader of R. Abraham Isaac Kook (1865–1935). It is here, I argue, deep within the recesses of a passionate and iconoclastic settler Zionism where we can perhaps cultivate a space for an alternative model, a diasporic post-Zionism that could supply the self-criticism necessary for American Jewry's problem with Zionism hegemony.

II

Before getting to Kook and Froman I begin with a brief synoptic view of post-Zionism. The term post-Zionism became part of the Israeli lexicon sometime in the 1980s although arguably it has a pre-history that goes back to the mid-1970s when settlement in the occupied territories became government policy with the election of the Likud party and Menachem Begin as prime minister in 1977.[12] In the 1980s a group of historians became known as the "new historians," distinguishing themselves from the previous generation of historians of Israel who were largely part of the "1948 generation." Some of these "new

---

11 In terms of its contestation of mainstream Zionism, contemporary post-Zionism is certainly not unique. The Canaanite Movement led by Israeli poet Yonatan Ratosh offered challenges to Zionism from a more autochthonous point of view beginning in the 1920s; see Diamond (1986).

12 For what is still a very good overview of the post-Zionist terrain see Silberstein (1999), Safir (1996), Kimmerling & Migdal (1993), and Hilliard (2009). Cf. Goremberg (2007), and Eldar & Zartal (2004).

historians" gained access to recently declassified IDF documents regarding the War of Independence in 1948 and began constructing a revised version of the establishment of the state and its relationship to the indigenous population, known as Palestinians, who lived there. In the English-speaking world, the most well-known of these new historians is Benny Morris, whose book, *The Birth of the Palestinian Refugee Problem 1947–1949* (1989) exposed the falsity of previous denials of mass deportations of Palestinian civilians and other abuses that resulted in, among other things, the Palestinian refugee problem. Books by other "new historians" followed suit, but the real transition from the new historians to post-Zionism occurred in the aftermath of the Oslo accords in 1994 when, for the first time, a two-state solution to the Israel/Palestine conflict seemed possible. It was then that the left in Israel began taking serious stock of the way their "myth of origins" presented serious barriers to overcome if indeed the occupation would end and a Palestinian State would be created.

By 2000, Morris recanted his initial position and rejected the label post-Zionist, subsequently publishing a significantly revised edition of his 1989 book now newly titled *The Birth of the Palestinian Refugee Problem Revisited* (2004). Morris has since become a spokesperson for what can be called the Israeli pragmatic right. But there were other important post-Zionist voices writing by this time such as Tom Segev whose book *The Seventh Million* (2000) was read widely in America, Baruch Kimmerling, Ilan Pappe, Gershon Safir, Uri Ram, Avi Shlaim, Shlomo Sands, Tanya Reinhart, Daniel Gavron, among many others.[13] For the most part, though, those in the diaspora who do not read Israeli scholarship or follow the contemporary debates in Israel very closely will not be very familiar with these names, even though some do publish in English. This is in part because most American Jews, even the most ardently Zionist (and even those on the left), gather much of their information from media sources, popular literature, or official Israeli agencies and not from critical contemporary scholarship on the subject. In Israel, these figures are more well-known and are more widely read. They participate in Israeli intellectual life, writing for newspapers, appearing on television, etc. More significantly, however, I think the absence of the post-Zionist voice from American Jewry is because post-Zionism is really an indigenous Israeli discourse, a re-assessment of Israeli history, and an opportunity to think outside the standard Israeli "myth of origins" that the new

---

13 Segev focuses on the role the Holocaust played in the Israeli imaginary which may have contributed to its popularity in America as it was not simply about an internal Israeli debate of its nationalistic origins. Another example of this progressive approach that may constitute post-Zionism in Gans (2008).

historians undermined in their work in the 1980s and 1990s. Perhaps American Jews are largely left outside this Zionist/post-Zionist orbit because being pro-Israel for many primarily involves supporting Israel against its critics rather than an in-depth exploration of Israel's nationalistic origins.[14] On this reading post-Zionism is really an extension of an internal Israeli Zionist discourse. For many American Jews Israel is about advocacy; they are arguably pro-Israelists rather than Zionists (although they certainly identify as Zionists and thus that identity should constitute a certain form of contemporary Zionism), and thus feel little inclination to engage with this discourse.

English readers may be more familiar with Avraham Burg and Tony Judt, both of whom represent some form of post-Zionism. Burg is a native Israeli whose father Joseph Burg was a member of Ben Gurion's first Knesset as head of the National Religious Party. Avrum Burg served as speaker of the Knesset himself (as part of the Labor party) as well as serving as president of the Jewish Agency. He published numerous essays that could be considered post-Zionist. One essay, published in *The London Guardian* entitled, "The End of Zionism: Israel Must Shed its Illusions and Choose between Racist Oppression and Democracy" (Burg, 2003) argued that "the end of the Zionist enterprise is on our doorstep," and that a Jewish State may remain but "it will be of a different sort, strange and ugly." Similarly, Tony Judt published a celebrated, or infamous, essay (depending on one's perspective) "Israel: The Alternative" in *The New York Review of Books* (Judt, 2003) in which he argued that Israel had stalled itself into a corner where few choices remained whereby Israel could remain a democratic state that embodied the vision of its Zionist architects. Another Israeli figure Avi Shavit has recently gained notoriety in the English-speaking world with his book *My Promised Land: The Triumph and Tragedy of Israel* (Shavit, 2015). This book occupies an interesting space between post-Zionism and a kind of revised Zionism among many on the Israeli left. Predictably, the book has been criticized by the pro-Israel camp as giving too much credence to the Palestinian narrative and viewed as an apologia for Israel by the progressive left.

As one can imagine, the criticism of this work—of Judt and Burg in particular—was swift and fierce.[15] Accusations of both being "self-hating Jews"

---

14 See, for example, Sternhell (1998, pp. 46–73). The first study in English on post-Zionism is Silberstein (1999), which nicely sets out the historical rise of post-Zionism and the major issues it addresses. More recently see Nimni (2003).

15 A sustained critique was proffered in Hazony (2000). Hazony does acknowledge that the post-Zionist perspective has become deeply embedded in Israeli society and, precisely for that reason, must be confronted and contested. There were many critical responses to

"Arab lovers" and "turncoats" (especially Burg) flooded the Jewish media. Leon Weiseltier, the literary editor of the ostensibly "liberal" *The New Republic* even removed Judt's name from the magazine's masthead (Hillard, 2009, p. 102). My aim here is not to enter the turgid waters of allegiance versus treason but to try to move the debate in a different direction. There is little doubt among both right and left that, to borrow a phrase, Zionism today is in a state of transition (Davis, 1980). Some have deemed settler Zionism "neo-Zionist" precisely to distinguish it from classical Zionism, while the left has increasingly moved toward a post-Zionist position.

In the diaspora, new forms of "diasporism" in the works of Daniel and Jonathan Boyarin, Judith Butler, Marc Ellis, and Jaqueline Rose now stand alongside more classical positions of anti-Zionism that still reside in the *haredi* camps of Satmar and its satellites.[16] Terms such as "queer diasporism" have been suggested by Jonathan Freedman in his book *Klezmer America* (2009, pp. 90–92) to describe a specific kind of Jewish identity that seeks to make its home in the complex web of what I would call, following David Hollinger (1995 and 1998), post-ethnic American life (Magid, 2013). It is true that much of this discourse exists primarily among intellectuals and university professors and has not breached the walls of the Zionist mainstream that is still protected by gatekeepers such as AIPAC, the ADL, and the American Jewish Committee. Hillel International Guidelines on Israel still do not permit Hillels from inviting speakers who are not Zionist (Magid, 2014d). This position has recently been challenged by the Open Hillel Movement. These diasporists, anti-Zionist, or post-Zionist positions do not get air time on news shows or other media in the US. The farthest left the mainstream media is willing to go is Peter Beinart who cogently and patiently makes his left-wing "Zionist" case to Jewish and American audiences (Beinart, 2012). Beinart does not, to my knowledge, identify as a post-Zionism even though some of the criticisms of Israeli government policy are shared by some post-Zionists. He fashions himself as solidly inside the Zionist orbit, in some way an American version of Avi Shavit, more critical of Israel in some ways and less critical in others.

Post-Zionism, like Zionism, is not one thing. There are post-Zionists who are focused on revising Israel's "myth of origins" but maintain that Israel has a right to self-identify as a "Jewish" state in some form, those who are one-staters,

---

post-Zionism in the Israeli press, far less in the US media. See, for example, Shehori (2004), Asseroff (2008). See also Shavit interview with Benny Morris (2004). C.f. Hilliard (2009 pp. 105–117).

16 See Ravitzky (1996, pp. 40–78) and Magid (2014c, pp. 92–107).

those who believe Israel should be a full liberal democracy with equal rights of all its citizens in both principle and practice, those who believe Israel is a racist state that should not exist at all. The diasporists and anti-Zionists mentioned above would likely not identify as post-Zionists since for many of them, the problem is not Zionism per se. Rather, many of them argue that living in the diaspora where, as Boyarin argues, Judaism as we know it really began, is the best, or most fruitful, way for Jews to fulfill their Jewishness (Boyarin, 2015; Boyarin, 1994, pp. 228–260; D. Boyarin & J. Boyarin, 2002).[17] The exclusivism and moral problems that arise with living in a "Jewish" state, the militarism necessary for political sovereignty, or the theological mandate to remain in exile until the coming of the messiah, are all deployed to argue for remaining in the diaspora, especially in a time, and in a place, where Jews are not facing an existential threat.

Post-Zionism, however, is not really about the diaspora, it is about Israel. It is about what kind of country Israel is, or wants to be. This may explain why American Jews are not interested in post-Zionism since for many American Jews, Israel as the homeland of the Jews, as a "Jewish" state, is all that is required to be pro-Israel. Most American Jews do not have to live with the choices Israel makes, be it in regards to security or the erosion of its democracy. One can see small cracks in that façade around the American Jewish responses to be new "Nationality Law" that arguably threatens Israel's democratic core, but even there, those murmurings will not likely erupt into any open rebellion. The one thing that seems to raise the collective blood pressure of American Jewry is church-state issues in Israel, for example, egalitarian prayer at the Kotel, non-Orthodox rabbis performing marriages in Israel, or the acceptance of non-Orthodox conversion from America. What seems to matter most to American Jews is that their religious sensibilities have legitimacy. For most Israelis, even those who are sympathetic to those concerns, these are not burning issues.

For the most part, post-Zionism in Israel has taken a secular form. That is, it is promoted by secular scholars and intellectuals who view Zionism as a secular Jewish ideology that is in need of significant revision. While this is arguably the case (hence the term "neo-Zionism" to describe settler ideology, distinguishing it from classical Zionism) there have been a few significant religious voices in Israel who have tried to make what may be called a spiritual case for post-Zionism. My interest, though, is not in an Israeli post-Zionism but a diasporic one. Can there be a post-Zionist critique from the diaspora that is not specifically about Israel's national tenor but rather about the nature and

---

17 Also see Butler (2012). On the reception of Butler, see Magid (2014a).

limits of Zionism as a source of Jewish identity in the diaspora? Can there be a diasporic post-Zionism that is not anti-Zionist or even diasporic but makes room for both, as well as for Zionism? Below I try make a spiritual case for a decidedly diaspora post-Zionism that is founded on negation as a spiritual exercise whereby the corruption of true religiosity—what Rav Kook called "true faith" and which I would call here "the secular dogma of Zionism in the diaspora"—is countered by a post-Zionism that cracks the hegemony of Zionism as the *sine qua non* of twenty-first-century Jewish identity.

It is interesting to note here that Zionism early on defined itself through negation known as "negating the diaspora" (*shlilat ha-golah*). The reasons for this had empirical, ideological, and ideational roots. Empirically it was a response to the dire state of the Jewish diaspora in the first part of the twentieth century. Ideologically Zionism was a revolutionary movement that for some sought to redefine Jewishness and in some cases replace Judaism. Practically, Zionist leaders knew that a flourishing Jewish diaspora would impede on immigration and make the case for the *need* for a Jewish nation-state difficult. This doctrine requires some revision in large part because most Jews today live in democratic countries where their rights are protected. Yet it still remains operative in part of the Zionist camp. Ben Gurion early on recognized that a vibrant Jewish diaspora would not serve the Zionist program (for Ben Gurion, the primary purpose of American Jewry was to support Israel). Today this can be seen by the growing number of Israelis who choose lives in the diaspora (something I think Ben Gurion could not have imagined) and the emergence of "Israeli diasporas" in countries such as the US, Germany, and to a lesser extent France. In response to the challenges of globalization, Eliezer Schweid arguably one of the most powerful intellectual voices in Israel today on questions of Jewish identity, called to reinstate Zionism's early "negation," arguing that without a renewed sense of "negation of the diaspora," Zionism would be in peril as the power of globalization is simply too strong to resist (Schweid 1996, pp. 133–160; also see Eisen, 2014).

While diaspora Jews who do not identify as Zionist may be critical of Israel, as well as Zionists such as JStreet and Peter Beinart, circumstantially or even structurally that is not my point. Rather, I am interested in how Zionism is *used* today in the diaspora and ask whether that usage is healthy for the flourishing of contemporary Jewish discourse. I make my case below not by engaging in the secular post-Zionist debates but by engaging with two Zionist thinkers, Rabbis Menachem Froman and Abraham Isaac Kook, to offer a prolegomenon for what one might call a spiritual post-Zionism in the diaspora.

III

Rabbi Menachem Froman (1945–2013) is not very well-known among Diaspora Jews, although he should be.[18] He was a highly visible and iconoclastic voice in Israel for the last four decades before his death at the age of 68. He was raised in a Zionist home in the Israeli town of Kefar Hasidim in northern Israel and spent years as a close disciple of Rabbi Zvi Yehuda Kook. Kook's father Abraham Isaac was the first chief rabbi of Palestine and arguably the main source of contemporary religious Zionism. The elder Kook died in 1935 and did not see the establishment of the State of Israel and thus could not predict the challenges political sovereignty would present. His more militant son Zvi Yehuda served as the dean of the Rav Kook yeshiva in Jerusalem until his death in 1982 and was the architect of the neo-Zionism of the settler movement (known as *Gush Emunim*, the Bloc of the Faithful, and *Yesha*, the Council of Judea, Samaria, and Gaza).[19] Froman was raised in the epicenter of settler ideology. Yet in his tenure as rabbi of Tekoa, a settlement in the occupied West Bank, known among settlers and their supporters as Judea, Froman developed a decidedly anti-militant worldview that was deeply committed to the idea that religion, instead of being that which made peace improbable, is precisely that which held the key to the solution to the conflict. A committed activist, Froman professed openly that he was willing to meet with any religious leader, friend or foe, who was willing to meet with him. He subsequently met with Yassar Arafat of the PLO, with Sheikh Yassin of Hamas, and with many other leaders in the Palestinian community, all in an attempt to foster dialogue and mutual understanding.[20] But Froman was not naïve. He did not believe "talking spirituality" would melt away decades, perhaps centuries, of hatred and acrimony. Rather, he believed that the realm of the spiritual, if it could be expansive rather than insular, if it could be inclusive instead of isolationist, was the best path toward fostering human flourishing; that "God talk" could lead to respect for human dignity, that the problem was not religion but politics or, more specifically, religion *as* politics. For Froman, religion had the power to bring

---

18   There was an obituary for Froman in *The New York Times*, March 9, 2013: http://www.nytimes.com/2013/03/10/world/middleeast/menachem-froman-rabbi-who-sought-mideast-peace-dies-at-68.html.

19   On the history of the settler movement see Sprinzak (1991); and Eldar & Idit (2004).

20   On the possibility of dialogue with Palestinians, even radical ones, see Froman (2014, pp. 115–117). On what he learned from meeting with Palestinian leaders see "Specifically a Primitive Settler like me" (pp. 141–143).

disparate people together while politics divided even like-minded people.[21] It is noteworthy that Froman remained to his last day a believer in the right of all Jews to live anywhere in Erez Yisrael.[22] In July 1996 he wrote, "As a primitive religious Jew who is connected to the land that God gave my ancestors I can attest: This is also the reason that the connection between those who support Greater Israel (*Erez Yisrael ha-Shelamah*) and the Palestinians have far greater potential [for success than the left].[23] This is because the Palestinians are also generally religious, or at least have a strong connection to their tradition, to their people, and to their land. What severs our connection is [only] hatred of the other."[24] Froman exhibits a kind of "spiritual nativism" that grew from his teacher R. Zvi Yehuda Kook but arguably moves beyond him in that he acknowledges, and affirms, the Arab connection to the land as well. Here he comes closer to the nativism of Yonatan Rotosh and the Canaanites, albeit the latter are radically secular. Both Froman and Ratosh held a nativist position, the former religious and the latter secular, that could potentially include the Arabs in their vision of a shared polity.[25] Froman argued that a solution to the crisis had to keep that in mind. One of his novel solutions, which may be itself a form of "settler post-Zionism," was to distinguish between the state and the Jewish attachment to the land—that is, to enable settlers to remain in their homes in the West Bank and become citizens of the State of Palestine. While certainly impractical, even utopian, its mere mention cuts through the religious Zionist narrative as it has heretofore been presented by the Kookian school.

---

21 See, for example, his essay "Politics and Humanism: Can They Co-Exist?" in Froman (2014, pp. 87–90). Here we find interesting similarities, from different perspectives between Froman and Martin Buber. See, for example, the "National and Zion" section in Buber's *Israel and the World* (1997, pp. 197–263). While Froman was coming from the more traditional Kookian and not Buberian tradition, a comparison of Froman and Buber on Zionism would be a desideratum.

22 See, for example, in Froman (2014, pp. 115–117, 121–126).

23 Froman (2014, pp. 141–3) argues that what the settlers and the Palestinians share is a connection to the land and thus if it these two groups, and not the urban Israeli elite who can truly reach a resolution to the conflict.

24 See "Peace without Limits," Froman (214, p.136). This was originally published in the settler journal *Nekudah* in July, 1996 a few months after the assassination of Rabin and right after Benjamin Netanyahu defeated Shimon Peres in the election for prime minister. Froman's position vis-à-vis religion as that which brings the settlers and people like Hamas together is spelled out in an interview in the Israeli newspaper *Hadashot*, March 1, 2011: www.news.walla.co.il/item/1798900.

25 Rotosh's case is made most forcefully in (1944). For a discussion of this text in English see Diamond (1986, p. 49–75.)

Viewed as a renegade in his community, Froman nonetheless enjoyed a kind of immunity due in part to the fact that he was one of R. Zvi Yehuda Kook's first generation of disciples and was respected by his teacher and his circle of colleagues. Rabbi Froman's death after a long illness was mourned by both Israelis and many Arabs with whom he developed close ties. He also cultivated a small circle of followers who began to see another way besides the militarism and dogmatism of the settler community. More of a teacher and activist than a writer, and more well-known for the force of his personality rather than his prose, Froman nonetheless published many short essays, and poetry, in Israeli journals and newspapers. Some of his essays have recently been collected and published in a slim volume entitled *Sakhaki Aretz, (Laugh My Beloved Land): Peace (Shalom), People (Am), Land (Adamah)* (Froman 2014).[26] The essays in this volume span the breadth of Froman's interests, from the crisis in religious Zionism, to education, ecumenism, politics, and secularism. Included in this volume is an essay entitled "Placing Limits on Faith" that was originally published in 1998. Froman structures his remarks around a short and penetrating passage from R. Abraham Isaac Kook's *Orot Emunah (Lights of Faith)* and then renders it applicable to his generation. Taking Froman's lead, I will extend his reading of Kook as the basis of my spiritual case for post-Zionism in the diaspora.

While Froman surely did not identify as a post-Zionist, he does mention post-Zionism numerous times in his writings (not in the essay below), and often in a positive light. Deeply committed to religious Zionism, Froman stayed solidly in the Zionist orbit but, taking license from Kook's dialectical thinking, he was able to see the ways in which critique is itself born from within in order to push the limits of any ideology beyond itself to a new articulation.[27] Below is a translation of one of his essays included in *Sakhaki Aretz, (Laugh My Beloved Land)*.

---

26 On his writing, see Froman (2014, p.7, p. 8). It is significant that some Canaanites, like Ratosh, became quite right-wing, while other such as Shlomo Avneri, became very left-wing. The nativist ideology could support both positions. The same might be true of Froman's teachings. The title and subtitle of the book is vexing. Rabbi Froman was a poet and author of a number of plays. The title suggests a play on words that speaks to the context of the book. "*Sakhaki*" can mean both playing and laughing. He may be implying that the land (*aretz, adamah*) is the root issue that we must play with which will lead us to laugh. "*Sakhaki*" is the opposite of the similar word "*Shakhaki*" which means grinding, laughing, and playfulness at the land root will allow motion instead of grinding things down. I want to thank my friend and student of R. Froman, Moshe-David Ha-Cohen for these suggestions regarding the title of the book.

27 Examples of Kook's dialectical thinking permeate his writings. One particularly schematic and salient illustration can be found in an early essay, written around 1910, entitled, "The Development of Ideas in Israel" in *Orot* (pp. 102–118).

IV

Placing Limits to Faith
(R. Menachem Froman, *Sakhaki Aretz*, pp. 79–82)

In relation to the upcoming festival of Hanukkah there has already been talk of comparing the natural, historical, and spiritual realms of the holiday. In terms of nature, the days are growing shorter and the light passes and is limited by increasing darkness. Historically, this was a time when Israelite culture was being diminished and limited by Greek culture. Nevertheless, the Israelites were able to overcome that challenge. Spiritually, Israelite faith was diminished by means of the influence of faithlessness [*hoser emunah*: perhaps, dominance of reason] of the Greeks.

With these ideas in mind I thought about citing a section from Rav Kook's *Orot Emunah* and include some observations and comments of my own (Kook, 1985, p. 47).

> Faith that extends beyond its measure brings destruction to the world. And this is not only regarding faith in things that are false (*emunah shel sheker*) but even true faith (*emunah emet*). When faith works on the individual and collective soul beyond its appropriate measure it becomes diluted with other physical and spiritual forces. This then becomes destructive.

The Rav raises an issue here that should be surprising, especially when coming from the chief rabbi of Israel. He claims that faith—even true faith—when it extends beyond its limit becomes destructive. What is implied here? Apparently, the Rav equates the experience of faith with mystical experience. When the individual or collective soul gets too caught up in divine perfection (*hashlamot ha-gedola be-yoter*) that which is beyond cosmic perfection, this admixture destroys the individuality of the singular person. In this respect, it is a death-force (*koah meimeit*) or at least a force of confusion and destruction.

> For this reason there are always those in the world that will rebel against faith despite the inherent strength of faith—in order to bring the situation under control. This way the world can receive the good that is in faith in proper measure.

The drive to rebel against faith comes to ensnare the power of faith [moving toward its overextension] so that it will not exceed its limits and cause destruction. The Rav envisions a positive role for these forces who ensnare faith. Through them, faith can contribute to the elevation of goodness in the world. It is precisely by the means of this limiting power that the world can receive the goodness that faith has to offer.[28]

> This is not only the case with faith, it is also true with wisdom, ethics, and all creative forces (*kisharon*). When we see some positive phenomenon there is also that which prevents it. From a narrow perspective (*mabat perati*) it appears that this positive phenomenon helps the world and that which prevents it does the opposite. But from a broader perspective (*mabat kelali*) we see that both of these build the world, one through positive expression, the other through negation.

Wisdom, ethics and all forms of creative expression need to be limited. One cannot remain stuck in the narrow perspective by saying, for example, that everything that limits ethics is destructive. It is precisely the limits to ethics—according to what the Rav says regarding limits to faith—that enables the good in ethics to become operative. The power of the negation of wisdom and ethics and all other forms of creativity construct the world the same way the forces [that drive these things] construct its very values.

> The final generation of every epoch (*tekufa*) generally comes with the power of negation. No epoch is complete without utilizing the most refined dimensions of its spiritual influence. By means of this influence it almost certainly extends beyond its limit.

When we mark the end of an epoch we can see certain spiritual forces reach the final stages of their power. And the spiritual force that was emblematic of that previous epoch often extends beyond its measure. Therefore, the divine (lit. the master of history, *adon ha-historia*) comes to limit its power.[29]

---

28 There is a similar, although surely not identical, approach taken by the Hasidic master Shmuel Bornstein of Sochaczev in regard to Jesus' role in redemption. See Magid (2014b, pp. 113–136).

29 Froman's use of the phrase "the master of history" to refer to the divine seems to me a covert reference to Hegel.

> The goodness that [this force] can bring often cannot be absorbed by the world and turns to shatter it. Therefore the last generation brings its measure, the generation that seals one epoch and begins another [and this measure comes in the form of] negation.

The final generation of an epoch that comes to rebel against the emblematic spiritual movement that defines that epoch guards—from the perspective of providence—the reconciliation of the world (*takinut ha-olam*) so that that spiritual movement will not be destructive in its overextension.

> As soon as that negation is revealed and exercises its strength to erase the measure, the weakness (*rifayon*) and nullity (*afsiyuto*) of that negation is revealed.

The power of negation does not have an independent value. Its strength and value lie in its power to limit the overextension of the spiritual movement that it negates. If it continues with its negation beyond its purpose to limit what exists, it reveals its nullity.[30]

The Rav wrote these words regarding the secularism/apostasy (*tenu'at kefira*) of his time. His claim was that secularism had a positive function in that it served to prevent the overextension of faith.[31] But in and of itself it had no intrinsic value. In our time, I feel that it is possible to claim the same thing regarding different forces and creative impulses. Just as the Rav saw his role not only to offer a correlation between faith and the secular, but also to correlate wisdom to its limits, ethics to its limits, as well as other creative forces, I feel in our time when Jewish nationalism—that is being expressed through Zionism—has also reached its limit, its power needs to be contained (*le-hagbil'et kokhah*) so that it too does not overextend its measure. But the required negation itself, without viewing its purpose as acting as a limiting force, loses its worth and value.

---

30 Elsewhere Froman notes from a psychological perspective that negation is never the end human beings seek but rather a preamble to constructing alternatives. See his "Happy Are the People, Whose lot is Thus," in Froman (2014, p. 43).

31 Rav Kook wrote about apostasy (*kefira*) often. One example that is very germane to Froman's argument can be found is the following: "There are thus many heretics (*apikorsim*) in whom we find heresy in a certain measure but when we understand the depths of their soul we will find in them a connection to the divine in a concealed state. And this is actually quite frequent regarding the merit and kindness in our generation, even among those who are total heretics" (2004, p. 100).

V

For those familiar with the writings of Rav Kook, the text cited above from *Orot Ha-Emunah* that serves as the basis for Froman's ruminations is not remarkable. One of Kook's most audacious claims is the notion that the secular, specifically secular Zionists who were devoting their lives to the establishment of a Jewish homeland, were unwittingly fulfilling God's will even as they may have claimed otherwise.[32] Kook takes this even one step further to argue that without these secularists, whose concerns were not tied up with ritual practice and ceremony, a Jewish homeland likely could not have been built. His relationship to heresy is perhaps best captured in an oft-cited passage from his collected letters. "A general principle in the war of ideas is that in regards to every idea that comes to destroy the Torah, we should not seek to destroy it but build a castle of Torah on its foundations. It will be elevated as a result and through this elevation its true nature will be revealed" (Kook, 1962, p. 164).

While Kook could not be called a Hegelian in any formal sense (his direct knowledge of Hegel is uncertain), he did adapt Hegel's dialectical model, which arguably extends in a different form back to Plato. This way of thinking also appears in Kabbalistic literature with which Kook was intimately familiar. He adopts this dialectical method as a way of understanding the role played by the secular Zionist of this time within a traditional perspective. The notion of epochs (*tekufot*) that frame both Kook's essay and Froman's reading, and the necessary negation of one ideology as a prerequisite to inaugurate the next, is an idea common in the anonymous fourteenth-century mystical work *Sefer Temumah* with which Kook was familiar as well as the Christian theologian Joachim of Fiore (Gershom Scholem suggests some possible confluence between the two).[33] The dialectical model was also made popular among certain Sabbatean thinkers and some earlier Greek and Hebrew forms of this thinking may have influenced Paul's view of messianism as well.

In any event, Kook and Froman merge these two related but not identical ideas (the dialectic and epochs or "world cycles") to make a case for negation as a spiritual dimension that both completes and also manages a previous ideology that, in the waning moments of the epoch in which it flourished,

---

32 There is literally a library of scholarship on Rav Kook that addresses this central issue in his thought. For some examples in English see Kaplan & Shat (1995), Ish-Shalom (1993), and Mirsky (2014).

33 On the "world cycles" of *Sefer ha-Temunah*, see Scholem (1979, pp. 1–84) and Scholem (1990, pp. 460–475).

naturally overextends itself to become a destructive force. It is not simply, in my view, that negation for Kook in this essay is preventative, but it is also constructive. Negation does not simply prevent the object from overreaching its productive nature; it also in due course changes the nature of the object it negates. This draws Kook closer to the Hegelian position. How much Kook was willing to acknowledge religious change as part of what Tamar Ross calls Kook's "evolving Torah" is an important discussion but not at issue here (Ross, 2004, pp. 205–207). Rather, I want to point out that for Kook negation is a spiritual exercise in that its purpose is the continuation of the good and the prevention of evil; the proliferation of peace through negation, the work done to enable the "truth" to remain "good" at the very instant that truth can express falsehood.

In Kook's time the "carriers of true faith" adhered to a strict rendering of the miraculous scope of exile and redemption whereby human agency in regards to settling the land and political sovereignty could not be understood.[34] In Kook's mind this stifled the divine progress of redemption that unfolded through this dialectical process. Kook fully acknowledged that the classical sources, if not read dialectically, are not in his favor. Apostasy is generally not viewed as progress, except in heretical cases such as the Sabbatean movement and in illusions in the Kabbalistic literature of the Zohar and Lurianic Kabbalah that inform both the Sabbateans and Kook.[35] For Kook and for Froman, the power of negation manifested as the secularist's negation of "faith" for the sake of returning to the Jewish homeland exposed how the truth was rendered false by its overextension. Too much faith (that is, the anti-Zionism of the traditionalists who denied the validity of the secular to be an arbiter of truth, even provisionally) makes the true false, or at least prevents the true from producing the "good." Thus for Kook, at least, without Zionism, tradition would not have maintained a status quo but would have become a destructive force in the world. This claim is founded on Kook's idea that as epochs end, truth necessarily overreaches, becoming destructive, and thus arouses its negation. From the "narrow view" (*mabat perati*) of the past, the negation appears false (which for Kook it ultimately is!) but it is precisely in its capacity to negate that this force does its positive, and redemptive, work.

---

34 A great example of this thinking is the lengthy discussion on miracle in the wake of the Six-Day War in Teitelbaum (1968, pp. 3–27).

35 One can see this in kabbalistic and Hasidism renderings of the Talmudic dictum "sin for the sake of heaven" an idea perhaps most prominently elucidated in the work of R. Zaddok ha-Cohen of Lublin.

In his somewhat surprising summation, Froman offers an updated version of Kook's dialectical formula as it relates to his own community. Regarding the crisis he witnessed in religious Zionism, Froman writes, "I feel in our time when Jewish nationalism—that is being expressed through Zionism—has also reached its limit, its power needs to be contained so that it too does not overextend its measure." What exactly does Froman mean here? Does he mean something close to what Avrum Burg suggests in his 2003 *London Guardian* article that this may be the last Zionist generation? Unlikely. This was first published in 1998, after Rabin's assassination but before the second Intifada, in fact before the euphoria of Oslo had fully worn off. What is Froman's evidence of Zionism having reached its limit? Froman remained a believer in Greater Israel as a spiritual ideal but not necessarily a political one, and he claims elsewhere that the operative question of his community is how to deal with human freedom, as "this is the essence of Zionism." The crisis of religious Zionism for him is thus not about history but about human will. What will Zionists do with freedom?[36] While one cannot know for sure, in other writings Froman stresses the choice of politics over culture, jingoism over humanism, and land over spirituality as the widening crack in the "Golden Bowl" of Zionism, the imperfection that undermines its true merit.[37] As a movement that was intended to establish Jewish sovereignty and freedom, in Froman's mind, Zionism in general and religious Zionism in particular had become a tool to control another people, thereby limiting their freedom and by extension, making Zionism itself an emblem of unfreedom. In effect, according to Froman it was in danger of losing its moral foundations. In a 1995 op-ed in the Israeli daily *Haaretz*, "The Right to Stand," Froman wrote, "In school we were taught a formal principle that if a person wants to build his world (as beautiful as it may be) by means of destroying the world of another (as impoverished as it may be), this is 'the sin and its punishment.'[38] The lesson one learns from this is simple: It is forbidden for Jews to build their return to Zion (*shivat Zion*) at the price of the Arabs. It is forbidden for settlers to build their settlements—even if they are beautiful and rooted—in the midst of the destruction of the world of the Palestinians" (Froman, 2014, 119).

---

36 See Froman's "Re-Evaluating Ourselves" (2014, p. 69, 70); see also pp. 93–95. One can also see similar sentiments in the Zionist writings for Yeshayahu Leibowitz. See, for example, Leibowitz (1992, pp. 185–190).

37 This refers to Henry James's novel *The Golden Bowl*.

38 See Midrash Shmuel on "Ethics of the Fathers" 6:2.

Here and elsewhere Froman seems to echo sentiments of many in Brit Shalom and Ichud, two short-lived binational movements comprised of mostly German-Jewish intellectuals who advocated for a binational state and equal rights for Arab citizens. In an interview in May 1972 Gershom Scholem, who was for a time a member of Brit Shalom, remarked, "The Land of Israel belongs to two peoples, and these peoples need to find a way to live together ... and to work for a common future."[39] The aspiration for coexistence is quite common, among left and right, but the declaration that the land itself *belongs* to two peoples is a far more audacious claim, certainly for religious Zionists, that Froman seemed quite open to considering. Can we say that for Froman, Zionism as a tool, or justification, of oppression is its overextension whereby a positive idea turns destructive not only for the oppressed but also for the oppressor (to gesture to Hegel's "master-slave" narrative)? Froman does not specify a particular event to which he is reacting; instead, on my reading, he is responding to a radicalizing trend that is exposing the destructive nature of the ideology to which he remained wed.[40]

In another essay in his volume, "Politics and Humanity: Can They Co-Exist?" Froman writes, "For my people I hope that nationalism will be expressed less through political means and more through cultural means. And one who, in any case, expresses their song of hope in that which exceeds the boundaries of Zionism—it is possible to respond that this is a claim to be a post-Zionist and not a pre-Zionist. And I would not recoil here in using the elder and great Hegel: It is possible to hope that the Jewish people will, in the future, succeed in building a synthesis of an intimate collective religious form of Judaism and a positive and passionate vision of Zionism" (Froman, 2014, pp. 88–9). Froman's reading of Kook fits into the positive or totalizing nature some make of Hegel's dialectic; that the process will reach a point of final synthesis where the Absolute will emerge, where non-identity will yield identity, where synthesis will achieve a finality whereby it will not have to repeat itself. For Hegel, the Absolute Spirit manifests finally in philosophy as the overcoming of both art and religion; for Kook and Froman, messianic redemption and, in Kook's case, the unification of the secular and the religious (or the disclosure of the former rooted in the latter). One could also posit on a more radical reading that for Kook it is the completion of the spiritual which might be viewed as its

---

39 Cited in Buber (1983, p. 72).
40 For perhaps the most comprehensive discussion of religious Zionism and particularly its radicalizing trend in the past 25 years see Fischer (2007), especially pp. 318–405.

liberation from formal religion. Perhaps this explains why both Froman and Kook deny any independent value to negation: negation exists only to prevent the form it negates from being destructive, it does not replace it; negation has no intrinsic value, only utility. Negation for Kook and Froman works to hold back the truth from becoming false and thereby pushes the truth to its final fulfilment, the truth of redemption and ultimate reconciliation.

I wonder if there is a way for contemporary Israeli post-Zionism to fit into this formula of negation as a spiritual exercise, as a necessary preventative of the overextension, and thus destructiveness, of present-day Zionism, especially religious Zionism, without necessarily adopting the totalizing view of a final synthesis as the necessary trajectory of all history. Kook was making a case for Zionism through its own force of negation, negating the ultra-traditional worldview that claimed Zionism was impossible. Can we formulate Kook's equation in reverse? That is, as viewing post-Zionism as the instrument of Zionism's overextension. Perhaps we can posit that the overreach for Froman may be viewed in the move from a Greater Israel ideology in people such as Menachem Begin who still retained a humanistic side, or his predecessor Ze'ev Jabotinsky whose militarism was coupled with a deep humanism and belief in minority rights, to the radical religious Zionism (or is it neo-Zionism?) of people such as Naftali Bennett, Yizhak Ginsburgh, Moshe Levinger, or Moshe Feiglin whose Zionism appears to be void of humanism and any deep respect for the integrity of the other.[41] And this too will be a stage with no obvious *aufheben*, or overcoming, of opposites. Froman appears committed to reinsert (religious/spiritual) humanism into the religious Zionist discourse, that is, *his* personal negation.

Whatever the case, Froman clearly felt that by 1998 religious Zionism had run its course, as indicated by its overreaching and destructive side (whatever he meant that to be), and thus negation was inevitable. In an essay a few years earlier, in 1996, Froman quotes Uri Elizur who wrote earlier in the settler journal *Nekudah*, "There is a contradiction between hating the Arabs and loving the land. We have to decide which of the two we want to choose." Froman continues, "To be more specific, if the movement for the land is not successful in overcoming its weaknesses and does not realize that it must develop ties with the Palestinians, it will not succeed in building a country that can stand the pressure from the outside, and more importantly, from the inside." From here we see Froman still believed the settler movement could succeed, but only

---

41 On his views of "Greater Israel," see Froman (2014, p. 106).

by enacting its own negation of those destructive forces ("hating the Arab") that were becoming dominant. Whether he viewed post-Zionism as another external negation or whether he felt religious Zionism could indeed pull itself back from the precipice where truth becomes falsity, I do not know. In any case, this is certainly an internal Israeli debate that is ongoing. For Jews in the diaspora, however, the challenges of Zionism are different and thus its negation will also have to different. It is to the manifestation of this negation I now turn.

VI

The excerpts of Kook and Froman above express a Hegelianism whereby totality is achieved through negation. The radical quality of their position is founded on the notion that the necessary negation can come, or must come, through the resistance against what appears as truth ("true faith"), in Kook's case, through heresy (*kefira*), in Froman's case though humanism. For a notion of negation as a foundation for a diasporic post-Zionism, I would suggest an approach perhaps closer in some way to Adorno's (1973) "negative dialectics" whereby the dialectic achieves no totality because no totality is in the offing. Adorno's negative dialectic is a critique of Hegel founded on Adorno's rendering of Auschwitz as the destruction of all theodicy and all totalizing history, that the Holocaust has taught us that the good is not the necessary outcome of humanity or history, that the Hegelian identity of identity and non-identity can still too easily exclude and lead to destructive consequences.[42] Adorno writes, "identity is the primal form of ideology," and ideology, as identity, can too easily lead to "subjugation to dominant purposes" (Adorno, 1973, p. 148). The danger then is not the dialectic but its *aufhebung*, the moment where the dialectic reaches its totalizing conclusion in what Hegel optimistically calls "freedom of the Spirit" or the "end of history," but, as Adorno notes, can also yield far worse consequences. We need not go into the complexities of Adorno's critique here except to suggest that perhaps in the case of Zionism in the contemporary diaspora the negation may take the form of resisting the very notion of a totalizing narrative regarding Zionism and Jewishness—that is, resistance to the notion that one Jewish ideology (Zionism) has become the litmus test of Jewish authenticity, where identity replaces discourse. Here

---

42 C.f. Wolfe (2008). See also Bernstein (2001, pp. 372–384). "Adorno thinks that any philosophical theodicy, that is, any attempt to demonstrate how despite and in light of the existence of evil we are at home in the world, is 'refuted' by Auschwitz."

I posit negation simply as a spiritual exercise in contesting hegemony and its negative consequences.

In today's American Jewish diaspora, rather than viewing the hegemony of Zionism as an example of its overextendedness, as Froman seems to do—unlike Israelis, few American Jews actually experience or witness the oppressive nature of contemporary Zionism—many view Zionism as a requirement of Jewish identity. While Yosef Hayim Yerushalmi famously claimed in his *Zakhor* (1982) that in modernity, history has become the "religion of the fallen Jew," today Zionism, or pro-Israelism, has arguably become "the civil religion of the American Jew." There is an old joke in America about "three day Jews"; Jews who attend synagogue two days of Rosh Ha-Shana and one day Yom Kippur. I recently heard a new LA version; the "three dinner Jews": Jews who go to the annual synagogue dinner, the Jewish Federation dinner, and the AIPAC dinner. Pro-Israelism has become an integral part of American Jewish civil religion.

As a result, Zionism often functions as Jewish identity, sometimes as "Jewishness" itself, and as a litmus test that closes off all other alternatives. Thus when Zionism moves from part of Jewish discourse to a hegemonic form of Jewish identity that deflects all challenges, it becomes dogma. And, more troubling, it becomes totalizing.[43]

I suggest that the overreaching of contemporary diaspora Zionism is its hegemonic control of public Jewish discourse. This operates in numerous ways. Perhaps on the most base level it is the equation of non- or even anti-Zionism with antisemitism, a sure way to prevent any serious consideration of its position. More subtly, albeit along similar lines, it is the innate suspicion that any non-Zionist position is an attempt to destroy the State of Israel. This is simply not the case. Many non-Zionists, and many diasporists, are not primarily focused on Israel. Or they are so largely to protest that the extent to which Israel gets to dictate the politics of the Jewish diaspora. Rather, they are interested in creating a viable cultural, religious/spiritual, political, and moral case for Jewish life in the diaspora without support of Israel at its center.

The hegemonic role of Zionism is not new to late twentieth- and early twenty-first-century American Judaism. Its beginnings are rooted much earlier, arguably with the establishment of the State of Israel in 1948. For example, in her essay "To Save the Jewish Homeland," published in 1948 Hannah Arendt

---

43 As one example of the totalizing nature of Zionism, see my essay (Magid, 2014a) on the reception of Judith Butler's work on Israel, especially the controversy that arose about her speaking about Franz Kafka at the Jewish Museum in Manhattan in February, 2014.

wrote, "From the time of the Balfour declaration the loyal opposition in Zionist politics was constituted by the non-Zionists. But for all practical purposes the non-Zionist opposition longer exists today. This unfortunate development was encouraged, if not caused, by the fact that the United States and the United Nations finally endorsed an extremist Jewish demand that non-Zionists had always held to be totally unrealistic. With the support of a Jewish state by the great powers, the non-Zionists themselves believed themselves refuted by reality itself" (Arendt, 2007, pp. 39–34). While Arendt is certainly correct that the reality of the state rendered non-Zionism (if we understand non-Zionism simply as opposing the establishing of a state) a position that stood in opposition to reality, her lamentation is more about the ways in which the non-Zionist position offered a salient and relevant critique to some of the decisions being made early on about the nature of the state more than about the existence of the state, in particular regarding the return of Arab refugees after the 1948 War of Independence. Yet I would still argue that the weakening of non-Zionism after 48 has reached new heights in twenty-first-century America whereby non- and anti-Zionism is totally rejected as a kind of secular Jewish heresy the likes of which did not exist when Arendt wrote her essay. And it is precisely this stage of rejection, what I suggest is an example of Kook and Froman's "overextension" of the Zionist narrative, that has, or perhaps should, evoke, a resistance of "negation."[44] Diasporic post-Zionism, still undefined, might serve as a skeleton of that negation.

My suggestion for an American post-Zionism is not to deny Zionism but to negate its hegemony in public discourse which might then free some diaspora Jews from the confines of Zionist affiliation or pro-Israelism, in order to encourage the development of new alternatives to Jewish life in the diaspora. Zionism has functioned for most of its history as one among many Jewish alternatives. And while the destruction of European Jewry in the Holocaust and the establishment of Israel certainly thrust Zionist from the margin (where it was until the late 1930s in America) to the center of Jewish life, it did not necessarily mandate Zionism's hegemonic status for diaspora Jews.[45] The extent to which that is the case is, in fact, quite recent, beginning after

---

44 On the move from rejection to censorship to excommunication of non-Zionism in contemporary America, see Magid (2014a).

45 For example, in 1933 the ZOA (Zionist Organization of America) had a membership of 9,000. In 1939 it was 43,000. Hadassah moved from 24,000 to 66,000 in those years. In a letter in 1939 on his way back to Palestine from America, David Ben-Gurion wrote, "The Zionists can hardly do anything that the non-Zionists oppose." Cited in Gal (1992, p. 46).

1967 (as I mentioned above, in the early 70s Norman Podhoretz wrote in *Commentary Magazine*, "We are all Zionists now!") and gained ground with the rise and success of AIPAC and Jewish neo-Conservatism in the 1980s.

Kook legitimized Zionism as the negation of the traditionalism that refused to view Zionism's (heretical) negation of tradition as the inauguration of a new stage toward the messianic era. Froman adopts this to criticize the defects in religious Zionism—its disappearing humanism, its choice of politics over culture—as a way to view his critique as a new form of negation, one that will prevent religious Zionism's excesses from becoming destructive. My suggestion of a post-Zionism in the diaspora is a negation of the totalizing narrative of Zionism as the defining factor of American Jewish authenticity. As opposed to Kook or Froman, I do not think the totalizing nature of the Hegelian dialectic is productive precisely as it refers to the messianic era. How messiah will, or will not, come, is best left agnostic. One can still hope for the Messiah without supporting any one program toward that end aside from treating creation with dignity and respect. The post-Zionist negation I propose here is informed by but surely not identical to either Kook or Froman, neither in structure nor in substance. And it is not really about Israel *per se* but about the role of Israel in the diasporic imagination. What one gains from reading Kook and Froman here is the notion of necessary negation as an applied dimension of the dialectic in relation to Zionism. One surely does not need Kook or Froman to get that but they both offer a reading of Zionism that uses that negation as a justification for ideas that exist outside the margins of legitimacy but in fact locate the very weakness in the thinking of the day.

Unlike Kook or Froman, we do not need to proclaim that negation itself has only instrumental value. Its value is that if implemented, it will break open the hegemonic nature of Zionism and enable other forms of identity-formation to flourish in conjunction with Zionism. As a result of subverting the hegemonic and totalizing nature of Zionism in the diaspora it can then begin to articulate a vision of identity that is not subservient to the Zionist narrative of "negation of the exile." It will resist the totalizing nature of one form of Jewishness, i.e. Zionism (this, I claim, is diaspora Zionism's present state of overreaching) while allowing Zionism to remain and develop (the "post" retains that which it reaches beyond) (Magid, 2013, pp. 2–4). Finally, it will be healthy for Zionism in that it will be released from the burden of all totalizing concepts; it will not have to be all things to all people. It will be kept honest by being confronted with resistance and a call to clarify its positions. It will become strengthened by being a part of, and not the overcoming of, the dialectic.

Rabbi Menachem Froman was a man of extraordinary courage and conviction. From deep within the recesses of the Zionist orbit he cracked open the tightly woven binary between right and left in Israel by arguing for humanism while maintaining that there is an unbreakable theological connection between the Jewish people and Erez Yisrael (e.g., Froman 2014, 139). While his practical solutions may not satisfy one interested in public policy, his vision of saving religious Zionism from overextension by exposing its destructive tendencies is noteworthy. In this he shared much with Kook, albeit Kook remained far more theoretical even than Froman who, even given his spiritual inclinations, lived amidst a radicalizing settler movement and had to respond to the daily challenges of occupation. Both viewed resistance and negation as a spiritual exercise that served both a preventative and constructive purpose. Jews living in the diaspora can learn much from them, not so much about the value or obligation to live in Israel (where diaspora Jews choose not to live) but about the dignity and importance of living spiritually engaged lives in the diaspora alongside, but not necessarily auxiliary to, the state of Israel.

Bibliography

Adorno, T. (1973). *Negative Dialectics.* E. B. Ashton (Ed.). London: Continuum.

Arendt, H. (2007). To Save the Jewish Homeland. In H. Arendt (Ed.), *The Jewish Writings.* New York: Schocken.

Asseroff, A. (2008). Post-Zionism: A Requiem for an Intellectual Fad. Retrieved from www.mideastweb.org.

Beinart, P. (2012). *The Crisis of Zionism.* New York: New York Times Books.

Berkowitz, M. (1996). *Zionist Culture and Western European Jewry before the First World War.* Chapel Hill, NC: University of North Carolina Press.

Bernstein, J. (2001). Auschwitz as Negative Theodicy. In J. M. Bernstein (Ed.), *Adorno: Disenchantment and Ethics* In: Cambridge: Cambridge University Press.

Boyarin, D. (1994). *A Radical Jew: Paul and the Politics of Identity.* Berkeley, CA: University of California Press.

Boyarin, D. (2015). *A Travelling Homeland: The Babylonian Talmud as Diaspora.* Philadelphia: University of Pennsylvania Press.

Boyarin, D. & Boyarin, J. (2002). *Powers of Diaspora: Two Essays on the Relevance of Jewish Culture.* Minneapolis, MN: University of Minnesota Press.

Buber, M. (1983). *Martin Buber: A Land of Two Peoples: Martin Buber on Jews and Arabs.* P. Mendes-Flohr (Ed.). Chicago, IL: University of Chicago Press.

Buber, M. (1997). *Israel and the World.* Syracuse, NY: Syracuse University Press.

Burell, D. (2014). *Toward a Jewish-Christian-Muslim Theology*. Oxford: Wiley Blackwell.

Butler, J. (2012). *Parting Ways: Jewishness and the Critique of Zionism*. New York: Columbia University Press.

Cohen, N. (2003). *The Americanization of Zionism 1897–1948*. Lebanon, NH: Brandeis University Press.

Davis, M. (1980). *Zionism in Transition*. New York: Herzl Press.

Diamond, J. (1986). *Homeland or Holy Land?: The "Canaanite' Critique of Israel*. Bloomington, IN: Indianan University Press.

Eisen, A. (2014). Zionism, American Jewry, and the "Negation of the Diaspora." In M. Meyer, & D. Myers (Eds.), *Between Jewish Tradition and Modernity, Essays in Honor of David Ellenson*. Detroit: Wayne State University Press.

Fischer, S. (2007). *Self-Expression and Democracy in Radical Religious Zionist Ideology* (unpublished doctoral dissertation). The Hebrew University, Jerusalem.

Freedman, J. (2009). *Klezmer America: Jewishness, Ethnicity, Modernity*. New York: Columbia University Press.

Foxman, A. (2007). *The Deadliest Lies: The Israel Lobby and the Myth of Jewish Control*. New York: Palgrave.

Froman, M. (2014). *Sakhaki Aretz*. Tel Aviv: Yediot Ahronot and Hemed.

Gal, A. 1992. *David Ben-Gurion and the American Alignment for a Jewish State*. Bloomington, IN: Indiana University Press.

Gans, C. (2008). *A Just Zionism; On the Morality of the Jewish State*. Oxford: Oxford University Press.

Goremberg, G. (2007). *Accidental Empire: Israel and the Birth of the Settlements 1967–1977*. New York: Holt.

Hazony, Y. (2000). *The Jewish State: The Struggle for Israel's Soul*. New York: Basic Books.

Hilliard, C. (2009). *Does Israel have a Future?* Lincoln, NE: Potomac.

Hollinger, D. (1998). Jewish Identity, Assimilation, and Multiculturalism. In Karen Mittlemen (Ed.), *Creating America's Jews*, Philadelphia, PA: JPS.

Ish-Shalom, B. (1993). *Rav Avraham Itzhak HaCohen Kooks: Between Rationalism and Mysticism* (O. Wiskind-Elper Trans.). Albany, NY: SUNY Press.

JTA. (2015, March 9). Hillel's Eric Fingerhut Withdraws from J Street Conference; Objects to Presence of Palestinian Negotiator Saeb Erekat. Retrieved from http://forward.com/articles/216303/hillel-s-eric-fingerhut-withdraws-from-j-street/

Judt, T. (October 23 2003). Israel: The Alternative. Retrieved from www.nybooks.com/articles/archives/2003/oct/23/israel-the-alternative/.

Kaplan, L., & Sat, D. (Eds.). (1995). *Rabbi Abraham Isaac Kook and Jewish Spirituality*. New York: NYU Press.

Kimmerling, B., & Migdal, J. (1993). *Palestinians: The Making of a People*. New York: Free Press.

Kolsky, T. (1992). *Jews Against Zionism: The American Council for Judaism, 1942–1948*. Philadelphia, PA: Temple University Press.

Kook, A. I. (1962). *Igrot 1*. Jerusalem: Mosad ha-Rav Kook.

Kook, A. I. (1985). *Orot ha-Emunah*. Jerusalem: Mossad ha-Rav Kook.

Kook, A. I. (2004). *Sheomeh Kevazim (Eight Notebooks)*. Vol. 1. Jerusalem: Mosad Ha- Rav Kook.

Leibowitz, Y. (1992). After Kibya. In E. Goldman (Ed.), *Judaism, Human Values and the Jewish State*. Cambridge, MA: Harvard University Press.

Magid, S. (2013). *American Post-Judaism*. Bloomington, IN: Indiana University Press.

Magid, S. (2014a). Butler Trouble: Zionism, Excommunication and the Reception of Judith Butler's Work on Israel/Palestine. *Studies in American Jewish Literature 33*(2), 237–259.

Magid, S. (2014b). *Hasidism Incarnate: Hasidism, Christianity, and the Construction of Modern Judaism*. Redwood City, CA: Stanford University Press.

Magid, S. (2014c). Is There an American Jewish Fundamentalism Part II: Satmar. In David Watt & Simon Wood (Eds.), *Fundamentalism: Perspectives on a Contested History*. Columbia, SC: University of South Carolina Press.

Magid, S. (2014d.) "Who is Boycotting Whom?" National Hillel Guidelines, Dissent, and Legitimate Protest. Retrieved from http://zeek.forward.com/articles/117993/

Magid, S. (2015). Stuck Between Berlin and Jerusalem: What Kind of Zionist was Gershom Scholem? Retrieved from http://tabletmag.com/jewish-arts-and-culture/books/189531/gershom-scholem-zionist

Mearsheimer, J., & Wald, S. (2006). *The Israel Lobby and U.S. Foreign Policy*. New York: Farrar, Straus, and Girou.

Mendelsohn, E. (1992). *On Modern Jewish Politics*. Oxford: Oxford University Press.

Mirsky, Y. (2014). *Rav Kook: Mystic in a Time of Revolution*. New Haven, CT: Yale University Press.

Morris, B. (1989). *The Birth of the Palestinian Refugee Problem 1947–1949*. Cambridge: Cambridge University Press.

Morris, B. (2004). *The Birth of the Palestinian Refugee Problem Revisited*. Cambridge: Cambridge University Press.

Myers, D. (Ed). (2008). *Between Jew and Arab: The Lost Voice of Simon Rawidowicz*. Lebanon, NH: Brandeis University Press.

Nimni, E. (2003). *The Challenge of Post-Zionism: Alternatives to Fundamentalist Politics in Israel*. London: Zed Books.

Raider, M. (1998). *The Emergence of American Zionism*. New York: NYU Press.

Ravitzky, A. (1996). *Messianism, Zionism and Religious Radicalism*. Chicago, IL: University of Chicago Press.

Rosenfeld, Alvin. (2013). *The End of the Holocaust*. Bloomington, IN: Indiana University Press.

Ross, T. (2004). *Expanding the Palace of Torah: Orthodoxy and Feminism*. Lebanon, NH: Brandeis University Press.

Rotosh, Y. (1944). *Mas'a Ha-Petikha: be-Moshav Hava'ad 'im Shelihei Hata'im (The Opening Discourse)*. Tel Aviv.

Safir, G. (1996). *Labor, Land and the Origins of the Israeli-Palestinian Conflict 1882–1914* (Rev. Ed.). Berkeley, CA University of California Press.

Sasson, T. (2013). *The New American Zionism*. New York: NYU Press.

Scholem, G. (1979). *Ha-Kabbalah she Sefer Ha-Temunah ve-shel Avraham Abulafia*. Jerusalem: Akadamon.

Scholem, G. (1990). *Origins of the Kabbalah* (A. Arkush, Trans.). Princeton, NJ: Princeton University Press.

Schweid, E. (1996). The Rejection of the Diaspora in Zionist Thought: Two Approaches. In J. Reinharz, & A. Shapira (Eds.), *Essential Papers on Zionism*. New York: NYU Press.

Segev, T. (2000). *The Seventh Million: The Israelis and the Holocaust* (Haim Watzman, Trans.). New York: Holt.

Shavit, A. (2004). Survival of the Fittest? An Interview with Benny Morris. Retrieved from https://www.haaretz.com/1.5262454

Shehori, D. (2004). Post-Zionism is Dead or in a Deep Freeze? Retrieved from https://www.haaretz.com/1.4783563

Silberstein, L. (1999). *The Post-Zionism Deate*. New York: Routledge.

Sprinzak, E. (1991). *The Ascendance of Israel's Radical Right*. Oxford: Oxford University Press.

Staub, M. (2004). *Torn at the Roots: The Crisis of Jewish Liberalism in Postwar America*. New York: Columbia University Press.

Sternhell, Z. (1998). *The Founding Myths of Israel* (David Maisel, Trans.). Princeton, NJ: Princeton University Press.

Teitelbaum, R. (1968). *Al Ha-Geulah ve 'al ha-Temurah*. Jerusalem Book Store.

Wolfe, R. (2008). Adorno's Critique of Hegel's Theodical Philosophy of History in *Negative Dialectics*. Retrieved from https://thecharnelhouse.org/2008/06/20/adornos-critique-of-hegels-philosophy-of-history-in-negative-dialectics/

Yakira, E. (2009). *Post-Zionism, Post Holocaust*. Cambridge: Cambridge University Press.

Yerushalmi, Y. H. (1982). *Zakhor: Jewish History and Jewish Memory*. Seattle: University of Washington Press.

Zertal, I. &, Eldar, A. (2004). *Lords of the Land: The War over Israel's Settlements in the Occupied Territories 1967–2007*. New York, NY: Nation Books.

Jewish Educators Don't Make Jews: A Sociological Reality Check About Jewish Identity Work

Tali Zelkowicz

Introduction

Those of us who work in or study liberal Jewish educational settings will likely have noticed a curious case of miscommunication between teachers and students. The teachers believe, and often are told, that their job is to form the students' Jewish identities for life. But they genuinely believe that this process of identity-formation is consistent with an attitude of openness and acceptance. In other words, they believe that their job is to make students Jewish, but not to make them into any particular kind of Jews. The students, on the other hand, do not experience the teachers' efforts in the way that they are intended. So Jewish educators are utterly baffled when, no matter how accepting of any theologies or Jewish practices, or how open they may be to any of their students' Jewish ideas or practices, students still claim that Jewish Studies classes infringe egregiously upon their freedoms, stifling their ability and right to become whom they want. One student even wrote an article in her high school newspaper about how Jewish Studies classes become an infringement of the First Amendment (Hyman, 2008, p. 166).

At the same time, many Jewish educators feel that if they were any more open-minded, "their brains would fall out," as one teacher at the same school put it. It seems that although students are being *told* they are permitted and invited to engage openly in Jewish identity-formation, they are not *experiencing* that permission or those invitations. On the contrary, they are experiencing their teachers' and schools' agendas and expectations for their life choices well beyond school, in college, marriage, and their own childrearing. For students, their experience of Jewish Studies, or more generally the Jewish educational mission of their schools, stands in stark contrast to, say, their experience of mathematics. Their math teacher simply wants her students to do their best with the material presented in that particular course, no lifelong strings attached.

There is something terribly askew in this Jewish educational teacher-student culture. This chapter argues that the all too common mutual agony between Jewish educators and their learners stems from, and is indicative of, a prevailing assumption that the central task of Jewish educators and Jewish education is to make Jews. In other words, the Jewish community is nourished by the very conviction that educators and the educational institutions that employ them can actually excavate or even manufacture something called "Jewish identity" for their learners, which I contend contributes significantly to the enervating power struggles prevalent across Jewish American educational cultures (for a classic example, see Schoem, 1989).

Even before entering a classroom, we hear the assumption proclaimed in the language used by Jewish leaders. Rabbis speak frequently about "creating Jewish identity in our young people."[1] Countless Jewish day schools and Jewish summer camps promise to "build [develop or foster] a solid Jewish identity" in their students.[2] Organizations, too, such as the American Jewish Joint Distribution Committee, claim that "positive Jewish identity is created for families and young children…"[3] From the schools and camps whose mission statements promise to *instill* Yiddishkeit or *build* Jewish identities, to the parents who send their children to those schools and are taught to collude with the belief, to the sociologists who strive to measure the impact of various forms of Jewish education upon "Jewish identity," to the funders whose investments bank on the assumption that Jewish identities can be produced in bulk, the fantasy is rarely questioned. It has become axiomatic that the purpose of Jewish educational projects and programs is to build Jewish identity, to make Jews Jewish, or to use my shorthand, to make Jews.

However, this ubiquitous belief is based on a delusion. Neither individuals nor institutions possess control over another's identity forming processes. That is not how education or identity formation works. In short, Jewish educators

---

1 http://blogs.rj.org/osrui/2014/07/08/creating-jewish-identity-at-camp/.

2 See http://www.nemjds.org/welcome.html, and http://www.chicagojewishdayschool. org/mission_vision.

3 See http://www.jdc.org/news/features/creating-jewish-identity-on.html.

don't make Jews; Jews make themselves Jews. The distinction, as I will strive to show, represents a deep paradigm shift in the way we think about both identity formation and the work of education. Drawing upon cultural studies theory and ethnographic research of identity and schooling, this chapter reframes identity formation as a form of situated sociocultural work, rather than a static product that can be shaped in others.

In order to provide concrete illustrations of the implications of this paradigm shift in educational practice, I open and close with two contrasting ethnographic descriptions; the first features an educator who teaches as if she can and must "make Jews" while the second depicts a rare instance of a teacher who believes he should not and cannot "make Jews." Between these two snapshots, I analyze the origins of the fantasy that educators can make Jews, and then discuss the two chief dangers—one theoretical and one political—of harboring the fantasy. Finally, if we take seriously the fact that Jewish educators do not make Jews, then we must clarify what it is that Jewish educators can do, realistically and productively. To this end, I conclude with an alternative purpose for Jewish educators, which focuses on facilitating genuine, ongoing Jewish identity work, as opposed to the engineering of people's Jewish futures.

Ultimately, I strive to show that educators can and should help learners to navigate among multiple and competing values and cultures. Whereas the project of making Jews or seeking to guarantee the survival of the Jewish people is not based in reality, serving as what I call professional *Jewish identity-work navigators* is sociologically and educationally feasible. It can also be mutually inspiring for educators and their learners. Consequently, and most importantly, it bears the potential to transform the unnecessary and exhausting battles over cultural reproduction that are too typical of contemporary Jewish education, into exciting, intergenerational, collaborative processes of creative Jewish American cultural straddling.

The Misery of Making Jews

As a backdrop for our examination of the role of educators and identity formation, I invite you into an all-too-typical eleventh-grade Jewish Studies class at a large Jewish community high school in the United States. In sharp contrast to the setting that we will visit at the end of this chapter, here we will see a culture where teacher and learners engage in an ongoing power struggle over who gets to determine the direction of the learning, and what ultimately matters. The class focuses on Jewish values through the study and translation of

Jewish legal texts from Hebrew to English, but reveals negligible opportunities for the students to engage in real, live, productive Jewish identity work.

Towards the beginning of this class, one of the students, Andy, does try to connect with the material that day which happened to be the role of rebuke ("*tochecha*") in Jewish tradition. Andy expresses a desire to wrestle with it but his passionate and dedicated Jewish Studies teacher, Sonya Klein, holds on tight to her Jewish content goals and immediately steers the discussion away from Andy's concerns:

> Andy: We're talking about this in a way that makes me feel like there's an easy way out. But I enjoy confrontation; maybe I was just raised that way. I enjoy arguing politics.
>
> Ms. Klein: But is that *tochecha*? That's not *tochecha*. *Tochecha* is telling someone they've behaved or done wrong in the world. So there's potential for us not to do it, because it takes a lot out of us. What did [classical medieval Jewish commentator] Ibn Ezra say about that?

Andy is expressing a genuine desire to engage, and his comment could be related easily to the topic at hand if the teacher were willing to listen to her learner's goals, in addition to her own.

Moreover, were Andy invited to probe, it would likely demonstrate that it is safe for others to do so, as well. Indeed, Andy is not the only one ready and willing to engage in rigorous exploration. The students do so freely and impressively in their daily secular General Studies classes. Jewish Studies teachers frequently miss, dismiss, or avoid these openings. In this case, Klein asserts her need to bring Andy and the class back to twelfth-century Spain and listen to the great Jewish medieval commentator Abraham Ibn Ezra, as opposed to first listening to twenty-first-century Andy, and later bringing Ibn Ezra's twelfth-century Spain to Andy and his classmates. The teacher's need to *cover* her material trumps the students' need to *uncover* it.[4] As such, teacher and students are locked in a mutually and continuously disappointing power struggle in which the teacher is not willing to engage in the students' cultural world, and the students grow resentful of entering their teachers'.

---

4 "Coverage" refers to the material that a teacher needs to present to students and "uncoverage" involves the unpacking, deconstructing, and internalizing that students need to experience in order to learn. Grant Wiggins and Jay McTighe coined the distinction in *Understanding By Design* (1998).

Klein then asks if *tochecha* is easy to give. The students know there is a right answer and drone out meek "no's." "Is it easy to give?" she repeats, raising her voice, indicating that their mumbling is unacceptable. A few sharper "no's" are dutifully uttered. The class proceeds with Klein doing most of the talking, and the students obediently offer their laconic, perfunctory responses. Klein proceeds with a class dominated by her telling as opposed to student asking. She asks for a volunteer to read the next Talmudic passage. A female student offers to read, but struggles with the initial word, stuttering "B-b-urur-" "Be*ruriah*," Klein rushes in with the correct pronunciation for the main character of the passage. Answering her own question, Klein asks, "Okay so what's going on? There's a lot going on," and proceeds to explain that the crux of the meaning lies in a careful reading of two Hebrew words which share the same root, *chotim* [sinners] versus *chata'im* [sins]. "We've discussed previously about 'sin' at the High Holidays, remember?" she asks, again rhetorically.

Didactically, Klein reminds them that, "Judaism considers us good people who do bad things," and then asks another leading question with a one-word right answer. "So, *chotim* and *chata'im* come from where—what do we need to look for?" A female student offers softly, "Proof-text?" "Bingo!" Sonya exclaims, in an exquisite example of IRE, the familiar and problematic pattern of Initiation (in which the teacher asks a question), Response (the student answers the teacher's question) and Evaluation (the teacher blesses the response as the correct one). But IRE classroom discourse communicates loud and clear to the students that the teacher sets the agenda, the teacher knows the answers, and the teacher determines the rightness of all answers. It is tailor-made for student alienation.

Sonya then tells the students that they need *Tanachim* [Hebrew Bibles] in order to check the full context of the proof text, in Psalms 104:35. She directs students to the back of the Hebrew Bible, where the Psalms are located. She asks for a volunteer to read it aloud. In a monotone English, a male student recites, "May sinners disappear from the earth and the wicked be no more. Bless Adonai, O my soul. Halleluya." In a moment very common to Jewish Studies classes, the teacher proceeds to demonstrate the philological move that the rabbis of the Talmud were making, between sinners versus sins, namely, that sins can and should be eradicated, but not sinners. Klein sermonizes, "So, as humans we do *Teshuvah* [repentance]." We are good people who do bad things. "We make mistakes. Hello! That's the whole purpose of *tochecha*, right? This proof text seems to work fairly well. It's not taken totally out of context, right?" Her questions are merely rhetorical, to punctuate her point.

Klein's unwavering commitment to her content could be viewed as heroic, especially if her students and their families are, as she believes, constantly at risk for Jewish apathy or even opting out of Jewish life altogether. She is so focused on her students' future Jewish identities and what their doubts and resistance today might mean years from now, she clings desperately to a "recipe" of a monolithic Jewish identity she believes her students need in order to survive as Jews in an open American culture she experiences as riddled with risks of assimilation. This future and fear-oriented focus can also be squarely self-defeating. Jon A. Levisohn (2010, p.12) provides us with two reasons to indict rigid adherence to educational recipes. First, Levisohn would say it is blinding Klein to the sociocultural reality of her learners, which is clear from her classroom. The second danger of sticking assiduously to recipes is not only that educators lose sight of their learners. It is that they actually distort the learners. Quoting Rosenzweig's 1920 essay "Towards a Renaissance of Jewish Learning," Levisohn warns us that, "all recipes produce caricatures of men, that become more ridiculous the more closely the recipes are followed."

In the final minutes of class, Klein concludes with an act of deferring student learning gratification. She tells them to "look at the characters of the passage and then it will all become clear," but then quickly counters, "Actually, it won't be clear until next class. This text takes a little time to get through," she explains. Remarkably, after plumbing the depths of texts in which students are not greatly invested to begin with, and after being told, rather than asked, about the significant points via a stream of rhetorical questions, now, moreover, the big juicy, meaningful "it" is postponed until further notice. In fact, it is not uncommon in Jewish Studies classes to hear teachers tell students that it will take days, weeks, or even until the end of the semester, to grasp the full import and meaning of a text. What a starkly different experience it must be for students in their biology class earlier that same day when they learned to do an oil immersion in order to see bacteria cells under a microscope, all within minutes.

Anxieties over Jewish Survival Impede Jewish Identity Work

Under the weight of such high-stakes extreme pressures to save and preserve the next generation of American Jews, even the best teachers can become insecure, didactic and moralizing. Stepping into Klein's classroom in this way provides us with nuanced understanding about how and even why teachers—even strong pedagogues with great intentions—can become fixated on coverage at the expense of its lack, perpetuating an overwhelmingly *teacher and content-*centered approach to Jewish identity formation. My argument is not ultimately about pedagogy, but rather how assumptions about identity formation tend to promote certain kind of pedagogic practice. Of course, starving their students intellectually or emotionally is not part of this teacher's or any school's intended goals. However, how the Jewish Studies department interprets a goal of the school that *is* explicit in their Assessment Standards, demonstrates how static constructs of "Jewish identity" as something that can be seized upon and guaranteed can distort otherwise sound pedagogical goals. Take, for example, their goal to help students become "self-directed and lifelong learners." Jewish Studies teachers at Zerin invariably interpret that to mean the future Jewish choices students make in their lives after graduation and beyond. In an honest sharing of panic at a faculty meeting, one Jewish Studies teacher needed the future to be read to him so that he could be consoled definitively that he was, in fact, making Jews. Almost confessionally, he exclaimed, "Do we know that it's happening? That's like my main goal in life, I just want to make sure it's happening!" Here is the future-oriented, survivalist driven goal in action, ablaze with urgency, tormenting the Jewish Studies department and haunting their Jewish identity-building mission Zerin to the school with unrealistic and unattainable guarantees about students' *future* Jewish choices and behaviors.

Many Jewish Studies teachers inadvertently create classroom cultures where what matters most is what students will do with the learning one, five, or 25 years into the future, and not what it means to them in the present, this week, this day, and this class. Consequently, the focus in Jewish Studies classes shifts, tacitly and explicitly, to what happens later in life, as opposed to what tools and experiences students have here, and now. Jewish educators frequently view each student as if s/he is carrying the weight of the Jewish future, while simultaneously failing to entrust them with the tradition or genuine Jewish identity work. In this way, the fantasy that educators can make Jews is largely rooted in widespread communal fears and anxieties about the survival of the Jewish people.

As such, a significant part of the fantasy seems to stem from a stance of fear. Although Jewish educators tend to treat their subject matter of God, Jewish ethics, morals, values, the Holocaust, Israel, sacred texts, and the Torah scroll itself with respect, they also relate to their Jewish content with considerable apprehension. Jewish educators are plagued by the constant fear that students will reject the Jewish identities they believe it is their sole job to provide, and not only for that class, but for the rest of their students' lives. Unfortunately, this is frequently what it means when people declare that Jewish identity education "works."

For example, in a moment of candid reflection upon her own Jewish education and identity formation, Head of School Helen Shapiro framed what "works" in these blunt terms:

> I grew up going to synagogue, *davening* ["daven" is Yiddish for "pray"], and even led a children's minyan, but did I even *know* what the prayers meant! But I stayed Jewish, but my brother and sister didn't. They both married non-Jews. So it worked for me, and not for them.

When Jewish education works, it means that Jews "stay Jewish," not just throughout school but even more importantly, afterwards. Never mind that all of our data indicate that Jews in North America, of all ages, whether they are educated Jewishly or not, whether they are married to other Jews or not, whether they engage in Jewish practices or not, actually report that they are happy and proud to be Jewish in astonishingly high numbers. When Jewish educational success is framed in terms of whom the learners choose to become *after* their schooling, teachers and communal leaders come to believe that their task must be to produce Jewish identities.

To be sure, the idea that Jewish educators and the apparatus of Jewish education could make Jews and ultimately save them from intermarriage, assimilation, and declining birth rates, is comforting.[5] After all, it is not clear whence other interventions could come if not from educators. Imagining that educators can make and save Jews is an understandable coping mechanism in the climate of the last seven decades of Jewish communal life.[6] Lay decision-makers, professionals, policy makers and funders, alike, look to American Jewish education to be, as Jonathan Woocher has put it, "the guarantor of Jewish survival" (foreword to Reimer, 1997, p.xi). The implication is that "strong" and

---

5 Until recent years, the master narrative of Jewish American identity research has consisted of a pervasive survivalism (for example, see Barack Fishman, 1993; Cohen, 1988; Cohen, 1991; Heilman, 1995; Himmelfarb, 1980; Liebman, 1973; Liebman, 2001; Liebman 1987; Schoem, 1989; Shrage, 1992; Sklare & Greenblum, 1967; Sklare, 1993; Tobin, 1999).

6 Numerous new pressures have emerged with Jewish life in America. First, historically, Jews in the modern period developed strategies that ultimately strove to render Jewish and American cultures utterly complementary and compatible. American Jewish historians refer to this cultural strategy of navigating American and Jewish identities as the "cult of synthesis" (Sarna, 1999; Sorin, 1997). Add to this cult of synthesis, the major shift away from the millennia-old classical approach to Jewish education of enculturation, to instruction, which meant Jewish education was no longer primarily the purview of the home but was now "outsourced" to schools (Sarna, 1998).

"meaningful" Jewish identities will secure the survival and continuity of the Jewish people in America.

However, the flipside to the premise that Jewish education has salvational potential, is that it can equally become the enemy:

> [T]here is also evidence of an abiding dissatisfaction and discomfort with the Jewish education that many American Jews actually encounter. If Jewish education now benefits from the conviction that it is American Jewry's last, best bulwark against assimilation, it also suffers from a widespread perception of failure and mediocrity (Reimer, p. xii).

Accordingly, contemporary American Jewish communities have engaged with Jewish education in ambivalent ways. Jewish education is held up as the great hope of communal, religious, spiritual transformation and renewal, very much as education in America in general is treated as a potent lever for social change. Both educational enterprises—Jewish and American—are similarly blamed when they fail to deliver on those grandiose expectations. With stakes that could not be higher, it should come as no surprise that there is resistance to questioning assumptions about the potential of teachers and institutions with regard to Jewish identity-building.

Identity as an Activity, not a State

Making Jews and saving Jewry are hefty burdens, which are exhausting and even impossible to carry. With these very long-term goals in focus, Jewish identity is treated as if it were an object that could somehow be manufactured and delivered to the future, rather than a dynamic and ongoing activity, full of human unpredictability and variability. Ironically, these great anxieties about American Jewish survival serve to limit rather than to foster the bold, adventurous spirit of Jewish living that most Jewish educators yearn to ignite in their students. Specifically, the fantasy of making Jews proves to be counterproductive to the goal of a durable and healthy Jewish future in America in two major ways. The first is theoretical, while the second is political, but both are equally detrimental.

First, the theoretical issue. Most people are willing to acknowledge, on reflection, that identity formation is not a simple prospect. Identities are not systematically and externally imposed. To assume so would require us to think of "identity" as a sort of static object or product, or a *thing* that one person somehow installs, like an app, "into" another person. Jewish identity formation involves the work required to navigate the cultural straddling for Jews in any host nation of an inherently unstable process of always *becoming* Jewish.

The instability of Jewish identity work is twofold. First, it involves confronting what American Jewish historian Jonathan Sarna called, "the most fundamental question of American Jewish life," namely, "how to live in two worlds at once, how to be both American and Jewish, part of the larger American society and apart from it" (Sarna, 1998, pp. 9–10). Add to this the additional challenge that the Jewish part of this bicultural dance is "marked," or bears lower status, because it differs from the dominant (American) norm. As an "unmarked" and naturalized norm, American identity formation enjoys a more pervasive and invisible power (Bucholtz and Hall, 2004, p. 372). The identity work required to navigate this acute Jewish American identity forming dilemma alone, is sufficient for making Jewish identity an unpredictable, shifting, and iterative process. Ironically, in their anxious pursuit of ensuring ultimate Jewish survival, Jewish leaders often fail to address the dilemma directly, even though (or perhaps because) they, themselves, also face it regularly.

However, there is a second, even more neglected aspect of identity theory that contributes to the instability of Jewish identity work: all identities are intrinsically unstable. This component of identity theory has received even less attention from Jewish educational leaders. Identities are unstable because they are "socially situated action" (Bucholtz and Hall, 2004, p. 376). Indeed, it is more accurate to talk about identities as attributes of situations rather than of individuals or groups. Identities are what we do, what we enact or perform, in a particular situation. Moreover, they are "interactionally negotiated," and people must work to "shift and recombine to meet new circumstances" (p. 376). But if, to use a phrase from Bucholtz and Hall, "identity inheres in actions" rather than in people, then it is hard to see how identity could be somehow doled out in advance by educators. Although identity is a noun that allows us to speak about it as a thing, sociologically speaking it is an active and iterative process, the product of constant cultural work.

Cultural studies theorists Siebren Miedema and Willem Wardekker (1999) illustrate this distinction best when they describe identity as an *activity* (p. 76).[7] Underscoring the role of flux, they invoke a metaphor from theater

---

7 For just a few of the numerous other scholars who theorize identity as an activity, see for example: Côté & Levine, 2002; Elder, 1985; Gergen, 2000; Giele & Elder, 1998; K. Hall, 2002; S. Hall, 1992; Swidler, 1986.

and argue that "[i]dentity presupposes distance from the self, and being able to handle different, mutually inconsistent roles. The individual in contemporary society must learn not to play a role, but to play *with* roles" (p. 76, emphasis in original). Further underscoring the fluidity inherent in identity formation, they argue that individual identity is,

> ... created again and again, for a short period, in a specific situation, and before a specific public. *Identity is not a given, but an activity, the result of which is always only a local stability...* If we are to understand identity in a different way, we also need a new theory of the development of identity (1999, p.79, emphasis in original).

New theories of identity are precisely what recent decades of cultural studies scholars have begun to offer us. In her ethnography *Shades of White: White Kids and Racial Identities in High School* (2002), Pamela Perry demonstrates that "race, culture, and identity are not static, immutable *things*, but are social *processes* that are created and recreated by people in their daily lives and social interactions" (Perry, 2002, p. 3, emphasis in original). Similarly, leading cultural studies scholar Stuart Hall (1996) emphasizes the need to treat identities as moving targets, and describes them as "points of temporary attachment to the subject positions which discursive practices construct for us" (p. 6). Hall contends that, "the concept of identity does not signal a stable core of the self" (p. 3).

For Jews worried about prospects of survival on American soil, this can be the most disturbing reality of all to face. This is the very stability they long for, since, with it, one Jewish identity can become the product, par excellence, that Jewish education is expected to able to deliver—to parents, community, and, ultimately, to the future. Conversely, to surrender the fantasy is to surrender the notion that Jews are products to be manufactured, and embrace them as the ever-emergent processes that they are.

So what options do we have? One option is to stop talking about Jewish identity and instead to talk about "Jewishness," a term used widely in popular and scholarly Jewish contexts. But insofar as "Jewishness" too connotes a static essence located within—or instilled within—a person, it doesn't help us. Another option is to use the gerund "identifying," as Bekerman and Rosenfeld (2011) do, in order to foreground the fluidity and contextuality of identity formation. It seems unlikely that we will be able to shake the persistent fantasy that we can make identity and hold it still, simply by jettisoning words like "identity" from our usage altogether, or by placing them in quotation marks to use them ironically. Instead, in an effort to help conjure an emergent and fluid process, I prefer the phrase *Jewish identity work*.[8]

To conclude this treatment of the theoretical ways in which the fantasy of making Jews proves to be counterproductive to the goal of a durable and healthy Jewish future in America, we might consider a way of talking about identity that sounds dramatically different than the typical way we talk about identity in the Jewish community. Identity, writes Hall (1990), is

> a matter of "becoming" as well as "being." It belongs to the future as much as to the past. It is not something which already exists, transcending place, time, history, and culture. Identities come from somewhere, have histories. But, like everything which is historical, they undergo constant transformation. Far from being eternally fixed in some essentialized past, they are subject to the continuous "play" of history, culture and power. Far from being grounded in a mere "recovery" of the past, which is waiting to be found, and which, when found, will secure our sense of ourselves into eternity, identities are the names we give to the different ways we are positioned by, and position ourselves within, the narratives of the past (p. 225).

This way of thinking about identity challenges us to relinquish a most cherished goal: to "secure a sense of ourselves into eternity." Frantic attempts to do so seem to achieve the opposite, actually limiting the ways Jewish educators can help Jews to manage a host of multiple values, images, symbols, and choices, as Jews, in America. Surviving, and even thriving, will come instead from focusing our creative energies on helping Jews to navigate their ways through the turbulent waters of history, culture, and power in their lives, not from trying to determine where those journeys should lead. This shift would orient the purpose of Jewish educators away from being producers of identity, toward facilitating identity-work.

Identity Work and the Politics of Authenticity

The second way in which the fantasy of making Jews proves to be counterproductive to the goal of a durable and healthy Jewish future in America involves the political question of who gets to determine what

---

8 Bucholtz & Hall (2004, p. 375) also acknowledge the problems of the term "identity" and its study, and recommend better theorizing in favor of eliminating the term.

counts as authentically Jewish. The new limitation here, of the fantasy that educators can make Jews, is that Jewish identities are treated not only as products, but *essentialized* products. Consequently, they are rife with charged investments over what count as the "right" components for the product. Passions surrounding this political contest for the "right" kind of Jew run high particularly in today's climate of austere scarcity (not only in terms of material resources, but also in terms of time and of actual numbers of Jews). For whichever identity "recipe" one favors affects how one teaches, leads, and ultimately informs one's definition of success. Indeed, the ideological debate over what counts as legitimately Jewish and most generative underlies much of the Jewish educational (and, arguably, the modern Jewish social scientific) enterprise.

Even if Vincent Cheng, author of *Inauthentic: The Anxiety Over Culture and Identity* (2004), is correct, and this pursuit of "copyrights" over identity serves as a way for individuals and groups to cope with "anxiety about losing cultural authenticity, subjectivity, distinctiveness," (p. 6), it is not a productive coping mechanism. Thus these politics of authenticity demonstrate just how high—life or death—the stakes are perceived to be in contemporary Jewish American communal discourse. Indeed, Cheng argues that it is a symptom of insecurity (p. 86). The quest for copyrights of one identity authenticity or another, like the belief that educators can and should make Jews, stems from what he calls "cultural nostalgia," or a longing for an "originally native difference, that once was, or maybe never was, but is imagined" (p. 117). If we can manage our fears and anxieties, however, there are ways of orienting the work of Jewish education away from such imaginary outcomes, and towards curricular and pedagogical choices that are grounded in real lived processes.

To be clear, the limiting problem is *not* that different people hold different criteria regarding what constitute good, legitimate, authentic, and ultimately generative Jews. As long as Jewish Americans exhibit diversity of practice, community, and ideology, these differing criteria will always exist. Rather, the trouble emerges when we fail to acknowledge how we are all subject to the same contextual positionality; everyone engages in identity work in the same socially situated ways. To claim that some of these ways are better than others is an ideological not an empirical claim. Ideologies, as sets of values, are important but they are often confused with facts. Academics and professionals collude with the resulting authenticity power politics that, in turn, yield unexamined competitions over who gets to deem which versions of Jewish identity count as authoritative.

The contours of two broad ideological camps, each with its own valid impulses and logic, can be outlined as follows: although few people are pure versions of either stance, social scientific literature variously refers to one of these groups as "survivalists," or sometimes "traditionalists," and the other group is consistently referred to as "transformationists." "Survivalism" (and traditionalism) can be defined as a stance based on a philosophical concern over standards of authenticity, in an effort to establish a normative definition of qualitative Jewish identity, and/or a quantitative concern over maintaining sufficient numbers of Jews. Both concerns are driven by a desire to guarantee the viability of Jewish life in America. Survivalists/traditionalists tend to experience changes in Jewish life as loss.

"Transformationism," conversely, is a stance based on a neutral or positive role for change, where change need not be loss, and can be experienced even as gain. Although not all changes may be good or useful, for transformationists, change is normalized. Transformationists tend to have few prescriptions for what count as ideal Jewish identities, while traditionalists tend to be invested in one or another set of criteria for Jewish authenticity. Both stances bear indispensable ways of thinking and acting for Jewish educators. Traditionalist orientations emphasize the importance of boundary *keeping*, while transformationists could teach the significance of responsible boundary *breaking*. The first stance helps educators to exercise their leadership in cultural authority, while the latter supports their leadership in cultural fluidity.

Rarely, if ever, however, are these stances presented in a balanced way. To traditionalists, transformationists lack investment and commitment in received Jewish tradition, and they are viewed as irresponsible or naïve about prospects for Jewish continuity. To transformationists, traditionalists appear nostalgic for obsolete times and emerge as the specious group, with distorted essentialist claims and visions. The position-oriented battles result in highly polarizing either-or contests for Jewish authenticity. Consider, for example, this exchange between transformationist Shaul Magid and traditionalists Steven M. Cohen and Jack Wertheimer. Presenting a classic transformationist stance, Magid proclaims that change is inevitable, and without anxiety, declares that there will simply be a new type of Jew,

> [In post-ethnic America] Jewishness, Judaism, and the Jewish people . . . may "disappear" according to a previous paradigm, but the Jew will survive—a new Jew, a figure who not only participates in the larger society, but is integrally, and even biologically, a part of it. Like Israelis,

these new Jews will foster a new sense of self. It will just be a different Jewish self. (Magid, 2011, p. 4)

Cohen and Wertheimer sound the survivalist alarm and argue that these post-ethnic changes are far from neutral and will actually compromise the quality of Jewish life, and counter that,

> Post-ethnic Judaism ... puts us at risk of abandoning a critical aspect of our "thick" Jewish culture, our obligation and familial ties to the Jewish people in Israel and around the world—in effect, trading our Jewish birthright for a thin gruel. (Cohen & Wertheimer, 2011, p. 6)

The point here is not whether Magid or Cohen/Wertheimer are correct, but rather, that the debate between traditionalists and transformationists is alive and well, and typically framed in either/or terms. Indeed, the successful Jewish educator must know how to draw from both traditionalist and transformationist stances, and develop keen judgment and strategies for how to integrate components from both impulses, at various times, under various conditions. Both camps bear great merits, but neither one of them holds the whole truth for Jewish educators. We cannot simply stick our heads in the sand as the survivalists do, insisting that we should keep doing what we're doing and teaching what we're teaching. And, we cannot simply celebrate whatever is new and different. This is why we need to find ways to talk about *how*, as individuals and as communities, we draw and re-draw boundaries, shifting the focus of the debate away from the question of whose prescriptions are the most "authentic," and invest more time and energy examining the underlying principles for these prescriptions. Most counterproductively, disregarding positionality denies Jewish educators the powerful opportunities they need and deserve in order to sophisticate a role I would like to argue they can and should assume: *boundary navigators*.

A Realistic and Productive Role for Jewish Educators

Although I agree with sociologist of modern Jewry Charles Liebman who once said that it is absurd to claim that there are as many Judaisms as there are Jews (Liebman, 2001), I do not think it is absurd to maintain that there are as many ways to *navigate* Jewish identity work as there are Jews. This is consistent with educational scholar Jerome Bruner's nuanced claim that a system of education "must help those growing up in a culture to find *strategies*" for engaging in identity work within that culture (Bruner, 1997, p. 42, emphasis added). Bruner knows that educators cannot do their learners' identity work for them, and assigns them at once a more realistic and a more powerful role: to help learners develop tools and strategies they need to engage in their own work of becoming Jews. When Jewish identity is treated as an activity, and Jewish leaders are ready and able to discuss openly the genesis and foundation for their various prescriptions of Jewish identity, Jewish educators can be freed to do this most important work of helping to develop strategies, rather than trying to make Jews.

Determined to live in two worlds at once, to be both American and Jewish, requires complex identity work that features an array of boundary navigations. Jews of all kinds regularly face dilemmas of differentiation (when, how, and to what extent to be apart from mainstream American society) and synthesis (when, how, and to what extent to be a part of it). They need to find strategies for deciding when and how to be selective and permeable, integrating American culture under some conditions, while filtering it out under others. This is tricky, and proves especially frustrating without the cultural tools and strategies to navigate the situation productively.

Contemporary American Jews of all ages need their educators to be models of Jewish identity-work navigators. They do not need their educators to tell them whom to become. As such, they must let go of the urge to want or expect to make Jews and control the outcomes of their students' Jewish futures, while holding on, closely and carefully, to the students' processes of grappling with Jewish subject matter and its methods. So far, most Jewish educators seem to struggle with making this trade-off effectively. This is not surprising since few schools of education seek to prepare their graduates for this role. However, the second ethnographic account of instructor Carl Silver's eleventh-grade Jewish studies classroom culture provides one vivid illustration of Jewish educator-as-navigator.

Navigating Identity-Work

Unlike his colleague Sonya Klein, Silver is not focused on the Jews his students could or should become, but on the tools they are developing for meaning making and boundary navigating, on that day and in that moment. To this end, Silver opens class with a bold dilemma, stemming from a rabbinic midrash, positing that Jewish tradition should be rejected on grounds that it robs us of free will,[9] and he asks the students how they and the rabbinic sages might recover from such an allegation, *if at all*. This question of whether Jewish tradition will be redeemed from the sharp allegation that it robs Jews of free will is neither rhetorical nor a trick. The students know it is acceptable for them not to redeem the tradition. Silver's invitation to "unpack the text" is genuine and elicits equally genuine responses. One student asserts, "It means that it is supposed to be our choice whether we accept the Torah. And it could, in extreme, lead us to change our minds over whether we want to follow Torah anymore." One student, Oren, like Andy in Ms. Klein's class, is contrary and strident. But in Silver's identity-forming culture, Oren has full range of expression. He contends that the rabbis' language is directly related to the question of free will and asserts that "God is forcing us," adding, "If the Torah is a contract, even if the rabbis believed it, *which I don't*, in modern times, I think we perfectly deserve to make such a declaration now." Silver is entirely unfazed by Oren's renouncing of Torah and, following that lead inquires, "So is there anything wrong with an authority forcing someone to do something like this?"

A range of energetic responses erupts from the class. "Not if it's for a life and death issue! Then the rules are all thrown out!" "But this isn't about crossing the street!" "But then, later on, they won't accept it!" "So once there's no mountain being held over their heads to threaten them, then what!" "At one point, they're going to need to learn from their mistakes." Thus, the students make a resounding case against forcing someone to accept something, even if it seems to be for one's own health and welfare. Silver then brings the text even closer to home, telling them, "You know, all this makes me think of a parent who once said, 'I'm ready to send my kid by forcing them.'"

Reflecting on this loaded example enables a student to conclude, "I find that the most efficient means are *not* the best." "For example," she continues, "torture might be efficient but then the 'acceptance' is not accurate. And that's maybe why they rebel against it later." Silver is delighted and announces gleefully, "This one goes in the book!" actually writing the comment down in a notebook. In Silver's Jewish identity-work culture, it is acceptable to compare Jewish education to torture and allow the students to recognize themselves in the ones who "rebel against it later." Silver even does his best to help them

---

9 Based on their reading of the biblical account, the rabbis of this midrash (Babylonian Talmud, Shabbat 88a) allege that Torah, all the teachings and laws, had been given at Sinai coercively, like a contract accepted by someone who was forced to sign under duress. The midrash objects to this, protesting that all of Torah could therefore be null and void, because it was not received of the people's own free will.

articulate these thoughts and feelings, without any concerns about where these sentiments may lead, now or later in their lives. Each class is treated as but one class, on one day, and not any indication of the sum total of students' thoughts even throughout that week, month or year, much less a sign of what choices they might make in college, in marriage, or in child-rearing. They permit students, and teachers too, to learn and grow in the moment, and for the moment, making choices for today, rather than anxiously projecting both teacher and students into a future that somehow matters much more.

At this point, Silver decides the students are curious enough to hear how the rabbis recover from the objection. Tracing the rabbis' thinking, Silver indicates that the clue they use lies in the use of the Biblical word pair *"kimu v' kiblu,"* "established and accepted." While these words may *appear* to be associated with coercion in the Exodus context, the rabbis search for an additional instance in the Hebrew bible when that same word pair is *not* associated with coercion or duress, which they find all the way in the Book of Esther, clear at the other end of the Hebrew Bible.

"It's always wrong! Do they ever get it right!?" Oren cries out in contempt. "The rabbis always bring some proof text, and never get it right," he continues. Oren takes issue with the rabbis' ahistorical decontextualization, and this Esther proof text becomes just another egregious example. Finally, almost threateningly, he asserts, "There better be another argument. That's all I have to say." He concludes in a poetic rage, now indicting the teacher, "You say the Torah is pregnant with meaning, but it can't be twins!" Upon hearing this, a flurry of debate ensues among the students about the context of the passage, arguing whether it was or was not coercive.

Even though Oren has renounced Torah and rabbinic methodology, the heart of Jewish tradition, Silver does not worry he is at risk for rejecting his Judaism. The truth is, he may or may not be. But losing him is simply not what is important or relevant at that teaching moment. What is at stake is how, in what spaces, with what tools, with what peer culture, and with what adult models, Oren navigates these and any other dilemmas in his Jewish identity work.

Meanwhile, Silver has not said anything. Silver does not have to because Oren is engaged by his peers. "Well," a quiet student begins thoughtfully, "when you're forced into something, like writing a paper or doing research in the library, after a while you can come to appreciate it." Another boy adds a sardonic retort, "or like an arranged marriage!" "But," Oren maintains, "it's not Torah." Finally, with time running out of class, a female student, in a very *midrashic* move of her own, uses the context of the holiday of Purim (when the Book of Esther is read), to wonder aloud, "But isn't Purim about accepting your identity as a Jew?" Rather than needing to literally say that Esther is part of Exodus, she suggests a thematic link. She posits that in the same way that Purim is a story about Jews accepting their identity, maybe so was the moment of revelation at Sinai an act of the Israelites accepting their separate, particularistic identity among the nations. Silver's students are comfortable with differentiated opinions and many of them are interested in exploring ways of redeeming Jewish tradition. Another female student got the final word for that day, suggesting, "The interconnection is only felt once you make it your own. We have to build it up for ourselves, because culture and traditions are passed down by us, it's not just what God forces on us."

While Silver may have had a sense of how these conversations might unfold, he had no guarantees that anyone in the class would make a move to redeem the tradition. He only knew that the risks he took were aligned with his largest goal of allowing his students to wrestle with Jewish tradition in their current moment, and not for some future purpose. To be sure, Silver's pedagogic moves are consistent with a progressive pedagogy of inquiry, in which the teacher plays the role of facilitating good questions and the shared effort to answer those questions, rather than transmitting information on his own. But what we see in this classroom is not only about pedagogy. Had Silver been oriented by a belief that his job is to make these kids Jews (urgently and forever), he would have been locked in an enervating power struggle based on an illusory goal. Although he of course has educational goals—skills, knowledge, values—that become the cultural tools his learners need to develop their own identity strategies, he is not desperate to make his students into anything. He leaves that job to them. If there is any urgency for Silver, it is to provide his students with the opportunity to get close enough to the tradition, and interact with it rigorously, dynamically and freely, that they might genuinely come to call it their own.

From listening carefully to his students over the years, Silver has learned that they feel as if they are being indoctrinated rather than educated in Jewish Studies. He knows they cite the First Amendment and he takes that claim very seriously. According to Silver, what the students seem to be railing against is "years of us telling them what to think. And it takes a while for students to arrive at this articulation because they're so pissed off about what they've had, that it's hard for them to look back." It has taken time, but Silver says he has learned to let go of their Jewish identity destinations, realizing that even if they were possible to control, nothing positive could come from that. Instead, Silver holds on carefully and lovingly to his role as a navigational guide who provides tools and strategies that his students need in order to engage in their own genuine and rigorous Jewish identity work.

Conclusion

Not only parents, but educators and many stakeholders in Jewish education will need successful role models like Carl Silver as well as support from respected leaders and institutions if they are to make the shift from expecting Jewish educators to make Jews, towards regarding Jewish educators as the valuable cultural navigators they can be. The situation is very different for secular studies teachers. Math teachers, for example, have the perceived luxury of teaching students without needing to make them into them math people. They are not responsible for cultivating math identities that will be strong enough to motivate them to date other math students, join math clubs in college, marry a mathematician, and ultimately raise good little mathematicians. While this may sound absurd in the context of math, Jewish educators and many others can say it all very seriously about their hopes for their students' Jewish identities.

To paraphrase the American philosopher of education John Dewey, education is not preparation for some future life; it is life itself.[10] So, too, is Jewish identity work an end in itself and not only a means to a larger future oriented purpose. As one of the coeditors of this volume put it, "[f]ocusing on the student as a future product distracts us from attention to the infinite value of the moment of encounter in the present" (Levisohn, 2005, p. 323). It is his attention to that infinite value of the moment of encounter that Carl Silver has turned into an art as he helps his learners to navigate their Jewish American questions, dilemmas, and struggles. But it will take discipline to relinquish Jews' most cherished treasure, the future.

Peter Kent, the non-Jewish principal, expresses a minority voice when he seeks to help parents release their impossible grip on the future. He imagines that,

---

10 I am grateful to Jon Levisohn's (2014) article "Should Jewish Day Schools Aspire to Create Educated Jews?" where he cites Dewey's adage in response to the highly utilitarian framing of Jewish youth education as a race to make children into adults.

people would come to school with an appreciation of the place they're at, and be in that place in the moment in time they're at, as opposed to thinking they are in control of their future, of every aspect of their future existence. What they control is the here and now, and this alone. I would call it insecurity. We have "paranoid parents." Well, not paranoid, but with a fear that their children won't be successful, that they won't carry on Jewish culture. (Hyman, 2008, p. 260)

Letting go in this way can feel like a massive and irresponsible risk. However, if we are to remain grounded in what is realistically possible when it comes to identity formation, trusting learners' own processes may be the only way to ensure that desperately sought after survival of the Jewish people.

In fact, survival actually depends on taking such risks. As Bruner avows,

education that emphasizes the powers of consciousness, reflection, breadth of dialogue, and negotiation all pose risks by opening discussion of currently institutionalized authority. And they are risky. Education *is* risky, for it fuels the sense of possibility. But a failure to equip minds with the skills for understanding and feeling and acting in the cultural world is not simply scoring a pedagogical zero. It risks creating alienation, defiance, and practical incompetence. And all of these undermine the viability of a culture (Bruner, 1996, pp. 42–43).

As if speaking directly to those invested in Jewish education, Bruner warns us that failing to take the risks necessary to permit learners to engage in genuine and rigorous exploration of Jewish boundaries and meaning making is riskiest of all, since Jewish culture becomes less, not more viable.

We still live in a world where Jewish education is very much expected to make Jews of one kind or another. To be sure, this has been a chief and weighty fantasy. But precisely when the concern is Jewish continuity, I argue that it is no longer productive, if ever it was. The unhealthy, adversarial relationships that so many Jews have with Jewish education stems from misguided expectations of educators and educational systems. Jewish education and educators, specifically, are capable of many wonderful things; guaranteeing Jewish survival is not one of them. Making Jews is not one of them. That so many thoughtful leaders cling to this imaginary outcome for Jewish education reflects the intensity of survivalist anxieties. Still, countless Jewish national organizations, philanthropic foundations, academics of Jewish life, communal leaders, and educators across the Jewish denominational spectrum not only believe in this cause and effect relationship, they bank on it. They treat Jewish education as a device, or independent variable, for making and saving Jews. But this is simply not how education, or identity formation, work. Jewish education is not for making Jews, but it *can* be for navigating the invaluable and necessary work that each Jew must undertake in order to be—and continue becoming—Jewish.

Bibliography

Barack Fishman, Sylvia, & Goldstein, Alice. (1993). *When They Are Grown They Will Not Depart: Jewish Education and the Jewish Behavior of American Adults.* Retrieved from *Stanford Berman Jewish Policy Archive* website: https://www.bjpa.org/search-results/publication/2896.

Bekerman, Zvi, & Sue Rosenfeld. (2011). Measuring Jews in Motion. *Journal of Jewish Education* 77(3), 196–215.

Bucholtz, Mary, & Hall, Kira. (2004). Language and Identity. In Alessandro Duranti (Ed.), *A Companion to Linguistic* Anthropology (pp. 369–394). Oxford: Blackwell.

Bruner, Jerome. (1997). *The Culture of Education.* Cambridge, MA: Harvard University Press.

Charmé, Stuart. (Winter 2000). Varieties of Authenticity in Contemporary Jewish Identity. *Jewish Social Studies* 6(2), 133–155.

Charmé, Stuart, & Zelkowicz, Tali. (2011). Jewish Identities: Education for Multiple and Moving Targets. In Helena Miller, Lisa D. Grant, & Alex Pompson (Eds.), *International Handbook of Jewish Education* (pp. 163–181). New York: Springer.

Cheng, Vincent. (2004). *Inauthentic: The Anxiety Over Culture and Identity.* New Brunswick, NJ: Rutgers University Press.

Cohen, Steven M., & Levitt, Joy. (April 2015). If You Marry a Jew, You're One of Us. Retrieved from *Jewish Telegraphic Agency* website: https://www.jta.org/2015/04/02/news-opinion/opinion/op-ed-if-you-marry-a-jew-youre-one-of-us.

Cohen, Steven M., & Wertheimer, Jack. (2011). What Is So Great about "Post-Ethnic Judaism?" Retreived from *Shma: A Journal of Jewish Responsibility* website: http://shma.com/2011/03/what-is-so-great-about-post-ethnic-judaism/.

Cohen, Steven M. (1987). The Quality of American Jewish Life: Better or Worse? *Jewish Sociology.* New York: American Jewish Committee, 23–49.

Elder, Glen H. (1996). Introduction: Who Needs Identity? In Stuart Hall & Paul du Gay (Eds.), *Questions of Cultural Identity.* London: Sage.

Elder, Glen H., Kirkpatrick Johnson, Monica, & Crosnoe, Robert. (2003). *The Emergence and Development of Life Course Theory.* New York, NY: Springer.

Hall, Stuart. (1990). Cultural Identity and Diaspora. In Jonathan Rutherford (Ed.), *Identity: Community, Culture, Difference* (222–237). London: Lawrence and Wishart.

Horowitz, Bethamie (2002). Reframing the Study of Contemporary American Jewish Identity. *Contemporary Jewry 23*, 14–31.

Hyman, Tali E. (2008). *The Liberal Jewish Day School as Laboratory for Dissonance in American Jewish Identity-Formation* (Unpublished doctoral dissertation). New York University, New York.

Levisohn, Jon A. (2010). Should Jewish Day Schools Aspire to Create Educated Jews? Retrieved from *Prizmah* website: https://prizmah.org/should-jewish-day-schools-aspire-create-educated-jews.

Levisohn, Jon A. (2005). Extending the Conversation on "Visions of Jewish Education": The Danger of Recipes. *Journal of Jewish Education 71*, 319–323.

Liebman, Charles S. (1987). The Quality of American Jewish Life: A Grim Outlook. Retrieved from *Policy Archive* website: www.policyarchive.org/handle/10207/10908.

Liebman, Charles S. (2001). Some Research Proposals for the Study of American Jews. *Contemporary Jewry 22*(1), 99–114.

Magid, Shaul. (2011). Be the Jew You Make: Jews, Judaism, and Jewishness in Post-Ethnic America. *Shma: A Journal of Jewish Responsibility 41*(678), 3–4.

Prell, Riv-Ellen. (2000). Developmental Judaism: Challenging the Study of American Jewish Identity in the Social Sciences. *Contemporary Jewry 21*(1), 33–54.

Sarna, Jonathan D. (1998). American Jewish Education in Historical Perspective. *Journal of Jewish Education 64*(1/2), 8–21.

Sarna, Jonathan D. (Fall 98/Winter 99). The Cult of Synthesis in American Jewish Culture. *Jewish Social Studies 5*(1/2), 52–79.

Schoem, David. (1989). *Ethnic Survival in America: An Ethnography of a Jewish Afternoon School.* Atlanta: Scholars Press.

Shrage, Barry. (1992). Jewish Continuity—Will Our Grandchildren Be Jewish? A Communal Response to the Challenges of the 1990 CJF National Jewish Populations Survey: Toward a Jewish Life Worth Living. *Journal of Jewish Communal Service 69*(4), 321–330.

Sklare, Marshall, & Greenblum, Joseph. (1967). *Jewish Identity on the Suburban Frontier: A Study of Group Survival in the Open Society.* New York: Basic Books.

Woocher, Jonathan S. (1985). Sacred Survival: American Jewry's Civil Religion. *Judaism 34*(1), 151–162.

Zelkowicz, Tali. (2013). Beyond a Humpty-Dumpty Narrative: In Search of New Rhymes and Reasons in the Research of Contemporary American Jewish Identity Formation. *International Journal of Jewish Education Research 5/6*, 21–46.

Beyond Language Proficiency: Fostering Metalinguistic Communities in Jewish Educational Settings

Sarah Bunin Benor and Netta Avineri

Introduction

When Jewish educators think about Jewish identity, they often think of practices, such as lighting Shabbat candles, studying texts, performing Israeli dance, and eating ritual foods (see Levisohn, this volume). A commonality that pervades these and many other Jewish practices is language. In some cases, we enact rituals with blessings, but we also need language to talk *about* the rituals, what to do and what not to do, and what meanings those rituals have. When we study texts, we read the text (in the original or in translation), and we use language to interpret it. Even food involves language, as we follow recipes, order off a menu, or participate in conversations around the dinner table. In all of these ways, language is an important component of Jewish religious and cultural practices. Of course, for language educators, the medium is also the message. Given the importance and ubiquity of language in Jewish life, this chapter offers a new framework for conceptualizing language, in particular Hebrew.

Many Jewish educational institutions maintain an ideal goal of competence in written and spoken Hebrew. The reality, however, is that most American Jews have little knowledge of Hebrew beyond decoding. In the 2013 Pew study, over half of the people who told phone researchers that they were Jews report knowing the Hebrew alphabet, but only 13% report understanding all or most of the words (Pew, 2013). This lack of Hebrew knowledge has been widely observed and criticized (Spolsky, 1998; Shohamy, 1999; Gedzelman, 2011; Wieseltier, 2011), and communal leaders have advocated devoting more philanthropic dollars to Hebrew education (Areivim, n.d.; Kaunfer, 2018). In fact, one Israeli writer calls American Jews' lack of Hebrew knowledge "the 800-pound falafel ball sitting in the room" (Hazony, 2012).

We agree that literacy and conversational ability in Hebrew are desirable for Jews, and we advocate for continued dedication of communal resources to educational programs that lead to these goals, especially Hebrew immersion programs in day schools, charter schools, summer camps, and Israeli institutions. At the same time, we are realistic in our expectation of what even increased communal resources can yield in the American Jewish population, most of which devotes only a small percentage of its time to Jewish communal engagement and education. Instead of aiming for their students to become proficient Hebrew speakers in just a few hours of instruction per week, supplementary schools and informal Jewish educational institutions should consider two more attainable goals. First, they should cultivate in their students and participants a sense of membership in a Hebrew-oriented "metalinguistic community" (Avineri, 2012, 2014, 2017, 2018), meaning that they feel attached to Hebrew and have some knowledge of Hebrew, even if they do not have full communicative competence (Canale & Swain, 1980). Second, they should help students develop competence in "Jewish English," English used by Jews that includes words from Hebrew and other distinctive features.

This paper introduces the concepts of metalinguistic community and Jewish English as they might be applied in Jewish educational settings. We explain how these notions fit into scholarly conceptualizations of language, identity, and community and the history of Jews' language use. We offer data from religious schools and summer camps to demonstrate that these notions are already being applied in certain Jewish educational contexts. And we explain how religious schools and other Jewish institutions might benefit from reimagining their pedagogical goals. We offer these suggestions as part of ongoing theorizing in Jewish educational forums on how to improve Hebrew education.[1]

The data in this paper come from several sources beyond published work, including Benor's research on the use of Hebrew at American Jewish summer camps, in collaboration with Sharon Avni and Jonathan Krasner, and Avineri's

---

1 E.g., Schachter, 2010; Greninger 2012; Moskowitz 2013; #OnwardHebrew (https://www.onwardhebrew.org/), and several threads in JEDLAB (https://www.facebook.com/groups/jdsmedialab/). See also Ringvald, 2011, and Wohl, 2005, for discussion of second-language pedagogy innovations in relation to Hebrew; Avni, 2014, for a historical and contemporary overview of research on Hebrew education in the US.

research in Yiddish educational institutions throughout the United States and on a Reform in religious school in California. In the past, our work, including in Avineri's analysis of metalinguistic communities and Benor's analysis of Jewish English, has been descriptive—describing, analyzing, and theorizing language use as we have observed it in American Jewish communities. In this paper, we venture into more prescriptive territory, offering suggestions for how Jewish educational institutions might reimagine their goals surrounding language.

In philosophical work on Jewish education, the concept "language" has been discussed in a metaphorical way to refer to the foundational texts of Judaism, in contrast to "literature," understood as commentary and experiences based on that foundation (Rosenak, 1995; see discussion in Levisohn, 2014). Our use of "language" is more concrete, referring to spoken and written interactions among individuals and within communities. Just as Rosenak's theorizing about "language" has had an impact on how Jewish educators understand their work, we hope our paper will lead educators to think in new ways about the relationship between language and Jewish identity.

Metalinguistic Community

Scholars have long recognized the significance of the relationships between language and group membership. In the eighteenth and nineteenth centuries, proponents of European nationalism conceptualized language as a primary connector of the nation (Fishman, 1973; Anderson, 1983). In the twentieth century, researchers began to investigate smaller language-based collectivities. Bloomfield (1933) introduced the "speech community" concept, characterizing it as "a group of people who interact by means of speech . . . the most important kind of social group" (p. 42). Gumperz (1968) highlighted additional traits of the speech community, including regular interaction, shared norms, and difference from other groups.

In Avineri's (2012) research on Yiddish clubs, classes, and festivals, she recognized that these conceptions of speech community did not accurately describe what she was observing. She found that people were forming communities based on a language that many did not use. Previous research on language-based community (e.g., speech community, linguistic community) addressed some (but not all) of the traits of these Yiddish-oriented groups. It became important to highlight that speech communities do not simply exist as categories in the world, but are created by individuals (who express diverse ideologies about language) in collaboration with one another via interaction

(Duranti, 1997). The notion that "community membership is a matter of degree" (Silverstein, 1996, 1998, as cited in Avineri & Kroskrity, 2014) resonated with aspects of what she found in her research, as well as shared values and ideologies that can be present in speech communities (Morgan, 2006). However, though aspects of these previous conceptualizations were useful, Avineri did not find a framework that perfectly described what she was observing.

Avineri therefore presented a new model: "metalinguistic community," defined as a community of people "engaged primarily in discourse *about* language and cultural symbols tied to language" (2012, p. ii). This concept offers a way to conceptualize situations where people experience "a strong connection to a language and its speakers but may lack familiarity with them due to historical, personal, and/or communal circumstances" (ibid., p. ii). This relates to Shandler's (2005) notion of post-vernacularity, in which the mere fact that Yiddish is being used at all is meaningful and worthy of note, beyond the actual content of what is said in the language. These traits apply not only to Yiddish but also to Hebrew in America today.

The model of metalinguistic community recognizes individuals' connections to a language and culture, in particular a range of affective affiliations. The five dimensions of the model of metalinguistic community are as follows:

1. "socialization into language ideologies is a priority over socialization into language competence and use,"
2. "conflation of language and culture,"
3. "age and corresponding knowledge as highly salient features,"
4. "use and discussion of the code are primarily pedagogical," and
5. "use of code in specific interactional and textual contexts (e.g., greeting/closings, assessments, response cries, lexical items related to religion and culture, mock language)" (Avineri, 2012, p. ii).

The metalinguistic community model casts the widest possible net to include a range of participants who would not otherwise be counted as members of a speech community. Although this model grew out of Avineri's research on Yiddish language engagement, it is also relevant to other heritage and endangered language contexts.[2] In this article, we explain how the model can also be applied in the case of Hebrew.

---

2 See Avineri (2012) for discussion of comparison cases, including Corsican (Jaffe, 2007), Miami (Leonard, 2011), Apache (Nevins, 2004), Gaelic (McEwan-Fujita, 2010), and Judeo-Spanish (Kushner-Bishop, 2001).

The metalinguistic community is "meta" to a linguistic community (historical and/or current), often involving discourse about the language. Those in the metalinguistic community have knowledge about the language and about what matters to communicators of that language. In the Yiddish case, this means for example that core members of the metalinguistic community recognize the difference between a Galitsianer and a Litvak (geographic categories involving different accents) and can evaluate their associated phonological features, but may be unable to produce those phonological features of interest.

The notion of metalinguistic community is connected to the construct "heritage languages" (He, 2010; Carreira & Kagan, 2011), languages to which individuals have a family connection following language shift among immigrant populations or among indigenous groups in colonial or postcolonial contexts. Polinsky and Kagan (2007) propose narrow and broad definitions of heritage language learners. The narrow definition is "individuals raised in homes where a language other than English is spoken and who are to some degree bilingual in English and the heritage language" (Polinsky & Kagan, 2007, p. 369; Valdes, 2000). The broad definition, which is more relevant to the present discussion, recognizes that some heritage language learners do not exhibit communicative competence but do have affective and communal ties to a language, as well as a range of motivations (Dornyei, 2005; Dornyei & Ushioda, 2009) and investments (Peirce, 1995). Because most immigrant families in America lack competence in their ancestral language beyond the third generation (Carreira & Kagan, 2011; Fishman, 1991; Silva-Corvalan, 2003; Veltman, 2000), the broad definition of heritage language—and the concept of metalinguistic community—can be useful in understanding how individuals relate to a language and how the language could be taught.

Among American Jews, Hebrew has similarities to and differences from heritage languages. Certainly for children and grandchildren of Israeli immigrants, Hebrew is a heritage language, similar to immigrant languages like Spanish, Russian, and Mandarin. Other American Jews do not have family ties to Israeli Hebrew but may have some knowledge of and connection to Textual Hebrew through their family and educational experiences (rituals like the Passover seder and Chanukah candle lighting, prayers, songs, and biblical and rabbinic texts). These ties are especially strong among Jews who are religiously observant and have intensive Jewish education. In addition, those who have spent time in Israel or with Israelis (including teachers and students in American Jewish educational settings) may have some knowledge of and connection to Israeli Hebrew. When American Jews arrive in college with some exposure to Textual and/or Israeli Hebrew, they have much in common with heritage learners of Spanish, Russian, Mandarin, etc.: some knowledge of the language and affective connection to it. (Notably, that affective connection may not be consistently positive.)[3] On the other hand, the situation of Hebrew is unique due to the ritualized nature of Textual Hebrew recitation (see Glinert, 1993, on Hebrew as "quasilect") and the institutionalized, rather than home-based, exposure to Israeli Hebrew. Even so, educators concerned with heritage languages (both immigrant and indigenous) and educators concerned with Hebrew might find the metalinguistic community approach useful in envisioning their educational goals.

Several of the features of metalinguistic communities that Avineri identified are relevant to Hebrew in Jewish educational settings:

1. Competence in the language is not necessary; one can be a member of the metalinguistic community even if one does not speak the language.
2. Members are socialized to have ideologies about the language.
3. The language is used in pedagogical ways.
4. A variety of selected words are used within the primary language.

Whereas Avineri's (2012) focus was description and analysis of what she observed in secular Yiddish educational contexts, in this paper we offer both description and a forward-looking set of recommendations regarding Hebrew in Jewish educational settings more broadly.

Competence in the Language is Not Necessary

Within metalinguistic communities, communicative competence is not necessarily the goal. Instead, individuals demonstrate their connections with the language in other ways. For example, the 2011 Orange County Yiddish Festival publicity flyer stated, "You don't have to know Yiddish to love Yiddish." This statement highlights the affective connection to the language as opposed to language competence, thereby making this metalinguistic community inclusive and open to all, and encouraging increased participation.

---

3 See Avineri (2017) for an in-depth discussion of "contested stance practices" in the Yiddish metalinguistic community.

Several Jewish educational institutions maintain as one of many goals instilling a love of Hebrew, as can be seen in the mission statements, blog posts, and Hebrew teacher job listings of contemporary synagogue schools, day schools, early childhood centers, and summer camps. For example, Yeshivah of Flatbush's early childhood program includes in its list of educational standards "Instilling a love of Torah and mitzvot, Promoting academic excellence, [and] Inspiring a love of Israel and Hebrew."[4] Temple Shir Tikva starts its educational philosophy statement with this: "There is no greater gift we can give our Jewish children than a love of Hebrew language, culture, and knowing how and when to do the right thing for others."[5] Even in the early 1940s, educators were emphasizing connection to Hebrew. Rosen and Chomsky (2003 [1940]) list as one of the objectives of Hebrew education: "To create in the child a sense of being a part of the Hebraic culture of our people, for Hebrew is the language bond which unites the child to his people throughout the world, as well as to Israel of the past." While some of these institutions, especially Jewish day schools, also strive for the cognitive and behavioral goals of language competence and use, the mention of an affective goal—love, connection, or positive feelings—indicates the relevance of the metalinguistic community model.

In Benor's research on summer camps, she found diverse uses of Hebrew, ranging from sporadic Hebrew blessings to Hebrew immersion programs. Many of these camps have love of Hebrew as a goal. The Conservative movement's Camp Ramah explains on its About Us webpage that Israeli staff members "help to inculcate in the campers a love of Hebrew language together with a familiarity with and connection to Israel."[6] Camp Harlam, a Union for Reform Judaism (URJ) residential summer camp in Pennsylvania, lists as one of its goals "Ahavat Yisrael," translated on its website as "Love of Israel and Hebrew."[7] Both Ramah and URJ camps incorporate Hebrew words into the mostly (Jewish) English of daily life. *Chanichim* (campers) and *madrichim* (counselors) eat in the *chadar ochel* (dining room) and participate in *chugim* (activities), *tefillah* (prayer), and *nikayon* ([cabin] clean-up). In addition, Ramah camps do announcements and theatrical productions in Hebrew and identify a few Hebrew-oriented staff members as "Daber fellows," tasked with encouraging more spoken Hebrew. At Ramah and URJ camps, campers are

4 http://www.flatbush.org/images/upload/FFvol7no9.pdf.
5 http://www.shirtikva.org/education.
6 http://www.campramah.org/content/aboutus.php.
7 https://campharlam.org/summer/.

not expected to be fluent in Hebrew by the end of the summer (even if some administrators hold that as an ideal). But the ubiquity of Hebrew words, songs, and blessings—in combination with the presence of Israeli staff members—helps these camps achieve their goal of campers loving Hebrew.

Members are Socialized to Have Ideologies About the Language

As Avineri writes, another hallmark of the metalinguistic community is that participants are socialized into holding specific ideologies regarding the language, beyond a particular affective orientation. Commonly, these ideologies involve ethnic/cultural connections: feeling a personal attachment to the language because of family ties or membership in the broader group with which the language is associated (see Hoffman, 2011; Morahg, 1993, 1999; Shohamy, 1999, on the relationship between Hebrew and Jewish communal identity and belonging). Ideologies like these encourage continued engagement with the communities within which the language is used, discussed, and/or valued. One way that educators can foster such connections is by collecting and analyzing students' language learner histories (Avineri, 2012, p. 134). Students would write or speak about their experiences with and feelings surrounding Hebrew and Hebrew learning, and those narratives would serve as a vehicle for class discussions about Hebrew.

Another type of ideology observable in metalinguistic communities revolves around sociolinguistic variation: discussion of dialects and their features becomes a site for negotiations around authenticity, identity, and correctness. In Avineri's Yiddish data, pronunciation of particular vowels became iconic of broader identities with which community members associated. For example, participants discussed their preferences for Galitsianer or Litvak pronunciations like *shayn* vs. *sheyn* (nice) and *kigel* vs. *kugel*, often based on family connections or the ideologies of teachers. In addition, contemporary Hasidic Yiddish was sometimes disparaged for its pervasive influence from English and changes in its case and gender systems.

In Hebrew-oriented Jewish educational settings, we find similar expressions of ideologies. Students are generally expected to understand Hebrew as important to Jewish identity for three reasons: it is the language of Jewish holy texts, it is the language of contemporary Israel, and it is the common language of Jews around the world. These three aspects of Hebrew are emphasized differentially in different educational settings. For example, in the camp research, Benor found that some camps primarily highlight the

Israel connection (as can be seen in the co-occurring mentions of Israel and Hebrew on the URJ and Ramah websites), while others focus on the textual and peoplehood connections, sometimes avoiding linking Hebrew with Israel (a case in point is the environmentally oriented Eden Village Camp, which calls its dining hall *Beit Shefa* [i.e., the house of abundance], has a *pe'ah* garden [employing the biblical term for the corner of field left for the poor], and highlights traditional values like *tza'ar ba'alei chayim* [(avoiding) the suffering of living creatures], but minimizes talk of Israel, which is seen as politically divisive).

The diverse rationales for Hebrew use relate to ideologies about which types of Hebrew are considered preferable or correct, similar to the Galitsianer/Litvak and Hasidic/non-Hasidic distinctions in Yiddish organizations. In some Hebrew-oriented institutions, like Sephardic Adventure Camp, near Seattle, and many Modern Orthodox synagogues and schools, there is some debate and negotiation about whether to use Ashkenazi, Israeli, or Sephardi Hebrew pronunciation. In educational settings of many backgrounds, some teachers—both Israeli and not—emphasize the correctness of Israeli Hebrew, while others emphasize the norms of Biblical Hebrew.

As an example of this negotiation, we offer data from Avineri's research at a Reform Torah school in California (Avineri, 2006, 2007). As preteen students prepare for their bar/bat mitzvahs, teachers and cantors spend many hours teaching students to chant from the Torah correctly, emphasizing the importance of accurate consonants and vowels and lexical stress on the appropriate syllable. Students learn "correct" pronunciation from the perspectives of their teachers, which sometimes conflict. While all of the teachers Avineri observed used mostly American phonology, they exhibited some variation in the realization of the *shva-na* vowel, which is pronounced as schwa in Biblical Hebrew and is silent in Modern Hebrew (e.g., *terumah* vs. *trumah*).

One teacher, David, corrected a student for saying *trumah*, the Modern Hebrew-influenced form the student had learned from the other teacher. David explained to the class:

35. So the tradition teaches
36. kay, this is the Torah tradition not Modern Hebrew,
37. it's a little different, Torah tradition says you
38. pronounce a sheva at~the~beginning~of~a~word (0.2)
39. nkay like a very short eh. A very a short and some
40. would even say a very short ay . . .

41. There are many people that I don't believe actually
42. (0.2) know the rules nkay. The rules are actually very
43. specific. A lot of people actually confuse the
44. pronunciation, (0.2) between Modern Hebrew and Torah
45. Hebrew tradition. And Torah Hebrew is what we're
46. actually learning.

While lengthy metalinguistic interactions like these may take time from students engaging with the text on an intellectual level, they express to the students that there are different ideologies of authenticity and correctness surrounding Hebrew. Avineri's conception of metalinguistic community helps us to see the significance of this interaction, not merely in terms of whether the students do or do not pronounce the shva-na but rather in terms of the presence of the linguistic-ideological discourse itself. The students are being socialized not to be competent speakers of Hebrew but into ideologies that value accuracy and certain variants over others. Particular pronunciation therefore becomes iconic of broader ideologies and communities (Irvine & Gal, 2000).

In Hebrew contexts, as in Yiddish ones, participants may be socialized into a diasporic language ideology, "focused on a language's complexity as a symbol for its speakers' mobile history" (Avineri, 2012, p. 9). And in many cases, participants in diasporic contexts, with their focus on what was lost, engage in "nostalgia socialization, a public attention to and affective appreciation of the past as a way to understand one's place in the present" (Avineri, 2012, p. 2). Hebrew- and Yiddish-oriented educational institutions therefore become central sites for socialization into these ideologies. Note that ideologies can be enacted but not necessarily always voiced (c.f. Giddens, 1984, on discursive and practical consciousness). For example, there can be a metalinguistic community that does not explicitly use metalinguistic discourse to discuss affective affiliations with the language but uses elements of it and debates correctness and authority.

Pedagogical Language Use

Another feature identified by Avineri (2012) is that "use and discussion of the code are primarily pedagogical" (p. ii). In the following example, a collective greeting sequence becomes an Initiation-Reply-Evaluation sequence (Mehan, 1979), a pervasive routine in educational settings. For example, at the start of a theatrical event celebrating the golden age of Yiddish radio, Avineri heard the following sequence:

Adam:	*Sholem aleichem!* [Hello!]
Audience:	*Aleichem sholem!* [Hello!]
Adam:	*Zeyer gut!* [Very good!]

Here, audience members producing the second pair part (*Aleichem sholem*) demonstrate their competence by inverting the syntax of the lexical items in the first pair part (*Sholem aleichem*). Their ability to produce a correct second pair part becomes an opportunity for Adam's positive assessment in the third turn (*Zeyer gut*), which transforms the sequence into an Initiation-Reply-Evaluation sequence. This moves participants into pedagogical roles in this local context, in which the language becomes an object to be assessed as opposed to one that is simply used to greet and converse. Although the opening lines of this event are in Yiddish, the subsequent interactions are primarily in English. This is quite similar to what Ahlers (2006) describes as "framing discourse" with native language use at American Indian events, marking them as culturally specific and inclusive events that invite a range of participants, whether or not they are competent in the heritage language(s).

In language classroom settings, one would expect language use to be primarily pedagogical. Interestingly, this type of language teaching also happens in Yiddish-oriented events that are not intended as linguistically pedagogical, like performances and festivals. We also see this in some Hebrew-oriented Jewish communal settings. In Jewish day schools, supplementary schools, and summer camps, one can often hear teachers teaching Hebrew words and praising or correcting students' use of Hebrew, even when students are not in Hebrew class. For example, at a Ramah camp, a cooking teacher conducted her smoothie-making lesson in English but asked a few times if students knew the Hebrew words for specific items, like ice cream (*glida*) and straw (*kash*). At a Habonim Dror camp, a counselor saw a new camper looking confused and explained: "*Machaneh* means camp. That's what we call camp—*machaneh*." And at an independent camp that used the word *amanut* for "art" in its camp song, a staff member took the initiative to explain to campers that that was incorrect and from now on they would be singing *omanut* instead. Although these teaching moments did not occur in a classroom intended to teach Hebrew, they serve to teach Hebrew terms and foster ideologies about correctness.

Selected Words Used Within the Primary Language

Related to pedagogical language use is the "use of code in specific interactional and textual contexts," including greetings, closings, assessments, and words related to religion and culture (Avineri, 2012, p. ii). Greetings and assessments are included in the brief exchange between Adam and his audience (described above), as well as in many similar interactions at Yiddish events. In addition, we see comparable language mixing in written materials from Yiddish-oriented organizations. The Yiddish Book Center, which "works to rescue Yiddish and other modern Jewish books and open up their content to the world,"[8] uses selected Yiddish words in their email newsletters. A donation thank you letter in English begins with "*A sheynem dank*—thank you—for renewing your membership with a generous gift of X" and ends with "We couldn't do any of this without your support and for that, we are deeply grateful. *A hartsikn dank*—my heartfelt thanks!" These Yiddish lexical items, framing the beginning and end of the text, provide a flavor of the language and bracket the text as a metalinguistic appreciation of the language (Ahlers, 2006). Their translation into English demonstrates sensitivity to the audience, providing the meaning of the words for those who demonstrate their appreciation of Yiddish through their monetary gifts but may not have competence in the language itself.

The use of selected Yiddish words within English can also be seen in Yiddish-oriented classrooms. In a UCLA Yiddish Language and Culture through Film class, the instructor would speak primarily in English. However, after an explanation or a student's response, she would often ask the class in Yiddish "*Farshteyt*?" (Do you [plural] understand?) with no translation. Similarly, when a student sneezed, the instructor responded "*Tse gezint*," meaning "to health," or "bless you." No translations were provided for the majority non-Yiddish-speaking students in the course, as the meanings were clear from context. These small verbal tastes of the language give the overall interactions a flavor of Yiddish, even when the vast majority of the time the language spoken is English.

Jewish educational settings of many kinds use words from Hebrew within otherwise English sentences. At the beginning of a class in a Hebrew school, the teacher greeted the children, "*Boker tov, yeladim*" (good morning, children), and they responded, as trained at the beginning of the year, "*Boker tov, Morah [Esther]!*" (Good morning, teacher Esther!). This framing discourse of an

---

8 https://www.facebook.com/YiddishBookCenter/info?tab=overview.

otherwise English-run class involves a ritualized greeting made up of a call and a response. At the beginning of a Jewish day school back-to-school night on a Thursday evening in September, the principal greeted the parents, "*Erev tov*" (good evening), and closed with "*Shabbat shalom, shana tova*" (Good Sabbath, happy new year). At an end-of-the-year show, the same principal praised the students' opening song with a Hebrew evaluation: "*Kol hakavod!*" (Well done! Literally, all the honor). Other evaluations we heard in Jewish educational settings include *yofi* (nice), *tov me'od* (very good), *metzuyan* (excellent), and *yasher koach* (good job. Literally, may it be for strength).

We can find many examples of Hebrew (and Yiddish) lexical items related to religion and culture by looking at the websites and newsletters of educational institutions. For example, Heschel Day School in Northridge, California, includes in its curriculum "Project *Chesed*/Community Service—*Beit* Issie Shapiro—We are all created in the image of God (*Batzelem Elohim*);" "Trope: This course helps students begin to learn how to read from the *Torah* and be *Shabbat* morning *tefilah* leaders;" and a unit that "explores *Eretz Yisrael* as our *Eretz Moledet*; (the land of Israel as our Homeland)."[9] Similarly, a newsletter sent home to parents of first-grade students at Pressman Academy in Los Angeles included these quotes: "*Kitah Alef* [first grade] finished the letter *het* this week. . . . We learned about the *Y'vaneem* [Greeks] and *Maccabeem* [Maccabees] and *nes kad ha-shemen* [miracle of the oil jug]. We enjoyed singing *Hanukkah* songs with *Morah* [Teacher] [Debby] and reciting the *brakhot* [blessings] when lighting the candles. 1C LOVES *parashat ha-shavua* [Torah portion of the week]!!! They are always so curious to know what will happen next in the *Torah*" (Pressman Academy first-grade newsletter, 12/11, quoted with permission; bracketed translations added). Hebrew words in educational materials are sometimes translated for the benefit of less Hebraically educated parents, but other times such parents are left to wonder, look words up, or ask their children.

Other Features

Two additional features of metalinguistic community that Avineri (2012) found to be relevant for Yiddish settings were conflation of language and culture, and age and corresponding knowledge as highly salient features. It was quite common to find advertisements for "Yiddish culture" festivals

---

9 http://heschel.com/upl/File/heschel_curriculum_guide.pdf.

or "Yiddish dance lessons" as a proxy for pre-war Eastern European Jewish culture, thereby conflating language and culture. This is generally not the case for Hebrew, as the language and culture(s) are seen as related but not conflated; people speak of "Israeli cuisine" and "Israeli dancing" rather than "Hebrew cuisine" and "Hebrew dancing" (although there are exceptions, such as the "Council for Hebrew Language and Culture")[10]. In Yiddish contexts, age and corresponding knowledge are highlighted frequently (e.g., Yiddish "elders" who hold essential cultural knowledge that must be captured, contrasted with young people's interest in Yiddish). Though there are discourses around Hebrew that relate to intergenerational transmission, this feature is not as salient as in the Yiddish context.

As the above section demonstrates, metalinguistic community provides a useful model for how Diaspora Jews relate (and could relate) to Hebrew. This framework is more inclusive and more expansive than a traditional language learning model, in that people are members of the community even if they are not fluent language users. In short, it acknowledges the range of meaningful ways that individuals and communities engage with history, tradition, and the present. At the same time, the metalinguistic community can be a springboard for linguistic competence: students who are socialized into ideologies about Hebrew and exposed to elements of it may be more likely than those without that exposure to pursue further Hebrew education as teens and adults.

Jewish English and Diaspora Jewish Language Varieties

The second construct that we propose as useful for Jewish education is the notion of Jewish English, which is related to the fifth dimension of metalinguistic community discussed above, the use of selected (Hebrew) words within the primary language (English). In most places where Jews have lived around the Diaspora, from Persia to India to Lithuania, they have spoken a variety of the local language (Weinreich, 2008 [1973]; Wexler, 1981). Yiddish and Ladino represent exceptions to this norm, as they were maintained for centuries away from their Hispanic and Germanic lands of origin (Benor, 2008). Most Jewish communities moved to a new land and learned the local language, distinguishing it, especially for in-group speech, with Hebrew words and other distinctive features. This process was facilitated by the maintenance of Hebrew

---

10 http://blogs.forward.com/the-arty-semite/217025/new-festival-celebrates-hebrew-language-and-cultur/.

(and Aramaic), used for liturgical and other ritual expression, study of biblical and rabbinic texts (especially among men), and sometimes business purposes. Jews' connection to the holy tongue led to Hebrew influence in their vernacular language and often the use of Hebrew letters in their writing systems.

Although contemporary Jewish communities do not use Hebrew writing systems to represent their local language, they continue the tradition of Jewish linguistic distinctiveness. The Jewish English of American Jews can be seen as a Jewish language, akin to Judeo-Greek, Judeo-Provencal, and Judeo-Aramaic (Gold, 1985; Benor, 2009), even sharing some features with more widely known—and more distinctive—languages like Yiddish and Ladino. Jewish English is an umbrella term referring to the English of diverse groups of Jews in the United States, the United Kingdom, Canada, and other former British colonies where English is spoken. It can be similar to non-Jewish English with the addition of a few Hebrew words, or, among Orthodox Jews, it can differ enough to require translations for non-Orthodox audiences (Benor, 2011a, 2012).

The repertoire of distinctive features (Benor, 2010) of Jewish English includes hundreds of words from Textual Hebrew, Aramaic, Yiddish, and Israeli Hebrew (as is evident from the examples from Jewish educational settings quoted above), and among specific immigrant communities, Ladino, Judeo-Arabic, Farsi, Russian, and other languages. It also includes influences from Yiddish in grammar and pronunciation, as well as intonational features stemming from traditional text study, discourse markers from Israeli Hebrew, and distinctive discourse style involving overlapping and argumentation (Benor, 2012, 2016).

To illustrate some of these features, consider the following quote from an Ashkenazi Orthodox woman in Philadelphia (non-English words underlined, other distinctive linguistic features **bolded**): "In another community, people might **tsk** [**click**] If they have . . . a different sort of yiddishkeit [Jewishness], **so** they might not daven [pray] in the same shul [synagogue]. They might send their kids to different yeshivas (study houses)." She uses four Yiddish words (some of which have Hebrew origins), and two discourse markers ("tsk" and "so") influenced by Israeli Hebrew. We see a different source of influence in a Jewish English song sung at Sephardic Adventure Camp, an Orthodox residential summer camp that emphasizes Ottoman Sephardic culture for the great-grandchildren of Ladino-speaking immigrants: "At Sephardic Camp we have *achdut* [Hebrew: unity]. We stick together like *yaprakis con aroz* [Ladino: grape leaves stuffed with rice]." This song is mostly English with the addition of some Hebrew and Ladino words and phrases.

Although the language most distinct from general American English can be heard among Orthodox Jews, non-Orthodox Jews also use Jewish English, especially in educational contexts. For example, a Reform rabbi wrote the following to a pluralistic Jewish professional email list (quoted with her permission):

> L'shem chinuch [for the sake of education], I am leading a "mock" seder [Passover ceremony] tomorrow for our Basic Judaism class. . . . I am wondering if anyone out there has already created . . . an "essence of" Haggadah [seder guide book] that is more explanatory than halachic [meeting the requirements of Jewish law]. . . . Thanks in advance for anything you might send my way. I'll teach it all b'shem omro/omrah [in the name of its speaker]!

This Jewish English quote includes several words and phrases from Textual Hebrew, which is common in many Jewish educational settings. At the Sholem Community's secular Jewish Sunday school, Yiddish is a more common enricher. They refer to their teachers as *lerer*, assistants as *belfer*, and the communal leader (with a role similar to that of a rabbi) as *vegvayzer* "guide." When Hebrew words are used, they tend to be rendered with Yiddish/Ashkenazi influence: "Beys [B] class . . . began by looking at a list of recipes for kharoyses/charoset [ceremonial Passover dish made with fruit and nuts] from around the world. . . . Afterwards, we sang the *fir kashes* [four questions] with Alef [A] class" (*Sholem* email newsletter, 4/14, quoted with permission). These examples of Jewish English from diverse groups of American Jews exhibit important differences, but all are primarily English with some influences from Hebrew and other Jewish languages.

Among American Jews, there is little awareness that their distinctive language patterns continue the centuries-old tradition of Diaspora Jewish language varieties. Cultural critic Leon Wieseltier writes:

> The American Jewish community is the first great community in the history of our people that believes that it can receive, develop, and perpetuate the Jewish tradition *not* in a Jewish language. By an overwhelming majority, American Jews cannot read or speak or write Hebrew or Yiddish. This is genuinely shocking. American Jewry is quite literally unlettered. The assumption of American Jewry that it can do without a Jewish language is an arrogance without precedent in Jewish history. And this illiteracy,

> I suggest, will leave American Judaism and American Jewishness forever crippled and scandalously thin. (Wieseltier, 2011, p. 16)

If one understands "Jewish languages" as including only Yiddish and Ladino, or "great community" as including only those who spoke Yiddish and Ladino, then this position is defensible. But by invoking "the history of our people," Wieseltier implies a broader comparison. Based on our understanding of "Jewish languages" as referring to both "languages" like Yiddish and Ladino and "dialects" or "language varieties" like Judeo-French and Judeo-Malayalam (see Benor, 2008, on the unclear boundary between languages and dialects), we disagree with Wieseltier's statement that American Jewry is attempting to "perpetuate the Jewish tradition *not* in a Jewish language."

Later in the article it becomes clear that Wieseltier is bemoaning not the absence of a distinctive Jewish language or dialect but rather the lack of literacy in Hebrew:

> Without Hebrew, the Jewish tradition will not disappear entirely in America, but most of it will certainly disappear. This gloomy premonition is owed not least to a proper understanding of the relationship of language to life. Our language is our incommensurable inflection of our humanity, our unique way of presenting, not least to ourselves, what is our unique way through the world. Our language is our element, our beginning, our air, the air peculiar to us. (Wieseltier, 2011, p.17)

We agree with Wieseltier that language is a primary determiner of group identity and that Hebrew is crucial for Jewish cultural continuity. We disagree, however, with his notion of a "proper understanding of the relationship of language to life." For us, the adjective "proper" means an understanding that is informed by contemporary sociolinguistic theory, and that kind of understanding should lead to a different conclusion: American Jews are expressing their "unique way" by using the local language, English, with influences from their religious tradition (Textual Hebrew), their Diasporic homeland (Israeli Hebrew), and their pre-immigration ancestral languages (Yiddish, Ladino, etc.). This linguistic hybridity allows American Jews to express both their Americanness and several aspects of their Jewishness, just as some Pakistani Americans use English with influences from Urdu and Arabic, and just as some African Americans use English with pronunciations reflecting their history in the American South, among other distinctive features. By using English as their base language, these groups present themselves as first and foremost American, and by incorporating distinctive features, they highlight their membership in their minority group (and subgroups within it). American Jewish educational institutions should encourage the use of Jewish English as a valid and productive expression of American Jewish identity and as a way of sustaining cultural transmission and continuing the linguistic distinctiveness of Diaspora Jews around the world and throughout history.

Our call for Jewish institutions to incorporate Hebrew words into English conversation is not without precedent. Deborah Lipstadt (1993), in making a case for Hebrew education for Jewish communal leaders, suggests compiling "*elef milim*," a compendium of 1000 Hebrew words, representing important concepts within Judaism and Jewish communal life. This suggestion is very much in line with our emphasis on Jewish English and on the specialized terminology that characterizes metalinguistic communities. Glinert (1999) describes a need for "Hebrew for Spiritual Purposes," which would involve "idioms, quotations, proverbs" as a "strategy to judaize our English," and emphasizes ideologies and values that are central to Jewish heritage, echoing Mintz's (2011) call to "approach Jewish education not through its formal grammar but through the concepts and values embodied in its three-letter roots" (p. 11). Our focus on Hebrew as a symbol of Jewish identification is also emphasized in Firestone's (2011) discussion of college students' engagement with Hebrew, Lanski's (2011) exploration of the relevance of Hebrew for high school students, and Paradise's (2011) "Rx for Hebrew in American Jewish communities", which includes visual stimuli, public speeches, and summer camps. Our proposal is also similar to Cutter's (2007) call for American Jews to understand Hebrew as a "second home."

Because Jewish English involves other distinctive features besides Hebrew words, educators who consider use of Jewish English to be a pedagogical goal must determine which distinctive features are important for students. While non-lexical features of Jewish English might occasionally be included in Jewish educational objectives, we expect that most institutions would be primarily interested in the use of Hebrew words. In some settings, words from Yiddish, Ladino, and other languages will be important. Because nonstandard grammar is often stigmatized, Yiddish-influenced constructions like "I want that you should see this" and "In a hotel she lives!" would likely not be promoted. Some constructions might be heard in Jewish educational settings, including "staying by us," "she has what to say," and "I don't know from physics," but these likely would not be part of any formal curriculum. Nor would most educators include the ability to participate in a highly interactive argumentation style associated with Jews (Tannen, 1981; Schiffrin, 1984) as an explicit educational goal. On the other hand, Avineri (2006) found that students in a seventh grade Torah classroom were socialized into moral reasoning practices through mobilizing evidence during argument sequences, and that the teacher explicitly identified particular morals and values as distinguishing elements of what "makes us Jews." So it is possible that culturally relevant discourse styles in English may also be a desired outcome in Jewish educational settings.

In Gold's (1985) analysis of Jewish English, he writes, "Although [Jewish English], in various forms, has long been a medium of instruction (though unacknowledged as such), it has never been a subject of instruction (this is not surprising in view of its largely unrecognized status as a legitimate variety of English, an identity marker, and a necessary component of any anglophone Jewish community)" (Gold, 1985, p. 297). We do not advocate teaching Jewish English explicitly as a subject of instruction. However, we do advocate that teachers use Hebrew words and other elements of Jewish English in the classroom with the explicit goal of students acquiring them. Educators may think of instruction and enculturation as contrasting concepts: the former involves intentional design, and the latter involves learning that occurs organically. But once we identify the use of Jewish English as a goal, it may be possible to combine the two, in effect to enculturate planfully by identifying the terms and linguistic practices that we want to promote and using them in the classroom.

Conclusion

Among American Jewish educational institutions, there is a spectrum of language use. At one end is a metalinguistic community that uses the language in many regular interactions, like a Jewish day school with a Hebrew immersion program, and at the other end is a metalinguistic community with little to no everyday use of the language for everyday communication, like a religious school that uses only a few Hebrew words. We see this spectrum with other languages in the Jewish community. At one end of the spectrum are organizations that operate partly in immigrant languages, like Camp Gesher, a camp in California for Russian American Jews, most of whom hear Russian at home. At the other end are organizations that emphasize post-vernacular uses of Ladino and Yiddish, fostering metalinguistic communities surrounding those languages, such as the Ladino-oriented Sephardic Adventure Camp, and Camp Kinder Ring, a historically socialist, secular camp oriented toward Yiddish culture. These institutions all operate as metalinguistic communities, because they socialize Jews to have ideologies about the language and to use elements of it. And they all use some variant of Jewish English, even if they also use another language. We encourage Jewish educational institutions—whether they are oriented toward Hebrew, a Diaspora Jewish language, or a combination—to consider where they fall and where they would like to fall on this spectrum.

The cultivation of Hebrew-oriented metalinguistic communities and Jewish English cannot take place in a vacuum; it is made possible by the existence of a sector of the Jewish community that has strong ability in spoken Hebrew and/or Textual Hebrew. This includes Israeli Americans and other Jews who have spent significant time in Israel, on the one hand, and Jews who participate intensively in Jewish education and religious life, whom Benor (2011b) lightheartedly refers to as "Super Jews," on the other hand. When such Hebrew-proficient Jews interact with other Jews, in educational settings and in everyday communication, they spread Hebrew words, ideologies about Hebrew, and other elements that make up the Hebrew metalinguistic community and Jewish English.

Some Jewish educational institutions—especially Hebrew-immersive Jewish day schools and long-term Israel programs—are crucial in teaching Hebrew to this "Jewishly elite" sector of the community. And, in line with the calls for expanded Hebrew literacy (e.g., Gedzelman, 2011; Wieseltier, 2011; Hazony, 2012), we encourage such institutions to make Hebrew available to a wider swath of the Jewish community. A new crop of Hebrew-immersion camps funded by the Areivim Philanthropic Group and the Israeli American Council are a welcome addition to this landscape. Nothing that we have written above should negate this goal of deepening Hebrew linguistic competence among a broader cross-section of the American Jewish community.

At the same time, no matter how many philanthropic dollars are poured into Hebrew education, a large percentage of Jews will likely not devote the time necessary to make Hebrew (or Judaism) a priority for themselves or their children.[11] While many Jews do not participate in any Jewish communal or educational institutions, a large percentage are served by Reform, Conservative, and other religious schools that meet just a few hours a week, as well as Jewish summer camps, youth groups, and Israel trips. It is

---

11 See Chiswick, 2014, for a relevant economic analysis of Jewish life and education.

in these settings that the approaches described here—focused on nurturing a metalinguistic community and teaching Jewish English—are potentially most useful.

Whether or not they strive for Hebrew competence, all Jewish educational institutions can have an explicit goal of fostering a metalinguistic community: a community of Jews who have a personal connection to Hebrew (and/or Yiddish, Ladino, etc.) as *their* language(s), certain ideologies about authentic Hebrew, and use of selected Hebrew words for cultural terms, greetings, closings, and evaluations. This last aspect of the metalinguistic community model involves socializing Jews to use Jewish English: English with distinctive features, including words from Hebrew and in some cases Yiddish and other languages. This type of language use connects American Jews to their ancestors and to Jews around the world and throughout history, who have used and continue to use Hebrew for prayer and study while speaking a local vernacular with distinctively Jewish features.

Our emphasis on Jewish English and metalinguistic community is in line with some recent innovations in congregational education. One Reform synagogue offered a class for adults on the Hebrew and Yiddish words used in Jewish English (see Benor, 2009), and a rabbi-educator in Northern California has included in the curriculum a list of "Jewish life vocabulary" that Reform Jews should know, which matches up nicely with many of the Hebrew words used in Jewish English (Greninger, 2014).

The proposals we put forth in this paper are intended not only as an end, but also as a scaffolding approach to language education. Jews who learn in religious school to have certain ideologies about Hebrew and to sprinkle Hebrew words into their English are more likely than Jews without that exposure to pursue additional Hebrew education in the future. However, even those students who end their Hebrew education after their bar/bat mitzvah will have a richer sense of connection to Jews around the world and throughout history because of their strengthened relationship with Hebrew. Language education is not an all-or-nothing endeavor. In the absence of full Hebrew competence, there is deep value in a Hebrew-oriented metalinguistic community and in Jewish English. These concepts represent a reimagining of the goals of language education, a new understanding of the role of language in building community and fostering Jewish self-understanding.

Fishman (1976, p. 3) notes, "We continue miraculously, generation after generation, to raise children who venerate, respect, and value the Hebrew language even as we have failed to give them speaking, reading, or even praying facility in the language." This affective relationship to the language can be an end unto itself, as opposed to a lamentation. Metalinguistic community provides an inclusive model that goes beyond a deficit view of what students do *not* do to an additive framework by emphasizing the various relationships one can have to a language and culture.

Bibliography

Ahlers, Jocelyn C. (2006). Framing Discourse: Creating Community Through Native Language Use. *Journal of Linguistic Anthropology 16*, 58–75.

Anderson, Benedict. (1983). *Imagined Communities*. New York, NY: Verso.

Areivim Philanthropic Group. (No Date). Primary Areas of Focus. Retrieved from http://www.steinhardtfoundation.org/programs/primary-areas-of-focus/

Avineri, Netta. (2006). Socialization into Moral Reasoning in a Torah School Classroom Discussion (unpublished master's dissertation). UCLA, Los Angeles, California.

Avineri, Netta. (2007). Embodied Torah Chanting in a Community of Practice. Unpublished Course Paper.

Avineri, Netta Rose. (2012). Heritage Language Socialization Practices in Secular Yiddish Educational Contexts: The Creation of a Metalinguistic Community. Retrieved from https://escholarship.org/uc/item/9f50n171

Avineri, Netta. (2014). Yiddish Endangerment as Phenomenological Reality and Discursive Strategy: Crossing into the Past and Crossing out the Present. *Language & Communication 38*, 18–32.

Avineri, Netta. (2017). Contested Stance Practices in Secular Yiddish Metalinguistic Community: Negotiating Closeness and Distance. In I. L. Bleaman & B. D. Joseph (Eds), Jewish Language Variation and Contact: Fifty Years After Uriel Weinreich (1926–967). [Special Issue]. *Journal of Jewish Languages 5*(2), 174–199.

Avineri, N. (2018). Metalinguistic Communities and Nostalgia Socialization in Historical and Contemporary Yiddish Literature. Connecting across Languages and Cultures: A Heritage Language Festschrift in Honor of Olga Kagan. Slavica Publishers.

Avineri, Netta, & Kroskrity, Paul V. (2014). On the (Re-)Production and Representation of Endangered Language Communities: Social Boundaries and Temporal Borders. *Language & Communication 38*, 1–7.

Avni, Sharon. (2014). Hebrew Education in the United States: Historical Perspectives and Future Directions. *Journal of Jewish Education, 80*(3), 256–286.

Benor, Sarah Bunin. (2008). Towards a New Understanding of Jewish Language in the 21st Century. *Religion Compass 2/6*, 1062–1080.

Benor, Sarah Bunin. (2009). Do American Jews Speak a "Jewish Language"? A Model of Jewish Linguistic Distinctiveness." *Jewish Quarterly Review 99*(2), 230–269.

Benor, Sarah Bunin. (2010). Ethnolinguistic Repertoire: Shifting the Analytic Focus in Language and Ethnicity" *Journal of Sociolinguistics 14*(2), 159–183.

Benor, Sarah Bunin. (2011a). *Mensch, Bentsh,* and *Balagan*: Variation in the American Jewish Linguistic Repertoire. *Language and Communication 31*(2), 141–154.

Benor, Sarah Bunin. (2011b). Hameyvin Yavin: Language and Super Jews. Retrieved from http://perspectives.ajsnet.org/the-religious-issue-fall-2011/hameyvin-yavin-language-and-super-jews/

Benor, Sarah Bunin. (2012). *Becoming Frum: How Newcomers Learn the Language and Culture of Orthodox Judaism.* New Brunswick, NJ: Rutgers University Press.

Benor, Sarah Bunin. (2016). Jewish English. In Lily Kahn, & Aaron Rubin (Eds.), *Brill Handbook of Jewish Languages* (pp. 130–137). Leiden, The Netherlands: Brill.

Bloomfield, Leonard. (1933). *Language.* New York, NY: Henry Holt.

Canale, M., & Swain, M. (1980). Theoretical Bases of Communicative Approaches to Second Language Teaching and Testing. *Applied Linguistics 1*, 1–47.

Carreira, M., & Kagan, O. (2011). The Results of the National Heritage Language Survey: Implications for Teaching, Curriculum Design, and Professional Development. *Foreign Language Annals, 44*, 40–64.

Chiswick, Carmel. (2014). *Judaism in Transition: How Economic Choices Shape Religious Tradition.* Palo Alto, CA: Stanford University Press.

Cutter, William. (2007). A Language for Zionist Reciprocity. *CCAR Journal 54*(2), 7–26.

Dornyei, Zoltan. (2005). *The Psychology of the Language Learner: Individual Differences in Second Language Acquisition.* Mahwah, NJ: Lawrence Erlbaum.

Dornyei, Zoltan, & Ushioda, Emi. (Eds.) (2009). *Motivation, Language Identity and the L2 Self.* Bristol, UK: Multilingual Matters.

Duranti, Alessandro. (1997). *Linguistic Anthropology.* Cambridge, UK: Cambridge University Press.

Firestone, Wayne L. (2011). Hebrew: A Grassroots Campaign for Jewish Identity. Retrieved from http://www.steinhardtfoundation.org/contact/spring_2011/spring_2011-firestone.html

Fishman, Joshua A. (1973). *Language and Nationalism: Two Integrative Essays.* Rowley, MA: Newbury House.

Fishman, Joshua A. (1976). Interview on the Success and Failure in Language Education. *Melton Research Center Newsletter 4*, 3. Quoted in Avni, 2014.

Fishman, Joshua A. (1991). *Language and Ethnicity.* Amsterdam, The Netherlands: John Benjamins Publishing Company.

Gedzelman, David. (2011). The Possibilities and Potential of Hebrew in America. *Contact: The Journal of the Steinhardt Foundation for Jewish Life 13*(2), 3–4.

Giddens, Anthony. (1984). *The Constitution of Society: Outline of the Theory of Structuration.* Berkeley, CA: University of California Press.

Glinert, Lewis. (1993). Language as Quasilect: Hebrew in Contemporary Anglo Jewry. In Lewis Glinert (Ed.), *Hebrew in Ashkenaz: A Language in Exile* (pp. 249–264). New York, NY: Oxford University Press.

Glinert, Lewis. (1999). Smashing the Idols: Towards a Need-Based Method for Teaching Hebrew as Heritage. *Journal of Jewish Education 65*(3), 17–20.

Gold, David. (1985). Jewish English. In J. A. Fishman (Ed.), *Readings in the Sociology of Jewish Languages* (pp. 280–298). Leiden, The Netherlands: Brill.

Gumperz, John J. (1968). The Speech Community. In D. L. Sills (Ed.), *International Encyclopedia of the Social Sciences* (pp. 381–386). New York, NY: Macmillan.

Greninger, Rabbi Nicki. (2012). Hebrew & the B'nai Mitzvah Revolution. Retrieved from http://blogs.rj.org/blog/2012/06/29/hebrew-bnai-mitzvah-revolution/

Greninger, Rabbi Nicki. (2014). A New Approach to Hebrew in Congregational Jewish Education, Network for Research on Jewish Education, Los Angeles, 2014.

Hazony, David. (2012). Memo to American Jews: Learn Hebrew. Retrieved from http://forward.com/articles/154253/memo-to-american-jews-learn-hebrew/?p=all

He, A. W. (2010). The Heart of Heritage: Sociocultural Dimensions of Heritage Languagelearning. *Annual Review of Applied Linguistics 30*, 66–82.

Hoffman, Joel M. (2011). Hebrew: A Language Reborn. Retrieved from http://www.steinhardtfoundation.org/contact/spring_2011/spring_2011-hoffman.html

Irvine, Judith T., & Gal, Susan. (2000). Language Ideology and Linguistic Differentiation. In P. V. Kroskrity (Ed.), *Regimes of language* (pp. 35–83). Santa Fe, NM: School of American Research Press.

Jaffe, Alexandra (2007). Discourses of Endangerment: Contexts and Consequences of Essentializing Discourses. In A. Duchene, & M. Heller (Eds.), *Discourses of Endangerment: Ideology and Interest in the Defence of Languages* (pp. 57–75). London, UK: Continuum International Publishing Group.

Kaunfer, Elie. (2018) Make a Bolder Investment. Retrieved from https://www.mechonhadar.org/blog/make-bolder-investment-0

Kushner Bishop, Jill. (2001). From Shame to Nostalgia: Shifting Language Ideologies in the Judeo-Spanish Maintenance Movement. In H. Pomeroy, & M. Alpert (Eds.), *Proceedings of the Twelfth British Conference on Judeo-Spanish Studies* (pp. 23–32). Leiden, The Netherlands: Brill.

Lanski, Anne. (2011). *Charting the Course: Hebrew Language in Public High Schools.* Retrieved from http://www.steinhardtfoundation.org/wp-install/wp-content/uploads/2013/10/spring_2011.pdf

Leonard, Wesley Y. (2011). Challenging "Extinction" Through Modern Miami Language Practices. *American Indian Culture and Research Journal 35*, 135–160.

Levisohn, Jon A. (2014). What Work Do the Concepts of "Language" and "Literature" Do for Michael Rosenak?" *Journal of Jewish Education 80*(4), 411–433.

Lipstadt, Deborah. (1993). Hebrew Among Jewish Communal Leaders: Requirement, Elective, or Extra-Curricular Activity? In Alan Mintz (Ed.), *Hebrew in America: Perspectives and Prospects* (pp. 309–321). Detroit, MI: Wayne State University Press.

McEwan-Fujita, Emily. (2010.) Ideology, Affect, and Socialization in language hift and Revitalization: The Experiences of Adults Learning Gaelic in the Western Isles of Scotland. *Language in Society 39*, 27–64.

Mehan, Hugh. (1979). *Learning lessons: Social Organization in the Classroom*. Cambridge, MA: Harvard: University Press.

Mintz, Alan. (2011). *The Hebraist Movement in American Jewish Culture and What It Has to Say to Us Today*. Retrieved from https://www.bjpa.org/search-results/publication/12103

Morahg, Gilead. (1993). Language is Not Enough. In Alan Mintz (Ed.), *Hebrew in America: Perspectives and Prospects* (pp. 187–208). Detroit, MI: Wayne State University Press.

Morahg, Gilead. (1999). HEBREW: A Language of Identity. *Journal of Jewish Education 65*(3), 9–16.

Morgan, Marcyliena. (2006). Speech Community. In A. Duranti (Ed.), *A Companion to Linguistic Anthropology* (pp. 3–22). Malden, MA: Blackwell.

Moskowitz, Nachama Skolnik. (2013). Teaching "The Impossible" with Hebrew Through Movement. Retrieved from http://ejewishphilanthropy.com/teaching-the-impossible-with-hebrew-through-movement/

Nevins, Marybeth E. (2004). Learning to Listen: Confronting Two Meanings of Language Loss in the Contemporary White Mountain Apache Speech Community. *Journal of Linguistic Anthropology 14*, 269–288.

Paradise, Jonathan. (2011). Rx for Hebrew in American Jewish Communities. *Contact: The Journal of the Steinhardt Foundation for Jewish Life 13*(2), 12.

Peirce, Bonny N. (1995). Social Identity, Investment, and Language Learning. *TESOL Quarterly,29*(1), 9–31.

Pew Research Center. (2013). *A Portrait of Jewish Americans: Findings from a Pew Research Center Survey of U.S. Jews*. Retrieved from http://www.pewforum.org/2013/10/01/jewish-american-beliefs-attitudes-culture-survey/

Polinsky, M., & Kagan, O. (2007). Heritage Languages: In the "Wild" and in the Classroom. *Languages and Linguistics Compass 1*, 368–395.

Ringvald, Vardit. (2011). The Role of Second Language Pedagogy. Retrieved from http://education.jed.macam.ac.il/article/1222

Rosen, Ben and William Chomsky. 2003 [1940]. Improving the Teaching of Hebrew in Our Schools. *Journal of Jewish Education 69*(1), 57–63.

Rosenak, Michael. (1995). *Roads to the Palace*. New York, NY: Berghahn Press.

Schachter, Lifsa. (2010). Why Bonnie and Ronnie Can't "Read" (the Siddur). *Journal of Jewish Education 76*, 74–91.

Schiffrin, Deborah. (1984). Jewish Argument as Sociability. *Language in Society 13*, 311–335.

Shandler, Jeffrey. (2005). *Adventures in Yiddishland: Postvernacular Language and Culture*. Berkeley, CA: University of California Press.

Shohamy, Elana. (1999). Contextual and Pedagogical Factors for Learning and Maintaining Jewish Languages in the United States. *Journal of Jewish Education 65*(3), 21–29.

Silva-Corvalan, Carmen. (2003). Linguistic Competence of Reduced Input in Bilingual First Language Acquisition. In S. Montrul, & F. Ordonez (Eds.), *Linguistic Theory and Language Development in Hispanic Languages* (pp. 375–397). Somerville, MA: Cascadilla.

Silverstein, Michael. 1996. Monoglot 'Standard' in America: Standardization and Metaphors of Linguistic Hegemony. In D. Brenneis, & R. H. S. Macaulay (Eds.), *The Matrix of Language: Contemporary Linguistic Anthropology* (pp. 284–306). Boulder, CO: Westview Press.

Silverstein, Michael. 1998. Contemporary Transformations of Local Linguistic Communities. *Annual Review of Anthropology 27*, 401–26.

Spolsky, Bernard (1998, March 1). Language Policy and the Teaching of Hebrew, Acquisition of Hebrew as a First or Second Language, University of Maryland, 2014.

Tannen, Deborah. (1981). New York Jewish Conversational Style. *International Journal of the Sociology of Language 30*, 133–149.

Valdes, Guadalupe. (2000). The Teaching of Heritage Languages: An Introduction for Slavic-Teaching Professionals. In O. Kagan, & B. Rifkin (Eds.), *The Learning and Teaching of Slavic Languages and Cultures* (pp. 375–403). Bloomington, IN: Slavica.

Veltman, Calvin. (2000). The American Linguistic Mosaic: Understanding Language Shift in the United States. In S. L. McKay, & S. C. Wong (Eds.), *New Immigrants in the United States* (pp. 58–93). Cambridge, UK: Cambridge University Press.

Weinreich, Max. (2008). *History of the Yiddish Language.* 2 vols. Paul Glaser (Ed.). Joshua A. Fishman, & Schlomo Noble (Trans.). New Haven, CT: Yale University Press.

Wexler, Paul. (1981). Jewish Interlinguistics: Facts and Conceptual Framework. *Language 57*, 99–149.

Wieseltier, Leon. (2011). "Language, Identity, and the Scandal of American Jewry." *Journal of Jewish Communal Service 86*(1/2), 14–22.

Wohl, Aryeh. (2005). Teaching and Learning Hebrew—Steering or Drifting. Retrieved from http://www.lookstein.org/articles/wohl_steering.htm

Where is the Next Soviet Jewry Movement? How Identity Education Forgot the Lessons that Jewish Activism Taught

Shaul Kelner

In this chapter, I draw together two phenomena that seem to have little in common. One is an undercurrent of American Jewish nostalgia for the Cold War-era movement to free Soviet Jewry. The other is a more acute dissatisfaction with American Jewish education of the present day, and particularly with the fetishization of "identity" in Jewish educational discourse and practice. I argue that nostalgia for the Soviet Jewry movement contains an implicit critique of Jewish educational models that prioritize shaping individual identity above engaging people in world-changing collective action. American Jews valorize the Soviet Jewry movement as representative of the American Jewish community at its best—a moment when Jews in great number creatively and passionately engaged the world as Jews in order to change the world in specific ways. Jewish educators should pay heed to this, because it holds forth a vision of an ideal community toward which to educate.

As one who studies the American Jewish community's Cold War-era campaign to free Soviet Jewry, I lecture about the movement to Jewish groups. The talks tend to draw American Jews of a certain generation, people who remember the movement, many of whom had some personal stake in it. There is no shortage of people like that. The mobilization was so broad and so successful in penetrating the synagogues, federations, summer camps, Hebrew schools, and other institutions of American Jewish life, that it touched most American Jews in one way or another over the three decades that it was working to change the world. Today, few think often about the Soviet Jewry movement, but it does not take much to get American Jews waxing nostalgic about it. A simple mention of the Matzoh of Hope readings they added to their Passover seders to decry the suppression of Jewish religion in the USSR; or of the bar and bat mitzvah ceremonies they "twinned" with absent thirteen-year-old Russian Jewish boys and girls unable to celebrate freely in the Soviet Union; or of the Solidarity Sunday demonstrations that they marched in along with hundreds of thousands of others under the banner, "Let my people go;" or of the metal bracelets that they wore to remember refuseniks like Anatoly Shcharansky and Ida Nudel who were imprisoned for asking to emigrate; or of the blue jeans and medicines they gave to their rabbis to deliver to refuseniks in the USSR; or of the "Escape from Russia" simulation games they played year after year at Jewish summer camps—any of these will suffice to elicit responses like, "I remember when I . . .," "What ever happened to that?", and "We need another Soviet Jewry movement." Gal Beckerman, author of the National Jewish Book Award-winning history, *When They Come for Us, We'll Be Gone: The Epic Struggle to Save Soviet Jewry* (2010), found much the same thing as he traveled the country promoting his book. "[O]ften when I speak to Jewish audiences about this," he said, "I get asked, 'do Jews have another Soviet Jewry movement in them?' Or . . . what right now is 'the Soviet Jewry'—and sad to say that I don't know that one exists" (Springer, 2011, p. 12).

Why the desire among American Jews for a modern day equivalent to the Soviet Jewry movement? Considering the persecutions that gave rise to the struggle, one might think that the last thing Jews would want is a situation that would demand a mass mobilization. But American Jews are not thinking about Soviet Jews when they wish for a new version of the cause; they are thinking of themselves. Nostalgia for the movement contains an implicit recognition that although the Soviet Jewry movement was intended to help Jews in Russia, it ended up offering something of enormous value to American Jews—a galvanizing cause that inspired them to action and stirred their feelings of Jewish pride and empowerment. Those who wish for "another Soviet Jewry movement" are giving voice to their sense that the mobilization for Soviet Jews enabled the American Jewish community to realize its best version of itself, and that the movement's end, successful though it was, also entailed a certain form of loss.

There is wisdom in this. Those who care about American Jewish education would do well to look at how the Soviet Jewry movement ignited American Jews. The campaign succeeded in accomplishing what most people who care about Jewish education want Jewish education to do, but what identity-centered education has generally struggled to deliver on: At the individual level, it inspired Jews to care passionately about living their Jewish values in practice. At the collective level, it created a vibrant, engaging and optimistic Jewish public culture, revitalizing holiday and life-cycle rituals with new meaning that was both timely and timeless. In the process, it brought Jews together in proud, joyful self-assertion. Working toward a cause, American Jews took ownership of their heritage and creatively treated Jewish tradition as a resource for engaging their world, for expressing their value commitments and for engaging young and old in a mass mobilization. If Jewish educators today aspire to recreate a community capable of such creativity, then they should look to how the Soviet Jewry movement managed to accomplish this, and ponder the contrast between the mission-oriented, "I am my brother's keeper" model that guided the movement's activity and the more determinedly individualistic, "All Jews are Jews by choice" model that supplanted it.

In the pages ahead, I will try to make the case that the American Soviet Jewry movement's success in achieving the types of educational and communal outcomes that have eluded the enterprise of identity-centered Jewish education, stems from the fact that the movement conceptualized its goals around realizing a vision of the public Good, in contrast to identity-centered education which places the cultivation of individual sentiment and self-concept at its center. In examining how Jewish communal interest in identity was informed by late twentieth-century sociological theorizations of American ethnicity, I will argue that alternative streams of social scientific research are better suited for translating the approach of the Soviet Jewry movement into educational practice. In place of the overly individualistic social-psychological notion of "identity," I propose that educators look to the anthropological concept of "subjectivity," which better articulates the socially situated, action-oriented character of people's self-understandings and their behaviors.

A Lesson from Viktor Frankl

From the founding in 1963 of the Cleveland Committee on Soviet Anti-Semitism, America's first Soviet Jewry movement organization, to the closing in 1994 of the United Jewish Appeal's $900 million Operation Exodus campaign to help Israel absorb hundreds of thousands of emigrants from the former Soviet Union, the struggle to free Soviet Jewry engaged millions of American Jews in myriad ways. There was nothing inevitable about such broad-based participation. Anyone inclined to think otherwise should ask why the movement really only got underway in the US in the 1960s rather than the 1950s, or why it was only in the 1970s that attendance at demonstrations began topping 100,000? Jacob Birnbaum, the founder of one of the first Soviet Jewry movement organizations in the US, adopted the shofar as an emblem for his Student Struggle for Soviet Jewry (SSSJ), not only to symbolize the ram's horn's call for freedom, but to indicate that American Jews needed to be roused from their apathy toward the Soviet Jewish plight (J. Birnbaum, personal communication, December 11, 2003; Rubin, 1966).

American Jews were rallied to action by leaders who engaged in a process that scholars of social movements call "micro-mobilization"—the development of strategies and tactics to recruit people as participants in a social movement campaign (Snow, Rochford, Worden & Benford, 1986, pp. 464–481). In the American movement for Soviet Jews, the micro-mobilization was broad based. Activists tried to reach and engage American Jews in their synagogues and Jewish community centers, in their religious schools and summer camps, in their homes and on the streets, in their work and in their leisure pursuits. Success required them to think creatively. Activists treated Passover, Simchat Torah and almost every other Jewish holiday including the Fast of the Tenth of Tevet as resources to be used to rally people for Soviet Jews, and they developed new holiday rituals to that end. They did the same with life cycle ceremonies, especially bar and bat mitzvahs (Kelner, 2008; Kelner, 2011). Synagogues added liturgies for Soviet Jewry and adapted their physical space, reserving empty chairs on the pulpit to remind people of Soviet Jews denied the right to worship with them. In the winter, educator-activists engaged Jewish children through Hebrew school curricula focused on the Soviet Jewish plight, and handed over the work of publicizing the cause to the children themselves, sponsoring poster competitions that let each student become a social movement artist. In the summer, they closed the books and used play instead, transforming campgrounds into imaginary USSRs where campers pretended to be refuseniks running the gauntlet of Soviet bureaucracy as they tried to escape to Israel. (Counsellors played the role of KGB agents). Seizing the opportunities presented by the rise of mass tourism, activist groups recruited vacationers in the thousands to cross the Iron Curtain and clandestinely deliver material and moral support to refuseniks, and they even tailored the tourist-engagement through profession-based affinity groups. Visiting doctors diagnosed and treated Soviet Jews' ailments. Visiting lawyers collected information for legal briefs. Visiting academics addressed home seminars for Soviet Jewish scientists fired from their positions. Visiting rabbis taught classes on religion. Thousands of these visitors wrote travelogues detailing their visits and describing what the experience meant for them as Jews and as Americans, sometimes even with a nod to James Bond (Kelner, forthcoming; Kelner, 2019; Kelner, 2013).

Through the Soviet Jewry movement, American Jews of all ages and of all religious stripes embraced new roles as creators of ritual, producers of political art, smugglers and spy novel writers, organizers of demonstrations, and more. They treated traditional Jewish culture as a storehouse of resources to be creatively developed. They did the same with contemporary American culture as well, and they intertwined the two to create new modes of acting as Jewish-Americans. (When else in history have Jews invented a "Passover walk-a-thon?")[1]

How did the American movement for Soviet Jewry foster such a generative form of Jewish engagement? Not by embracing pabulums like "building," "strengthening," or "cultivating" Jewish "identity." Instead, activists—from the professional leaders of national organizations to thousands of volunteers in synagogue Soviet Jewry committees—were preoccupied with working to change the world in specific ways. Sometimes, the work focused on changing the life of a single human being, whether it was writing one's senator to request intervention for one's bar or bat mitzvah twin, or smuggling a two hundred-day supply of Enalapril to a Leningrad refusenik suffering from severe hypertension (Kelner, 2015; Graber, 1987, p. 12). Sometimes, it focused on making systemic change, such as lobbying Congress to pass the Jackson-Vanik legislation so that US economic leverage could be used to pressure the Kremlin to liberalize its emigration policies (Lazin, 2005; Peretz, 2006; Galchinsky, 2007).

Activists understood that there were no quick or simple solutions to the problem they were trying to address and that any hope of success would depend on sustaining a decades-long mass mobilization of American Jews. It was their pursuit of this strategic imperative to keep people mobilized that led them to treat Jewish culture as a creative resource to be continually adapted and re-adapted in the service of the cause. Just as this imperative led them to weave the movement into the rhythms of the Jewish calendar and the Jewish life-course, it also led them to try to bring the movement into as many different types of American Jewish institutions as they could, tailoring their efforts to

---

1 An account of this is found in "Political and Civic Notables to lead Walkathon for Soviet Jewry on Sunday April 11" (press release; no date) in the Records of the Student Struggle for Soviet Jewry [hereafter, SSSJ], Yeshiva University Archives, New York, box 16, folder 8.

each. Their efforts made the Soviet Jewish cause (and the array of particular American and Jewish values that it invoked and elicited) a vital part of the Jewish lives that American Jews' lived during the late Cold War era. Simply put, the Soviet Jewry movement *moved* American Jews.[2] And yet, the movement's effect on American Jews' identities was a by-product of activism, not the campaign's manifest goal. The point was to get Soviet Jews out. Rousing American Jews to take action and then to stay motivated, decade after decade in the face of setbacks as well as successes—this was only a means to an end.

Contrast this with a Jewish education that defines its mission as cultivating Jewish identity, and consider this in terms of Viktor Frankl's dictum regarding success and happiness. "Don't aim at success," the psychotherapist and Holocaust survivor famously wrote in *Man's Search for Meaning*. "The more you aim at it and make it a target, the more you are going to miss it. For success, like happiness, cannot be pursued; it must ensue, and it only does so as the unintended side effect of one's personal dedication to a cause greater than oneself or as the by-product of one's surrender to a person other than oneself" (Frankl, 1985, p. 16–17).

The same is true of identity. Two aspects of Frankl's approach have special bearing here. First is the folly of pursuing something which can only "ensue." The endemic problems faced by educators working in an identity-centric model are not accidental, but inhere in the attempt to treat an unintended consequence as the specific object of pursuit. Second, and related, is the anchoring of salient social identities in dedication to "a cause greater than oneself" or to other human beings. Here, the psychiatrist introduces the sociological into the conversation, for causes and relationships are collective matters, not individual ones. Yet a Jewish educational enterprise preoccupied with identity—how *individuals* think and feel—is ill-prepared to come to terms with this, for it would mean, among other things, defining success in terms of collective outcomes that cannot be measured in student progress reports. True success for the Soviet Jewry movement was the emigration of

---

2   It is important not to impute individual mental states from public collective behaviors (Kelner, 2008). Still, there is ample evidence from personal testimony that people engaged by the Soviet Jewry movement found their involvement deeply meaningful. See, for instance, memoirs of former activists written after the movement ended such as Eisen (1995); Weiss (2015). See also the travelogues written by American Jews who met with refuseniks in the USSR during the years of the movement itself (thousands of which are available online at the website of the American Jewish Historical Society's Archive of the American Soviet Jewry Movement.) Contemporary nostalgia for the movement can also be interpreted as a window onto the movement's effect on private sentiment.

Soviet Jews. And yet, the pursuit of this outcome inspired American Jews to engage the world as Jews, acting from a Jewish standpoint. Through their actions, they gave life to a mode of Jewish being-in-the-world in which the values of Jewish peoplehood, unity and mutual responsibility were vital, operative forces.[3]

All this came to an end with the collapse of America's Soviet adversary and the ensuing mass emigration of Russian-speaking Jews. American Jews stopped marching in Solidarity Day rallies, stopped singing *Am Yisroel Chai* in front of Russian diplomatic offices, stopped twinning bar and bat mitzvahs, stopped placing empty chairs on synagogue pulpits, stopped raising a fourth matzah "of hope" at Passover seders, stopped wearing Prisoner of Zion jewelry, stopped flying to Moscow to smuggle in contraband prayer books. In short, they stopped everything that they had been doing over the past three decades to shout, "Let my people go!"

There were profound consequences to demobilizing. Behavior actively shapes how people think and feel. Too often, we assume that the process works the other way around—that people first come to know or feel something and then act on the basis of that understanding. But such a view forgets the sound sociological wisdom contained in the Talmud's interpretation of the line in Exodus 24:7, *na`aseh v'nishma*, "[first] we will do and [then] we will understand." Explaining why, when accepting the Torah, the Israelites did not say the converse, "We will read it and understand it and then based on that understanding we will follow its teachings," which would seem to be the more logical statement, the rabbis (b. Shabbat 88a) explained that it is only by doing that understanding actually emerges. Action generates meaning.

The converse also holds. In the absence of action, meanings cease to be created. The understandings that were once grounded in action dissipate. Once we recognize this, it is no longer surprising that the understandings and sentiments that the movement generated—that is, the particular type of Jewish self-understandings that Soviet Jewry movement activism fostered—began to erode once people stopped marching, stopped twinning, stopped all the activities through which they demonstrated to themselves that all Jews were responsible for one another, *kol yisrael arevim zeh lazeh,* and that they were, in fact, their brothers' keepers (Kelner, 2008).

---

3   These values were part of what Jonathan Woocher (1986) referred to as the ethic of "Sacred Survival," the civil religion that gave transcendent legitimation to Jewish ethnic mobilization of the 1970s. For a treatment of the relationship between the Soviet Jewry movement and Woocher's notion of Sacred Survival, see Kelner (2008).

This helps makes sense of the odd situation in which leaders of the same Jewish organizations that in 1987 had managed to demonstrate American Jewry's passion for saving Soviet Jewry by rallying 250,000 at the National Mall in Washington, D.C., were, not five years later, worrying that American Jews were so apathetic about their Jewishness that the American Jewish community itself was at risk of disappearing through assimilation. In retrospect, it seems reasonable that the loss of what, for three decades, had been one of the community's major rallying points might lead to a sense among American Jewish leaders in the 1990s that their community was adrift.[4] By winding down its mass mobilization for Soviet Jews, the American Jewish community stopped engaging the rank and file in the activities that powerfully generated peoplehood sensibilities. And since the sensibilities emerged through the behaviors that people engaged in, when the na`aseh ("we will do") stopped, its particular nishma ("we will understand") evaporated (Kelner, 2008).

Few recognized this at the time, however, and it was more common to argue that the "continuity crisis" (to use the language of the era) was a result of the fact that Jews' ethnic identities were weakening, and that the younger generations did not feel the same pull of peoplehood as prior generations had. This was a nishma v'na'aseh argument that flipped the rabbinic sociology on its head: People stopped caring, and so they stopped acting, or so the argument went. The educational prescription to focus on identity flowed from this. If educators could get people to care again about being Jewish, then they would start acting on those sentiments.

The logic was consistent. The problem was that it got the sociology backwards. When Jewish leaders mobilized action to realize compelling visions for changing the world, they stirred Jewish commitment and engagement. This was true of activism on behalf of Jewish peoplehood, which inspired people for decades and ended not due to any waning in individual Jewish caring for other Jews, but as a result of leaders' decisions to demobilize once Jews were no longer trapped in the Soviet Union. It was also true of Jewish feminist activism, whose powerful mission-oriented na'aseh engaged an increasingly large and diverse population of women and men of all ages, mushrooming in the 1990s even as "continuity crisis" talk was portraying a community suffering from an epidemic of disengagement (see, e.g., Fishman, 1993; Prell, 2007).

---

4   Nor could Israel serve as the common rallying point that it had in the decade or so after the 1967 Six Day War. By virtue of bitter disagreements over the 1982 Lebanon War, 1987 Intifada, and 1993 Oslo Accords, Israel had become a source of division among American Jews, and not only a source of unity (Sasson 2013; Waxman 2016).

Perhaps if conveners in the world of Jewish education had placed commitment to realizing the mission of a Jewish social movement at the top of the educational agenda, they would have filled the vacuum created by the end of the Soviet Jewry mobilization. Certainly, there was no shortage of new educational materials emerging out of Jewish feminism, Jewish environmentalism, and other movements, all of which made their impact felt in various ways. But ultimately, what ended up being placed at the fore of the broader communal agenda for Jewish education was oblivious to the social movements of the era and quite the opposite of the model suggested by the Soviet Jewry movement. Focusing on the individual over the community and on the personal sense of self over any collective mission, educators operating in the "identity" paradigm adopted a *nishma v'naaseh* approach—a cart-before-the-horse reversal of the traditional formulation which, ignoring Frankl, actively pursued that which could only ensue from focusing on something else.

Identity Education and the Social-Psychological Turn in Jewish Social Science

The rise of Jewish identity discourse in Jewish education was well underway even at the height of the Soviet Jewry movement. This was part and parcel of changes in the field of applied research in the social science of American Jewry, a change that can be described as a "social-psychological turn" away from the field's origins in the discipline of sociology.

There are many reasons why the notion of "identity" gained currency in the social scientific and educational conversations about Jewish life in America since the 1970s. Other contributors in this volume will be better positioned to trace the genealogy of the concept from scholar to scholar as it diffused throughout the research literature in Jewish education. But leaving aside the field-specific history that is crucial for understanding the concept's rise in American Jewish educational discourse, there is also a broader enabling context to be considered.

If one steps outside the communal conversation about Jewish identity to examine the concept that stands at its center, it becomes easier to recognize certain key features of the concept that mark it as a product of its time and place. To speak of "identity" is to speak of the individual, and to give primacy to the importance of self-concept—a reasoned, reflexive awareness of an autobiographical story that one is able to put into words and tell to oneself. It becomes a relevant concept—appropriately so—in a society that values the individual above the group, and that permits a great deal of individual autonomy, where choice is privileged over socially imposed obligation and constraint. It also arises in a free society that values human reason and tends to presume a behavioral model that imagines—Freud be damned—rational actors making decisions based upon clear and well-articulated self-knowledge. (Consider the slogan, "All Jews are Jews by choice.")

Can anyone be surprised that such a strongly individualistic concept rose to prominence as Baby Boomers, finally adults, were being re-christened the Me Generation (Wolfe, 1976)? And yet while it certainly tapped broader shifts in American culture, the popularity of the concept in the social scientific and educational discourse about American Jews is replete with ironies. One is simply that, of all the conceptual tools for thinking about a community that cares about itself as a community, "identity" is perhaps the most atomistic, with the least to say about anything beyond the individual. To the extent that it even suggests a theory of collective change, such a theory can be little more than aggregate psychology.

This points to a second irony. The field of research on Jewish identity is colloquially known as the "sociology" of American Jews. But if any discipline is, at its core, antagonistic to the notion of psychological reductionism in the explanation of social phenomena, it is sociology. At the foundation of the discipline is Emile Durkheim's argument that society exists *sui generis*—that social phenomena cannot be understood simply as the sum of their individual parts (Durkheim, 1966; 1982). Once people begin to interact with each other, dynamics are set in motion that are beyond the choice or control of any single person, and social facts are created that exist at a level that is not reducible to any single individual or what is going on inside his or her head. Anyone who has ever tried to navigate a complex bureaucracy will understand this.[5] But as a result of Jewish communal policy makers' embrace of "identity" as a primary object of applied research and as a key target of intervention, this foundational insight of sociology has largely been lost to the American Jewish community.

And yet, there are sound sociological explanations for the appeal of identity discourse in the American Jewish conversation. These too can be traced back to the 1970s, when sociological research on European ethnic groups in the United States took up the question of whether the social-structural groundings of ethnicity were on the wane, and if so, what this would portend for the future of these ethnic groups. Framed initially by Herbert Gans

---

5   For the classic analysis of bureaucracy by another of sociology's founders, see Weber (1958).

(1979) who referred to the rise of "symbolic ethnicity," and developed by Mary Waters (1990), who spoke of "ethnic options," this research showed erosion in the sources of social cohesion that had previously created tightly knit ethnic communities. Ethnic neighborhoods were on the wane, as were vernacular use of pre-migration languages, work in economic niche industries (in some cases), intra-ethnic friendships and marriages, and exclusionary social barriers that reinforced group boundaries from the outside. In such a situation, the folk cultures that emerged from the lived experience of people embedded in highly bounded face-to-face ethnic communities had lost much of their structural and interactional grounding. Ethnic organizations could serve as an alternative base, but the persistence of ethnic cultures in a newly fluid social environment would depend much more, the argument went, on the choice of individuals to make ethnicity a priority in their own lives. But unlike the grounded ethnicity that preceded it, this "symbolic ethnicity," Gans argued, did not shape actual life chances. Rather, it was a cultural resource to be invoked episodically, offering some flavor or variety or meaning to those who opted to embrace it.

I will not enter into the critiques of this conception of ethnicity. Here, I only wish to point out that to an organized Jewish community concerned about its future, the analysis rang true. Prominent sociologists were arguing that the future of ethnic community in America was no longer a function of sociology, but of social psychology. If the neighborhood could no longer sustain Jewishness in America, the community's future would perforce rest on the *choices of individuals* to think of themselves as Jews and to act on this self-concept. The role of Jewish organizations, in this context, would be to encourage Jewish choices. And of all the enterprises in the Jewish community that bore on the Jewish future, education would carry the greatest burden.

Identity, choice and the Jewish future were thus welded together into a model that has shaped the mission of Jewish education over the past several decades. The model's own struggles to live up to the lofty hopes pinned on it to produce dramatic changes in Jewish demography, institutional affiliation and other communal-level outcomes were probably inevitable, given the limitations of the concept at its core. To speak of "identity" is to imagine selfhood in static, ahistorical, non-interactional terms, divorced from the larger contexts in which people create and re-create themselves. Simply put, the concept is too individualistic and too generic to be of use as a concept for making any significant change in the world. It is too focused on how people feel alone in their own minds rather than how they are shaping their world even as they are being shaped by it. And without adjectives and hyphens to modify the term, it gives no guidance as to what type of Jewishness educators should be educating toward.

What Jewish educators need is a more dynamic, historicized, interactional concept, one that can speak coherently to the relationship between self and society. The point is not to eschew social psychology, but to draw out the social dimensions by showing how the act of thinking of oneself in a certain way simultaneously imagines the world in a certain way, and vice versa. By examining how people and their social worlds are mutually constituted, educators might better understand how particular ways of acting Jewishly rise and fall with the different contexts that create (and are created by) them. And this understanding will help them better articulate and educate towards the specific communal outcomes they hope to realize.

How People and Their Social Worlds are Mutually Constituted: The Case of Soviet Jewry Activism

This brings us back to the Soviet Jewry movement, a case well-suited to illustrate the point. Consider the efforts of movement leaders to turn Jewish holidays into mobilization opportunities. Such efforts were a hallmark of the campaign. Protest activities around Passover and Chanukah began early in the 1960s, with other holidays sometimes being drafted in an ad hoc manner. By the early 1970s, however, activist groups were circulating action plans to synagogues and Jewish community centers calling upon them to tailor specific Soviet Jewry-related activities to each holiday in the Jewish calendar (Kelner, 2011). Listing each festival one by one in calendar order, these documents suggested ways of tying holiday themes to the plight of Soviet Jews. Greeting cards could be sent to refuseniks for Rosh Hashanah. Night after night for eight nights, Chanukah programs could emphasize the struggle for religious freedom. Trees could be planted in Israel in honor of Soviet Jews on Tu Bish'vat. Purim shpiels could tell the story of Anatoly Shcharansky as a modern-day Moredecai, with Avital in the role of Esther and Brezhnev in the role of Haman. A "Matzoh of Hope" could be held aloft every Passover seder in solidarity with those awaiting a new exodus. And so on.

This was neither the first nor the last effort to use holidays for political causes or to reflect on the issues of the day. That is not what is notable about this effort. What is notable is the extent to which this effort to use the holidays was systematic, rational, and mapped out in advance. The Soviet Jewry movement's holiday program calendars could be produced only by people who decided to look systematically at each holiday, scrutinizing it for its potential to be enlisted into the service of the cause. Whether one views such an enterprise as holy work or chutzpah or both, notice how unusual it is to relate to Jewish holidays in such a way. Holidays in the Jewish tradition are typically treated as ends in themselves, observed and celebrated for the sake of fulfilling divine command, linking the generations past and future, or experiencing the rhythms of the sacred calendar. They are not commonly picked apart, one by one, to determine how they can be put to use. The American activists in the Soviet Jewry campaign did precisely this however.

Many Jewish educators would look at this example as an ideal to educate towards: Here were people knowledgeable about Jewish culture, confident in their own sense of ownership over their heritage such that they were willing to assert their right to do something new and unconventional with it, and capable of creatively developing Jewish cultural resources in ways that made a difference in the world. What should educators be doing to raise Jews to act like this? In answering this question, the concept of "identity" is useless, its many shortcomings revealed by its inability to account for the phenomenon or to offer guidance about how to reproduce something similar to it. We cannot make sense of this fascinating and consequential form of Jewish practice through the conventional lenses of identity for the simple reason that "identity" only points inward to the individual mind. It gives us no conceptual tools for moving beyond the activists to consider the other elements in the configuration—the holidays, the people they were trying to rally, the context in which all this was occurring.

Soviet Jewry movement leaders who adopted an instrumental approach to the Jewish holiday calendar behaved as political actors trying to mobilize a Jewish public for political action. This mode of being was not simply an "identity" because it not only made claims about the activists themselves but it also made claims about the other people whom they had in mind when they were acting (Claim: Jews are a political constituency to be mobilized), the Jewish cultural forms they were engaging (Claim: Holidays are resources to be utilized), and the context in which they were doing all this (Claim: In a democratic political culture, protest in religious spaces should be seen as legitimate. Claim: In Jewish religious culture, it should be legitimate for individuals to play with the sacred forms).[6] All these were claims, subject to

---

6   It is important to recognize that none of these claims were natural or inevitable. To see that this is so, consider some alternatives: B'nai mitzvah tutors typically do not think of their

contestation, and it is only the fact that the claims generally went uncontested in this instance (as opposed to the cases of Jewish feminism and the Jewish New Left, which did face opposition) that the boldness of the move is not immediately apparent.

At that particular moment in Jewish history, a group of individuals created a Jewish reality in which they were activists, other Jews were human resources to be deployed for a cause, holidays were political resources, and synagogues and homes were sites of political mobilization. As a result, hundreds of thousands of American Jews turned their Passover seders and Simchat Torah celebrations into moments of solidarity with Soviet Jews. A generation of American Jews—the b'nai mitzvah who twinned their ceremonies with children of refuseniks—came of age in a Jewish culture that enshrined activism on behalf of oppressed Jews in its holidays and life cycle rituals.[7]

None of this is about "identity." Some leaders of the Soviet Jewry movement might have acknowledged, if asked, that they were interested in cultivating the identities of Jews as "Soviet Jewry activists" —in helping Jews to start to see themselves in that way, by wearing a bracelet or attending a march—but that was just a means to the real end, freeing the Jews of the USSR. Some anticipated that activism could also spark a Jewish revival in the United States.[8] But they certainly would not have said that they were in the business of promoting Jewish identity, simpliciter. None of the activism focused on the lone individual searching for meaning. None of it was about Jewishness in the abstract, nor about holidays whose meanings are fixed and eternal.

So if it was not about "identity," what was it about? What conceptual language can we find to help educators articulate the phenomenon in ways that might guide educational practice? For this we turn away from social psychology, away even from sociology, and look to the discipline of anthropology, which offers the concept of "subjectivity."

---

charges as a political constituency to be mobilized. Gabbais scheduling Torah readers for the year's upcoming festivals tend to relate to the holiday calendar as a schedule to be filled, not as a resource to be put to use. A bereaved family saying kaddish graveside would likely be horrified were others to treat the funeral as a moment for political protest.

7 Ferziger (2015) refers to these religious politics, among Modern Orthodox American Jews, as "Solidarity Orthodoxy."

8 Writing of Jacob Birnbaum's vision for Student Struggle for Soviet Jewry, Kelner cites Yossi Klein Halevi (2004) who wrote that "[O]ne of his basic contentions [was] that SSSJ would save not only Soviet Jewry, but American Jewry—by kindling the Jewish passion of its youth."

Subjectivity: All Meanings are Situated Meanings

Before introducing a technical definition of *subjectivity* from the anthropological literature, it might be helpful to try to convey the concept in more colloquial terms (with the relevant caveats that come with a translation of this sort). When thinking about subjectivity, do not mistake it for the opposite of objectivity. That is not the meaning of the term being invoked here. Imagine instead the grammatical notion of the subject of a sentence. Outside of the sentence, you may have a noun, but you do not have a subject. Only by putting that noun together with a verb to form a sentence, does a subject come into being. It is a relational concept. Subjectivity, in the anthropological sense, can be understood, metaphorically speaking, as the gestalt experience of being the *subject* of the sentences that you write through your actions.

Because the subject is defined through its relationship with other parts of the sentence, as the verb changes, or as the direct object changes, the nature of the subjectivity changes, too. Thus, the "I" that cleans a floor is not the same "I" that carves a sculpture. The experience of self in each of these moments is radically different. Likewise, the Jew who mobilizes a holiday embodies a different subjectivity than the Jew who celebrates a holiday—even if that Jew is the same person. And as the subjectivity changes, the objects of action change too. Marble takes on a different meaning when it is treated as a chore to clean rather than an opportunity to create art. Passover takes on different meanings depending on whether it is treated as a resource to be used for a political mobilization, or as a divine command to be obeyed, or as an opportunity to showcase culinary creativity in the kosher kitchen, or as a stress-inducing family reunion to be navigated, etc.

Moreover, sentences take on meaning and are constrained by virtue of the larger paragraphs, chapters, dialogs and documents in which they are embedded. The sentence, "They were rushing," means different things if it appears in a paragraph about a work deadline, a college sorority, or a football game. Its meaning also changes as the people referred to by the word "they" changes. So too, subjectivities are embedded in the particular social contexts that enable and constrain them. Even what nominally appears to be the same act takes on different meanings as the *Sitz im Leben* changes. Who would argue that sitting in a rickety sukkah in New Orleans elicited and expressed the same meanings in 2005 after Hurricane Katrina had swept away peoples' homes as it had in the years prior? Or that a Passover seder on a kosher cruise off the coast of Florida in 2017 is the same thing as a Passover in the Warsaw ghetto? Sukkot is sukkot and a seder is a seder, no? No.

A key problem with the concept of "Jewish identity" is that one can speak of it without paying any regard to such changes in context. But this makes the concept so generic as to be almost meaningless. By contrast, it is impossible to speak of "subjectivity" in such a way, and this is part of that concept's strength. Subjectivity implies the contexts that create *all* meanings as *situated* meanings. For almost the entirety of Jewish history, there was not a Jew alive who could utter as a meaningful sentence the words, "Let's organize a Passover 5K walk/run for freedom." In its 1970s American Soviet Jewry movement context, the sentence makes perfect sense. But the subjectivity that would allow these words to come from someone's mouth could become possible only in a time and place that allows the notion of mobilizing holidays to become a thinkable thought, *and* that frames running as a leisure activity to promote good health, *and* that permits people to organize their own public events, etc.

With this in mind, a more technical definition of subjectivity offered by Sherry Ortner (2005) in the journal *Anthropological Theory* will not seem as mystifying as it otherwise might. Ortner begins by defining subjectivity as "the ensemble of modes of perception, affect, thought, desire, fear, and so forth that animate *acting* subjects." That is, subjectivity refers to one's experience of self—cognitively, emotionally, motivationally—*in the context of situated action.* She immediately extends this, however: "But I will always mean as well the cultural and social formations that shape, organize, and provoke those modes of affect, thought and so on" (p. 31, emphasis added).

Ortner's decision not to limit a definition of subjectivity to the first sentence alone seems to highlight an aspect of the concept that makes it somewhat confusing. To which level of analysis does the term subjectivity refer? The individual, or the societal? How can something simultaneously be an individual mode of perception and a social formation that provokes an individual mode of perception? It is important to recognize that the duality in Ortner's definition is intentional. Unlike the psychologists' *identity*, which presumes that we can treat the individual and society as separable from one another, the anthropologists' *subjectivity* insists that the two thoroughly interpenetrate one another. To speak of one, there is no choice but to speak of the other at the same time. The mindset and emotions of the person who says, "Let's organize a Passover 5K," exists only in a context that enables someone to treat holidays as useful resources. But such contexts are rare, and it requires no stretch of the imagination to think of Jewish communities where people could not even begin to think such a thought, let alone utter it.

These other contexts create very different types of Jewish subjectivities. If Jewish educators want to understand and influence how Jews think and act as Jews, they should strive to keep the embedded character of social action in mind.

Variations on the Theme

Ortner's is not the only approach to subjectivity, and educators exploring the concept might find that other variants will serve their particular interests better. I will mention two here, briefly, as examples and as enticements for Jewish educators to delve deeper on their own into the rich literature on the topic. Both examples maintain the conceptual duality that is one of the concept's key strengths, simultaneously pointing to the individual actor's motivated action as well as the societal context that enables and constrains such action. Each nuances the argument differently, however.

Anthropologist T. M. Luhrmann's (2006) approach highlights the inherently political character of subjectivity. Defining subjectivity as "the *emotional* experience of a *political* subject" (emphasis in the original), she redefines Ortner's "cultural and social formations that shape, organize, and provoke" as an embedding system of power relations. There is no subjectivity that is not political, in the broad sense, because every subjectivity is a product of larger configurations of power. (This does not mean that subjectivity necessarily reproduces those power relations, however. Much anthropological work focuses on subjectivities of resistance among oppressed groups.)

Luhrmann's approach draws in yet another meaning of the term "subject," different from the grammatical meaning that I introduced above. This meaning is, per the *Oxford English Dictionary*, "Someone or something under a person's rule or control." No person is entirely the author of his or her own situation. We are all political subjects insofar as power relations bear upon all of us. Broader political forces act on us, whether we know it or not, whether we like it or not. So too, we all act to advance various types of politics, whether we know it or not, and whether we or others like it or not. For Jewish educators, whether they are laying the groundwork for resistance to antisemitism or to patriarchy or to assimilation or to fundamentalism, or trying to foster commitment to social justice or to kashrut observance or to Israel or to the Yiddish language, Luhrmann's approach suggests the importance of recognizing that this work always contains a Jewish politics (preferring one way of being Jewish over others) and often participates in broader politics as well.[9]

Another approach to subjectivity, offered by Michel Foucault, shares Ortner's interest in looking at how self and society shape one another as people act in the world, but frames subjectivity in more narrowly cognitive terms than does Ortner, whose expansive approach also encompasses the emotions that animate action. In *Birth of the Clinic* (1973), Foucault shows how the emergence of modern medicine entailed new ways of observing, speaking about, applying categorizations to, and behaving toward the human body— ways of observing, speaking, categorizing and acting, that were grounded in a new type of medical institution, the clinic. The ability to know a human body in the ways that modern medicine does is inconceivable without, 1) the knowers simultaneously adopting orientations to themselves that enable them to see bodies in this way and, 2) an institutional context that legitimates these interrelated orientations to object and self.[10]

What Foucault wrote in the self-important style of French post-structuralists, *Saturday Night Live* made lowbrow comedy of in its classic 1977 sketch, "Theodoric of York, Medieval Barber," with Steve Martin in the title role.

> Announcer: In the Middle Ages, medicine was still in its infancy. The art of healing was conducted not by physicians, but by barbers. The medieval barbers were the forerunners of today's men of medicine, and many of the techniques they developed are still practiced today. This is the story of one such barber . . .
>
> [Theodoric approaches Joan, who stands next to her daughter]
>
> Joan [Jane Curtin]: Hello, Theodoric, Barber of York.
>
> Theodoric of York: Hello, Joan, Wife of Simkin the Miller. Well, how's my little patient doing?

---

9 I am not speaking of partisan politics here. I am speaking about politics in the larger sense. For example, there is a politics to a Jewish education that puts Israel at its center just as there is a politics to a Jewish education that does not put Israel at its center. There is a politics to a Reform Jewish education that presumes gender egalitarianism as there is a politics to an Orthodox Jewish education that does not. I am arguing here that it would be better for Jewish education if educators were to admit this, make themselves aware of it and choose consciously among their alternatives.

10 This Foucauldian approach to subjectivity is applied to analyze Soviet Jewry activists' mobilizations of ritual in Kelner (2011).

Joan: Not so well, I fear. We followed all your instructions—I mixed powder of staghorn, gum of arabic with sheep's urine, and applied it in a poultice to her face.

Theodoric of York: And did you bury her up to her neck in the marsh and leave her overnight?

Joan: Oh, yes. But she still feels as listless as ever, if not more.

Theodoric of York: Well, let's give her another bloodletting. Broom Gilda.

Broom Gilda [Gilda Radner]: Yes, Theodoric.

Theodoric of York: Take two pints.

Broom Gilda: Yes, Theodoric.

Joan: Will she be alright?

Theodoric of York: Well, I'll do everything humanly possible. Unfortunately, we barbers aren't gods. You know, medicine is not an exact science, but we are learning all the time. Why, just fifty years ago, they thought a disease like your daughter's was caused by demonic possession or witchcraft. But nowadays we know that Isabelle is suffering from an imbalance of bodily humors, perhaps caused by a toad or a small dwarf living in her stomach.

Joan: Well, I'm glad she's in such good hands.[11]

Medieval barbers probably shared with modern doctors an interest in healing and a concern for the well-being of others. In this sense, they share an identity as healers. But as the sketch makes clear, this is meaningless. What really matters, what makes the medieval barber a medieval barber and not a modern physician has nothing to do with identity and everything to do with a contextually embedded subjectivity. Calling the sick daughter "my patient," reviewing the caregiver's adherence to a treatment regimen that combines the not entirely implausible (a pharmaceutical prescription) with the blatantly absurd (overnight burial in a marsh), specifying the precise volume of the bloodletting (in pints, no less!), and taking pride in new medical claims that indicate the march of scientific knowledge even though here the medical advances have

---

11   Saturday Night Live (Season 3, Episode 18). The sketch can be viewed at https://www.nbc. com/saturday-night-live/video/theodoric-of-york/n8661

simply replaced one superstition with another—the sketch builds its humor through the mismatch of placing a modern medical subjectivity into a social context that clearly does not legitimize, enable or sustain it. Since we know that no medieval barbers could ever approach their work as modern physicians do theirs, seeing one do so strikes us as ridiculous, and ridiculously funny.

Vivid and memorable, the "Theodoric of York" sketch offers a helpful analogy for Jewish educators who want to shift from thinking about identity to thinking about subjectivity. If medical schools were operating with the discourse prevalent in American Jewish education, and focusing on strengthening students' *identities* as healers, they could just as easily churn out medieval barbers as modern physicians. But medical educators know very clearly what type of medical subjectivity they are and are not trying to cultivate, and this is why, when you suffer your next heart attack, you won't have to worry that your barber will bury you up to your neck in the marsh.

The challenge for Jewish educators is to come to similar clarity about what type of Jewish subjectivities, what institutionally and contextually grounded ways of Jewish being-in-the-world, they are and are not hoping to create. But to do this requires that educators focus less on how people think and feel about being generically Jewish and more on training them in specific ways of engaging the world as Jews, and specific ways of behaving with regard to Jewish culture, institutions, people, etc.

Conclusion

For decades, Jewish educators have been using the term *identity* as a proxy for what they really seek to create, which are communal outcomes that are vaguely defined. The concept has not served those ends well, because its atomism makes it inherently unsuited to the task. In contrast to identities, subjectivities, as orientations to action in the world, are always bound up in the worlds that they create.

Thinking about subjectivities demands more of educators than does educating for identity. Subjectivities are, by their nature, never generic. Because they are manifested in concrete, situated behavior, they implicitly assert claims about how the world is and how it should be. It is as meaningless to say that one's goal is to "educate for a Jewish subjectivity" as it would be to say that one's goal is to teach children to speak language. Which language? What type of Jewish subjectivity? These categories exist only in their specific instances.

Educators will not be able to answer the question of which type of Jewish subjectivities they hope to cultivate until they embrace a vision of the type of Jewish world they are trying to build. Only if educators know what type of society they are trying to create can they begin to think about how to cultivate the orientations to action that could realize it. Do they envision a world where environmental concerns will drive a broad reevaluation of Jewish theology and practice, including changes in the definition of what is kosher and what is treyf? Do they envision a world where da`as torah reigns and Jews eagerly defer to rabbinic authority? Do they envision a world where authority over liturgy and ritual rests with artists instead of clergy? These are different worlds, and they would be created by people with very different orientations to themselves, to others, to elements of Jewish culture, and to their behaviors towards all of these.

Whatever the vision of the greater good may be, vision must come first. But vision should not be understood in atomistic terms (e.g., "the educated Jew"). Nor should the burden for articulating these visions fall primarily to educators, *per se*. Instead, the model of the Soviet Jewry movement reminds us that it is in social movements trying to change the world where compelling Jewish visions of the Good are to be found, framed not as conceptions of the Good Life (on an individual level) but as conceptions of a redeemed (or Redeemed) world. There is no shortage of Jewish social movement visions out there: environmentalism, feminism, religious Zionism, Jewish renewal, Open Orthodoxy, the Jewish social justice movement, the Jewish food movement, Chabad, and on, and on. If activists are mobilizing effectively, educators will not have to seek them out. The movements will find them. They will enlist funders, co-opt institutions, train teachers, develop curricula, and engage people in specific forms of na`aseh that create new types of nishma in the process. And if activists are mobilizing broadly and deeply, leaving no stone unturned, then American Jews will stop asking, "Where's the next Soviet Jewry movement," because they will be too busy engaging in it.

Bibliography

Beckerman, Gal. (2010). *When They Come for Us, We'll Be Gone: The Epic Struggle to Save Soviet Jewry.* Boston, MA: Houghton Mifflin Harcourt.

Durkheim, Emile. (1966). *Suicide: A Study in Sociology.* New York, NY: Free Press.

Durkheim, Emile. (1982). *The Rules of Sociological Method.* New York, NY: Free Press.

Eisen, Wendy. (1995). *Count Us In: The Struggle to Free Soviet Jews, a Canadian Perspective.* Toronto, Canada: Burgher Books.

Ferziger, Adam S. (2015). *Beyond Sectarianism: The Realignment of American Orthodox Judaism.* Detroit, MI: Wayne State University Press.

Fishman, Sylvia Barack. (1993). *A Breath of Life: Feminism in the American Jewish Community.* New York, NY: Free Press.

Foucault, Michel. (1973). *The Birth of the Clinic: An Archaeology of Medical Perception.* London, UK: Tavistock.

Frankl, Viktor E. (1985). *Man's Search for Meaning.* New York, NY: Simon and Schuster.

Galchinsky, Michael. 2007. *Jews and Human Rights: Dancing at Three Weddings.* Lanham, MD: Rowman and Littlefield.

Gans, Herbert J. (1979). Symbolic Ethnicity: The Future of Ethnic Groups and Cultures in America. *Ethnic and Racial Studies* 2(1), 1–20.

Graber, A. (1987). *Trip to a Closed World Chicago Action for Soviet Jewry* (Collection I-530, Box 156, Folder 1, p, 12). Archive of the American Soviet Jewry Movement, American Jewish Historical Society, New York.

Kelner, Shaul. (2008). Ritualized Protest and Redemptive Politics: Cultural Consequences of the American Mobilization to Free Soviet Jewry. *Jewish Social Studies* 14(3), 1–37.

Kelner, Shaul. 2011. The Bureaucratization of Ritual Innovation: The Festive Cycle of the American Soviet Jewry Movement. In Simon J. Bronner (Ed.), *Revisioning Ritual: Jewish Traditions in Transition* (pp. 360–91). Oxford, UK: Littman Library of Jewish Civilization.

Kelner, Shaul. (2013). Tinker, Tourist, Soldier, Spy: American Visits to Soviet Jewish Refuseniks, 1972–1988, Association for Jewish Studies Annual Meeting, Boston, MA.

Kelner, Shaul. (2015). Sub-Cultural Diversity in American Cold War Culture: The Case of the Soviet Jewry Movement. *Association for Jewish Studies Annual Meeting.* Boston, MA.

Kelner, Shaul. (2019). Foreign Tourists, Domestic Encounters: Human Rights Travel to Soviet Jewish Homes. In Sune Bechmann Pedersen & Christian Noack (Eds.), *Tourism and Travel during the Cold War: Negotiating Tourist Experiences across the Iron Curtain.* London, UK: Routledge.

Kelner, Shaul. (Forthcoming). À la rencontre des Juifs de l'autre côté du rideau de fer: récits de voyage de Juifs américains et représentation du judaïsme en Union soviétique. Andreas Nijenhuis-Bescher (Ed.), *Frontières et Altérité Religieuse: La Religion dans le Récit de Voyage.* Rennes, France: Presses Universitaires de Rennes.

Klein Halevi, Yossi. (2004). Jacob Birnbaum and the Struggle for Soviet Jewry. *Azure* 27(5764), 27–57.

Lazin, Fred A. (2005). *The Struggle for Soviet Jewry in American Politics: Israel Versus the American Jewish Establishment.* Lanham, MD: Lexington Books.

Luhrmann, Tanya M. (2006). "Subjectivity." *Anthropological Theory* 6(3), 345–61.

Ortner, Sherry B. (2005). Subjectivity and Cultural Critique. *Anthropological Theory* 5(1), 31–52.

Peretz, Pauline. (2006). *Le Combat pour les Juifs Soviétiques: Washington-Moscou-Jérusalem, 1953–1989.* Paris, France: Armand Colin.

Prell, Riv-Ellen. (Ed.). (2007). *Women Remaking American Judaism*. Detroit, MI: Wayne State University Press.

Records of the Student Struggle for Soviet Jewry. No date. "Political and Civic Notables to lead Walkathon for Soviet Jewry on Sunday April 11," Press Release. Records of the Student Struggle for Soviet Jewry, Yeshiva University Archives, New York, Box 16, Folder 8.

Rubin, R. I. (1966). Student Struggle for Soviet Jewry. *Hadassah Magazine* 48(4), 7, 34–35.

Sasson, Theodore. (2013). *The New American Zionism*. New York: NYU Press.

Saturday Night Live. (2017). Theodoric of York: Medieval Barber. Retrieved from http://snltranscripts.jt.org/77/77rtheodoric.phtml

Snow, David, Rochford Jr., E. Burke, Worden, Steven K., & Benford, Robert D. (1986). Frame Alignment Processes, Micromobilization, and Movement Participation. *American Sociological Review* 51(4), 464–481.

Springer, Brandon. (14 March 2011). Interview With Gal Beckerman. Retrieved from https://localhistory.boulderlibrary.org/islandora/object/islandora%3A36204?solr_nav%5Bid%5D=6b5718d94c93ef1b4c0f&solr_nav%5Bpage%5D=0&solr_nav%5Boffset%5D=0

Waters, Mary C. (1990). *Ethnic Options: Choosing Identities in America*. Berkeley, CA: University of California Press.

Waxman, Dov. (2016). *Trouble in the Tribe: The American Jewish Conflict over Israel*. Princeton, NJ: Princeton University Press.

Weber, Max. (1958). Bureaucracy. In Hans Gerth, & C. Wright Mills (Eds.), *From Max Weber: Essays in Sociology* (pp. 196–244). New York, NY: Oxford University Press.

Weiss, Avraham. (2015). *Open Up the Iron Door: Memoirs of a Soviet Jewry Activist*. London, UK: Toby Press.

Wolfe, Tom. (1976). The Me Decade and the Third Great Awakening. Retrieved from http://nymag.com/news/features/45938/

Woocher, Jonathan S. (1986). *Sacred Survival: The Civil Religion of American Jews*. Bloomington, IN.: Indiana University Press.

Jewish Education as Initiation into the Practices of Jewishness

Jon A. Levisohn

Introduction

One version of the story of Jewish identity—or to be more precise, the story of the discourse of "Jewish identity" in North America—goes like this. Beginning around the 1950s, leaders of the Jewish community found themselves faced simultaneously with the collapse of a traditional, religious self-conception and with the demographic challenge of increasing exogamy. Jews were moving out of ethnic enclaves to the suburbs, and while suburban American norms certainly did demand membership in a house of worship (and suburban synagogues fit the bill quite nicely), they did not support intensive Jewish practice, and the social integration of Jews in white middle-class American life started to make itself felt in the diminishment of the taboo against intermarriage. Given these challenges, the leaders of the community seized upon the continued existence of the Jewish community—"Jewish continuity"—as an intrinsic good, a value in itself.[1]

Why? One can interpret this valuation of continuity for its own sake as an admirable embrace of a pluralistic attitude; on this charitable interpretation, Jewish leaders were saying, in effect, that they were not willing to bet on any

---

1 Google's NGram viewer tool partially corroborates this account. The phrase "Jewish continuity" only emerges in the postwar period, and then its usage increases—but only incrementally—until the early 1980s, at which point it spikes. At around the same time (the early 1980s), the phrase "continuity crisis" also begins to emerge (it was nonexistent beforehand), then spikes in the late 1980s, and then spikes much higher in the early 1990s. In other words, while the language of "continuity crisis" seems to have entered into communal discourse later in the twentieth century, the language of "Jewish continuity" makes its appearance and becomes established in the late 1940s and 1950s.

particular form of Judaism or Jewish practice to the exclusion of others, so instead they would simply commit themselves to the continuity of the Jewish people. Less charitably, the continuity agenda may have simply emerged from an unreflective, tribalist survivalism (Glazer, 1989, 162 and ff.), unwilling to confront the hard questions about the purposes of individual or communal existence.[2] We might also consider a deeper critique, from a feminist perspective, that argues that the focus on Jewish continuity has the effect—and perhaps even the intent—of objectifying women as wombs (Ungar-Sargon, 2017; Rosenblatt, Corwin Berman, & Stahl, 2018).

In either case, whether we are inclined to interpret the continuity agenda more charitably or less so, what is important for the present purposes is that it coalesced with a particular conception of Jewish identity, a conception according to which having a "strong" Jewish identity was aligned with Jewish continuity while having a "weak" Jewish identity was aligned with the opposite. Why were these aligned? The answer seemed obvious. If you have a strong Jewish identity, you "remain Jewish"[3] despite the buffeting winds of assimilation

---

2   There is a fascinating and complicated relationship between the ideology of American Jewish continuity and American Zionism. By the second half of the twentieth century, they go hand-in-hand; the leaders of the continuity agenda are also, typically, fervent supporters of the State of Israel. Usually, however, they operate as twin commitments rather than a single integrated one. That is, there is lip service paid to the contribution of the Jewish State to American Jewish pride (especially for the generation that experienced the anxiety and the euphoria of 1967) and there is an acknowledgement that Israel serves as potential safe haven, and some argue on political grounds that Israel needs a strong American Jewish community, but these rhetorical moves do not amount to a well-developed vision for the future of world Jewry located in two centers, one in a majority Jewish culture and one in the diaspora (as one finds, for example, in Rawidowicz, 1986). In the absence of such a well-developed vision, one may well wonder why it is so important for the American Jewish community in particular to persist. If one is concerned about Jewish continuity, why not simply invest emotionally or financially in the place most likely for that continuity to happen, namely, in Israel?

3   The scare quotes are intended to signal that the concept of "remaining Jewish" is anything but clear. It seems to assume, first, that religion or ethnicity is something, a fixed pole, at which one begins (historically or in one's personal biography) and from which one (sometimes) moves away, to a greater or lesser degree; and second, that the movement in question may be sufficiently extensive that it then calls into question whether the person at the end of the process shares an identity with the person at the beginning of the process. All of this is highly questionable. Of course it is true that people change, as they become adults, and one of the dramatic ways that they change is by abandoning practices of their families of origin or by taking up new ones. So people who grew up keeping kosher stop doing so (and vice versa), and people who grew up going to synagogue stop doing so (and vice versa). But the cessation of a particular practice is not correlated with a self-perception of "being Jewish," and it is hard to see why it should be interpreted as such.

and the attractions of other, non-Jewish options. You've got a strong Jewish core that holds you firm against those buffeting winds. Equally, because you are more likely to marry another Jew and raise children as Jewish and initiate them into Jewish practices and community, your children are also likely to "remain Jewish." We might even be tempted to say that you transmit identity to your children (although it's not clear what kind of thing identity is, such that it might be transmitted from one person to another). And thus, if enough people have strong Jewish identities, then Jewish continuity would be, if not guaranteed, at least promoted.

Conversely, if you have a weak Jewish identity, you are already on the way out the door. At the extreme, you are Jewish in name only (unless you give that up too, changing your name in order to "pass"). To borrow from the sociologist Herbert Gans (1979), you have only a residual "symbolic identity" instead of a real or authentic ethnic identity. Implicitly, those with weak Jewish identities are "at risk," unreliable, even suspect. If the occasion happens to arise, the weakness of your Jewish identity may lead you to make the wrong choice, betray your people, leave the fold—or at least, will fail to prevent you from doing so. You do not have that Jewish spine, the Jewish "moral fiber" that those with strong Jewish identities have, to stand up to the assaults or the seductions. Again, this applies both to you and, because of your likelihood of exogamy and the weaker Jewish environment that you will provide for your children, to them as well. Hence continuity is threatened.

This is the picture within which it makes sense to think about "strengthening Jewish identity" as the desired outcome of Jewish educational projects and programs. But I have taken the time, at the outset of this chapter, to spell out these apparently obvious linkages because, on closer examination, they are so problematic. It is problematic, first, whether the concept of "weak" or "strong" identity means what it has been taken to mean. If, to use a psychological formulation, identity has to do with self-conception—who I imagine myself to be in the world, the various roles that I play, the stories that I tell myself about myself—then it would seem more appropriate to talk about the centrality of certain aspects of one's identity rather than its strength or weakness. I may or may not have an identity as a musician or an athlete, and those aspects of how I see myself in the world may be more central to me or more marginal. But that is only circumstantially related to whether I am a good musician or athlete, whether I live up to someone else's conception of the norms of musicianship or athleticism. I can think about myself as a flutist, even if I am a bad one. Likewise, I can think about myself as a runner even if, by the norms of the running community, my efforts do not amount to much. I might even have a firm identity—a very strong self of myself—as a poor flutist or a slow runner.[4]

Second, the apparently obvious linkage is problematic because the notion that weak identity causes intermarriage or even communal exit is no longer valid, if it ever was. The much-belabored 2013 Pew Report documents, in vivid detail, that people continue to identify as Jews even when raised with minimal Jewish education and communal involvement—in many cases, even when not being raised as Jews at all (Sasson, 2013). In fact, this phenomenon has strengthened over time. So it is not correct that Jews—those with weak identities—are choosing to exit the community. And if that is not actually occurring, then linking the supposed "cause" (weak Jewish identity) to that supposed "effect" (communal exit) is obviously illogical.[5] Likewise, the causal link between "weak identity" and intermarriage is poorly conceived; whatever reason individuals have for choosing a life partner, it hardly seems accurate to say that their weak Jewish identities made them do it.[6]

---

4 Scholars (e.g., Thompson, 2013b) have recently begun to explore the idea of the self-identified "bad Jew," a rhetorical move that simultaneously gestures towards a normative conception of Jewishness while also positioning oneself at a distance from that normative conception.

5 It is certainly true that there continues to be a significant population of people "of Jewish background" who do not consider themselves Jewish. The online Pew Research Center calculator—http://www.pewforum.org/2013/10/01/jewish-population-calculator/—produces a number of 2.4 million. Typically, these are children of intermarriage who now practice another religion (two million). In other words, it remains true that there is a significant population of people with one Jewish parent who have embraced another religious affiliation and therefore do not consider themselves to be Jewish. Presumably, the religion of choice, for most of these people, is the religion of the non-Jewish parent, or possibly, the religion of their own non-Jewish spouse. I thank Sarah Benor for pointing this out to me.

6 In fact, we ought to challenge the conceptual framework that implicitly emphasizes making "Jewish choices" in general. There are, to be sure, moments in life when choices must be made. And sometimes, those choices do reflect our values. Will I make time for a student when a manuscript is overdue? Will I act in my own interest, in a particular situation, or in the interest of others? But the idea that "making Jewish choices" is the paradigmatic mode of interacting with the world is false to the lives that real Jews live. The choice of a marriage partner is incredibly important to one's life path, and for educational purposes, it may well be helpful to think about, and prepare for, that choice. But people making a "Jewish" versus a "non-Jewish" choice does not explain the actual incidence of intermarriage, any more than it explains the decision to eat sushi rather than matzah ball soup, or the decision to enroll in a hip hop class rather than an Israeli dance class, or the decision to vacation in Italy rather than Israel. See the argument in Levisohn (2012), especially p. 65, and on

Expressions of this unexamined, commonsensical, but in fact highly questionable conception are legion. In one that recently crossed my desk, Yedidia Stern (2015) writes that "some Jews choose . . . to ignore the pull of Jewish particularism on their lives. They dilute their Jewish identity to such an extent that their offspring may lose any connection to the Jewish people within a generation or two." In Stern's picture, some Jews are making choices, the wrong choices, that reflect deep-seated convictions about particularism (which exerts a "pull" but which can be ignored) versus what he proposes as the alternative, "Western liberalism." What are these choices? He does not enumerate them, but they represent a "dilution" of Jewish identity. Apparently, Jewish identity can be full-strength or it can be a weaker version, diluted through the introduction of some other substance, something other than Judaism, that makes it less pure, less potent, and less transmissible. But how is this supposed to work, exactly, on a psychological or sociological level? What evidence do we have of such "dilution"? Does reading Kant or Mill dilute your Jewishness? Does advocating for the poor or the homeless dilute your Jewish identity? Once one begins to examine the metaphors, it becomes clear that they do not amount to much.

In another fairly recent example, a great Jewish hero of the twentieth century, Natan Sharansky, borrows elements of the picture in explaining the Prime Minister's Initiative, an initiative "to take more responsibility for strengthening the identity of Jewish communities" that gathered some headlines in 2014.[7] According to Sharansky, "In the non-Orthodox world nothing stops assimilation with the exception of a connection to Israel." Israel, that is, functions as the anchor that keeps non-Orthodox Jews from floating away. Sharansky doesn't explain what he means by "assimilation" here, but since he has already explained that he is talking about non-Orthodox Jews, it cannot mean the absence of traditional ritual observance; presumably, "assimilation" here is code for exogamy. He then continues, "When you move [beyond the Orthodox community,] you find that [awareness of Jewish identity] is becoming thinner and thinner." So Jewish identity is weak, and a connection to Israel is a mechanism for strengthening or anchoring it. Without such an anchor, there's nothing to stop "assimilation."

---

the phenomenon of intermarriage in particular, see Thompson (2013a), which carefully documents the experience of intermarried couples and disrupts the casual association between intermarriage and "assimilation."

7   The quotes that follow are taken from the account by Sales (2014). In general, the saga of this initiative over the last few years is replete with expressions about Israel undertaking a strategic effort to "strengthen Jewish identity."

These phrases are taken from an interview, not a carefully crafted argument, but they do seem to represent the picture that we have been discussing—a picture which assumes that there is a substance called "Jewish identity" which can grow "thinner and thinner." Moreover, on the specific policy question, Sharansky is wrong that nothing has an effect other than Israel trips; in fact, research consistently demonstrates the positive effects of all types of Jewish education other than the least intensive. Sharansky, however, seems clear that thin Jewish identity leads to exogamy, and that the goal of his educational intervention is to strengthen Jewish identity in order to preclude that unhappy outcome.[8]

The argument here is that Jewish identity discourse oversimplifies a complex set of phenomena. To be clear, those phenomena are real. We have abundant empirical evidence that those Jews who are less embedded in Jewish social networks, for example, are also less active in Jewish practices and marry other Jews less frequently. We have abundant empirical evidence that those Jews who participate in more, and more intensive forms of, Jewish education are more highly engaged in all kinds of Jewish activities as adults and in-marry more frequently. There is an important and undeniable correlation between these various phenomena. What we need, therefore, is a way to talk about these phenomena that captures these correlations without inventing something called "Jewish identity" as a pseudo-explanation for them.

The Instrumentalization of Jewish Education

To this point, I have presented some of the problems with Jewish identity discourse, as it purports to explain a large and complicated set of phenomena by collapsing them under the framework of "stronger" and "weaker" Jewish identity. I called this a "pseudo-explanation." While Jewish identity clearly exists as a psychological and sociological phenomenon—people think about themselves as "Jews," and "being Jewish" means something in the world—it cannot do the explanatory work that it is often called upon to do. Strong Jewish identity does not cause us to act Jewishly (including marry Jewishly), and weak Jewish identity does not cause the opposite. The takeaway, then, is that when we do talk about Jewish identity, we ought to avoid such naïve and

---

8   Sharansky and Naftali Bennett, of Israel's Ministry of Diaspora Affairs (and Ministry of Education), may have been on opposing sides of the political struggle over control of the Prime Minister's Initiative, but on this topic they are united: Bennett consistently talks about the initiative, and other efforts of his ministry, as efforts to "strengthen Jewish identity." For a recent example, see his remarks to the 2018 First Global Jewish Education Summit (Buckman, 2018).

simplistic formulations, and instead develop and employ a far more nuanced understanding of how Jewish identity works. I trust that my colleagues, the authors of the other chapters in this volume, would concur.

But the purpose of my introduction has been to lay the groundwork for the rest of this chapter, which will focus more specifically on Jewish education, because the problem with the pseudo-explanation of "Jewish identity" is not just that it is an invention without empirical or conceptual justification. From the perspective of Jewish education, the problem is actually much worse than that, because when Jewish identity discourse dominates how we talk about the goals of Jewish education, it has the effect of *corrupting* that conversation. Rather than a principled discussion about the richness and vitality of Jewish life and culture, and what aspects of that Jewish life and culture we most value and most want to cultivate in our students, the conversation becomes flattened by the supposedly shared purpose of "strengthening Jewish identity." Rather than an exploration of the challenges and opportunities of teaching particular subjects, particular aspects of Jewish life and culture—the kind of exploration that can improve pedagogic practice—the conversation becomes a homogenized, generic one with little connection to teaching and learning.

To illustrate, consider the following hypothetical example. Imagine Vered, a teacher of Israeli dance to a troupe at a Jewish summer camp. Vered has taught dance professionally for two decades. She has performed and taught a variety of styles of dance, but is particularly committed to, passionate about, and experienced in Israeli dance. Is Vered in the Jewish identity business? Well, that depends.

If we were to speak with Vered about her work with this group of kids, what she does with them and especially why she does it—the goals of this particular educational intervention—we can imagine that she would respond initially by saying, "I want the kids in the troupe to love dancing!" Educators often fall into this trap, employing vapid and vague formulations about kids "loving" a particular subject or about building "self-esteem." But that response is insufficiently nuanced and does not tell us why Vered does the specific things she does. When we push her on this, when we encourage her to be more specific, Vered might offer other formulations of her goals like the following:

1. I want the kids to learn these particular classical dance steps.
2. I want them to perform well in front of the camp community.
3. I want them to learn dance moves that are just a bit harder than things they've learned before, so that they really have a sense of advancing in this art form.

4. I want them to become a healthy and mutually supportive and smoothly functioning group, to have a positive shared experience that is challenging but that leads to collective success.

Any and all of these responses begin to provide a window into her vision of dance education, and thus begin to help us understand why she makes the pedagogic choices that she does.

But perhaps Vered says more. Perhaps, when pushed to explain her pedagogic choices, she says something like this:

> I choose to teach this dance because it was the "CIT dance" of 1985. That CIT cohort will be coming for their 30th reunion on Shabbat. I want the current campers to perform for the 1985 cohort, and thereby to feel a connection to the history of dance in our camp, and to feel their own place in the chain that connects past generations of dancers to future ones.[9]

This response is interesting because Vered links her own practice and that of her students to the practice of others with a great deal of specificity and historical context. The choice of the dance carries a certain meaning, based on its history. Learning the practice of dance, in this context, is also about learning and linking to that history. What is particularly notable about this response is how "insidery" it is, how it draws on local knowledge of the practice and the setting in a way that is opaque to most of us but that makes perfect sense to those within the community of camp-dancers.

What our hypothetical dance teacher Vered almost certainly will *not* say, in talking about her practice and the pedagogic choices that she makes, is, "I want to strengthen their Jewish identities." To clarify, she may well believe that dance is an important part of Jewish culture, and that well-rounded Jews ought to have familiarity or even proficiency in dance, or most modestly, that dance is one powerful mode of Jewish communal participation among other options. She may find particular meaning in participating and helping others participate in a practice that has such a prominent place in her conception of Jewish culture. So she may think that, by teaching dance, she is actually helping her students become better (or more culturally adept, or more confident) Jews, in some sense. Better Jews? Yes. Not better at Shabbat-candle-lighting, because there is no reason to imagine that dancing and candle-lighting are correlated,

---

9 This is a lightly edited version of a response given to me by Erica Goldman (personal communication, July 13, 2015), a dance instructor at Camp Alonim.

and not better at Talmud or prayer (or tzedakah or tikkun olam), but better in the sense of having a firmer and deeper grasp of one particular Jewish cultural form, one particular enactment of Jewishness. The choice to teach this particular cultural form is not random; Israeli dance does not stand on its own as an isolated practice. Rather, it is informed by what Charles Taylor (1992, p. 39) calls "horizons of significance," which is to say, its meaning derives from the way in which it is embedded in larger cultural structures.

Still, "to strengthen Jewish identities" is not an explanation for any particular aspect of her practice. But let us now imagine that Vered has a meeting with a prospective funder. In order to figure out her pitch, she does some research on this funder. If Vered learns that the prospective funder is a dance enthusiast herself, someone who is as passionate about dance as Vered herself is, then we can expect that their discussion will be dance-specific, about styles and steps and particular dance-education-specific challenges. There may be points of disagreement. Perhaps the funder wants Vered to focus more on classical choreography and less on contemporary. Perhaps there are differences of opinion about the role of soloists versus the role of the collective. Those disagreements, however, are about dance and dance education. They are internal to the practice. Vered and the funder will be talking the language of dance, not the language of Jewish identity.

Compare, on the other hand, Vered's pitch to a funder who is not particularly invested in dance but rather is invested in Jewish identity. In that setting, Vered will offer arguments about the importance of the arts to strong identity, and how these kids feel good about being Jewish because of their experience. If the funder is particularly hard-nosed, Vered may find herself back on her heels since, after all, she has precious little evidence for the claims about impact on identity. And importantly, Vered's experience in talking with the funder (or in assembling a grant application) will feel, to her, curiously disconnected from her real passion, and her real work, including the pedagogic decisions that she has to make every day. Those decisions are driven by Vered's conception of this particular practice, not her conception of Jewish identity. This funder will have coopted Vered into a discourse external to the practice, an instrumentalist discourse in which dance is a means to the end of Jewish identity.[10]

---

10 This dynamic, in which educators adopt a discourse external to their practice, is described by Joseph Schwab (1957) as the "corruption of education by psychology." Joe Reimer pointed out this connection for me. Similarly, R. S. Peters expresses concern in the early 1960s (reprinted as Peters, 1973) about a trend that he notices, in which "the descriptions of what [a teacher] is doing [by behaviorists on the one hand and economists on the other]

The example is merely hypothetical, and to the extent that it is based on actual conversations with both practitioners and philanthropists, those conversations amount to merely anecdotal evidence. But the point of the example is to suggest that Jewish identity discourse has contributed to—or at least, is often a corollary of—a kind of instrumentalization of Jewish educational interventions. It may once have been sufficient for practitioners and policy makers to invest in dance or Israel trips or Talmud study "for their own sake"—which in this context means that the practitioners and policy makers appreciate the aspects of Jewish culture in question and want to promote them as an important element in their vision of a full Jewish life. Increasingly, however, this is not enough. And the search for a bigger, broader, more forward-looking goal leads many to the Jewish identity discourse that we have been worrying about.[11]

So what, then, is the alternative? If the discourse of Jewish identity fails to cohere with the educator's self-conception and her own articulation of her goals, what can replace it? The example of dance already begins to point the way to the alternative to which the remainder of this chapter will be devoted. The proposed alternative to "Jewish identity" is "Jewish practices." That is, the most helpful and constructive way to think about the goals of Jewish education is to identify the practices of Jewishness that we value, and then to conceptualize Jewish education as an initiation of students into those practices. The example of Israeli dance provides another helpful way of framing the same idea: we should think and talk about the Jewish cultural performances that we

---

seriously misrepresent what is distinctive of his calling by the generality of the description or by assimilating to something else . . . a conformist or instrumental way of looking at education [that deviates from] the point of view of someone engaged in the enterprise" (p. 82). These misconceptions are not just wrong; according to Peters, they are also potentially dangerous, if they are allowed to exert undue influence on the practice that they purport to describe.

11 My thinking about the instrumentalization of Jewish education was initially prompted by a conversation with Steven M. Cohen in May, 2012. In that conversation, he noted that, before Birthright, philanthropists and policymakers in the Jewish community supported trips to Israel because they believed that they were a good thing for kids to do—that an Israel experience has inherent or intrinsic value, we might say, as part of a well-rounded Jewish life. Subsequent to Birthright, Israel trips are legitimated because of their "impact," which is to say, their effect on a set of outcomes entirely unrelated to the practice of visiting Israel. The Israel experience, therefore, has been instrumentalized in the service of some other goal (often framed in terms of identity or continuity). That instrumentalization is an unintended byproduct of what is sometimes called "strategic philanthropy," with its greater focus on demonstrable and measurable outcomes. To focus on outcomes, while avoiding instrumentalization, requires a great deal of patience, intellectual humility, and wisdom.

value, and we should then conceptualize Jewish education as the development of the capacities and dispositions to enact those cultural performances.[12]

From Practices to Identity: Becoming What You Do

The argument, pursued above and throughout this book, that we ought to avoid "Jewish identity discourse" in Jewish education does not mean that there is no such thing as "Jewish identity." For the purposes of this chapter, what is particularly important is that identity is not the kind of thing that one just *has*, but rather, it is the kind of thing that one *performs*, in various ways and at various times. Judith Butler (1989) famously makes this claim in a radical form, regarding gender. "Gender," she writes, "is always a doing, though not a doing by a subject who might be said to preexist the deed." We should not imagine that we *are* male or female, essentially, and that our behavior is simply an enactment of this preexisting identity. She continues: "There is no gender identity behind the expressions of gender; that identity is performatively constituted by the very expressions that are said to be its results" (p. 25). This is complicated, however, in part because there are different kinds of identities, and different ways that identities relate to the practices that constitute their enactment. To be overly schematic about it, sometimes practices create identities, and sometimes identities create practices.[13]

Let us consider, first, the way in which what one does—or more specifically, what one *learns* to do—sometimes becomes part of who one is. A person might learn to speak Hebrew. Speaking Hebrew is a practice. And when this person acquires a certain level of proficiency in this practice, she starts to think of herself in a particular way. We can reasonably say that she now has an identity as a *doveret Ivrit,* a Hebrew speaker. A person might take a class to learn how to throw pots. Pottery is a practice. When she develops a certain level of skill and commitment to the craft, she starts to think of herself as a potter. The line between learning the language or the craft, and being that kind of person, is fuzzy. When exactly does the student of Hebrew become a *doveret Ivrit?* When

---

12 The example of dance may mislead the reader to think that a "cultural performance" or the enactment of a practice must necessarily be public. But it need not be. I can perform or enact a practice in private. However, a practice cannot simply be an idiosyncratic habit. That is: a practice need not be performed publicly but it must be shared with some community, real or imagined, contemporary or historical.

13 Butler would presumably not accept this second mode of the relationship, but I hope to show below how there is a reasonable and non-controversial sense in which it holds true.

exactly does the student of pottery become a potter? It's hard to say, but we know that there's a difference. We know that there are people who learn a bit of Hebrew but are not Hebrew speakers. We know that there are people who dabble a bit in pottery who are not potters. We also know that there's an element of subjectivity here, since after all we are talking about self-conceptions; where one person might start to consider herself a Hebrew speaker or a potter, another person might not. Still, conceptually, the distinction is clear, even if practically, we may be hard pressed to discriminate one from the other.

How does practice lead to identity? If a person happens to run to catch the bus in the morning, she is not a runner. In fact, even if she is habitually late and thus regularly has to run to catch the bus, she is still not a runner. Repetition, while important, is not sufficient. We might say, colloquially, that she is not *really* doing what runners do. Or we might say more conceptually that, while she is performing the action of running, she is not yet performing the practice of running. The adverb "really" in the first formulation points to the conceptual distinction in the second; it signals that there are norms that are internal to the practice that our bus-catcher does not meet. Joseph Rouse, who develops a "normative conception of practices" (2007), makes the point this way: "A performance belongs to a practice if it is appropriate to hold it accountable as a correct or incorrect performance of that practice" (p. 3). So in our case, the "performance" (running to the bus) does not belong to the "practice" (running) because we understand that it is not "appropriate to hold it accountable as a correct or incorrect performance of that practice." She's not a good runner or a bad runner. She's not a runner at all.[14]

---

14 Rouse makes a parallel point in writing about the practitioners of the practice. "Actors share a practice," he notes, "if their actions are appropriately regarded as answerable to norms of correct or incorrect practice" (Rouse, 2001, p. 199). This is important for our consideration of identity. Two people may be doing something that looks, superficially, like it is the same thing—but unless they share the same normative framework, the same basic idea of what it means to do this thing well, their actions do not represent a shared practice, which then raises the question of whether they can be said to have a shared identity (as practitioners of that practice). At the same time, Rouse (2007, p.4) cites MacIntyre about the way in which a tradition (or a practice) is not fixed but rather always contested: "What constitutes a tradition is a conflict of interpretations of that tradition, a conflict which itself has a history susceptible of rival interpretations." (MacIntyre, 1977, p. 460). MacIntyre, interestingly, then gives the following example: "If I am a Jew, I have to recognize that the tradition of Judaism is partly constituted by a continuous argument over what it means to be a Jew" (ibid.). Rouse glosses this comment as follows. "Judaism, like any other significant tradition, exhibits no elements shared throughout its history. What it is to be a Jew is instead at issue in the practices of Judaism in all their historical complexity... Working out what is at issue

What are these mysterious norms of running, that govern the practice of running (but not of bus-running)? One is intentionality: runners are people who intentionally go for runs. Another norm is intrinsicality: runners are people who run for the purposes intrinsic to the practice (fitness, the joy of movement, challenging oneself, training for competitions, achieving a "runner's high") rather than purposes extrinsic to the practice (catching the bus).[15] A third norm is regularity: runners are people who run regularly, on some kind of schedule that, while certainly not inviolable, is nevertheless fairly predictable at least to themselves. Then there are subtler and less universally observed norms, such as what runners wear (as opposed to what bus-catchers wear) or how runners run (steadily and smoothly, rather than in a mad dash to the bus). To be sure, some of these norms are contested (the training technique of "fartlek" rejects the smooth-and-steady norm).[16] And importantly, we all violate the norms of our practices from time to time; runners go through periods where they stop running. But the very idea of a "violation of the norm" reinforces the point. I could only consider myself to be on a hiatus from running (because of injury, busyness, or boredom) if I also have a sense of the norm of regularity that I am violating.

The point of the elaboration of all these norms, in the preceding paragraph, is that a practice is never just about *doing*. It also involves the adoption of a set of value commitments, not just to the value of the practice itself but to the values internal to the practice. Becoming the person, adopting the identity, involves a combination of the doing and the valuing. So if our bus-catcher begins a program of running regularly for fitness or for competition or for joy, if she sticks with it over some time, if she runs intentionally rather than only when she's late, then

---

in these practices and how the resolution of that issue matters is what the practice is about" (Rouse, 2007, p. 5). Also see Rouse (2006, p. 506–7).

15 Space does not permit a full exploration of the norm of intrinsicality, or what we might call *lishma-ness,* in contrast to the kind of instrumentalization discussed above. But it is frequently noted that, for those who are inside a practice, the very question about the purpose of the practice seems to not quite make sense. The answers that the insider provides, to the outsider, do not capture the meaning of the practice for the insider. For example R. S. Peters (1973) writes, in a related way, about teaching things that one loves: "To ask [the teacher] what the aim or point of the form of life is, into which he himself has been initiated, seems an otiose question" (p. 103). Notably, Peters makes this point in the context of his argument on behalf of "initiation," which includes the student coming to adopt the norms of (what he calls) a "form of life" as her or his own.

16 As discussed above in note 14, Rouse (2007, pp. 5–6) argues that, rather than imagining a set of fixed rules that a practice must adhere to, it is more accurate to see the contest over the norms—which are historically located and inevitably evolving—as part of the practice itself.

she can and may in fact begin to think about herself as a runner. In one small sense—and of course this identity easily and seamlessly coexists with other identities that she holds and enacts—she will have become what she does.[17]

Education as Initiation into Social Practices

This, then, is the primary way to think about the relationship between practices and identity: we become what we do. We are never one thing, because we never do just one thing. (There is also a secondary way to think about the connection between identities and practices, to which I referred earlier and to which I will turn later on.) But this does not yet explain why education in general, or Jewish education specifically, ought to focus on practices. To develop that explanation, we can turn to the argument of one of the central figures in twentieth-century analytic philosophy of education, Paul Hirst.

In an early and very influential paper, "Liberal Education and the Nature of Knowledge" (1965), Hirst argues that liberal education is an education that systematically encounters each of several forms of knowledge, and in fact, enables the student to pursue each of those forms of knowledge on her own. Those forms of knowledge, perhaps not surprisingly, map onto what we usually call "disciplines." While the argument is about "liberal education," in fact Hirst is working out the paramount aims of education more generally, and doing so within a distinctly rationalist conception of human flourishing. According to this conception, all action ought to be preceded by a highly cognitive process, analyzing all available information, in order to decide the right thing to do. In McLaughlin's paraphrase, "the cognitive capacities of the person ... are seen as structuring ... all other capacities ... thereby making possible rational emotions and rational action: the 'rational life' to which all should aspire" (McLaughlin, 2001, p. 196).[18]

---

17 In Rouse's terms: "Our participation in [particular social] practices enables us to become the agents we are through our mutual accountability to the possibilities those practices make available and to what is thereby at stake for us in how we respond to those possibilities" (2007, p. 8).

18 Parenthetically, Jewish identity discourse may share such a rationalist conception when it imagines that those with "strong Jewish identities" will, because of the influence of those identities, make Jewish choices. Jewish education, at least in its more traditional forms, focuses on the acquisition of knowledge, on the reception and internalization of a set of texts and ideas that comprise a highly intellectual tradition. The implicit theory is that, if one acquires a sufficient body of knowledge, one will have that knowledge at one's disposal when the time comes to make one's decisions.

By the 1980s, however, Hirst begins to rethink some of his positions.[19] He becomes skeptical about the picture of detached human reason, calmly surveying the landscape and making judicious decisions about human purposes; he now calls this a view of "the good life as the exercise of the will enthralled in the service of reason" (p. 188). Instead, Hirst proposes a different picture, in which the "differentiation [of desires] in terms of richly alternative satisfactions means that what constitutes the good life for an individual can in detail be determined only by that particular person" (p. 189). So we all have different specific understandings of what the good life entails, not because some of us are more rational and some of us are less rational but simply because the good life is not the kind of thing that reason is going to determine once and for all. To be sure, we can still differentiate between a well-ordered life and a poorly ordered one, between choices made on the basis of self-understanding and those made on the basis of dimly understood external influences. Autonomy is still important. But "reason should not be conceived as separable from, or having determining status over, other capacities of the person" (McLaughlin, 2001, p. 197). Hirst has given up on the idea that reason alone can deliver us the answers.

And more than this, the way that Hirst thinks about reason itself also undergoes a shift, and practical reasoning emerges as more primary and fundamental than purely theoretical reasoning. "The knowledge that is . . . developed in practice," he writes, "is from the start not simply propositional knowledge, or 'know-that.' It is rather a matter of 'know-how,' of skill and judgment, that is, in major respects, tacit or implicit rather than consciously recognized" (p. 191). Implicitly borrowing from Gilbert Ryle's (1946/1971) distinction between "know-how" and "know-that," and from Michael Polanyi's (1958/1998) concept of tacit knowledge, Hirst—like Ryle and Polanyi—demonstrates a newfound respect for the practical, for the embodied and the enacted. Knowing what to do, how to get around in the world, how to act within a particular domain, is a not a secondary by-product of having a lot of ideas in one's head. On the contrary, being able to articulate ideas that one supposedly has in one's head is now understood to be the secondary, derivative phenomenon. We might put it like this: to know my way around, say, the domain of biology means to know how to do a lot of things within that domain, to handle a lot of practical problems. Yes, I can also answer questions that are

---

19 See especially Hirst (1993 and 1999). The citations to follow are from the former essay.

put to me about this or that aspect of the domain, but that's just a by-product of being able to *do* things.[20]

Furthermore, the prior rationalist picture, Hirst now believes, is too individualistic. He writes that a society is not merely a contingent joining together of individuals for their various instrumental purposes. Instead, a society or community is "a network of socially constructed individuals who, within that network, have the capacities for choice for the formation of their patterns of life and the modification of their social networks" (p. 194). Of course we do make choices, but we make those choices within social networks, and those choices affect not only our own individual paths but also reverberate out into those networks. Practices are, by their very nature, social. They are public, not private. We can enact a practice privately, of course. We can run on a treadmill in our basement with no one watching. We can throw a pot in a closed studio. We can meditate or pray privately. We can even pursue our biological research on our own. But even when we are alone, our practice is inevitably shared with the community of other practitioners, whether or not we know them, whether or not they are even living, because we are participating in the same activity governed by the same norms.[21]

What are the implications of the shift away from the rationalist picture? Hirst arrives at the dramatic conclusion that "we are mistaken if we conceive of the purpose [of education] as primarily the acquisition of knowledge" (p. 195). Education is not about knowledge! Instead, he writes, "the content of education must . . . be conceived as primarily initiation into certain substantive social practices" (p. 195).

Hirst contrasts initiation with immersion, picking up a particular social practice though a kind of unconscious osmosis, or what others call enculturation or socialization (Reimer, 2007). Surely this happens as well, when we begin speaking or acting as those around us do without even noticing it. But for

---

20 There is a significant literature on the relationship between practice and language—including both those who argue that practice contains a kind of knowledge or understanding that is inexpressible in language and those who argue that language is itself a social practice (one among many, or perhaps, a paradigmatic practice). See Rouse (2006, pp. 515–523).

21 In his focus on the social quality of learning, and the rejection of the common assumption about learning as primarily an individual process, Hirst echoes the "situated learning" or "situated cognition" movements (see Lave & Wenger, 1991, and Brown, Collins, & Duguid, 1989). Note, however, that Hirst's claim that practice is always social is distinct from Lave & Wenger's influential concept of "communities of practice;" not every practice has a community of practice, according to their definition.

Hirst, this kind of immersive development of habits is not worthy of the name "education." Nor is education, properly understood, the teaching of a practice blindly, with the expectation that the student will mimic the master.[22] This too is not worthy of the name. In the move from a focus on knowledge to a focus on practice, Hirst refuses to give up on the normative element. Within the rationalist or cognitivist conception, normativity is embedded in the distinction between true and false ideas; only the former represent knowledge and thus only the former ought to be taught, together with the capacity for developing new knowledge and critiquing claims to knowledge. Within this new, practice-focused conception, normativity is embedded in the distinction between good and poor practice; education in a practice aspires to the former rather than the latter, together with the development of the capacity for critique.[23] Or, as I wrote above, a practice is never just about *doing*; it also involves the adoption of a set of value commitments. So this is not an education merely of the hand, with no education of the mind. It is more accurate to say that mind and hand are engaged in a shared, embodied practice.

What I am proposing, then, is that we in Jewish education should follow Hirst's lead. Instead of the individualist, cognitivist paradigm, we ought to embrace a picture of human existence and human flourishing in which practice is primary, and to reimagine Jewish education as an initiation in Jewish social practices. This is not an argument on behalf of certain pedagogic approaches; I do not mean that we should focus exclusively on skills or hands-on activities. Nor is this an argument for practices that look at first glance more like "cultural performances," like Israeli dance, over others that look more like traditional learning, like studying classical Jewish texts. On the contrary, thinking about Jewish social practices pushes us to articulate how the intellectual engagement with the Jewish textual tradition can also be—how it *is*—a Jewish social practice, not just an exercise in knowledge transmission. Once we do that, we can ask ourselves: what are the habits and dispositions that we want to cultivate among our students, within this engagement with the Jewish textual tradition?

---

22 There are connections here both to Lave & Wenger's (1991) idea of "legitimate peripheral participation" and to Collins, Brown & Newman's (1989) idea of "cognitive apprenticeship." For the philosopher of education Hirst, however—as for the philosopher of science Joseph Rouse (2001 and 2007), as we saw above—the normative element is particularly important. In Jewish education, see Aron (1989) for a normative conception of enculturation.

23 The ongoing significance of critique saves the social-practices view from an uncritical conservatism. It also points to the way in which reason, while demoted from its primacy in the prior view, is still an essential element (see Yoo, 2001, pp. 621–622).

To use old-fashioned philosophical language, what are the excellences or virtues of this practice?

From Identity to Practices: Performing Who You Are

I have been discussing the way that practices can lead to identity; the shorthand for this is that "we become what we do." But I also mentioned that there is a secondary relationship between practice and identity, a relationship that goes in the other direction. Sometimes, that is, we begin with a certain self-conception, even if we do not enact—or have not yet enacted—that self-conception in practice. That seems to be the case with our identities as people in certain kinds of relationship to others (spouses, parents, siblings), perhaps with our professional identities, and typically, with ethnic and religious identities. We start out with a sense of being an *x*—a parent (once we have a child), a professor (once we are hired into an academic position), a Jew—and the work in front of us, then, is to perform who we are.[24] Seligman, Weller, Puett, and Simon (2008) note in their study of ritual that ritual is a way of becoming a certain kind of person. But the mode of ritual is complemented by the mode of (what they call) "sincerity," when we bring our actions into alignment with our self-understanding. "Rather than *becoming what we do in action* through ritual," they write, in this second mode, "*we do according to what we have become* through self-examination" (p. 103). These two modes correspond to the two kinds of relationship between identity and practice.

Consider the following example from the political sphere, in the not-too-distant past. According to reports that emerged after the American presidential election of 2012, the Obama campaign employed a set of strategies that year—innovative at the time, even if they now seem both quaint and innocent—that relied both on new data analysis technologies as well as the ongoing advice of some astute social scientists.[25] Those social scientists taught the campaign staff what they had learned about the depth of voter identity: the vast majority of the voters were already identified as Obama voters or Romney voters, and in fact, those identities were fairly well known (or could be known, for those who

---

24 Joe Reimer first helped me to appreciate this point.

25 The topic was discussed in a wide range of journalistic outlets in late November and December, 2012. Perhaps the most extensive report is Isenberg (2012).

know how to deal with large data sets), not just on the basis of registered party affiliation but also on the basis of a whole set of other data points.

Armed with that knowledge, the Obama campaign undertook a Get Out The Vote effort unlike anything that had happened before—more extensive, more comprehensive, and far more individualized. They did not try to convince Obama supporters to become who they already were. Their main focus was convincing Obama supporters to do what Obama supporters are supposed to do. We might say that the campaign was not trying to create identity, or transmit identity, or even strengthen identity. Instead, they were finding ways to encourage people to enact the practices that are associated with the identities that they already held.

This example looks remarkably like the situation of contemporary Jewry, at least in North America. Jews claim and embrace their Jewish identities. Ninety-eight percent of non-Orthodox Jewish singles in a 2008 study said that they're proud to be Jewish Cohen & Kelman, (2008). In 2011, 93% of the Jews in New York say that being Jewish is important to them (Cohen, Ukeles, and Miller 2012). In a 2012 study, 85% of Jews on campus report that they like people to know that they're Jewish (Cousens, 2012). In the Pew Study in 2013, even the "Jewish nones"—respondents who answered "no religion" but subsequently identified themselves as Jews, and who are mostly the children of inter-marriage with little Jewish institutional affiliation—express pride in their Jewish identities at a very high rate, 83% (Sasson, 2013). Some Jews choose to participate in Jewish cultural and religious activities and Jewish communal projects, and some choose not to. But they all tend to know that they are Jews, identify as Jews, and are proud of being Jewish. When a Jew marries another Jew, they raise their children as Jews 98% of the time (Cohen, Ukeles, and Miller 2012). These are astonishingly high numbers.[26]

---

26 It is worth thinking about the ways in which all these findings are, themselves, examples of certain kinds of cultural performances (or discursive practices). If I answer the phone and engage in a conversation with a poll-taker, and if in that conversation I am asked "What religion are you?", and if in response to that question I answer, "Jewish," it is of course true that I have said something about myself—but it is also true that I have enacted a particular cultural performance with its own sets of norms and context-specific expectations. I know the "right" answer, the answer that the poll-taker is looking for in a case such as mine, and unless I am in a particularly ornery mood, I am prepared to comply. I don't say, "I'm a Patriots fan"—nor do I say "I'm a lefty" nor "I'm a father of three." The point of this digression is that, while the general thrust of my argument in the main body of the text is that many American Jews have identities (self-conceptions) without practices, another way of describing their condition is to notice how they *do* enact certain cultural performances of Jewishness, such as responding that they are Jewish (when asked) and even responding that they are proud to be Jewish, just not traditionalist ones.

At the same time, in any sociological study, most Jews are assessed as having weak Jewish identities, because of their lack of affiliation with Jewish institutions and the absence of significant Jewish activities. So there is a disconnect between identity and practice. Even those of us who are critical of the rhetoric around "making Jewish choices" recognize that an affirmation of Jewish identity without an engagement in Jewish practices lacks richness, depth and meaning. Jews, that is, ought to "perform who they are." This is an unabashedly normative statement—they *ought* to—and that normativity might make some readers uneasy. Who are we to say what other people ought to do? But notice that the normativity emerges from a diagnosis of the disconnect between identity and practice. In this sense, it is no more and no less normative than saying that someone who claims the identity of being a runner ought to enact the practice that is constitutive of that identity, by running regularly. Or, that someone who claims the identity of being an Obama supporter ought, at the very least, to vote. Any identity carries with it an implicit conception of what it means to uphold that identity, to enact it well.

Of course, there are various ideas about what a Jew ought to do, various images of what a Jew ought to be. The implicit conception may well be a contested one. So the diagnosis of a disconnect between identity and practice does not prescribe precisely how to overcome that disconnect. It is normative without being narrowly prescriptive. To say that Jews ought to "perform who they are" leaves open the question of who, exactly, they are—whom they understand themselves to be—and what it means to be that kind of person. As Alasdair MacIntyre writes, "If I am a Jew, I have to recognize that the tradition of Judaism is partly constituted by a continuous argument over what it means to be a Jew" (MacIntyre, 1977, p. 460).[27]

If I claim an identity as a father, we can ask what that identity means to me. What are the practices that are constitutive of being a father? There is room for disagreement here. My conception of what fatherhood entails might diverge from that of others. And there is no reason that "fatherhood" needs to be a fixed concept rather than one that evolves over time. Nevertheless, we should notice that my conception of fatherhood is not my own idiosyncratic invention; I have been influenced by what we might call a "tradition of fatherhood," or perhaps by more than one. And thus, my own conception is, implicitly at least, in dialogue with the conception of others. Moreover—and this is the main point about the relationship between identity and practice, between who I consider myself to be and what I do in the world—even as I

---

27 See above, note 14.

may have my own conception, it still makes sense to ask about the enactment of that conception.

Thus, we can ask contemporary Jews: What is the Judaism or Jewishness that they affirm, when they identify as Jews? (The use of the sociological term "Jewishness" instead of the more religious term "Judaism" may help to disrupt the assumption that Jewish practice is synonymous with traditional Jewish religious ritual practice.) What are the practices associated with those ideals? (The plural "practices" instead of the singular "practice" may also help to disrupt the assumption that Jewish practice is synonymous with the practice of the ritual aspects of *halakha*.) Nor is this even a matter of denominationalism or of belief. Maybe enacting a Jewish identity means carrying out the rituals of Jewish religious practice as codified in the tradition. Maybe it means carrying out some of those rituals in new ways. Maybe it means supporting Israel in the face of external threats, or helping Israel to live up to its ideals. Maybe it means caring for the elderly. Maybe it means tikkun olam. Maybe it means appreciating or engaging with Jewish culture, literature, art in particular ways. Maybe it means Chinese food and a movie on Christmas. The point is simply that it is not possible to have that identity—to have a conception of who you are in the world—without also having a sense of the practices that are constitutive of that identity, what it means to enact the identity.[28]

Earlier, drawing on the idea that we become what we do, I proposed that practice is primary, and that we ought to conceptualize Jewish education as an initiation into a set of Jewish practices. What we now see

---

28 Sagi (2016), drawing on Heidegger, observes that, in the standard case, we do *not* reflect on identity or on the practices that constitute identity. "Full reflection on practices or on identity occurs only at times of crisis, when the continuity and the duration typical of action are disturbed" (p. 5). Given the radical diversity of contemporary Jewish self-understandings, we might say that, for many, our age is an age of crisis. Here again, however, we also have to acknowledge the contemporary "bad Jew" phenomenon, which is important in this context because it represents an instance in which individuals identify the norms or practices associated with a particular identity—but self-consciously situate themselves outside those norms or practices. Earlier, I compared the "bad Jew" to the "poor runner," but this analogy does not quite capture the phenomenon. After all, the "poor runner" would like to be a "great runner," if it were not for physiology, or the absence of time for training, or weakness of will. The "bad Jew" is saying, "I know what it means to be a 'good Jew' and I have no interest in doing that." One way to solve the conundrum—the conceptual conundrum, not the practical-educational problem—is to say that "bad Jews" do have a sense of the practices that are constitutive of their identities, not as "Jews" but as "bad Jews." They are indeed performing who they are.

is that this second way of thinking about the relationship between practice and identity—the idea that we should perform who we are—leads us to a very similar educational conclusion. Even if identity precedes practice, as it seems to do for many Jews, the educational task is to articulate the set of practices that will meaningfully fulfill that identity and to educate towards those practices. In neither case do we "educate for Jewish identity" or "strengthen Jewish identity." For thoughtful educators, those terms are impossibly abstract and monolithic. In place of Jewish educational discourse that focuses on Jewish identity, a Jewish educational discourse that focuses on Jewish practices (or, equally, Jewish cultural performances) will be specific, concrete and plural.

Conclusion

In the blizzard of reactions to the Pew study of American Jews in 2013, perhaps the most unexpected came from the prominent public intellectual Noah Feldman, who jumps from the Pew study to some observations about, surprisingly, the Lakewood yeshiva (Feldman, 2013). Lakewood is a massive all-male ultra-Orthodox educational institution focused almost entirely on the study of Talmud. Feldman claims that its educational model is "astonishingly egalitarian and democratic," that it demonstrates that "one kind of authentically Jewish experience is flourishing in America." He concludes that, "by privileging ideas and thought over identity, [Lakewood] proudly stakes out a position of genuine durability."

At first glance, this seems like a naïve and uncritical embrace of the authenticity of old-time religion. But Feldman is no apologist for traditionalism. He is well aware of the ways in which Lakewood is not egalitarian and not democratic, as those terms are conventionally used; women are not permitted in the space, and decisions about institutional policies are determined by the senior leadership with little consideration of the wishes of the masses of students. Nevertheless, what he notices about Lakewood, astutely, is that they have identified a particular practice that they value above everything else—a particular cultural performance—and they have set up an educational system to pursue that cultural performance with singleminded focus and discipline. That is what makes Lakewood admirable. That focus and discipline is the quality to which Feldman points in his phrase "privileging ideas and thought over identity." What he really means to say is that Lakewood does not spend time or energy worrying about the

Jewish identity of its students, and does not believe that vacuous phrases like "strengthening Jewish identity" are sufficient to inform an educational vision. Instead, Lakewood wants students to learn Talmud, and to do so in a particular way that they value. It doesn't matter that that particular methodology is only a couple hundred years old; they're not interested in history. Nor, for that matter, are they particularly interested in "ideas and thought," if we take that phrase to indicate philosophy or theology, which are also not part of the curriculum. It's all Talmud, all the time.

The rest of the Jewish community is not about to mimic the Lakewood model for any number of good reasons. Nevertheless, we ought to ask ourselves how our educational visions might achieve the clarity that Lakewood's seems to have—not theological clarity but educational clarity— and how our educational institutions might pursue our goals with similar focus and discipline. That educational clarity requires identifying the cultural performances that we value most, and then figuring out how to help students achieve the capacities to pull off those cultural performances.

What do we want students to know and be able to do? Read texts in certain ways? Speak certain languages or participate in certain metalinguistic communities?[29] Enjoy Jewish culture? Produce Jewish culture? In what ways do we want them to be engaged with their local Jewish and non-Jewish communities? Who do we want them to be, as interpreters of Jewish history and tradition? How do we envision the connection of Jews to other Jews, locally or globally? What is our picture of engaged citizenship, and in what polities? What are our aspirations for the inner, spiritual lives of Jews? What does it mean to live a life on behalf of others, or to pursue justice, or to create beauty in the world, or to serve the Divine?

Contemporary American Jews are perfectly comfortable with their Jewish identities, and the discourse of "Jewish identity" does not help us to make principled and effective decisions about our educational purposes and practices. Instead, we ought to be talking about Jewish practices. Educators must help Jews become what they do, and help them perform who they are: educators must initiate students (of all ages) into particular practices of Jewishness, so that they become what they do, and at the same time, educators must help Jews to identify and articulate the particular practices that are constitutive of their sense of Jewishness, so that they perform who they are. In these two

---

29 On Jewish languages and metalinguistic communities, see the chapter by Benor and Avineri in this volume. Also see above, note 20.

complementary senses, Jewish education is not about transmitting identity or strengthening identity. Instead, the desired outcome of Jewish education is an initiation into the practices of Jewishness.

Bibliography

Aron, I. (1989). The malaise of Jewish education. *Tikkun* 4(3), 32–34.

Brown, J. S., Collins, A., & Duguid, P. (1989). Situated Cognition and the Culture of Learning. *Educational Researcher* 18(1).

Buckman, L. (2018). Israel's Shifting Focus. Retrieved from https://ejewishphilanthropy.com/israels-shifting-focus/

Butler, J. (1989). *Gender Trouble.* London, UK: Routledge & Kegan Paul.

Cohen, S. M. & Kelman, A.Y. (2008). *Uncoupled: How Our Singles are Reshaping Jewish Engagement.* Retrieved from http://research.policyarchive.org/14578.pdf

Cohen, S. M., Ukeles, Jacob B., & Miller, Ron. (2012). *Jewish Community Study of New York.* Retrieved from https://www.ujafedny.org/assets/785329

Cousens, B. (2012). *Hillel: New Jewish Adults.* Unpublished report.

Collins, A., Brown, J. S., & Newman, S. E. (1989). Cognitive Apprenticeship: Teaching the Craft of Reading, Writing and Mathematics. In L. B. Resnick (Ed.), *Knowing learning and instructions: Essays in honor of Robert Glaser.* Hillsdale, NJ: Erlbaum.

Feldman, N. (2013). Where Jewish Life Thrives in America. Retrieved from http://www.bloomberg.com/news/2013-10-03/where-jewish-life-thrives-in-america.html

Gans, H. (1979). Symbolic ethnicity: The Future of Ethnic Groups and Cultures in America. *Ethnic and Racial Studies* 2(1), 1–20.

Glazer, N. (1989). *American Judaism* (2nd ed.). Chicago, IL: University of Chicago Press.

Hirst, P. (1965). Liberal Education and the Nature of Knowledge. In R. D. Archambault (Ed.), *Philosophical Analysis and Education.* London, UK: Routledge & Kegan Paul.

Hirst, P. (1993). Education, Knowledge and Practices. In Robin Barrow, & Patricia White (Eds.), *Beyond Liberal Education: Essays in Honour of Paul H. Hirst.* London, UK: Routledge.

Hirst, P. (1999). The Nature of Educational Aims. In R. Marples (Ed.), *The Aims of Education.* London, UK: Routledge.

Isenberg, S. (2012). How President Obama's Campaign Used Big Data to Rally Individual Voters. Retrieved from https://www.technologyreview.com/s/509026/how-obamas-team-used-big-data-to-rally-voters

Lave, J., & Wenger, E. (1991). *Situated Learning: Legitimate Peripheral Participation.* Cambridge, UK: Cambridge University Press.

Levisohn, J. A. (2012). Rethinking the Education of Cultural Minorities to and from Assimilation: A Perspective from Jewish Education. *Diaspora and Indigenous Minority Education 7.*

MacIntyre, A. (1977). Epistemological Crises, Dramatic Narrative, and the Philosophy of Science. *The Monist* 60(4), 453–472.

McLaughlin, T. (2001). Paul H. Hirst—1927. In J. A. Palmer (Ed.), *Fifty Modern Thinkers on Education: From Piaget to the Present* (pp. 193–199). London, UK: Routledge.

Peters, R. S. (1973). *Authority, Responsibility and Education.* London, UK: George Allen & Unwin.

Polanyi, M. (1958/1998). *Personal Knowledge: Towards a Post-Critical Philosophy.* London, UK: Routledge.

Rawidowicz, S. (1986). State of Israel, Diaspora, and Jewish Continuity: Essays on the "Ever-Dying People." Hanover, NH: Brandeis University Press.

Reimer, J. (2007). Beyond More Jews Doing Jewish: Clarifying the Goals of Informal Jewish Education. *Journal of Jewish Education, 73*(1), 5–23

Rosenblatt, K., Corwin Berman, L., & Stahl, R. (2018). How Jewish Academia Created a #MeToo Disaster. Retrieved from https://forward.com/opinion/406240/how-jewish-academia-created-a-metoo-disaster/

Rouse, J. (2001). Two Conceptions of Practices. In T. R Schatzki, K. Knorr-Cetina, & E. von Savigny (Eds.), *The Practice Turn in Contemporary Theory.* New York, NY: Routledge.

Rouse, J. (2006). Practice Theory. In S. Turner & M. Risjord (Eds.), *Handbook of the Philosophy of Science, Volume 15: Philosophy of Anthropology and Sociology.* New York, NY: Elsevier Science.

Rouse, J. (2007). Social Practices and Normativity. *Philosophy of the Social Sciences 37*(1), 1–11.

Ryle, G. (1946/1971). *Collected Papers* (Vol. 2). London, UK: Hutchinson.

Sagi, A. (2016). *Reflections on Identity: The Jewish Case.* Boston, MA: Academic Studies Press.

Sales, B. (2014). Big-Money Israel Plan to Engage Diaspore is Approved—Details Still Fuzzy. Retrieved from http://forward.com/news/israel/199461/big-money-israel-plan-to-engage-diaspora-is-approv/

Sasson, T. (2013). New Analysis of Pew Data: Children of Intermarriage Increasingly Identify as Jews. Retrieved from https://www.tabletmag.com/jewish-news-and-politics/151506/young-jews-opt-in

Schwab, J. J. (1957). On the Corruption of Education by Psychology. *Ethics 68*(1), 39–44.

Seligman, A., Weller, Robert P., Puett, Michael J., & Simon. (2008). *Ritual and Its Consequences: An Essay on the Limits of Sincerity.* Oxford, UK: Oxford University Press.

Stern, Y. (2015). The Spirit of Jewish Particularism. Retrieved from https://mosaicmagazine.com/response/2015/04/the-spirit-of-jewish-particularism/

Taylor, C. (1995). *The Ethics of Authenticity.* Cambridge, MA: Harvard University Press.

Thompson, J. (2013a). *Jewish on Their Own Terms: How Intermarried Couples Are Changing American Judaism.* New Brunswick, NJ: Rutgers University Press.

Thompson, J. (2013b). Good and Bad Jews in American Jewish Discourse and Experience. Paper presented at the Association of Jewish Studies, New York.

Ungar-Sargon, B. (2017). How the Obsession with Jewish Continuity Perverts Our Liberal Values. Retrieved from https://forward.com/opinion/382679/how-the-obsession-with-jewish-continuity-perverts-our-liberal-values/

Yoo, J-B. (2001). Hirst's Social Practices View of Education: A Radical Change From His Liberal Education? *Journal of Philosophy of Education 35*(4), 615–626.

Jewish Sensibilities: Toward a New Language for Jewish Educational Goal-Setting

Lee Moore and Jonathan Woocher, zl

Talking About the Goal(s) of Jewish Education

What is the goal of Jewish education? In this chapter we use several terms—goals, desired outcomes, objectives—essentially interchangeably. In some contexts, it makes sense to define and differentiate these terms more precisely. However, for our purposes, they all refer to whatever it is that an individual or entity involved in the educational process seeks to achieve through that process. The question—what do I seek to achieve—is simple enough, but answering it has proven devilishly difficult.

The reasons for this difficulty are many. First, there is the question of goal (or goals) for whom? Jewish education has multiple stakeholders involved in the process who often bring with them very different perspectives on the desired outcome(s). Learners, parents (if the learners are children), institutions, educators, communal authority figures, funders—all may seek different things.

Second, there is the question of the time frame with which we are concerned: are we looking at immediate learning objectives at the end of a session or particular short-term intervention, outcomes at the end of some reasonably proximate period (e.g., by the time of Bar or Bat Mitzvah, when a student graduates, etc.), or goals for the distant future (how will a student now relate to her Jewishness in twenty years, or when she has children of her own)? Are there links between the more immediate and the more distant goals?

Third, there is the question of individual goals versus collective goals. Education is not only about preparing people for a good life; it is also about the transmission or reproduction of culture across generations. How much weight do we give to that collective dimension in our thinking about goals? Are our goals for individuals shaped by a commitment to a clear goal (e.g., continuity) at the collective level? Can individual and group goals be in tension, and what happens if they are?

Fourth, there is the question of the proper domain to which our goals belong. In much of the discourse in general education, the primary focus is on cognitive achievement: the knowledge we have learned and can put to use. In Jewish education, there are other things we might choose to place above cognitive achievement as measuring rods for success, e.g., qualities of character (generosity), patterns of behavior (engaging in prayer), emotional dispositions (gratitude). Increasingly, these kinds of goals—sometimes called "socio-emotional learning" or "whole child education"—are receiving greater emphasis in the world of general education, bringing with them practical challenges in terms of how to measure them.

Finally, there is the question of whether we define the outcomes we seek strictly in "Jewish" terms, or whether our goals are more broadly "human." Clearly, there is distinctively Jewish knowledge that we may wish learners to acquire (e.g., an understanding of the meaning of traditional texts or familiarity with historical events affecting and affected by Jews). And, there are distinctively Jewish practices that we might want students to adopt (e.g., observing Shabbat, saying b'rachot). Often, these have provided the operative goals for Jewish education. But, there are other goals, having to do with how individuals see themselves and act in the world, which, at least for today's Jewish population, involve dealing with ideas, emotions, and behaviors that transcend a narrow focus on "Jewishness" (though, as we will argue, Jewish wisdom has much to say about these). Jewish education is being asked to embrace "whole person" learning, which means that its goals will be even broader and, quite likely, more diverse.

It turns out, then, that "what is the goal of Jewish education?" is not a simple question at all. Current discourse around this question reflects that reality. For many years, the conversation about Jewish educational goals focused largely on two concepts: Jewish "identity" at the individual level (e.g., "strengthening Jewish identity") and Jewish "continuity" at the collective level ("ensuring Jewish continuity"). Recently, though, the use of these concepts as desired educational outcomes has come under assault from several angles (see, e.g., Levisohn, 2014a, as well as the other chapters of the present volume). Philosophers, social scientists, and educators have critiqued the vagueness of these concepts, the conventionality of the ways in which they are usually defined and measured, and their lack of meaningfulness to newer generations of Jews for whom Jewish identification is largely a given, but who seek rationales for why that identification should be important and how it actually affects their lives. Although the language of Jewish identity and continuity is still present in the discussion of educational goals, it is increasingly evident that it is insufficient to guide educators today from both a conceptual and practical perspective. We need goals that are more specific, more in tune with what learners are seeking, and more ambitious in terms of their potential impact.

The price of moving in this direction is that we will have to give up the idea that any single phrase or concept, at a high level of generality, can serve as a singular, comprehensive goal for Jewish education. Specific goals will inevitably reflect specific values, specific ways of understanding Judaism, specific understandings of the purposes of education generally, and specific empirical circumstances. These differ dramatically among Jews, and not only along denominational lines. What is reasonable to seek, therefore, is not consensus on one goal, or even a limited set of goals, but a common framework within which the discussion can be carried out—a vocabulary for talking about the desired outcomes of Jewish education.

Existing Frameworks

Several such frameworks that aim to provide a richer, more nuanced vocabulary for speaking about educational goals have achieved some prominence in recent years. One approach, associated with the work of the Mandel Leadership Institute in Jerusalem and building on work in philosophy of general education that focused on "the educated person," begins with the concept of "the educated Jew" (Fox, Scheffler, & Marom, 2003). By identifying the characteristics of an individual whom we would consider "educated" from a Jewish perspective, we can work backwards to the educational program that would produce such an individual. A variation of this approach focuses on the "ideal graduate" of an educational institution or program. By envisioning an ideal product of the school or camp or other educational program, we can begin to lay out the educational pathways that will lead to this outcome.

The approach to goal-setting that seeks to define specific characteristics of the "educated Jew" or "ideal graduate" needs, of course, to flesh out the domains in which these characteristics lie. For many years, educators have spoken about educational goals in terms of three domains signified by the mnemonic "ABC": the affective, the behavioral, and the cognitive domains.[1]

---

1 This is actually a slightly skewed version of the original taxonomy of educational goals associated with Benjamin Bloom (1956). He and those who have followed in his approach

More recently, a fourth domain has been added that might be termed "relational" (how students connect with others and with their environment), and some have suggested a fifth that focuses on the values that learners hold. The Jewish Education Project in New York, which has done work on defining educational outcomes in several settings, uses a four-element model which it designates as "KDBB"—encompassing knowing, doing, believing/valuing, and belonging—to describe what it calls a "whole-person" approach to learning and assessment (Coalition of Innovating Congregations).[2] Institutions are encouraged to elaborate the goals they have for students in each of these domains: what should students *know*, what should they *do*, what should they *believe* and *value*, and what *connections* should they feel to their school or synagogue, their Jewish community, the Jewish people? Here again, a "backward design" process can then translate these goals—identified for a class session, a year, or the entirety of a program—into a lesson plan or a curriculum that makes their realization feasible.

These approaches do provide a language in which to discuss, compare, weigh, and ultimately select the goals that are most meaningful for a particular institution, program, family, or even individual. Even more importantly, identifying three (or more) domains serves to subvert the long-established tendency of educational institutions—schools, especially—to default to the cognitive, as if getting kids to know stuff is the core mission of schools. On the other hand, in practice, educators are familiar with what happens when they are asked to come up with multiple objective for each of multiple domains: the ABCs approach (and its expanded versions) often leads to rather lengthy and poorly integrated "laundry lists" of desired outcomes.

How do we do justice to the interconnection of knowledge, emotion, valuing, relationships, and behavior? Analytically, we can distinguish among

---

divide goals into three domains: cognitive, affective, and psycho-motor, all of which have behavioral objectives attached to them. Nonetheless, the "ABC" version, which allows for specific Jewish behaviors to be postulated as desirable outcomes, has become the popular approach in Jewish educational discourse.

2 The KDBB framework for articulating educational goals was developed by Cyd Weissman, who brought it with her to the Jewish Education Project and who headed up its work in the area of congregational educational improvement for a number of years. In her unpublished paper (2008), "A Framework for Meaning Making Learning: Reaching Deeper and Broader," Weissman proposed general goals for each of the domains: Know—"Learners have a body of knowledge and know how to access the information of the concepts, values, tools of Jewish tradition"; Belong—"Learners develop a sense of connection to and identification with the Jewish community, land of Israel, *Klal Yisrael*"; Believe—"Learners are actively engaged in a spiritual journey"; Do (originally, Live)—"Learners apply teachings to daily life choices, practice ritual, *tzedakah*, etc."

several domains using a model like ABC or KDBB. But, in actual life, the separation among these domains is artificial—what we know, feel, believe, and do are deeply affected by one another. Indeed, often it is precisely their melding together that gives an experience its power and its meaning. This is especially true when it comes to knowledge, value judgments, emotions and practices that may be characterized as "religious." The anthropologist Clifford Geertz has argued that the distinguishing characteristic of religion is that it uses symbols (including rituals) in such a way as to make statements about the nature of reality and prescriptions for how we ought to behave in the world feel "right" and even inevitable because they are interwoven so as to support one another in ways that transcend rational analysis (Geertz, 1966). Creating lists of desired outcomes—e.g., for a student to know the Biblical origins of Shabbat and the thirty-nine categories of "work," to be able to make Kiddush, to feel and value Shabbat as a day to step back from the business of daily life, to join with others to celebrate and pray in synagogue, or any of dozens of other possible goals relating to Shabbat—may actually have little to do with designing experiences that make Shabbat feel compelling in that student's life. Can we find a vocabulary for speaking about Jewish educational goals that respects both the holistic way in which we as humans engage the world, with our minds, hearts, and hands all at once, and the holistic way in which Jewish tradition organizes its insights, teachings, and guidance for our lives?

There are also other languages for discussing goals that are beginning to make their way into current Jewish educational discourse. One focuses on so-called twenty-first-century learning skills, often described mnemonically as consisting of multiple "C's": curiosity, communication, collaboration, creativity, critical thinking, complex problem solving, citizenship, and others (see, e.g., National Education Association, 2014; San Carlos School District; and many more). A second speaks of developmental competencies, with its own set of "C's": competence, confidence, connection, caring, character, and contribution. These skills or competencies are desirable because they enable students to successfully traverse the course to adulthood in the contemporary world (Woocher, 2014). Notably, these languages take us still further from the old discourse about Jewish identity. In fact, the goals of Jewish education are not limited to specifically "Jewish" knowledge, attitudes, or behaviors at all. Instead, they seek to place Jewish education squarely in a larger framework of human development; Jewish learning and experiences are seen as vehicles for achieving broader human goals as well.

This movement from relatively narrow, "identity"- and "continuity"- driven educational goals—knowing and doing more "Jewish" things, feeling more "Jewish," spending more time with Jews in Jewish settings—to goals that connect directly to individual growth, fulfillment, and purposefulness is, on the whole, a good and necessary development. In a sense, it represents a recovery of the Jewish tradition's own vision of Torah as a vehicle for living a better, nobler, richer life and creating a better, more just and peaceful world. One thinks, for example, of Maimonides' claim in the twelfth century (in *The Guide for the Perplexed* 3:27): "The general object of the Law is twofold: the well-being of the soul, and the well-being of the body." The goal is not to know the 39 categories of work or to know how to make Kiddush; the goal is spiritual and physical flourishing.

On the other hand, as educational guidance, it carries with it the potential to reduce the particulars of Jewish learning—the knowledge, the practices, the connections, the settings—to mere stepping-stones to outcomes that are articulated in entirely general terms. If the goals of Jewish education are general, and only the means are particular, then other means leading to the same goals may be of equal value. If, on the other hand, there is a vocabulary for speaking about the goals of Jewish education that is distinctively Jewish, if the goals can best be expressed and understood in this language, then Jewish education may be able to contribute unique value to the lives of Jewish learners.

Thus, the concept of the "educated Jew," on its own, is too abstract. The framework of ABC or KDBB is artificially fragmented. Twenty-first-century skills and developmental competencies are generic rather than rooted in a particular tradition. Is there a vocabulary for thinking and talking about educational goals that addresses the broadest human purposes in a distinctively Jewish voice?

Jewish Sensibilities

We propose a framework that addresses many of these challenges—using what we call "Jewish sensibilities" to carry on a constructive discussion about educational outcomes. Vanessa Ochs may have been the first to use the term, in an essay in *Sh'ma* titled "Ten Jewish Sensibilities" (Ochs, 2003), where she describes sensibilities as "particularly Jewish ways of thinking about what it means to be human, ways that guide and orient a person's actions and choices."[3]

---

3 Ochs' list reads as follows: (1) Making Distinctions (*Havdalah*), (2) Honor (*Kavod*), (3) Turning (*Teshuvah*), (4) Dignity; Being in the Image of God (*Tzelem Elokim*), (5) Saving

Sensibilities can be seen as mindsets through which the core activities of perceiving the world, processing those perceptions, and responding to them take place. Sensibilities are culturally informed memes that cut across those categories of knowledge, emotion, valuing, relationships, and behavior because they can be applied toward life situations in such a way that constructs meaning. Thus, we do not use the term "sensibility" as a technical or scientific term, nor to propose a philosophical theory of mind or behavior. Rather, we are drawing on a number of different constructs, like frame theory and cultural memes, and using "sensibilities" as a general descriptive term for the constructs that we employ in making sense of what we encounter.[4]

How? Take, for example a sensibility we might call *Elu v'Elu*—"both these and those." Drawn from a Mishnaic narrative[5] where it is applied to the opposing views of two groups of scholars, the term refers to that particularly Jewish—not necessarily uniquely Jewish, but still particularly Jewish—way of approaching the world that suggests there may be two correct answers to a given question. Consider the common joke with many derivatives: "Two Jews, Three Opinions." To those who know Jewish families, Jewish communities, this is funny because it rings so true. When set against American culture, it is an example of one of the distinguishing characteristics of Jewish culture and points toward not only a specific piece of knowledge or a specific ritual action, but a way of being in the world—one that makes room for diversity, engenders

---

a Life: *Pikuach Nefesh*, (6) Being a Really Good Person ("Be a *Mensch*"), (7) Keeping the Peace (*Shalom Bayit*), (8) Repairing the World (*Tikkun Olam*), (9) Maintaining Hope (*Yesh Tikvah*), (10) Memory of One's Ancestors (*Z'chut Avot*). Ochs subsequently expanded her discussion of Jewish sensibilities in an essay, "The Jewish Sensibilities," published in an issue of *The Journal of Textual Reasoning* (2006) devoted to that topic. In that essay she defines Jewish sensibilities as: "a largely unarticulated code of behaviors which [American Jews] try to follow and which they use to judge both themselves and others." She emphasizes further that "the code is certainly supported by traditional Jewish practices, texts and regula, but it is not necessarily synonymous with them," and claims that these sensibilities are present in the lives of both religiously observant American Jews as well as those who are not traditionally observant. The issue of the journal in which Ochs' essay appears also includes responses by Nancy Fuchs-Kreimer (2006) and Daniel Weiss (2006) that raise several interesting questions about how Jewish sensibilities are selected, elaborated, and transmitted, and how they reflect both traditional sources and environmental factors.

4 For a cross-cultural comparison, see Cornel West's references to the "tragicomic *blues sensibility* of African Americans"—a sense that humans are flawed creatures with complex and sometimes hopelessly tangled agendas—as a complement to the Greek Socratic tradition of questioning and speaking out, and the Jewish prophetic tradition of taking action against injustice (2004).

5 Babylonian Talmud, Eruvin 13b

humility and provides a powerful relationship technique, if applied correctly. *You don't have to be wrong for me to be right*, as Rabbi Brad Hirschfield has phrased it (2007). The emotional resilience, genuine curiosity and nuance of thought that a learner can develop by employing this sensibility can surely help them thrive as a human. And, it's so Jewish.

What does it mean when we say that someone is thinking Jewishly, speaking Jewishly, acting Jewishly and feeling Jewishly? Perhaps we mean that this person is exhibiting certain specific sensibilities that emanate from the cultural storehouse of Jewish history, tradition and habits.

In principle, every culture has distinct sensibilities that can be unearthed, identified, and understood as values-based lenses through which the world is perceived, responded to, and therefore comprehended multi-dimensionally. Sensibilities can be heuristically powerful because they put emphasis on process, not content. A sensibility pertains to the way in which a person perceives, and then responds. In other words, a sensibility gets employed at the moment that a person takes in information about what is happening (like a "lens"), and then again when responding to that stimulus. In this way, sensibilities describe the ways in which our cultural predilections impact how we build our awareness of what the world is, and in turn then shape how we respond to it.

Sensibilities are also powerful as a framework because they authentically emerge from cultural stories, patterns and habits, while at the same time enabling an individual to autonomously perceive-and-respond as herself, not echoing a rote response, but rather acting within a range of responses that all represent legitimate interpretations of that sensibility. How does this work? One might adopt, e.g., a sensibility that we might call *Gerim Heyitem* ("you were strangers"), perceiving and responding to instances of marginalization through a cultural lens that says, "(It is central to my self-understanding that) my people were once slaves and strangers in the land of Egypt; therefore I attempt to always exercise empathy for any person that is being marginalized." How exactly such an individual will respond to seeing an act of marginalization will vary according to other factors that make that person unique—including personal style, additional cultural mores, etc. She may choose to protest, to empathetically stand alongside the victim of marginalization, to create a new setting where the marginalized individual will be included with dignity. All these are legitimate expressions of the sensibility *Gerim Heyitem*.

It is not the case that empathic responses *require* this particular sensibility—surely others (who do not identify with the idea of having been strangers in Egypt) achieve empathy for the marginalized in other ways—so we do not claim that Jews are uniquely empathic, or even necessarily more empathic than others. Nevertheless, by witnessing and responding to an act of marginalization in this particular way, a person can see herself as "acting Jewishly," even as she will still be acting as herself. Perhaps her sense of self will become even stronger because she is able to root her response in a framework of meaning that connects her to a long history of similar situations and similar responses. Embracing sensibilities that emanate from one's cultural heritage enables an individual to perceive and respond more similarly to her ancestors' patterns of perceiving-and-responding.

In pre-modern settings, sensibilities were learned mimetically through family life and histories as much as through institutional educational means. Their almost instinctive adoption lies at the heart of cultural transmission—the way in which any culture replicates its memes across generations. As the social density of Jewish communities has decreased and integration into the larger society has increased, a form of mimetic transmission continues but now often through the vehicle of popular culture. Young Jews often learn more about what it means to be Jewish, to speak Jewishly and to act Jewishly, from Jon Stewart and Jerry Seinfeld than they do from formal educational transmission and, at times, even their own families. Given the loss of an organic mimetic tradition as described by Haym Soloveitchik (1999), a critical question is where and how Jews today will encounter a rich set of Jewish sensibilities that extend beyond the few that contemporary culture has canonized.

What Does it Mean to Be Jewish?

Taken as a set of life-approaches, sensibilities offer one way of answering the question: what does it mean to be Jewish?—a question that lies at the heart of Jewish education, and yet can be difficult for many educators to answer. There is, of course, no single answer to that question. However, imagine a classroom of second graders, or a teen youth group, who when asked respond swiftly and clearly, "I know that being Jewish means recognizing that there are always many sides of an issue, so we should always be open to hearing views that are not our own." For this group of students, being Jewish clearly means (among other things) living by the sensibility of *Elu v'elu.*

What makes for a Jewish sensibility? Some characteristics we have found useful in our thinking include:

1. Jewish sensibilities are distinctively Jewish, arising from and widely attested in Jewish narratives, texts and practices. In saying that Jewish sensibilities are "distinctively Jewish" we do not mean to imply that they may not have analogs or parallels in other cultures or faith traditions. A belief that there may be truth in opposing opinions (or a special sensitivity to the plight of strangers) is not a uniquely Jewish characteristic. But, expressed in the ways these are in Jewish texts and historical experience, connected to specific stories, historical figures, and circumstances, they take on a distinctive character that cannot be fully captured in some more "universal" formulation. This is also not a matter of simply labeling any concept with a Hebrew word, but rather of identifying and articulating memes that are undeniably located in some fashion within the historical and literary corpus of Jewish experience, and reflected and described through lived experience of Jewish people.

2. Sensibilities describe particular junctures where cultural inheritance meets the human experience. Because sensibilities are carried by people, and are not simply what's found in a text, they may emerge or fade from focus over time, according to prevailing cultures that Jews are living in concert with/response to. As a result, sensibilities become more or less prominent as people adopt and use them within particular cultural contexts. For example *kana'ut*, zealotry, is a Jewish sensibility that has had strong valence in some Jewish communities, and not others. "Ironic humor" is another with modest, though real, ancient roots that has risen in prominence as a Jewish sensibility over the past two centuries.

3. Sensibilities integrate the cognitive, affective and behavioral domains. They encompass values, and move beyond them to include emotional dispositions, to offer guidance and to point toward a life of meaning.

4. Sensibilities can be described in a single word or short phrases and can act as gateways into and expressions of a world of Jewish texts, stories, personal family stories, jokes, and other expressions of Jewish culture. A person may know only one point of reference to the sensibility from the tradition. But, the more explicit and implicit references one can draw upon, the more meaningful, richer, and nuanced the sensibility becomes.

As with any cultural system, the best way to get a sense of this framework is through examples. *Elu v'elu* is just one Jewish sensibility. Here are a few others, several of which are on Ochs' list as well, that we think speak to the life situations that many Jews (and others) face today:

A. *Simcha* (Joy)—Find pleasure in life. Balance earnest efforts to repair the world with finding contentment and joy in our lives.

B. *b'Tzelem Elohim* ([All people are made] In the Divine Image)— Value the humanity in each person. Protect the life of every person, and ensure dignity and justice for all people.

C. *Na'aseh v'Nishmah* (We Will Do and We Will "Hear" ["understand"])—Try it. Learn by doing. Take action without necessarily knowing why it's important or how it will work out, recognizing you will gain insight along the way.

D. *Shevirah* (Brokenness)—Embrace imperfection. Make room for both the joys and sorrows of life, and acknowledge that we are shaped by our struggles and losses as much as by our victories. In order to be whole, one must also experience brokenness.

E. *Shabbat* (Day of Rest)—Make time for rest and renewal. Carve out time from the relentless pressure of the day-to-day, truly separating yourself from the never-ending drumbeat of life.

F. *Lech Lecha* (Take Yourself and Go)—Take the next step. Live life as a journey, not a destination. Take action and move forward—toward a place you don't yet know, but will discover.

G. *Teshuvah* (Return)—Take responsibility for your actions. Humans often fail to live up to our best selves, so we must learn from our mistakes. Change is always possible.

H. *Brit* (Partnership)—Nurture community. Forge relationships and communities—meaningfully connecting to others by agreeing to shared commitments.

We present each sensibility here along with a phrase that suggests what applying the sensibility might look like (e.g. Find pleasure in life, Value the humanity in each person). This language offers ways that these sensibilities might be acted upon, which are not exhaustive.

No group of Jews is likely to agree on any single list as "the most important sensibilities," any more than the rabbis of *Pirkei Avot* could agree on the most important principle of the Torah. The utility of sensibilities as a way to think about educational outcomes does not depend on getting agreement on a single list of ten or any specific number. Rather, it lies in the concept itself as a framework for naming and elaborating a wide range of Jewish ideas, values, attitudes, and practices.

Why Not "Values"? Why Not "*Middot*"?

In looking at this list of sensibilities an obvious question is how this language differs from one heard not infrequently today that proposes "Jewish values" as the essential content of Jewish tradition that we wish to convey and instill in learners. That there is a "family resemblance" is clear—many of the terms we use to designate "sensibilities" could well be seen and described as "values." We prefer the language of "sensibilities" in part because "values" can carry the connotation of being something abstract and idealized, something we hold in esteem and strive toward, but not necessarily something anchored in our whole being, something that calls forth an emotional and behavioral, as well as an intellectual and evaluative, response. We should note that perhaps the strongest modern proponent of "values" as the core language of Judaism, Max Kadushin, who wrote extensively about what he called Rabbinic "value concepts," recognized this issue. He argued that these value concepts were not just abstract concepts, but carried an inherent "drive towards concretization or actualization." In this way, the value concepts become "personal, subjectively felt and experienced, and thus capable of influencing character and personality" (Steinberg, 1995). Similarly, Michael Rosenak, the guiding force behind perhaps the most ambitious recent effort to build a Jewish educational curriculum around Jewish values, the Hebrew University Melton Centre's Jewish Values Project, argues that what he calls Jewish "value-ideas" are distinctive in large measure because they must

> be applied in every situation and to every aspect of life. Indeed, one of the dominant concepts of this language is that ideas that are not translated into action are worthless: knowledge must be reflected in noble character, and principles of belief and of reason must be brought down to earth and lived by 'a kingdom of priests and a holy people.' This idea remains peculiar to Judaism, even though many of its doctrines and its monotheistic world-view have been adopted by others. (Rosenak, 1986)

This notion that "Judaism [i]s a set of value-ideas striving for implementation," like Kadushin's that "value concepts" carry an inherent drive toward actualization, addresses the concern that "values" may be seen as abstract and detached from daily life. Thus, though we prefer and will use the language of Jewish sensibilities as one that is inherently multi-dimensional, much of our analysis could be applied to a discourse focused on Jewish values—at least as Kadushin and Rosenak use the term—as well.[6]

Another set of concepts becoming more prominent in Jewish educational programming involves *middot,* or character traits, that are seen as defining what a (Jewish) person should be and how she should behave. One notable example is Gann Academy's Chanoch LaNa'ar program, which aims to encourage "students to develop the habits of heart and mind necessary to build meaningful, ethical Jewish identities." In their description, they describe *middot* "as our responses to the world—points of intersection—a way of learning and growing. Learning about and developing character traits engages our intellectual, spiritual, social and emotional life and helps us build strong Jewish identities." This language echoes our emphasis on sensibilities as holistic responses to life experiences. We draw a distinction between sensibilities and *middot* however, in that *middot* are traits that dwell within individuals as building blocks of character, whereas sensibilities are collectively constructed.

Using Jewish Sensibilities to Frame and Assess Educational Outcomes

What, in practical terms, would it look like to use Jewish sensibilities as a vocabulary for framing and assessing the outcomes of our educational efforts, and how might doing so respond to the two questions posed earlier in this chapter: 1) How can we do justice to the inherent interconnectedness of knowing, feeling, valuing and doing? and 2) How can we frame broadly human goals in a distinctively Jewish language?

---

6 In addition to the Melton Jewish Values Project, there have been a number of other efforts in recent years to use Jewish values as a framework for educational programming. These range from full-scale values-based curricula (e.g., the one developed by Shalom Learning, a national organization seeking to revitalize supplementary education, that is built around seven core values: Teshuvah: Taking responsibility for your actions; B'Tzelem Elohim: Honoring the image of God in ourselves and others; Gevurah: Using one's inner strength to do what's right; Achrayut: Doing what you can to make the world a better place; HaKarat HaTov: Seeking joy and being grateful; Koach HaDibbur: Understanding the power of words; and Shalom: Helping to create a calmer, more peaceful world) to tools like the Jewish Values Challenge "cards" developed by Robyn Faintich and distributed by Behrman House with fifty-eight Jewish values that can be used by educators for a variety of experiential activities.

We will not pretend to provide a full blueprint for how Jewish sensibilities might be used to articulate and assess educational goals, but rather offer a general framework as a starting point. To do so, it is useful to draw on a fertile distinction made a number of years ago by philosopher and political theorist Michael Oakeshott (1962) between a "language" and a "literature," a distinction that has been picked up and used since by educators in a number of settings, including Jewish education (Rosenak, 2003; Rosenak, 1995; Levisohn, 2014b). A "language" (metaphorically) is, according to Oakeshott, a "manner of thinking" that characterizes a particular discipline, domain, or field of human endeavor. "Literature" is what is produced using that language. Although the usage may not be exact, we would suggest that "Jewish sensibilities" represent, as we have earlier described them in a less formal way, "Jewish language"—assumptions, perceptions, principles, and processes with which Jews approach the world, a Jewish "manner of thinking." Using this language, Jews have and continue to produce a vast "literature," both literal and metaphorical, in the form of texts, teachings, practices, cultural artifacts, and communal institutions. Oakeshott argues that we cannot (and should not try to) learn a language directly; we learn a language by studying its literature. Nonetheless, the ultimate goal for the educational process is not simply for the student to master the literature in a domain; rather, the goal is to become capable of using the language both to critique the existing literature (and perhaps the language itself) and to create new literature. The goal is to be able to "participate in the conversation" in a domain in a thoughtful, articulate, and productive way.

If we are prepared to accept the claim that Jewish sensibilities function in a way that is akin to Oakeshott's concept of "language," then our goal should be to help learners acquire facility in this language, primarily through the study of Jewish "literature," i.e., the full range of Jewish cultural and social product and experience, so that they can be participants in a conversation that uses this language and to create their own "literature." This is a more ambitious goal than simply knowing the "literature" of Jewish life—a purely cognitive outcome. Taking part in a conversation, being able to use and using a language both critically and creatively, is itself a multi-dimensional act. It inevitably involves knowing, doing, believing/valuing, and belonging.

How might students learn the language of Jewish sensibilities so that they can be part of the literary conversation? One approach is to focus on a number of sensibilities directly, examine their origins and development in Jewish literature and lived experience, and explore how they could be employed in one's life. For example, a class might study the origins of the sensibility of *Elu v'elu*, explore instances of arguments in Jewish text or history that illustrate this sensibility, discuss its relevance to contemporary situations—perhaps denominationalism in American Jewish life or alternative views on Israel. This approach is embodied most fully in a curriculum, *Jewish Sensibilities: An Interactive Guide* (2016), developed by Hillel International that is based on ten representative sensibilities identified by Lippman Kanfer Foundation for Living Torah and is intended to be used by Hillel professionals with college students. The curriculum includes source materials, both classical and contemporary, discussion questions, and activities that students can undertake to apply these sensibilities. In addition to this curriculum, individuals or educators interested in exploring these sensibilities directly can draw on other recently produced resources, including decks of cards and online source sheets.[7]

From a pedagogic standpoint, studying the sensibilities as specific content does, however, carry some risks. By looking at individual sensibilities as subject matter, one could come away with an artificial and compartmentalized picture of lived Jewish life. Focusing attention on particular sensibilities in the course of the educational process is in some ways similar to focusing on specific elements of language (vocabulary, grammar, usage, etc.). What may be lost is the way in which different sensibilities are woven together in historical Jewish experience and in lived life to form a more comprehensive whole—a full-fledged literature, not just a vocabulary. In the end, the goal is not to teach Jewish sensibilities as a subject; it is to enable learners to encounter and internalize them with increasing richness and depth as they engage with the "stuff" of Jewish life—texts, practices, history, community.

What is the "literature" that we hope Jewish learners will produce using the "language" of Jewish sensibilities? More than anything else, it is the narrative of their own lives. If Jewish sensibilities indeed become central elements in how learners approach the world, then the fruits of this will be seen in how they live—how they make major choices, develop careers, nurture families, build communities and strive for spiritual awareness. Some of the "literature" they create will be specifically and particularly "Jewish." It will consist of expressions and behaviors that are connected to specific Jewish times, places, customs, rituals, norms, and content. These are the familiar expressions of "Jewish identity" that much of Jewish education in recent decades has focused on. But, because the language of Jewish sensibilities is one that addresses the totality of our lives—how we approach the world, not

---

7 See, for example, www.jewishsensibilities.org.

only our Jewishness—much of the "literature" that can be created with it will not necessarily be particularly Jewish; it will be broadly human. A Jewish sensibility like *b'tzelem elohim*, seeing human beings as created in the image of God, challenges us to consider the implications of such a claim in every sphere of our lives. The "literature" through which we come to understand and commit to this piece of Jewish vocabulary may similarly include not only the text of *B'reishit*, classical midrashim, and the counter-experience of Jewish dehumanization under the Nazis, but contemporary struggles of gay, lesbian, bisexual, and transgender individuals to claim their full human dignity.

To summarize: We propose that the goals and outcomes of Jewish education can usefully and effectively be framed in terms of Jewish sensibilities. Learners should a) understand and appreciate how sensibilities function as Judaism's "language," characteristic and often distinctive ways of perceiving, thinking about, and responding to life situations (both individual and collective); and b) consciously use some number of sensibilities to inform and/or reflect upon their own attitudes, relationships, and behaviors as Jewish human beings. Adopting these goals as the desired outcomes for Jewish education means encouraging students to engage seriously with the "literature" of Jewish life, the products that those who have used Judaism's "language" in their own lives have produced—its texts, rituals, history, and institutions—but always with the aim of motivating and equipping them to become active participants in the Jewish "conversation" that takes place both verbally and via the "texts" we create through living our lives.

How Would This Framework Function?

We believe that motivating, empowering and equipping students to become active participants in the process of Jewish literary creation, critique, and application (in the way we have defined "literature") is a realistic aspiration for Jewish education, and one well-suited for an era when autonomy, diversity, and relevance are highly and widely valued. Without question, different institutions, educators, and learners will resonate strongly with different sensibilities. As is evident from both Jewish history and contemporary experience, one can say many different things in the Jewish language. But not everything.[8]

---

8 For example, one would be hard pressed to find a Jewish language to validate a wanton indifference to the suffering of other humans or the wholesale destruction of the natural environment. Similarly, it would be difficult to find language that exalts the individual's absolute freedom and denies any responsibility to the community. At a minimum, language

As long as the goal is to enable students to identify, engage with, and, hopefully, internalize and apply elements of that language that are recognizably "Jewish" (i.e., emanating from Jewish texts, stories, lived experience, etc.) and personally meaningful (i.e., that they want to use in producing their own "literature"), there is ample room for diversity in which sensibilities can be emphasized in various educational settings and programs. Ideally, it will be the cumulative effect of encountering multiple sensibilities in multiple pieces of "literature" that will enable learners to internalize the sensibilities and be able to deploy them in their lives spontaneously, naturally and authentically. In that sense, they will be "fluent conversationalists" in the language of Jewish sensibilities.[9] Again, what each individual has to "say" will be different. But, hopefully, in the course of acquiring sufficient fluency to become Jewishly articulate, they will also be able to recognize and appreciate how others are using Jewish language, even when they don't agree with what is said. Sensibilities lend themselves well to this approach to diversity in the particulars of educational goal-setting because they are themselves multi-vocal, subject to diverse interpretation and application. At the same time, like a language with specific vocabulary and grammatical rules, they establish a shared framework for the discourse. You and I may not agree on how to observe Shabbat, or even whether doing so is important or meaningful. But, if education has done its job, we share awareness of the term and some overlapping set of associations with it—it's a Jewish sensibility that we both recognize. This may not be the case with every sensibility. Some people have larger vocabularies and know grammar better than others. Even here, though,

---

in Jewish text or history that might validate such attitudes would be overwhelmed by expressions of the opposing stance.

9 "Fluency" is another metaphor from the realm of language that is worth exploring more deeply in the discourse on goals and outcomes for Jewish education. It has many of the same characteristics as other terms used more commonly, such as literacy, proficiency, or mastery, but evokes more than these do the idea of putting what one knows to use and a sense of comfort or "at-homeness" in the language one is speaking. We like these connotations. All of these terms carry some sense of a standard, a level of familiarity with and ability to understand and make use of content below which one cannot justly claim to be "fluent," "proficient," or "literate." At the same time, each also has gradations—one can be more or less fluent in a language, and, indeed, one's fluency may to some extent be content-dependent. (I may be fluent enough to carry on a conversation in the street, but not fluent when it comes to giving a lecture.) From a practical standpoint, we think it is less important to try to establish some minimal level of fluency in the language of Jewish sensibilities than it is to a) recognize that both levels and domains of fluency will vary, and b) make growth in fluency, both in terms of being aware of a greater number of sensibilities and in terms of being able to apply the sensibilities with which one is familiar more widely and naturally, a focus of educational efforts.

they are still able to participate in a conversation and may even have something worthwhile to say to one another.

Framing educational goals in terms of Jewish sensibilities leaves wide latitude for different formulations of these goals. We have proposed an overarching goal that involves learners coming to be aware of and to adopt as valuable in their own lives some of the distinctive ways in which Jews have perceived and responded to life's challenges and opportunities over the centuries. Individual educational frameworks may wish to go beyond this and to identify particular sensibilities, and perhaps even particular ways of understanding and applying these sensibilities, that they hope students will embrace. Putting forward these types of more prescriptive sets of goals—we might think of these as attempts to induce students to use the "language" to say specific things (beyond simply participating in the conversation)—will be seen by some as the essence of good education and by others as dangerously close to indoctrination. (Some may also see such prescriptive goals as simply unrealistic in the era of the "sovereign self," in which individuals are the ultimate arbiters of how they wish to be Jewish (Cohen & Eisen, 2000).) We would urge caution in using Jewish sensibilities to seek to produce or reproduce individuals and groups who think, feel, and behave in specific, predetermined ways. The beauty of Jewish sensibilities as a language in our view is that it invites diverse, creative expression while nevertheless always mapping to a common cultural core. It maps out a middle ground between autonomy and prescription. Using the language of sensibilities enables institutions and programs to talk about what it means to be Jewish in ways that are substantive and specific without prescribing particular behaviors as a "litmus test" of Jewishness. We can encourage and even require that learners grapple with the Jewish sensibility of 'Shabbat'—taking time out of weekly life to reorient ourselves to the world—via its many associated interpretations, rituals, and modes of observance as they encounter these in Jewish texts, halakha, history, and contemporary life. The responsibility, however, ultimately rests with the students (and their particular Jewish communities) to decide how they will embody this sensibility in their lives. Some individuals and communities will undoubtedly choose to follow more or less "traditional" pathways. But, by keeping the focus of our goal on the necessity of equipping Jews with the motivation and ability to understand and use the "language" rather than on what, specifically, they say with it, we also heighten the likelihood that new ways of understanding and applying the language (new "literature") will emerge that can enrich the culture as a whole and keep it vibrant and adaptive (e.g., the spread of Shabbat "unplugging" as a practice even among Jews who are not generally observant of *halakhah*).

The fact that Jewish sensibilities represent not just individual dispositions, but cultural memes (all "language" is shared), is important. By framing our educational goal as one of encouraging individuals to learn and use Jewish sensibilities as vehicles for shaping their responses to life situations we are simultaneously preparing them to participate in and add to the collective culture of which these sensibilities are a vital and generative part. More use of the language means more literature. For those who see "Jewish continuity" or "strengthening Jewish life" as primary goals of Jewish education, embracing the language of Jewish sensibilities allows them to give these rather vague and abstract goals concrete content. By creating a bridge between those who believe that the goals of Jewish education should be articulated in terms of how it affects the individual and those who believe that education's success should be measured by its impact on the collective (the Jewish community or people) and the transmission of a culture across generations, Jewish sensibilities can again serve as a common language for those holding diverse perspectives.

The language of Jewish sensibilities helps build two other bridges as well. Earlier in this chapter we asked how we can do justice in articulating educational goals to the interconnection of knowledge, emotion, valuing, relationships, and behavior, and also if there is an authentic Jewish vocabulary for articulating the whole-person goals that are replacing Jewish identity and continuity as the focus of our educational efforts. We believe that Jewish sensibilities provide a way of thinking and speaking about educational goals and outcomes that can answer both of these questions. As we have emphasized, sensibilities as they are elaborated in the rich "literature" of Jewish life are inherently multi-dimensional. They incorporate cognitive and evaluative judgments (the world is "broken," imperfect), emotions (therefore, I feel frustrated, sad, frightened, angered), behavioral responses (I feel called to help repair the world in some fashion and act on that), and point us toward relationships (to effectively do this, I seek allies and a community that embraces this mission). Stated in this fashion (as "language") the sensibility of 'shevirah' (brokenness) sounds dry and propositional. But, encountered and re-encountered in, e.g., the Biblical story and Rabbinic elaborations (*midrashim*) on the broken tablets, the cosmic drama of the Lurianic Kabbalah, or the experiences of individuals struggling with disappointments and heartaches in their lives who badly need a word of comfort and support, 'shevirah' can become a powerful theme that helps shape our understanding of and response to a myriad of life situations in which incompleteness, imperfection, and chaos may threaten to overwhelm us.

These are human life situations, not Jewish ones. And, we respond to them as whole persons, not just as Jews. Jewish sensibilities constitute a distinctive Jewish language, but one that is not only useful for speaking about "Jewish" things. We need not attempt to translate the broad human goals we have for our learners—becoming competent, caring, confident, creative, contributing individuals—directly into the language of Jewish sensibilities (or vice versa) to recognize that helping students engage deeply, thoughtfully, and consequentially with any number of Jewish sensibilities will in fact help them along that journey. Is there a gain in talking about '*brit*' (covenantal partnership) as opposed to simply "commitments" as something we aspire to build into our lives? Not, perhaps, in some absolute sense. (Is one language better than another? Is poetry better than science?) But, if we believe, as we do, that the approaches to life encapsulated in Jewish sensibilities have something distinctive to contribute to humanity's discourse—that we benefit from the existence of multiple languages that enable us to say somewhat different things differently (c.f., charity vs. *tzedakah*)—then we can legitimately adopt the goal of exposing Jews and others who may wish to do so to Jewish tradition's unique language for dealing with the universally human. We are decidedly *not* claiming that the language of Jewish sensibilities is the only one that Jews should learn. There is great value, especially in this day and age, in being multilingual, multicultural.[10] It is simply a reality that the vast majority of Jews today will draw on memes, norms, values, and sensibilities from a variety of sources as they go about the business of living their lives. And, "languages" themselves evolve as they come into contact with one another, sharing words and taking on new vocabulary, sometimes to the point where it is difficult, if not impossible, to say to which language a particular word or phrase "belongs." Nonetheless, having Jews who are becoming more fluent in the language of Jewish life, even in the form of a somewhat hybridized dialect, certainly can do

---

10 How the idea of "multi-linguality" fits into our thinking about Jewish education (i.e., how we relate to other sensibilities and meaning-systems in our educational practice) is an important issue that has not yet received great attention in the field. In a time when what Sylvia Barack Fishman (2000) calls "coalescence" of values is the norm for many learners and when familiarity with and adoption of cultural memes emanating from sources other than Jewish tradition is virtually universal, carving out an appropriate role for Jewish language among the several that our students likely speak requires attention to those other languages as well. One starting point may be the recent work of Ben Jacobs (2013) on "cosmopolitan Jewish education."

no harm to those individuals or to the world, especially since with that fluency comes the capacity (as Oakeshott reminds us) to be a more effective critic of both language and literature and a more fertile creator of new literary products (texts, rituals, institutions, modes of behavior). Indeed, we would argue that this is exactly what is happening in Jewish life today as a growing number of individuals seek to engage more deeply with Jewish teachings and then turn around to apply these in new and creative ways to rejuvenate Jewish life.

Assessment

If Jewish sensibilities are to serve as a vocabulary with which to carry on a conversation about Jewish educational goals, there is one additional question that must be addressed: How can we assess the extent to which goals articulated in terms of Jewish sensibilities (either general or specific) are being met? In reality, we would argue, assessing goals framed in terms of Jewish sensibilities is no more difficult—and also no easier—than assessing significant and aspirational Jewish educational goals framed in any of the other ways that have conventionally been used.

Methodologically, there are two fundamental ways of assessing Jewish educational goals and outcomes: We can ask learners or we can observe them. If our goals were solely in the realm of cognitive knowledge, we could measure their achievement using conventional academic approaches –everything from responses to closed-end questions (the classic multiple choice test) to complex simulations where students must employ knowledge to solve problems. But, nearly everyone would agree that the goals of Jewish education extend beyond the cognitive. We are trying to affect attitudes, emotions, and behaviors. To assess the extent to which changes in these areas have occurred (whether the goals themselves have been set by the institution, parents, educators, or learners) we can ask students what they think, feel, and do or have done. We can do this too in a variety of ways, ranging from a written survey to one-on-one conversations. Alternatively, we can observe what students say and do in "natural" situations and seek to infer from their articulations and behaviors what they know, how they feel, what they think, and what else they do. Asking and observing/inferring each have their strengths and weaknesses as methods for assessment. But, they represent the best options available to us.

The real question is what to ask about and what to look for. We are suggesting that the most telling thing to ask about and to listen and look for is whether, how, when, and for what purposes individuals use Jewish sensibilities to shape how they perceive the world and how they respond to it. Ideally, we will be able to witness action that reveals students using sensibilities in their lives, and being conscious of doing so. Experiential education in particular lends itself well to creating situations for students in which they can put various sensibilities to work. But, even when it is not possible to observe students employing sensibilities directly, it is still relevant to ask whether learners are able to and do in fact cite stories, texts, practices, Jewish historical experiences, jokes, or other cultural products as guides, supports, instigators of reflection, or in any other way useful points of reference when they consider and discuss various life issues and situations. Does the question of how far to go to help a friend elicit a recollection of the story of David and Jonathan? When something noteworthy and gratifying happens, do they recognize it as calling for an expression of gratitude, perhaps even through the words of the *Shehechiyanu*? When they face a situation that asks them to take a risk, do they find inspiration in Abraham and Sarah, or in Nachshon? Being able to connect a life situation with appropriate sensibilities and their referents in Jewish literature does not, of course, guarantee that the student will actually employ that sensibility—our ultimate goal. But, *not* being able to make those connections makes it less likely that the relevant sensibilities will in fact be deployed.

Beyond seeking to assess the extent to which students are aware of, able to cite, and use specific sensibilities, whether those identified as important by the educational institution or those they themselves select, we can ask a broader question: Are they motivated to and capable of participating in the ongoing Jewish conversation about how to live a worthy and fulfilling (some might say, sacred) life, one largely carried out using the language of Jewish sensibilities? Do they see that conversation and the people who participate in it as important and relevant to them? Do they want to be part of it and to contribute their insights to it? This may be too ambitious or generalized an aspiration for some. But, if we are concerned not only with how individuals live their lives, but also with how Jewish civilization is carried forward in the contemporary world, this is a valid goal and one that we can assess as we interact deeply with our students.

This approach to assessment encompasses a concern for what students know, what they value, how they feel, and what they do. But, the unifying focus is, on the one hand, on the core vocabulary that constitutes Jewish tradition's distinctive lens on the world, and, on the other, how this vocabulary and its cultural expressions actually operate in the lives of the learners. Getting at these dimensions of learning requires what has been called "authentic" assessment—understanding how what students have learned affects and is put to use by them not just in the classroom (or camp), but in their daily encounters and experiences. This is not an impossible task, and, in fact, some of the pedagogical approaches that are now gaining in popularity—project based learning, gaming, digital badging, and other forms of constructivist learning—lend themselves well to this approach to assessment. Jewish sensibilities-focused assessment will be messy for the reasons we have noted above: Jewish sensibilities allow for and have generated multiple and evolving interpretations. And, these sensibilities and the literature that embodies them certainly will not enjoy exclusive influence over how the vast majority of Jewish learners today will see and respond to the world. Nonetheless, we believe that using Jewish sensibilities in our efforts to assess the success of our educational endeavors will give these efforts a focus and a connection to the ultimate goal(s) of Jewish education that they otherwise often lack.

Adopting the language of Jewish sensibilities is not a panacea for Jewish education. But it is, we believe, a decided advance over the language of Jewish identity and continuity that has long dominated the discussion of what we seek from Jewish education. Jewish sensibilities provide a framework for describing how Jews (and others) have interacted and (in many instances) continue to interact with one another and with the world. When we ask what it means to identify as a Jew, or what it is that we wish to continue in our collective enterprise, it is the expression of these sensibilities, we suggest, that we most often have in mind. Jewish sensibilities are our language. By preserving, transmitting, and enlarging that language, Jewish education can help to ensure that Jews and others who know and love that language will continue to produce great literature—and a better world.

Bibliography

Bloom, B. (1956). *Taxonomy of Educational Objectives*. Boston, MA: Allyn and Bacon.

Coalition of Innovating Congregations. (2011). *The Lomed Handbook.* Retrieved from https://www.jewishedproject.org/resources/innovation-resources

Cohen, S., & Eisen, A. (2000). *The Jew Within: Self, Family, and Community in America.* Bloomington, IN: Indiana University Press.

Fishman, S. (2000). *Jewish Life and American Culture.* Albany, NY: State University of New York Press.

Fox, S., Scheffler, I., & Marom, D. (Eds.). (2003). *Visions of Jewish Education.* Cambridge, UK: Cambridge University Press.

Fuchs-Kreimer, N. (2006). Sensibilities, Transmission, and Deep Metaphors. Retrieved from http://jtr.lib.virginia.edu/volume-4-number-3/sensibilities-transmission-and-deep-metaphors/

Geertz, C. (1966). Religion as a Cultural System. In Michael Banton (Ed.), *Anthropological Approaches to the Study of Religion* (pp. 1–46). London, UK: Tavistock Publications.

Hirschfield, B. (2007). *You Don't Have to Be Wrong for Me to Be Right: Finding Faith Without Fanaticism.* New York, NY: Random House, Inc.

Jacobs, B. (2013). Problems and Prospects of Jewish Education for Intelligent Citizenship in a Post-Everything World. *Diaspora, Indigenous, and Minority Education* 7(1), 39–53.

Levisohn, J. (2014a). What I've Learned About Jewish Identity. Retrieved from http://ejewishphilanthropy.com/what-ive-learned-about-jewish-identity/

Levisohn, J. (2014b). "Languages" and "Literature" for Michael Rosenak. *Journal of Jewish Education* 80(4), 411–33.

Merriam-Webster Dictionary. (2015). Sensibility. Retrieved from http://www.merriam-webster.com/dictionary/sensibility

National Education Association. (2014). *Preparing 21st Century Students for a Global Society: An Educator's Guide to the "Four Cs."* Retrieved from http://www.nea.org/assets/docs/A-Guide-to-Four-Cs.pdf

Oakeshott, M. (1962). *Rationalism in Politics and Other Essays.* London: Methuen.

Ochs, V. (2003). Ten Jewish Sensibilities. *Sh'ma: A Journal of Jewish Responsibility* 34(606), 1–3.

Ochs, V. (2006). The Jewish Sensibilities. Retrieved from http://jtr.lib.virginia.edu/volume-4-number-3/the-jewish-sensibilities/

Rosenak, M. (1986). *Teaching Jewish Values: A Conceptual Guide.* Jerusalem, Israel: Nachala Press.

Rosenak, M. (1995). *Roads to the Palace.* New York, NY: Berghahn Press.

Rosenak, M. (2003). Educated Jews: Common Elements. In S. Fox, I. Scheffler, & D. Marom (Eds.), *Visions of Jewish Education.* Cambridge, UK: Cambridge University Press.

San Carlos School District. (2015). The 5Cs. Retrieved from https://www.scsdk8.org/apps/pages/index.jsp?uREC_ID=1101467&type=d&pREC_ID=1394190

Soloveitchik, H. (1999). Rupture and Reconstruction: The Transformation of Contemporary Orthodoxy. In R. Farber, & C. Waxman (Eds.), *Jews in America: A Contemporary Reader.* Hanover, NH: Brandeis University Press.

Sperling, A., & Yaros, L. (2016). *Jewish Sensibilities: An Interactive Guide.* Washington, DC: Hillel International.

Steinberg, T. (1995). Teaching Hebrew Through Value-Concepts. *Avar v'Atid: A Journal of Jewish Education, Culture, and Discourse* 1(2), 90–100.

Weiss, D. (2006). Some Reflections on Jewish Values, Jewish Sensibilities, and Their Transmission. Retrieved from http://jtr.lib.virginia.edu/volume-4-number-3/some-reflections-on-jewish-values-jewish-sensibilities-and-their-transmission/

Weissman, C. (2008). A Framework for Meaning Making Learning: Reaching Deeper and Broader. Unpublished paper.

West, C. (2004). Retrieved from https://www.youtube.com/watch?v=9ZzWWq_rQt8

Woocher, M. (2014). *Teen Development and Jewish Life: Insights from Research and Practice.* Retrieved from https://www.jewishedproject.org/sites/default/files/2017-01/Teen%20Development%20and%20Jewish%20Life%20-%20Insights%20from%20Research%20and%20Practice.pdf

Index

CPSIA information can be obtained
at www.ICGtesting.com
Printed in the USA
BVHW040330101019
560735BV00001B/1/P